Global Economic Prospects

A World Bank Group
Flagship Report

JANUARY 2025

Global Economic Prospects

WORLD BANK GROUP

ISSN: 1014-8906
ISBN (paper): 978-1-4648-2147-9
ISBN (electronic): 978-1-4648-2194-3
DOI: 10.1596/978-1-4648-2147-9

Cover design: Bill Pragluski (Critical Stages)

The Library of Congress Control Number has been requested.

The cutoff date for the data used in the report was December 20, 2024.

Summary of Contents

Contents

Acknowledgments

This World Bank Flagship Report is a product of the Prospects Group in the Development Economics (DEC) Vice Presidency. The project was managed by M. Ayhan Kose and Carlos Arteta, under the general guidance of Indermit Gill.

The report was prepared by a team that included Amat Adarov, Marie Albert, Francisco Arroyo Marioli, Mirco Balatti, Tommy Chrimes, Jongrim Ha, Samuel Hill, Phil Kenworthy, Joseph Mawejje, Kate McKinnon, Dawit Mekonnen, Alen Mulabdic, Hayley Pallan, Edoardo Palombo, Nikita Perevalov, Dominik Peschel, Peter Selcuk, Shijie Shi, Kersten Stamm, Max Rudibert Steinbach, Naotaka Sugawara, Takuma Tanaka, Garima Vasishtha, Guillermo Verduzco-Bustos, Dana Vorisek, Collette Wheeler, and Bart Wilbrink.

Research assistance was provided by Nour Bouzouita, Guillermo Caballero, Jiayue Fan, Shiqing Hua, Fuda Jiang, Yi Ji, Nikola Evgeniev Kolev, Maria Hazel Macadangdang, Rafaela Martinho Henriques, Kaltrina Temaj, Urja Singh Thapa, Matias Urzua, and Juncheng Zhou. Modeling and data work was provided by Shijie Shi.

Online products were produced by Graeme Littler, with assistance from the Open Knowledge Repository. Adriana Maximiliano handled design and production. Joe Rebello managed communications and media outreach with a team that included Nandita Roy, Kristen Milhollin, Leslie Yun, and Mariana Lozzi Teixeira, and with extensive support from the World Bank's media and digital communications teams. Graeme Littler provided editorial support, with contributions from Adriana Maximiliano and Michael Harrup.

Regional projections and write-ups were produced in coordination with country teams, country directors, and the offices of the regional chief economists.

Many reviewers provided extensive advice and comments. The analysis also benefited from comments and suggestions by staff members from World Bank country teams and other World Bank Vice Presidencies as well as Executive Directors in their discussion of the report on December 17, 2024. However, both forecasts and analysis are those of the World Bank staff and should not be attributed to Executive Directors or their national authorities.

The Prospects Group gratefully acknowledges financial support from the Policy and Human Resources Development (PHRD) Fund provided by the Government of Japan, which helped underpin some of the analytical work in this publication.

Foreword

As the twenty-first century dawned, world leaders were optimistic as seldom before. They vowed to make "the right to development a reality for everyone" and free "the entire human race from want." Fifteen years later, buoyed by the initial burst of progress, they set a tight deadline: "We resolve, between now and 2030, to end poverty and hunger everywhere." For a time, it seemed humanity might be on the brink of an era of extraordinary progress.

It was not to be. As the first quarter of the century winds to a close, it's clear that the lofty goals of the past few decades will not be met. The long-term growth outlook for developing economies is now the weakest it's been since the start of the century. Barring a sustained improvement in growth rates, only six of today's 26 low-income countries are likely to achieve middle-income status by 2050. By 2030, 622 million people will remain in extreme poverty. Hunger and malnutrition will remain the fate of roughly the same number.

This edition of *Global Economic Prospects* presents the first systematic review of the performance of developing economies since the dawn of the century—and assesses their prospects for the next 25 years. Developing economies, which began the century on a trajectory to close the income gap with the wealthiest economies, are for the most part now falling farther behind. Most of the forces that powered their rise have dispersed. In their place have come fierce headwinds: weak investment and productivity growth, aging populations in nearly all but the poorest countries, rising geopolitical tensions, and the escalating dangers of climate change.

These economies achieved considerable progress in the twenty-first century, the report finds: initially, they grew at the fastest clip since the 1970s. Developing economies also became more important to the global economy than they were at the start of the century. Today, they account

for nearly half of global GDP, up from just 25 percent in 2000. In short, within a generation, they transformed the global landscape.

The bulk of this progress occurred in the earliest years—before the Global Financial Crisis of 2008-09. It began to peter out after that. Overall economic growth underwent a series of downward shifts: from 5.9 percent in the 2000s to 5.1 percent in the 2010s to 3.5 percent in the 2020s. Since 2014, with the exception of China and India, the average per capita growth rates of income in developing economies have been half a percentage point lower than those in wealthy economies, widening the rich-poor gap. Domestic reforms stalled. Government debt surged to record highs as government expenditures as a share of GDP ballooned without an attendant rise in government revenues. Geopolitical tensions escalated, causing global economic integration to falter: as a share of GDP, foreign direct investment (FDI) inflows into developing economies today are at just half the level of the 2000s. New global trade restrictions in 2024 were five times the 2010-19 average.

The consequences were greatest for low-income economies, home to more than 40 percent of people struggling on less than $2.15 a day. These economies have been the focus of global efforts to end extreme poverty. Yet their progress has come to a virtual standstill amid rising conflict, frequent economic crises, and persistently weak growth. At the start of the twenty-first century, 63 countries were classified as "low-income." Since then, 39—including India, Indonesia, and Bangladesh—have entered the ranks of middle-income countries, meaning their annual per capita incomes were above $1,145 by 2023. The remainder, which were joined by South Sudan and the Syrian Arab Republic in the 2010s, have simply stagnated: on average, their inflation-adjusted GDP per capita has grown by less than 0.1 percent annually over the past 15 years.

These ups and downs underscore what developing economies got right and wrong in the first quarter of this century—and they shed light on what they can do in the coming years to chart their own progress regardless of what happens beyond their borders. It's worth remembering that these economies now have greater sway on growth outcomes in other developing economies. Today these economies increasingly trade with one another: more than 40 percent of the goods exported by developing economies go to other developing economies, double the share in 2000. They're also an increasingly important source of capital flows, remittances, and development assistance going into other developing economies.

Our analysis indicates that a 1 percent increase in GDP growth in the three biggest developing economies—China, India, and Brazil—boosts GDP in other developing economies by nearly 2 percent in all after three years. That's just half the effect of growth in the United States, the euro area, and Japan. In short, the welfare of developing economies is still strongly tied to growth in three biggest advanced economies. Still, the dependence is smaller than it was at the turn of the century—and that points to an opportunity for them.

Developing economies should have no illusions about the struggle ahead: the next 25 years will be a tougher slog than the last 25. A fresh game plan is needed—one that strengthens their capacity to fend for themselves and seize growth opportunities wherever they can be found. With the right policies, some challenges can be turned into opportunities. Given their tighter trade links with one another, developing economies can reap significant rewards by accelerating reforms to attract investment and deepen trade and investment ties with these economies. They can also accelerate growth by modernizing infrastructure, improving human capital, and speeding up the climate transition.

That work should start now—while the global economy remains stable. Our forecasts call for it to expand by 2.7 percent this year and next—the same rate as in 2024. That's below the 3.1 percent average that prevailed in the decade before COVID-19, but it could be accompanied by some welcome trends: an expected decline in both inflation and interest rates. In a time of exceptionally high global policy uncertainty, however, developing economies would be wise to take nothing for granted. Far better to redouble the effort to take control of their own destiny.

Indermit Gill
Senior Vice President and Chief Economist
The World Bank Group

Executive Summary

Global growth is expected to hold steady at 2.7 percent in 2025-26. However, the global economy appears to be settling at a low growth rate that will be insufficient to foster sustained economic development—with the possibility of further headwinds from heightened policy uncertainty and adverse trade policy shifts, geopolitical tensions, persistent inflation, and climate-related natural disasters. Against this backdrop, emerging market and developing economies (EMDEs)—which fuel 60 percent of global growth—are set to enter the second quarter of the twenty-first century with per capita incomes on a trajectory that implies substantially slower catch-up toward advanced-economy living standards than they previously experienced. Without course corrections, most low-income countries are unlikely to graduate to middle-income status by the middle of the century. Policy action at both global and national levels is needed to foster a more favorable external environment, enhance macroeconomic stability, reduce structural constraints, address the effects of climate change, and thus accelerate long-term growth and development.

Global Outlook. Global growth is stabilizing as inflation returns closer to targets and monetary easing supports activity in both advanced economies and emerging market and developing economies (EMDEs). This should give rise to a broad-based, moderate global expansion over 2025-26, at 2.7 percent per year, as trade and investment firm. However, growth prospects appear insufficient to offset the damage done to the global economy by several years of successive negative shocks, with particularly detrimental outcomes in the most vulnerable countries.

From a longer-term perspective, catch-up toward advanced economy income levels has steadily weakened across EMDEs over the first quarter of the twenty-first century. Heightened policy uncertainty and adverse trade policy shifts represent key downside risks to the outlook. Other risks include escalating conflicts and geopolitical tensions, higher inflation, more extreme weather events related to climate change,

and weaker growth in major economies. On the upside, faster progress on disinflation and stronger demand in key economies could result in greater-than-expected global activity.

The subdued growth outlook and multiple headwinds underscore the need for decisive policy action. Global policy efforts are required to safeguard trade, address debt vulnerabilities, and combat climate change. National policy makers need to resolutely pursue price stability, as well as boost tax revenues and rationalize expenditures in order to achieve fiscal sustainability and finance needed investments. Moreover, to raise longer-term growth and put development goals on track, interventions that mitigate the impact of conflicts, lift human capital, bolster labor force inclusion, and confront food insecurity will be critical.

Regional Prospects. Against a backdrop of heightened trade restrictive measures and subdued global growth, EMDE regions face varying growth prospects this year. Growth is projected to moderate in East Asia and Pacific, amid weak domestic demand in China, as well as in Europe and Central Asia due to decelerations in some large economies following strong growth last year. In contrast, a pickup is anticipated in Latin America and the Caribbean, the Middle East and North Africa, South Asia, and Sub-Saharan Africa, partly underpinned by robust domestic demand. In 2026, growth is expected to strengthen in most regions.

The year 2025 will mark the end of the first quarter of the twenty-first century—a good time to review the performance of emerging and developing economies since 2000 and assess their prospects. This edition of the *Global Economic Prospects* report features two analytical chapters that offer a quarter-century report card. One chapter provides insights into the prospects and challenges of middle-income emerging and developing economies; the other covers the performance of the poorest countries.

From Tailwinds to Headwinds: Emerging and Developing Economies in the Twenty-First Century. The first quarter of the twenty-first century has been transformative for EMDEs. These economies now account for about 45 percent of global GDP, up from 25 percent in 2000, a trend driven by robust collective growth in the three largest EMDEs—China, India, and Brazil (the EM3). Collectively, EMDEs have contributed about 60 percent of annual global growth since 2000, on average, double the share during the 1990s. Their ascendance was powered by swift global trade and financial integration, especially during the first decade of the century. Interdependence among these economies has also increased markedly. Today, nearly half of goods exports from EMDEs go to other EMDEs, compared to one-quarter in 2000. As cross-border linkages have strengthened, business cycles among EMDEs and between EMDEs and advanced economies have become more synchronized, and a distinct EMDE business cycle has emerged. Cross-border business cycle spillovers from the EM3 to other EMDEs are sizable, at about half of the magnitude of spillovers from the largest advanced economies (the United States, the euro area, and Japan).

Yet EMDEs confront a host of headwinds at the turn of the second quarter of the century. Progress implementing structural reforms in many of these economies has stalled. Globally, protectionist measures and geopolitical fragmentation have risen sharply. High debt burdens, demographic shifts, and the rising costs of climate change weigh on economic prospects. A successful policy approach to accelerate growth and development should focus on boosting investment and productivity, navigating a difficult external environment, and enhancing macroeconomic stability.

Falling Graduation Prospects: Low-Income Countries in the Twenty-First Century. Rapid growth underpinned by domestic reforms and a benign global environment allowed many low-income countries (LICs) to attain middle-income status in the first decade of the twenty-first century. Since then, the rate at which LICs are graduating to middle-income status has slowed markedly. The prospects for today's LICs appear much more challenging. In recent years, per capita growth has been anemic amid heightened levels of conflict and fragility and adverse global developments. Across a wide array of development metrics, today's LICs are behind where LICs that since turned middle-income stood in 2000. They are also more susceptible to domestic shocks, including those related to climate change.

Many LICs that graduated in the past underwent growth accelerations—extended periods of robust economic expansion, during which output became far more trade- and investment-intensive. These accelerations were generally preceded by reforms that tended to increase market orientation and channeled resources into rapid investment growth. To kick-start stronger growth, today's LICs can harness large resource endowments to, among other things, supply the green transition, and find advantage in youthful and growing populations, untapped tourism potential, and regional trade integration. However, harnessing these factors and improving productivity hinges on engineering increased investment in human and physical capital, closing gender gaps, addressing fiscal risks, and improving governance. For LICs in fragile and conflict-affected situations, attaining greater peace and stability is paramount. LICs will also need international support to mobilize additional resources and foster institutions that can drive durable reforms. Throughout, policy makers should be guided by deep knowledge of country circumstances—there is no one-size-fits-all recipe for growth and graduation to middle-income status in LICs.

Abbreviations

AE	advanced economy
AE3	the United States, the euro area, and Japan
AfCFTA	African Continental Free Trade Area
AI	artificial intelligence
BBL	billion barrels
CFA	African Financial Community
CPI	consumer price index
DFM	dynamic factor model
DSSI	Debt Service Suspension Initiative
EAP	East Asia and Pacific
ECA	Europe and Central Asia
EM3	China, India, and Brazil
EM7	Brazil, China, India, Indonesia, Mexico, the Russian Federation, and Türkiye
EMBI	Emerging Markets Bond Index
EMDEs	emerging market and developing economies
EU	European Union
FCS	fragile and conflict-affected situations
FDI	foreign direct investment
FY	fiscal year
G7	Canada, France, Germany, Italy, Japan, the United Kingdom, and the United States
GCC	Gulf Cooperation Council
GDP	gross domestic product
GEGI	Gender Employment Gap Index
GNAFC	Global Network Against Food Crises
GNI	gross national income
GVCs	global value chains
IDA	International Development Association
IMF	International Monetary Fund
KNOMAD	Global Knowledge Partnership on Migration and Development
LAC	Latin America and the Caribbean
LAC+	Latin America and the Caribbean, the United States, and Canada
LIC	low-income country
LNG	liquified natural gas
LTMs	LICs turned into middle-income countries
MMT	million metric tons
MNA	Middle East and North Africa
ODA	official development assistance
OECD	Organisation for Economic Co-operation and Development
OPEC+	Organization of the Petroleum Exporting Countries and other affiliated oil producers
PMI	purchasing managers' index
PPP	purchasing power parity
R&D	research and development
RRF	Recovery and Resilience Facility
SAR	South Asia
SSA	Sub-Saharan Africa

SVAR	structural vector autoregression
UN	United Nations
WDI	World Development Indicators
WTO	World Trade Organization

CHAPTER 1

GLOBAL OUTLOOK

Global growth is stabilizing as inflation returns closer to targets and monetary easing supports activity in both advanced economies and emerging market and developing economies (EMDEs). This should give rise to a broad-based, moderate global expansion over 2025-26, at 2.7 percent per year, as trade and investment firm. However, growth prospects appear insufficient to offset the damage done to the global economy by several years of successive negative shocks, with particularly detrimental outcomes in the most vulnerable countries. From a longer-term perspective, catch-up toward advanced economy income levels has steadily weakened across EMDEs over the first quarter of the twenty-first century. Heightened policy uncertainty and adverse trade policy shifts represent key downside risks to the outlook. Other risks include escalating conflicts and geopolitical tensions, higher inflation, more extreme weather events related to climate change, and weaker growth in major economies. On the upside, faster progress on disinflation and stronger demand in key economies could result in greater-than-expected global activity. The subdued growth outlook and multiple headwinds underscore the need for decisive policy action. Global policy efforts are required to safeguard trade, address debt vulnerabilities, and combat climate change. National policy makers need to resolutely pursue price stability as well as boost tax revenues and rationalize expenditures in order to achieve fiscal sustainability and finance needed investments. Moreover, to raise longer-term growth and put development goals on track, interventions that mitigate the impact of conflicts, lift human capital, bolster labor force inclusion, and confront food insecurity will be critical.

Summary

The global economic context has become modestly more favorable since last June, following several years characterized by overlapping negative shocks. Inflation appears to be moderating without a substantial slowdown in key economies, and monetary policy easing has now become widespread. In the next couple of years, deceleration in the two main engines of the global economy—the United States and China—is expected to be offset by firming growth elsewhere, including in many emerging market and developing economies (EMDEs; figure 1.1.A). In all, the post-pandemic global economic expansion is forecast to remain on a steady path. However, the global economy appears to be settling at a relatively low level of growth—one insufficient to foster sustained economic development and catch-up in per capita incomes—with the possibility of further headwinds from heightened policy uncertainty, growing trade fragmentation, slower-than-anticipated progress in reducing inflation, and weaker activity in major economies.

Global trade growth rebounded last year, despite weak manufacturing activity in some key advanced economies. The recovery was driven by goods trade, which firmed in the third quarter of last year, partly owing to inventory buildups. Meanwhile, services trade growth continued to moderate. In 2025-26, trade growth is set to pick up further but will still remain below its 2010-19 average pace in nearly two-thirds of economies (figure 1.1.B). Recourse to trade restrictions remains prevalent—with the number of new measures implemented in 2024 five times higher than the 2010-19 average.

Aggregate commodity prices softened by about 3 percent in 2024, primarily reflecting improving supply conditions for energy and food commodities, despite heightened geopolitical tensions. Commodity prices are projected to ease further over the forecast horizon. A small decline in oil prices last year reflected ample potential oil supply amid decelerating global oil consumption (figure 1.1.C). A significant further decrease in oil prices is expected in 2025-26 as production expands while global oil demand growth remains modest. Base metals prices are set to stabilize over the forecast horizon, mirroring steady global growth. Meanwhile, prices for staple food crops, having fallen notably in 2024, are expected to post a small further decline.

Global headline inflation has continued to gradually ease, in part reflecting falling commodity prices and the lagged effects of monetary tightening. Inflation is now close to targets in

---

Note: This chapter was prepared by Carlos Arteta, Phil Kenworthy, Nikita Perevalov, Peter Selcuk, Garima Vasishtha, and Collette Wheeler, with contributions from Mirco Balatti, Jongrim Ha, Samuel Hill, Dawit Mekonnen, Alen Mulabdic, Edoardo Palombo, Dominik Peschel, Shijie Shi, Naotaka Sugawara, Takuma Tanaka, and Bart Wilbrink.

TABLE 1.1 Real GDP[1]

(Percent change from previous year unless indicated otherwise)

Percentage-point differences
from June 2024 projections

	2022	2023	2024e	2025f	2026f	2024e	2025f	2026f
World	**3.2**	**2.7**	**2.7**	**2.7**	**2.7**	**0.1**	**0.0**	**0.0**
Advanced economies	**2.8**	**1.7**	**1.7**	**1.7**	**1.8**	**0.2**	**0.0**	**0.0**
United States	2.5	2.9	2.8	2.3	2.0	0.3	0.5	0.2
Euro area	3.5	0.4	0.7	1.0	1.2	0.0	-0.4	-0.1
Japan	0.9	1.5	0.0	1.2	0.9	-0.7	0.2	0.0
Emerging market and developing economies	**3.7**	**4.2**	**4.1**	**4.1**	**4.0**	**0.1**	**0.1**	**0.1**
East Asia and Pacific	3.4	5.1	4.9	4.6	4.1	0.1	0.4	0.0
China	3.0	5.2	4.9	4.5	4.0	0.1	0.4	0.0
Indonesia	5.3	5.0	5.0	5.1	5.1	0.0	0.0	0.0
Thailand	2.5	1.9	2.6	2.9	2.7	0.2	0.1	-0.2
Europe and Central Asia	1.6	3.4	3.2	2.5	2.7	0.2	-0.4	-0.1
Russian Federation	-1.2	3.6	3.4	1.6	1.1	0.5	0.2	0.0
Türkiye	5.5	5.1	3.2	2.6	3.8	0.2	-1.0	-0.5
Poland	5.3	0.1	3.0	3.4	3.2	0.0	0.0	0.0
Latin America and the Caribbean	4.0	2.3	2.2	2.5	2.6	0.4	-0.2	0.0
Brazil	3.0	2.9	3.2	2.2	2.3	1.2	0.0	0.3
Mexico	3.7	3.3	1.7	1.5	1.6	-0.6	-0.6	-0.4
Argentina	5.3	-1.6	-2.8	5.0	4.7	0.7	0.0	0.2
Middle East and North Africa	5.4	1.7	1.8	3.4	4.1	-1.0	-0.8	0.5
Saudi Arabia	7.5	-0.8	1.1	3.4	5.4	-1.4	-2.5	2.2
Iran, Islamic Rep. [2]	3.8	5.0	3.0	2.7	2.2	-0.2	0.0	-0.2
Egypt, Arab Rep. [2]	6.6	3.8	2.4	3.5	4.2	-0.4	-0.7	-0.4
South Asia	5.8	6.6	6.0	6.2	6.2	-0.2	0.0	0.0
India [2]	7.0	8.2	6.5	6.7	6.7	-0.1	0.0	-0.1
Bangladesh [2]	7.1	5.8	5.0	4.1	5.4	-0.6	-1.6	-0.5
Pakistan [2]	6.2	-0.2	2.5	2.8	3.2	0.7	0.5	0.5
Sub-Saharan Africa	3.8	2.9	3.2	4.1	4.3	-0.3	0.2	0.3
Nigeria	3.3	2.9	3.3	3.5	3.7	0.0	0.0	0.0
South Africa	1.9	0.7	0.8	1.8	1.9	-0.4	0.5	0.4
Angola	3.0	1.0	3.2	2.9	2.9	0.3	0.3	0.5
Memorandum items:								
Real GDP[1]								
High-income countries	2.9	1.7	1.7	1.8	1.9	0.0	-0.1	0.0
Middle-income countries	3.7	4.6	4.3	4.3	4.1	0.1	0.2	0.0
Low-income countries	5.1	3.0	3.6	5.7	5.9	-1.4	0.4	0.4
EMDEs excluding China	4.2	3.5	3.5	3.8	3.9	0.0	-0.2	0.0
Commodity-exporting EMDEs	3.3	2.6	2.8	3.2	3.4	0.0	-0.2	0.2
Commodity-importing EMDEs	3.9	5.0	4.7	4.5	4.2	0.0	0.2	-0.1
Commodity-importing EMDEs excluding China	5.3	4.6	4.3	4.4	4.6	-0.1	-0.2	-0.1
EM7	3.3	5.1	4.6	4.2	3.9	0.1	0.2	-0.1
World (PPP weights) [3]	3.4	3.2	3.2	3.2	3.2	0.1	0.0	0.0
World trade volume [4]	**5.9**	**0.8**	**2.7**	**3.1**	**3.2**	**0.2**	**-0.3**	**-0.2**

Level differences from
June 2024 projections

Commodity prices [5]								
WBG commodity price index	142.5	108.0	104.5	98.5	96.7	-1.5	-3.6	-4.8
Energy index	152.6	106.9	100.8	93.6	91.7	-3.2	-6.4	-7.3
Oil (US$ per barrel)	99.8	82.6	80.0	72.0	71.0	-4.0	-7.0	-7.1
Non-energy index	122.1	110.2	112.1	108.5	107.0	2.0	2.1	0.4

Source: World Bank.

Note: e = estimate; f = forecast. EM7 = Brazil, China, India, Indonesia, Mexico, the Russian Federation, and Türkiye. WBG = World Bank Group. World Bank forecasts are frequently updated based on new information. Consequently, projections presented here may differ from those contained in other World Bank documents, even if basic assessments of countries' prospects do not differ at any given date. For the definition of EMDEs, developing countries, commodity exporters, and commodity importers, please refer to table 1.2. The World Bank is currently not publishing economic output, income, or growth data for Turkmenistan and República Bolivariana de Venezuela owing to lack of reliable data of adequate quality. Turkmenistan and República Bolivariana de Venezuela are excluded from cross-country macroeconomic aggregates.

1. Headline aggregate growth rates are calculated using GDP weights at average 2010-19 prices and market exchange rates.

2. GDP growth rates are on a fiscal year (FY) basis. Aggregates that include these countries are calculated using data compiled on a calendar year basis. For India and the Islamic Republic of Iran, the column for 2022 refers to FY2022/23. For Bangladesh, the Arab Republic of Egypt, and Pakistan, the column for 2022 refers to FY2021/22. Pakistan's growth rates are based on GDP at factor cost.

3. World growth rates are calculated using average 2010-19 purchasing power parity (PPP) weights, which attribute a greater share of global GDP to emerging market and developing economies (EMDEs) than market exchange rates.

4. World trade volume of goods and nonfactor services.

5. Indexes are expressed in nominal U.S. dollars (2010 = 100). Oil refers to the Brent crude oil benchmark. For weights and composition of indexes, see https://worldbank.org/commodities.

many advanced economies and EMDEs, with the share of economies with above-target inflation on a downward trend and set to reach in 2025 its lowest level since the peak in 2022 (figure 1.1.D). Core inflation briefly edged up in some EMDEs and advanced economies at about the middle of last year on persistent strength in services inflation. However, it has since generally resumed a gradual decline.

Global financial conditions have eased slightly, in aggregate, since mid-2024, mainly owing to the onset of monetary easing in the United States and generally robust risk appetite. Advanced-economy policy rates are expected to decline somewhat further this year but remain well above the unusually low levels of the 2010s (figure 1.1.E). For much of last year, improving investor sentiment translated into capital inflows and improving financial conditions in EMDEs. Following the U.S. presidential election, risk appetite in the United States strengthened further. However, a general appreciation of the U.S. dollar, rising U.S. bond yields, and various idiosyncratic domestic risks pared back the easing in EMDE financial conditions late in the year, with many EMDE currencies weakening amid debt and equity outflows. Growing debt-service burdens continue to pose considerable headwinds to economic activity in countries with elevated financial vulnerabilities, particularly in many low-income countries (LICs). Among middle-income countries with weak credit ratings, sovereign spreads normalized substantially last year, although borrowing costs remain far higher than in the 2010s.

Fiscal policy is estimated to have been broadly neutral for global growth in 2024, with previously expected fiscal consolidation plans delayed in some major economies. Going forward, fiscal policy is generally anticipated to be modestly contractionary. The pace of fiscal consolidation is expected to pick up in EMDEs excluding China, and in some advanced economies—although not in the United States—as governments intensify efforts to realign spending with revenues. This is likely to exert a modest drag on near-term global growth.

FIGURE 1.1 Global prospects

Global growth is set to stabilize below its pre-pandemic pace, with a slowdown in China and the United States offset by firming growth elsewhere. Trade growth is poised to be lower than its 2010-19 average in nearly two-thirds of economies. Moderating oil prices partly reflect decelerating global oil consumption. The share of economies with above-target inflation in 2025 is set to decline to its lowest level since the peak in 2022. Monetary policy rates are generally expected to ease further over the forecast horizon, supporting growth, although advanced economy rates are set to remain well above the low levels of the 2010s. Risks to the global outlook remain tilted to the downside. Surging trade-distorting measures—to which EMDEs have been heavily exposed—could dampen global activity.

A. Contributions to global growth

B. Share of economies with average trade growth in 2025-26 lower than in 2010-19

C. Annual change in oil demand

D. Share of economies with headline inflation above target

E. Policy rates in advanced economies and EMDEs

F. New trade-distorting policy measures

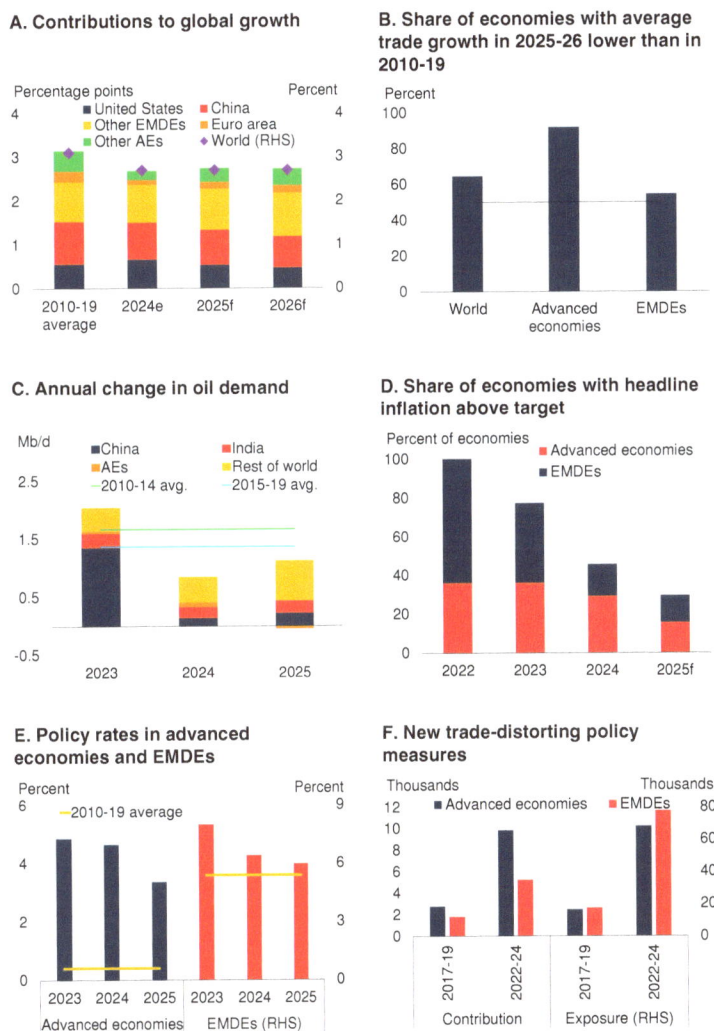

Sources: Bloomberg; Consensus Economics; Global Trade Alert (database); Haver Analytics; International Energy Agency (IEA); World Bank.

Note: AEs = advanced economies; avg. = average; e = estimate; EMDEs = emerging market and developing economies; f = forecast; RHS = right-hand scale. Unless otherwise indicated, aggregates are calculated using real U.S. dollar GDP weights at average 2010-19 prices and market exchange rates.

B. Horizontal line shows the 50 percent threshold. Sample includes 37 AEs and 101 EMDEs.

C. Data from IEA *Oil Market Report*, December 2024 edition. Mb/d = million barrels per day.

D. Data for 2024 use average monthly year on year inflation. Data for 2025 use December 2024 Consensus Economics surveys. Sample includes 16 advanced economies and 28 EMDEs.

E. AEs are GDP-weighted averages of policy rates for 2023-24 and policy rate expectations for 2025, based on futures curves on December 23, 2024. EMDEs are the median 3-month government bond yields for 2023-24 and the median Consensus Economics forecasts for 1-year-ahead yields (or policy rates) for 2025, based on December 2024 surveys. Sample includes 3 AEs and 16 EMDEs.

F. Panel shows implemented interventions by countries that discriminate against foreign interests. Contribution is the number of measures implemented by each country group. Exposure is the number of measures affecting each country group. Each measure can be implemented by and target multiple countries. Data as of December 19, 2024.

Against this backdrop, global growth is estimated to have stabilized at 2.7 percent last year and is forecast to hold steady at that pace over 2025-26. This forecast nonetheless implies that global growth will remain 0.4 percentage point below the 2010-19 average, with output continuing to lag its pre-pandemic trajectory. This reflects both the prolonged effects of the adverse shocks of recent years, and a structural decline in the fundamental drivers of growth. In particular, trade and investment are expected to expand at a slower pace relative to their 2010-19 averages across many advanced economies and EMDEs. The long-term weakening of economic dynamism is captured also by measures of potential growth: in all, global potential growth is estimated to have declined by about one-third since the 2000s.

Growth in advanced economies remained at an estimated 1.7 percent in 2024, as robust activity in the United States helped to offset subdued growth elsewhere. Over 2025-26, growth is forecast to remain around 1.7 percent—below the pace in the decade before the pandemic—as a projected slowdown in the United States is accompanied by modest recoveries in the euro area and Japan. This outlook assumes no major shifts in trade or fiscal policies.

Growth in EMDEs is forecast to remain about 4 percent in 2025-26. In China, following a moderate deceleration last year, subdued consumption amid a continuing secular slowdown is expected to reduce growth further in 2025-26. Excluding China, EMDE growth is projected to firm from an estimated 3.5 percent in 2024 to an average of 3.8 percent in 2025-26. The pickup in growth is anticipated to be broad-based, with growth set to strengthen in nearly 60 percent of these economies. Global monetary easing, recovering real incomes, improving domestic demand, and gradually expanding trade and industrial activity are expected to support overall economic activity going forward. Nevertheless, the pandemic and subsequent shocks have left a lasting mark, with the level of output in EMDEs as a whole expected to remain more than 5 percent below its pre-pandemic trend by 2026.

Growth in LICs is estimated to have been subdued at 3.6 percent in 2024, much weaker than previous expectations, on account of escalating conflict and violence. Growth is forecast to firm to 5.8 percent in 2025-26, but this is contingent on the stabilization of activity in some LICs affected by severe conflict last year.

The global outlook is surrounded by substantial uncertainty, and the balance of risks remains tilted to the downside. Global growth could be weaker than projected on account of potential adverse changes in trade policies and heightened policy uncertainty. A surge in trade-distorting measures, implemented mainly by advanced economies but often disproportionately affecting EMDEs, poses a risk to global trade and economic activity (figure 1.1.F). Beyond specific trade-related policy shifts, a sustained increase in global economic policy uncertainty could dampen growth, particularly in EMDEs (figure 1.2.A). Heightened geopolitical tensions and conflict escalations relating to Russia's invasion of Ukraine, events in the Middle East, and instability elsewhere could disrupt global trade and commodity markets, hurting growth. In affected EMDEs, intense conflicts could set back a wide range of development goals and result in large and long-term output losses.

In addition to the possible inflationary effects of trade policy shifts and conflict-related shocks, inflation could prove to be more persistent than expected if services sector inflation remains elevated even as labor market tightness diminishes. Growth in major economies could also be weaker than projected on account of several factors. U.S. growth could slow more than in the baseline if trade protectionism increases sharply or if the labor market cools more quickly than envisaged. In China, a deeper or more prolonged property sector downturn could lead to further weakness in overall activity. More frequent climate-change-related disasters with worsening impacts could hurt near-term growth while amplifying the slowdown in the fundamental drivers of long-term growth.

On the upside, faster-than-anticipated global disinflation could result from lower commodity prices or stronger productivity, enabling central banks to cut policy rates faster than expected in the baseline. Additionally, growth in major economies could exceed expectations for other reasons. In the United States, more expansionary fiscal policy and resilient consumption—for instance, supported by strong household balance sheets—could push growth above expectations. Growth could also surprise on the upside in China if policy makers were to implement further stimulus measures, boosting domestic demand. Stronger-than-expected growth in the United States or China could boost economic activity substantially across other EMDEs, with spillovers from U.S. growth being especially pronounced (figure 1.2.B).

The timing and magnitude of possible changes in U.S. trade and fiscal policies are currently unclear, with resulting impacts on U.S. and global growth and inflation clouded by uncertainty. Illustrative simulations suggest that a 10-percentage-point increase in U.S. tariffs on all trading partners could reduce global growth this year by 0.2 percentage point compared to baseline forecasts, assuming no retaliatory action. The expected negative effect could be amplified if proportional retaliatory tariffs are factored in—global growth would be lower than the baseline by a total of about 0.3 percentage point in 2025, while EMDE growth would be lower by a total of about 0.2 percentage point. Conversely, the extension of U.S. tax provisions set to expire this year would likely result, all else being equal, in fiscal expansion and stronger near-term growth in the United States. This would take effect in 2026, potentially boosting U.S. growth that year by 0.4 percentage point relative to the baseline, albeit with only small global spillovers.

From a longer-term perspective, the prevailing economic climate—broadly slowing potential growth, elevated government debt, substantial policy uncertainty, and notable downside risks—will see most EMDEs depart the first quarter of this century with per capita incomes on a trajectory that suggests substantially slower catch-up toward advanced-economy living standards in the second quarter. Even without downside risks materializing, EMDE per capita income growth is projected to remain relatively subdued over 2025-26, at about 3.1 percent, which is notably weaker than the average pace over 2000-19. This slowdown was well underway prior to the

FIGURE 1.2 Global prospects (*continued*)

Among various downside risks, a sustained increase in global economic policy uncertainty could result in notably slower growth. On the upside, stronger-than-expected growth in China or, in particular, the United States, would lead to substantial output spillovers across other EMDEs. The pace of EMDE income convergence with advanced economies is expected to remain sluggish, with earlier gains reversing in LICs. Based on 2010-19 growth rates, less than one quarter of LICs appear on course to graduate to middle-income status by 2050. Poverty reduction in EMDEs has stalled since 2020, with the incidence of extreme poverty excluding China and India still higher than before the pandemic. Regaining momentum on income catch-up will require boosting human capital and job creation in EMDEs, especially where working-age populations are rapidly expanding.

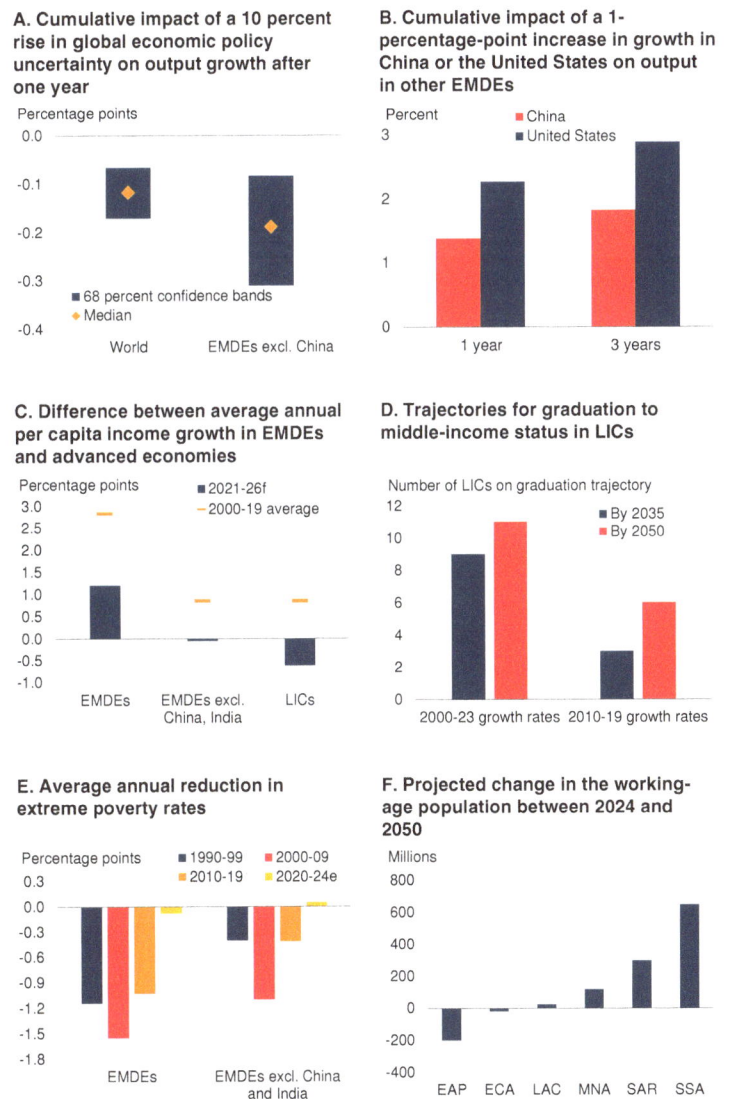

A. Cumulative impact of a 10 percent rise in global economic policy uncertainty on output growth after one year

B. Cumulative impact of a 1-percentage-point increase in growth in China or the United States on output in other EMDEs

C. Difference between average annual per capita income growth in EMDEs and advanced economies

D. Trajectories for graduation to middle-income status in LICs

E. Average annual reduction in extreme poverty rates

F. Projected change in the working-age population between 2024 and 2050

Sources: Haver Analytics; Mahler, Yonzan, and Lakner (2022); UN Population Prospects (database); WDI (database); World Bank Poverty and Inequality Platform; World Bank.
Note: AEs = advanced economies; EAP = East Asia and Pacific; ECA = Europe and Central Asia; EMDEs = emerging market and developing economies; e = estimate; f = forecast; LAC = Latin America and the Caribbean; LICs = low-income countries; MNA = Middle East and North Africa; SAR = South Asia; SSA = Sub-Saharan Africa.
A. Data are GDP-weighted cumulative impulse responses of output growth to a 10 percent increase in global economic policy uncertainty. Three types of Bayesian vector autoregressions are estimated over 1998Q1-2023Q4, with four lags. Sample includes 32 AEs and 39 EMDEs excluding China.
B. Cumulative impulse responses of output in EMDEs excluding Brazil, China, and India to a 1-percentage-point increase in output growth in China and the United States.
D. Graduation trajectories assume that the threshold for middle-income status increases at the same average pace as over 2000-23. Data use GNI per capita in U.S. dollars (Atlas method).
E. Extreme poverty is defined as living below the International Poverty Line of $2.15 per day.
F. Working-age population is defined as individuals aged 15-64 years.

pandemic, as earlier gains from international integration and domestic reforms faded in many EMDEs, dampening the catch-up process toward advanced-economy incomes.

As the first quarter of this century progressed, EMDE per capita income gains relative to advanced economies diminished. Per capita GDP in the two largest EMDEs, China and India, has continued to move closer to advanced-economy levels, but at a slowing pace. Excluding China and India, per capita GDP in EMDEs peaked as a share of advanced-economy incomes at nearly 11 percent in 2013. This share has not been regained over a decade later, and the near-term outlook does not portend well for income catch-up.

Following the 2020 global recession, outright divergence from advanced-economy incomes has been pronounced in many of the most vulnerable EMDEs, with earlier progress reversing in LICs (figure 1.2.C). Indeed, even assuming average 2010-19 growth rates, less than one-quarter of LICs appear on course to graduate to middle-income by 2050, down from close to two-thirds of eligible countries in the last 25 years (figure 1.2.D). Meanwhile, contrasting with steady progress in reducing extreme poverty during the decades prior to the pandemic, the extreme poverty rate in EMDEs last year was little changed from its 2019 level—and higher when excluding China and India (figure 1.2.E).

As the first quarter of the twenty-first century concludes, the overarching challenge facing policy makers is to sustainably raise growth rates and put a wide range of development objectives on a better trajectory. This will entail addressing multiple pressing concerns. Enhanced international cooperation is needed to address growing trade fragmentation and limit its damage, safeguarding a rules-based multilateral trade system. Decisive and coordinated policy action is also needed to tackle high debt burdens and avoid the economic and social costs of sovereign defaults, particularly in some of the most vulnerable EMDEs. It is critical for the global community to boost concessional financing in light of the sharp decline in grants to LICs in recent years. Global cooperation is also essential to tackle climate change and biodiversity loss, mounting food insecurity, and conflict.

Although inflation continues to decline overall, its uneven path in some EMDEs underscores that monetary policy makers may need to reduce the pace of monetary easing or even tighten policy, as appropriate, to maintain credible inflation-targeting frameworks. Moreover, against a backdrop of heightened policy uncertainty and a stronger U.S. dollar, adverse shifts in investor sentiment could trigger sizable capital outflows from EMDEs, resulting in additional inflationary risks from currency depreciation. In EMDEs with rapid credit growth, it will be crucial for financial regulators to guard against threats to financial stability by strengthening oversight and risk management systems for banks and nonbank financial institutions. Rising debt-servicing costs, particularly for LICs, highlight the need for vulnerable EMDEs to rebuild fiscal buffers and shore up market confidence. EMDEs will also need to mobilize fiscal resources to undertake investments geared toward achieving sustainable growth, addressing development challenges, and providing targeted support to vulnerable populations.

Over the longer term, comprehensive and wide-ranging reforms will be necessary to foster greater prosperity and address the root causes of insufficient growth prospects in many EMDEs. Tackling the rising incidence of conflict is crucial to reversing declines in living standards in some of the most vulnerable countries. Targeted policies are needed to boost growth-enhancing investment, including in human capital, and advance labor force inclusion, especially in EMDE regions where the working-age population is projected to increase substantially (figure 1.2.F). Bolstering food security is paramount. Acute food insecurity remains elevated, with conflict as a key driver, posing dire implications for both the immediate well-being and the lifetime prospects of those affected.

Global context

The global economic context has become somewhat more favorable, even in the face of various headwinds and risks. Global trade rebounded last year, despite being hindered by weak manufacturing activity in some advanced economies and continued trade-restrictive measures. Commodity prices edged down due to improving supply conditions, in spite of heightened geopolitical tensions. This decline, in turn, enabled further progress on disinflation globally, notwithstanding some upward pressure from services prices. With widespread gradual easing in monetary policy and mostly solid risk appetite, EMDE sovereign spreads have generally been stable, despite significant recent volatility in exchange rates. Among less creditworthy sovereigns, credit spreads have normalized substantially from elevated levels in recent years, but borrowing costs remain high. Still, about half of LICs are in, or close to, debt distress.

Global trade

Global trade in goods and services rebounded in 2024, growing by an estimated 2.7 percent after a tepid expansion in the previous year. Growth in goods trade accelerated in the second half of 2024, following a weaker-than-expected recovery in the first half. The pickup was partly driven by precautionary inventory buildup in anticipation of possible trade dislocations, including those resulting from dockworker strikes on the U.S. East Coast and the Gulf of Mexico, as well as announced and potential higher tariffs in the United States. Maritime transit and freight rates increased in the latter half of 2024, reflecting disruptions in maritime transport and higher shipping volumes. However, these costs remain well below the peaks seen during the pandemic and have not had a significant impact on the availability of goods or global delivery times thus far.

The recovery in global goods trade last year was uneven across country groups. Goods trade expanded steadily in EMDEs, while it remained weak in most advanced economies, except for the United States, as a result of sluggish growth (figure 1.3.A). Moreover, leading indicators signal continued weakness in advanced-economy goods trade. Among EMDEs, the expansion in goods trade in 2024 was broad-based across regions—except in the Middle East and North Africa (MNA), where trade contracted because of oil production cuts by OPEC+ members.

FIGURE 1.3 Global trade

Global goods trade growth accelerated in the second half of 2024, following a subdued recovery in the first half. The recovery was uneven across country groups, with goods trade expanding steadily in EMDEs and the United States while remaining weak in most other advanced economies. Leading indicators point to continued softness in advanced economy goods trade alongside a stabilization in global services trade. The use of trade-distorting policies has been growing, especially among countries whose voting patterns at the UN General Assembly align closely with China and the United States. Global trade growth over 2025-26 is forecast to remain well below the 2010-19 average, with the slow pace partly reflecting proliferating trade-restrictive measures and heightened geopolitical tensions.

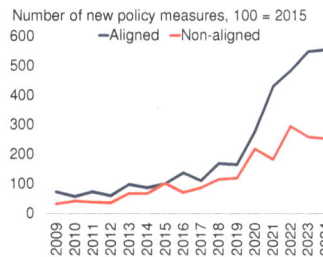

A. Goods trade growth

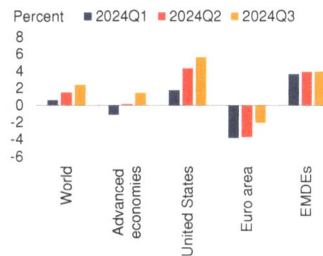

B. Global PMI: New export orders

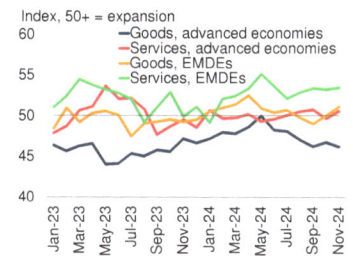

C. Trade-distorting policy measures, by UN voting alignment

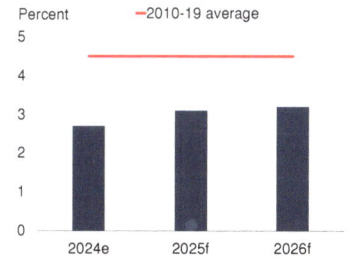

D. Global trade growth

Sources: Aiyar, Malacrino, and Presbitero (2024); Bailey, Strezhnev, and Voeten (2017); CPB Netherlands Bureau of Economic Policy Analysis; Global Trade Alert (database); Haver Analytics; World Bank.
Note: AEs = advanced economies; EMDEs = emerging market and developing economies; e = estimate; f = forecast; PMI = purchasing managers' index. Trade in goods and services is measured as the average of export and import volumes.
A. Panel shows the annual percentage change in goods trade volumes. Last observation is September 2024.
B. Panel shows the manufacturing and services subcomponents of the global purchasing managers' index (PMI) new export order series. PMI readings above (below) 50 indicate expansion (contraction). Last observation is November 2024.
C. Panel shows implemented interventions that discriminate against foreign commercial interests. Each measure can be implemented by multiple countries. "Aligned" countries are those in the top quartile in terms of UN General Assembly voting alignment with the United States or China. All other countries are considered "non-aligned." Adjusted data (for reporting lags) as of December 19, 2024.
D. Panel shows growth in global trade in goods and services.

Global services purchasing managers' index (PMI) for new export orders suggest that the recovery in services trade has stabilized, reflecting a slowdown in the growth of travel services (figure 1.3.B). Recent data on tourist arrivals indicate that tourism activity has recovered to pre-pandemic levels in nearly all regions except for EAP, where strict pandemic-control measures remained in place for longer.

Trade policy uncertainty and trade-restrictive measures remain elevated. Trade policy uncertainty has increased amid recent electoral outcomes and new trade policy announcements in several large economies—most notably in the United States. Globally, the number of new trade-restricting policies introduced in 2024 was five times higher than the 2010-19 average and is close to the record high observed in 2023. The growing use of trade-restricting policies in recent years has been more prevalent in countries whose voting patterns at the United Nations General Assembly align closely with those of China or the United States—for these countries, the number of distorting measures increased five-fold since 2015, compared to a two-fold increase for non-aligned countries (figure 1.3.C).

Against this backdrop, global trade growth is forecast to pick up to an average of about 3.1 percent in 2025-26, supported by slightly firming trade growth in the euro area—which accounts for one-fourth of global trade—as well as in Japan and EMDEs excluding China (figure 1.3.D). Nevertheless, global trade growth over the forecast horizon is projected to remain below pre-pandemic averages, in line with heightened trade-restrictive measures and the overall relative softness in output and investment growth. Nearly two-thirds of countries are expected to experience lower trade growth in 2025-26 compared to their 2010-19 averages—a period that was also characterized by subdued trade growth. A major downside risk to the trade outlook is the increased likelihood of surging trade restrictions and related uncertainty in light of policy shifts following key elections. Other downside risks include weaker-than-expected global demand, escalating geopolitical tensions, and further disruptions in maritime transport.

Commodity markets

After falling by about 3 percent in 2024, commodity prices are forecast to decline further by 6 percent in 2025 and 2 percent in 2026, which would bring prices to their lowest level since 2020

(figures 1.4.A and 1.4.B). Nevertheless, most commodity prices remain well above pre-pandemic levels, supporting economic activity in many commodity exporters.

The price of Brent crude oil averaged $80/bbl in 2024, about 3 percent lower than a year earlier but 40 percent above the 2015-19 average. This annual price decline reflected an ample global oil supply given modest consumption growth, which offset the impact of escalating geopolitical tensions (figures 1.4.C and 1.4.D). Under the baseline, Brent crude oil prices are expected to decrease further, to an average of $72/bbl in 2025 and $71/bbl in 2026. The fall in prices is anticipated to be driven by increasing supply among non-OPEC+ producers—mainly Brazil, Canada, Guyana, and the United States—coupled with modest growth of global oil demand owing to slowing oil consumption in China and advanced economies. A substantial downside risk to the oil price forecast could materialize if OPEC+ unwinds supply cuts based on its announced schedule. Meanwhile, the recent strengthening of the U.S. dollar could, if sustained, dampen global oil demand and prices further. Upside risks include a prolonged escalation of conflict in the Middle East and shortfalls in U.S. shale oil production.

U.S. natural gas prices are projected to increase steeply in 2025-26 as new liquefied natural gas (LNG) terminals enhance export capacity, increasing competition for domestic supply. European gas prices are forecast to rise by 11 percent in 2025, reflecting strong global LNG demand and reduced supplies, before falling 8 percent in 2026 as more LNG supply comes online. Upside risks include conflict-related developments that curtail gas exports from the Middle East and uncertainty around LNG supplies from the Russian Federation to Europe, particularly given recent declines in the amount of LNG shipped to the European Union. On the downside, weaker-than-expected demand growth in fast-growing markets in East Asia and Pacific (EAP) and South Asia (SAR) could lead to lower prices.

Base metal prices (excluding iron ore) increased by 6 percent in 2024, driven by aluminum and copper, mainly reflecting tight supply conditions. Meanwhile, gold prices surged to record highs, reflecting strong private and official demand. In contrast, iron ore prices dropped by 10 percent, reflecting ample supplies and weaker steel demand, notably from the real estate sector in China (figure 1.4.E). Base metal prices are expected to be broadly stable in 2025-26, in line with steady global growth. Precious metal prices are projected to remain elevated, underpinned by heightened geopolitical tensions. Upside risks to the price forecasts include additional policy stimulus in China and mining disruptions.

Food commodity prices decreased by 8 percent in 2024, aided by strong supplies. Grain prices led the decline, dropping 15 percent, amid solid harvests (figure 1.4.F). Food prices are expected to ease by an additional 5 percent in 2025 owing to favorable growing conditions in key exporters, before stabilizing in 2026. Upside risks to prices include extreme weather disrupting production, while lower-than-expected crude oil prices would put downward price pressure on energy feedstocks such as maize, sugar, soybean oil, and palm oil. Despite declining food commodity prices, global acute food insecurity remains elevated. Conflict, extreme weather events, and economic shocks have severely disrupted food access in many affected locations, and further adverse developments along any of these dimensions could worsen food insecurity.

Global inflation

Global headline inflation continued to recede last year amid easing energy and food prices, healing supply chains, and the lagged effects of tight monetary policy stances (figure 1.5.A). As a result, headline inflation by late 2024 was at or below target in over 60 percent of economies and remained only slightly above target elsewhere.

In many advanced economies, year-on-year inflation has fallen below targets as fuel prices declined through last year and food prices stabilized. In EMDEs, headline inflation has continued to decline, coming within a percentage point of pre-pandemic levels by late 2024, despite briefly edging up in some economies in the second half of last year. Further moderation in year-on-

FIGURE 1.4 Commodity markets

Commodity prices fell modestly in 2024 and are forecast to decline further, dropping 6 percent in 2025 and 2 percent in 2026, although they are expected to remain above pre-pandemic averages. The price of Brent crude oil, which averaged $80/bbl in 2024, is expected to drop to $72/bbl in 2025 and $71/bbl in 2026, with robust supply and subdued consumption growth in major economies more than offsetting the effects of geopolitical tensions. Metal and mineral prices are expected to edge down in 2025-26, with the decrease led by declines in iron ore prices due to subdued demand, notably from China's ailing real estate sector. Food commodity prices fell last year amid a rebound in grain supply growth.

A. Commodity price indexes, monthly

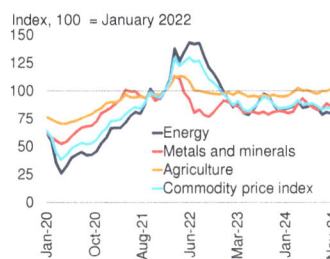

B. Commodity price projections

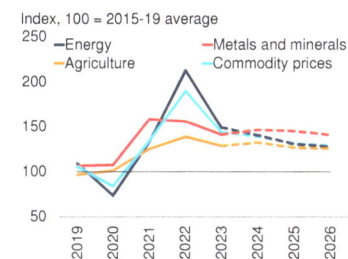

C. Brent crude oil price around major events

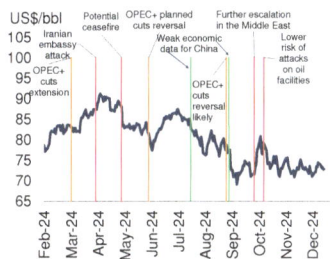

D. Global oil market balance

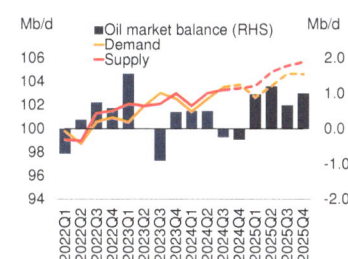

E. Fixed-asset investment growth in China

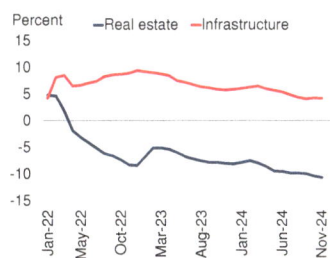

F. Global grain supply growth

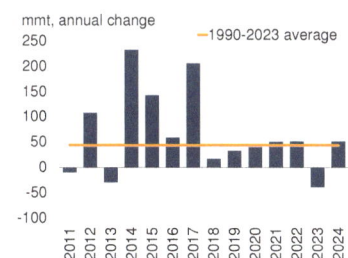

Sources: Bloomberg; Haver Analytics; International Energy Agency (IEA); U.S. Department of Agriculture; World Bank.
Note: bbl = billion barrels; Mb/d = million barrels per day; mmt = million metric tons; OPEC+ = Organization of the Petroleum Exporting Countries and other affiliated oil producers.
A. Last observation is November 2024.
B. Commodity prices refer to the World Bank commodity price index annual average, excluding precious metals. Dashed lines indicate forecasts.
C. Orange lines indicate events related to OPEC+ supply management, red lines indicate geopolitical events, and green lines indicate selected economic news. Last observation is December 20, 2024.
D. "Oil market balance" is the difference between supply and demand in each quarter. Data from IEA *Oil Market Report*, December edition. Dashed lines indicate IEA forecasts for 2024Q4 to 2025Q4, based on the IEA's assumed extension of voluntary OPEC+ cuts.
E. Year on year change in real estate and infrastructure investment. Last observation is November 2024.
F. Supply is the sum of beginning stocks and production in the crop season. Data as of December 20, 2024.

FIGURE 1.5 Global inflation

Global inflation continued to recede last year amid easing energy and food prices, healing supply chains, and the lagged effects of tight monetary policy stances. As a result, the share of economies with above-target inflation is set to fall in 2025 to its lowest level since the peak in 2022. Core inflation remained elevated last year, moderating the disinflationary impact of a sharp decline in energy and food inflation. Inflation is expected to decline in 2025, owing to softening core prices as demand cools and labor markets ease, as well as a further decline in commodity prices. However, a wide range of inflation outcomes remains plausible, partly due to heightened policy uncertainty.

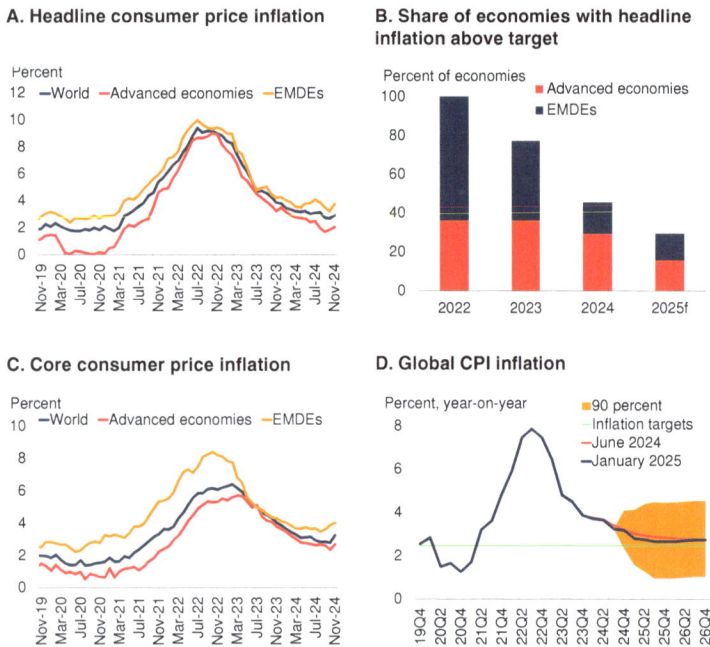

A. Headline consumer price inflation

B. Share of economies with headline inflation above target

C. Core consumer price inflation

D. Global CPI inflation

Sources: Consensus Economics; Haver Analytics; Oxford Economics; World Bank.
Note: CPI = consumer price index; EMDEs = emerging market and developing economies.
A. Panel shows median headline inflation. Sample is unbalanced and includes 35 advanced economies and up to 100 EMDEs. Last observation is November 2024.
B. Data for 2024 are based on average monthly year on year inflation across all available months. Data for 2025 are based on December 2024 Consensus Economics surveys. Sample size includes 16 advanced economies and 28 EMDEs.
C. Panel shows median core consumer price inflation. Sample is unbalanced and includes 32 advanced economies and up to 46 EMDEs. Last observation is November 2024.
D. Model-based GDP-weighted projections of consumer price inflation using Oxford Economics' Global Economic Model. Forecast starts in 2024Q4. Sample includes 68 countries, of which 34 are EMDEs (excluding Argentina and República Bolivariana de Venezuela). The horizontal line is the GDP-weighted average inflation target across the sample. The 90 percent confidence bands are derived from Consensus Economics forecast errors using the longest available sample for each country before 2020.

year inflation in EMDEs is likely to follow, with the share of economies with above-target inflation set to fall in 2025 to its lowest level since the peak in 2022 (figure 1.5.B).

Despite trending downward, core inflation remained elevated last year, in contrast to the disinflationary impact of a sharper decline in energy and food inflation (figure 1.5.C). Some EMDE regions and advanced economies

experienced a pickup in the pace of core price gains in the middle of last year due to accelerated services inflation. In some of these economies, wage growth and demand for services has boosted core prices, prompting some central banks to begin reassessing the pace of monetary easing. More recently, global core inflation began to cool again, partly as a result of slowing wage gains and weakening demand for services. Meanwhile, goods inflation stabilized at subdued levels, no longer supporting the decline in overall inflation.

Going forward, global headline inflation is forecast to decline to an average of 2.7 percent in 2025-26, broadly consistent with target levels in many advanced economies and EMDEs (figure 1.5.D). That said, the range of plausible paths for global inflation over the forecast horizon is wide, in part reflecting substantial policy uncertainty amid the possibility of marked shifts in fiscal policy and notable increases in global tariffs. In the baseline forecast, the decline in inflation is expected to be driven by softening core prices as services demand moderates, labor markets ease, and wage growth slows, accompanied by a further decline in commodity prices. Consistent with these projections, surveys of inflation expectations indicate a continued moderation in inflation globally this year and next.

Global financial developments

Global financial conditions have generally eased slightly since mid-2024 as major advanced-economy central banks—most notably, the U.S. Federal Reserve—reduced policy interest rates (figure 1.6.A). However, some of this improvement unwound in late 2024, with financial conditions tightening in EMDEs. Monetary policy in the United States is expected to become gradually less restrictive over the course of 2025, with real policy rates expected to align with median neutral-rate estimates by the end of the year (figure 1.6.B). Even so, U.S. government bond yields picked up substantially over the final quarter of last year, reflecting in part the continued resilience of economic activity. In the euro area, real policy rates are likely to become somewhat accommodative by the end of 2025, reflecting a more subdued economic outlook.

Risk appetite in advanced economies generally remained robust in the second half of 2024. In particular, investor sentiment in the United States continued to strengthen, as reflected by gains in equity prices. U.S. credit and equity risk premia, as indicated by corporate bond spreads and cyclically adjusted equity earnings relative to the risk-free rate, fell to their lowest levels in a decade in November (figure 1.6.C). Nonetheless, a spike in equity volatility in August illustrated that markets remain highly sensitive to swift changes in sentiment, especially related to policy shifts. Indeed, in the euro area, concerns over prospects for trade relations with the United States and an increase in political uncertainty in some large economies pared back investor optimism late last year.

Investor sentiment toward EMDEs excluding China has fluctuated in recent months, but the cost and availability of external credit have shown modest improvement overall since mid-2024. Government bond issuance in foreign currencies has picked up for mid-rated sovereigns (figure 1.6.D). Meanwhile, sovereign spreads generally remained low and stable for most EMDEs last year, declining significantly for those with weak credit ratings (CCC+/Caa1 and below)—about one-fourth of EMDEs rated by the major agencies (figure 1.6.E). However, nonconcessional external debt remains unusually expensive in these economies, reflecting the elevated level of advanced-economy bond yields compared to the 2010s.

In late 2024, EMDE financial conditions deteriorated somewhat amid slower-than-expected disinflation in some regions, uncertainty about shifting U.S. trade policies, and moderating expectations for future U.S. policy rate cuts. EMDE currencies became more volatile, with some depreciating notably against the U.S. dollar in the fourth quarter amid a concerted bout of EMDE debt and equity outflows (figure 1.6.F). The combination of inflation upside surprises in mid-2024 and weaker currencies also gave rise to a moderate scaling back of expectations of further EMDE interest rate cuts, contributing to equity market losses in some large EMDEs. In China, despite accommodative monetary policy actions

FIGURE 1.6 Global financial developments

Global financial conditions have eased since mid-2024 amid advanced-economy policy rate cuts, but some prior improvement in EMDEs has been recently reversed. U.S. real policy rates are expected to become less restrictive, reaching neutral estimates by end-2025, while euro area real rates may become somewhat accommodative, reflecting a more subdued outlook. U.S. risk appetite has strengthened, as evidenced by falling equity risk premia. Aided by easing advanced-economy financial conditions, government bond issuance has picked up for mid-rated sovereigns. Sovereign spreads have remained low and stable for most EMDEs, declining for those with weak credit ratings. However, EMDE financial conditions deteriorated in late 2024, as reflected in currency depreciation.

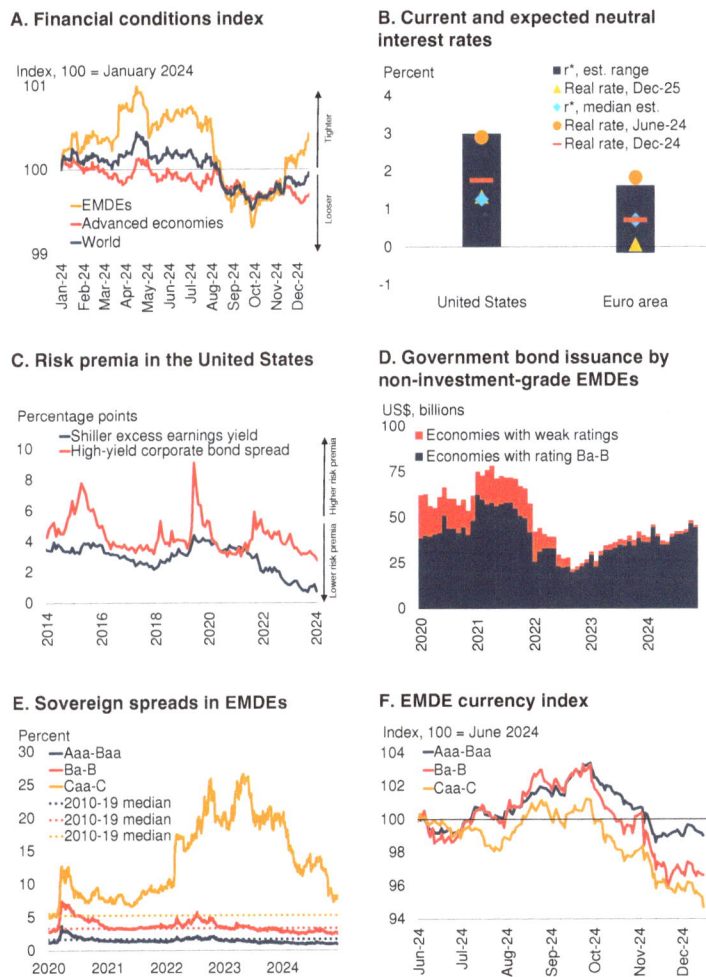

A. Financial conditions index

B. Current and expected neutral interest rates

C. Risk premia in the United States

D. Government bond issuance by non-investment-grade EMDEs

E. Sovereign spreads in EMDEs

F. EMDE currency index

Sources: Barclays Investment Bank; Bloomberg; Dealogic; European Central Bank; Federal Reserve; Federal Reserve Bank of New York; Federal Reserve Bank of St. Louis; Fitch Ratings; Goldman Sachs; Haver Analytics; Holston et al. (2023); Hördahl and Tristani (2014); J.P. Morgan; Laubach and Williams (2003); Lubik and Matthes (2023); Moody's Analytics; S&P 500 Index; World Bank.

Note: EMDEs = emerging market and developing economies. Credit ratings based on Moody's long-term foreign currency sovereign credit ratings, with weak ratings defined as Caa+/CCC+ and below.

A. Higher index values represent tighter financial conditions. Last observation is December 17, 2024.

B. Blue bars represent the range of the latest estimates of r* from various semi-structural, DSGE, and VAR models since 2024. Real rates are calculated by subtracting 12-month ahead inflation expectations implied by inflation swaps from the actual or expected policy rate.

C. Shiller excess yield is the inverse of the cyclically adjusted price-to-earnings ratio minus the yield on 10-year U.S. Treasury inflation-protected securities. Last observation is November 2024. High-yield corporate bond spreads are measured by ICE BofA Option-Adjusted Spreads (OASs). These represent the calculated differences between a computed OAS index for all bonds rated below Baa-/BBB and the spot U.S. Treasury curve. Last observation is December 2024.

D. Panel shows rolling 12-month totals for bond issuance by EMDE governments denominated in U.S. dollars, euros, pound sterling, Swiss francs, and yen. Sample includes 15 EMDEs with weak ratings and 30 with ratings of Ba-B. Last observation is November 2024.

E. Aggregates are the median from a sample of 77 EMDEs. Last observation is December 17, 2024.

F. Sample of 49 EMDE currencies relative to the U.S. dollar. The index starts at 100 from June 1, 2024, takes the median of the daily currency movements across each ratings classification, and compounds it. An increase (decrease) in the index indicates EMDE currency appreciation (depreciation). Last observation is December 17, 2024.

and news of supportive shifts in fiscal policy, investor sentiment remains subdued against the backdrop of weak domestic demand and worries about intensifying trade disputes with the United States.

Major economies: Recent developments and outlook

Advanced economies

Advanced economics expanded by an estimated 1.7 percent in 2024, as steady U.S. growth and a modest pickup in the euro area were accompanied by a sharp slowdown in Japan. Assuming no major shift in economic policies, growth over 2025-26 is forecast to average about 1.7 percent, as modest recoveries in the euro area and Japan help counter a slowdown in the United States. Although aggregate growth is envisioned to proceed in line with previous forecasts, activity over 2025-26 is expected to be weaker on average in nearly 60 percent of advanced economies than previously assumed.

In the **United States**, although growth in the first half of 2024 was slightly stronger than anticipated, activity showed tentative signs of deceleration toward the end of last year, reflecting easing labor market conditions and softening consumer sentiment. The pace of job creation has been gradually diminishing, while the unemployment rate increased by 0.8 percentage point through November of last year, after reaching a trough in April 2023. Compared to rises in unemployment after previous troughs, job losses have played a smaller role in driving the current increase so far (figure 1.7.A). In line with reduced labor market turnover, as reflected in declining job openings and falling quit rates, wage growth has eased, after hovering at about 4 percent in the middle of last year.

U.S. consumer spending has recently shown signs of moderating, as households adjust to the cooling labor market and slowing disposable income growth. In addition, the personal saving rate has been below pre-pandemic levels since early 2022, leading to a gradually diminishing stock of the

excess savings accumulated during the pandemic. Investment spending, which boosted growth significantly in 2024, is not expected to support activity to the same extent going forward (figure 1.7.B). At the same time, support from fiscal policy began to wane last year; however, policy proposals being considered by the incoming U.S. administration could provide an additional boost to near-term growth.

Overall, recent data suggest that the U.S. economy may be approaching a soft landing, with growth projected to slow as inflation gradually declines toward its target level over the forecast horizon. Growth is expected to ease to 2.3 percent in 2025 and 2 percent in 2026, alongside continued progress on disinflation, allowing the Federal Reserve to proceed with further easing of monetary policy. The somewhat higher U.S. growth outlook relative to June projections reflects stronger-than-expected activity last year, particularly in consumer spending. The upward revision to the outlook also accounts for trend growth going forward, as recent elevated productivity gains and labor supply expansion are expected to be more resilient.[1]

In the **euro area**, growth remained feeble last year owing to anemic consumption, business investment, and industrial activity, with the latter partly reflecting the dampening effects of high energy prices on export competitiveness and consumption. High-frequency indicators suggest that manufacturing and industrial production remain weak—particularly in Germany, which accounts for nearly 30 percent of euro area GDP. Across the broader euro area, although private consumption has been rising since the second half of last year, it has been somewhat curbed by still-subdued consumer confidence, with household saving intentions remaining high, as indicated by survey data and reflected in an elevated personal savings rate (figure 1.7.C).

---

[1] These baseline forecasts do not incorporate the impact on U.S. growth from potential policy changes that may be implemented by the incoming U.S. administration, as their timing and magnitude are uncertain. Possible implications of some of these changes are explored in the "Risks to the outlook" section below.

Over 2025-26, euro area growth is projected to pick up to about 1.1 percent as the cyclical recovery firms. Nevertheless, this is slightly weaker than previous forecasts, largely owing to sharp rises in policy and domestic political uncertainty, particularly in some major economies. The euro area outlook remains uncertain and is predicated on an improvement in investment and trade growth—both of which have been notable areas of weakness in recent years. After contracting last year, investment is expected to benefit from a further decline in interest rates. Meanwhile, and assuming no major change in trade relations with the United States, trade growth is anticipated to firm, as exports pick up alongside improving global manufacturing activity and imports are supported by strengthening domestic demand. At the sectoral level, euro area growth is expected to be supported by an expansion in the services sector, underpinned by solid consumer spending as real incomes continue to recover from the earlier erosion caused by high inflation.

In **Japan**, output is estimated to have stagnated in 2024, undershooting last June's growth forecast by 0.7 percentage point. This weakness reflected longer-than-expected auto plant shutdowns and a limited recovery in consumption amid subdued consumer confidence, despite a pickup in wage growth. Over 2025-26, growth is projected to rise to an average of 1.1 percent, with capital investment firming and consumer spending improving in line with rising wages. Meanwhile, the Bank of Japan tightened monetary policy twice last year, and policy rates are expected to increase gradually in 2025-26 as the economy recovers.

China

Growth in China declined to an estimated 4.9 percent in 2024, marginally stronger than projected in June but the slowest pace in over three decades excluding pandemic-affected years. Activity moderated in the second half of the year, dampened by further falls in real estate investment and slower consumption growth amid weak consumer confidence. Retail sales growth remained subdued relative to its pre-pandemic

FIGURE 1.7 Major economies: Recent developments and outlook

In the United States, labor market conditions have been easing, with job losses contributing less to the rise in unemployment than in previous episodes. Investment spending, which boosted growth significantly in 2024, is not expected to support activity to the same extent going forward. In contrast with the United States, euro area growth was feeble last year. The euro area personal savings rate remains high, suggesting subdued consumer confidence. In China, consumption growth continues to be tepid, with retail sales rising at a slower pace than before the COVID-19 pandemic.

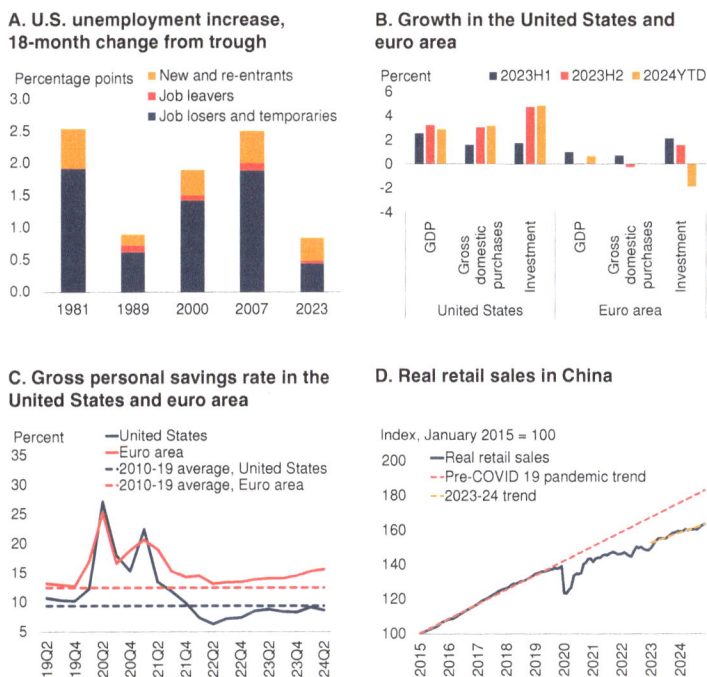

A. U.S. unemployment increase, 18-month change from trough

B. Growth in the United States and euro area

C. Gross personal savings rate in the United States and euro area

D. Real retail sales in China

Sources: Federal Reserve Bank of St. Louis; Haver Analytics; World Bank.

A. Bars show the contribution to the increase in the number of unemployed, scaled by the labor force, from the month and year (year indicated on the horizontal axis) when the trough in the unemployment rate occurred, using comparable 18-month periods. The current period, which is labeled 2023, shows data over April 2023 to November 2024. Classification follows the Bureau of Labor Statistics' definition for job leavers, job losers and persons who completed temporary jobs, and new and re-entrants.

B. Bars show the average year on year percent change in GDP components for corresponding periods. Investment is gross fixed capital formation. Gross domestic purchases (domestic demand) are defined as GDP minus net exports of goods and services. Last observation is 2024Q3.

C. United States: Gross personal savings as a percentage of gross disposable income. Euro area: Gross savings as a percentage of gross disposable income, adjusted for the change in net equity in pension fund reserves, including nonprofit institutions serving households. Dashed lines show 2010-19 averages.

D. Nominal retail sales deflated by headline consumer price inflation. Red line trend based on observations between January 2015 and December 2019, extended to November 2024. Orange line denotes the trend between January 2023 and November 2024. Last observation is November 2024.

trend (figure 1.7.D). In contrast, infrastructure and manufacturing investment were resilient, with the latter benefiting from solid external demand. Exports rebounded, driven by the global trade recovery, but weak domestic demand weighed on imports. Subdued domestic demand alongside economic slack continued to dampen price pressures, with both headline and core inflation remaining well below pre-pandemic averages.

Amid low inflation, weak domestic demand, and monetary policy easing in major advanced economies, the People's Bank of China implemented several measures in late 2024 to support the property market and broader activity, building on earlier policy changes. Policy interest rates, rates applied to existing mortgages, and reserve requirement ratios for banks were reduced, though their impact was somewhat dampened by weak sentiment and subdued credit demand. An expansion in government bond issuance enabled a pickup in public spending, but mounting local government fiscal pressures continued to constrain overall fiscal support.

In 2025, growth is projected to slow further to 4.5 percent—0.4 percentage point higher than envisioned in June, mainly reflecting a boost to activity from recent support measures and strong export momentum in late 2024. Consumption is anticipated to remain weak due to soft labor market conditions, subdued consumer confidence, and mounting wealth effects from declining property prices. With construction starts falling further in the second half of 2024, a broad-based stabilization of the property sector is not expected until later this year, weighing on overall investment growth. Following last year's rebound, export growth is expected to ease, while import growth will be dampened by subdued domestic demand. Tepid demand will also continue to weigh on inflation pressures, with headline consumer price inflation expected to remain well below the target of around 3 percent.

In 2026, growth is projected to edge down to 4 percent, as rising corporate sector and public debt weigh on investment, and slowing productivity growth constrains incomes and consumption. In tandem, potential growth will be further depressed by continued declines in population, with the fertility rate now well below the replacement rate. The growth outlook for China is, however, subject to a number of risks—most notably, the evolution of trade relations with the United States.[2]

---

[2] For further details, see the "Risks to the outlook" section below and EAP regional outlook in chapter 2.

Emerging market and developing economies

After edging down to 4.1 percent last year, EMDE growth is projected to remain near that pace over 2025-26, broadly in line with potential growth estimates. Decelerating activity in China is anticipated to be mostly offset by firming growth among other EMDEs, albeit with variations across regions (box 1.1). Growth in EMDEs excluding China is projected to rise from 3.5 percent in 2024 to 3.8 percent on average over 2025-26. Firming investment and solid consumption growth are anticipated to drive this pickup in growth, largely supported by continued monetary easing, improving financial conditions, recovering real incomes, and gradually expanding trade and industrial activity. Nevertheless, the recovery among EMDEs is expected to remain insufficient to make up for lost ground since 2020, particularly in vulnerable economies, including LICs and fragile and conflict-affected situations (FCS).

Recent developments

Activity in EMDEs generally steadied over 2024, as indicators of domestic demand—led by an ongoing expansion in the services sector—remained broadly supportive, despite some moderation in the second half of the year (figure 1.8.A). Gradually improving domestic demand was aided by generally easing financial conditions and improving credit growth (figure 1.8.B). This helped offset some softening in the expansion of manufacturing activity in the second half of 2024, which partly reflected still-modest external goods demand and ebbing industrial production growth (figure 1.8.C).

Growth continued to diverge across EMDEs in 2024, with slower-than-expected activity in some energy-exporting EMDEs and generally more solid conditions across other economies. In some major energy exporters, softness in global energy demand and ongoing OPEC+ production cuts weighed on net exports, revenues, and investment (figure 1.8.D). In energy-importing EMDEs excluding China, growth remained generally steady throughout 2024, supported by a broad-based pickup in consumption and investment.

Consumption was underpinned by declining inflation and easing energy prices, improving real wage growth, and generally favorable consumer confidence. Similarly, despite some softening in late 2024, business confidence and industrial production remained favorable for investment activity.

In LICs, growth is estimated to have been subdued in 2024, at 3.6 percent (box 1.2). This represents a downward revision of 1.4 percentage points relative to June projections, following a previous downgrade of 0.5 percentage point in the January 2024 report. In large part, downgrades to LIC growth in 2024 have reflected increased violence in several major LICs, resulting in significant disruptions in economic activity and large output losses, notably in Sudan and, to a lesser extent, the Democratic Republic of Congo. In both cases, conflict has caused a large displacement of the population.

EMDE outlook

Growth in EMDEs is forecast to remain at about 4 percent over 2025-26 on average, as the projected slowdown in China is offset by an aggregate pickup in other EMDEs. Growth in EMDEs excluding China is projected to firm from 3.5 percent in 2024 to an average of 3.8 percent in 2025-26. This improvement is expected to be broad-based, with average growth over 2025-26 accelerating in nearly 60 percent of EMDEs. These baseline forecasts do not incorporate possible shifts in U.S. economic policies, as their overall scope and final form remain uncertain.

The acceleration in growth in EMDEs excluding China over 2025-26 mainly reflects firming domestic demand (figure 1.9.A). Investment is expected to strengthen in many EMDEs, mirroring steadily rising business confidence, improving domestic demand, and the ongoing recovery in global trade. Consumption is also expected to remain solid across EMDEs, supported by receding inflation, improved real household incomes, and stronger consumer confidence. In many EMDEs, increasingly favorable domestic and global financial conditions—in part due to monetary policy easing in both advanced economies and EMDEs—are

FIGURE 1.8 Recent developments in emerging market and developing economies

Activity in EMDEs steadied over 2024. Amid an ongoing expansion in the services sector, domestic activity was supported by generally easing financial conditions and improving credit growth, despite a slowdown in manufacturing activity in the second half of 2024. Growth remained robust in many energy-importing economies excluding China, underpinned by consumption and investment and bolstered by improving business and consumer confidence. In contrast, growth softened in some energy-exporting EMDEs.

A. Services PMIs: Headline and new orders component

B. Credit impulse across EMDEs

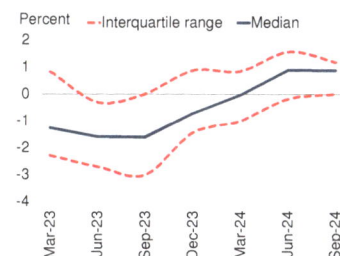

C. Manufacturing PMI: New export orders and industrial production growth

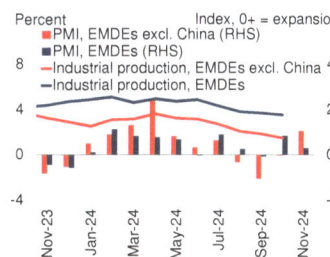

D. Share of EMDEs with accelerating growth in GDP and components

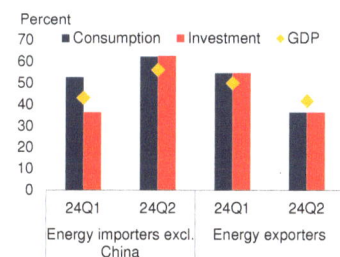

Sources: Haver Analytics; World Bank.
Note: EMDEs = emerging market and developing economies; PMI = purchasing managers' index; RHS = right-hand scale.
A. Panel shows the weighted average of a sample that includes 21 EMDEs. Readings above (below) zero indicate expansion (contraction). Monthly readings are recentered at 0, the expansionary threshold. Last observation is November 2024.
B. The credit impulse is calculated as the change in the ratio of the four-quarter sum of the change in total credit to the private sector to the four-quarter sum of nominal GDP. The unbalanced sample includes up to 36 EMDEs. Last observation is September 2024.
C. Lines show the three-month moving average of the growth rate (year over year) of the industrial production index, seasonally adjusted. Bars show a weighted average of monthly PMI readings for sample that includes 21 EMDEs. Readings above (below) zero indicate expansion (contraction). Monthly readings are recentered at 0, the expansionary threshold. Last observation is November 2024 for PMI data, and October 2024 for industrial production.
D. Panel shows the share of economies with a higher growth rate (year over year) on a quarterly basis, relative to the prior quarter. The sample includes up to 59 energy-importing and 12 energy-exporting EMDEs for GDP data and up to 40 energy-importing and 11 energy-exporting EMDEs for components data. Last observation is 2024Q2.

anticipated to support credit growth and bolster consumption and investment. In contrast, fiscal policy among EMDEs is broadly expected to either dampen or have a neutral effect on activity over 2025-26, as fiscal consolidation proceeds or as policy shifts toward a more neutral stance after earlier tightening (figure 1.9.B).

FIGURE 1.9 Outlook in emerging market and developing economies

Growth in EMDEs excluding China is anticipated to average 3.8 percent in 2025-26, driven by firming domestic demand, with fiscal policy remaining broadly neutral or modestly restrictive. Activity in commodity-importing EMDEs is anticipated to expand more slowly than in the decade prior to the pandemic, despite robust investment growth in some major economies. EMDEs with weak credit ratings remain on a lower growth trajectory than other EMDEs. Despite a projected cyclical upswing in growth in EMDEs excluding China over 2025-26, significant output losses are expected to persist.

A. Contributions to growth in EMDEs excluding China

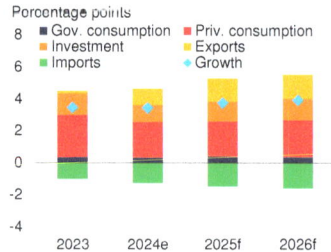

B. Fiscal impulse stance as a share of EMDEs excluding China

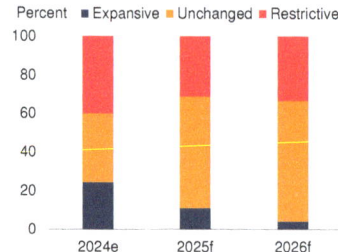

C. GDP growth versus 2010-19 averages

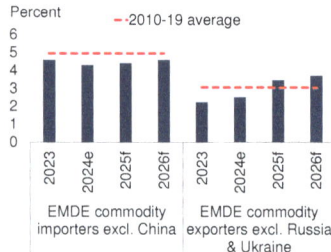

D. Investment and consumption growth in EMDE commodity importers excluding China

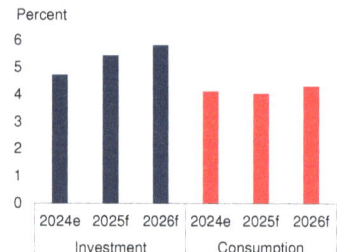

E. GDP growth in EMDEs, by credit rating

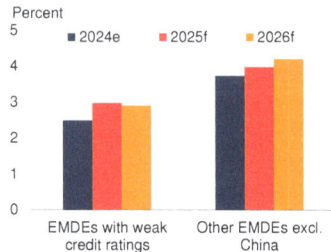

F. Output losses relative to the pre-pandemic trend

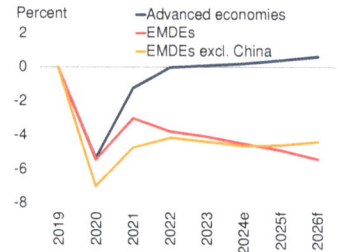

Sources: International Monetary Fund; Moody's Analytics; World Bank.
Note: EMDEs = emerging market and developing economies; e = estimate; f = forecast.
A. Panel shows the projected annual GDP growth for EMDEs excluding China and the contributions to growth of GDP sub-components. Any discrepancy between GDP growth and the sum of its components is explained by inventories and statistical residuals.
B. Panel shows the share of EMDEs with negative, unchanged, and positive changes in their fiscal impulse measured by the cyclically adjusted primary balance. The impulse indicates fiscal stance: expansive (positive) or restrictive (negative). An "unchanged" fiscal stance is defined as the change in fiscal impulse falling within the +/- 0.5 percent of GDP range. Sample includes 46 EMDEs.
C. Bars show the annual percentage change in real GDP for each country group. Dashed lines show the simple average of annual real GDP growth for each country group over 2010-19.
E. Sample includes 28 EMDEs with sovereign bond rating grades at CCC+/Caa1 and below.
F. Panel shows the percent deviation between the latest projections and projections released in the January 2020 edition of the *Global Economic Prospects* report (World Bank 2020). For 2023 and beyond, the January 2020 baseline is extended with a trend using projected growth for 2022. Sample includes 179 countries, of which 37 are advanced economies and 142 are EMDEs.

Growth in commodity-exporting EMDEs is expected to accelerate to 3.3 percent over 2025-26, up from 2.8 percent in 2024, mainly reflecting stronger investment spending. Following some weakness in 2024, investment is anticipated to pick up in many energy-exporting EMDEs, aided in some cases by ongoing domestic investment programs. Many oil-exporting economies are also expected to see net exports improve, as oil production increases modestly in the later part of 2025, in line with fading OPEC+ production cuts. Among metal-exporting EMDEs, the pickup in investment and growth is set to be stronger than in energy exporters. Over the forecast horizon, many metals prices are anticipated to remain broadly stable, staying well above pre-pandemic levels, and supportive of investments in expanded production, particularly for metals linked to the green transition.

In commodity-importing EMDEs excluding China, growth is projected to accelerate from 4.3 percent in 2024 to an average of 4.5 percent over 2025-26, slightly below the pre-pandemic pace (figure 1.9.C). Solid domestic demand is expected to accompany a steady firming of global manufacturing and trade, supporting employment and an improvement in investment growth, particularly in economies with substantial manufacturing sectors (figure 1.9.D). Consumption is also anticipated to remain solid, similar to that in most other EMDEs.

In the roughly one-fourth of EMDEs with weak credit ratings (defined as those with sovereign bond ratings at CCC+/Caa1 and below), growth is expected to pick up to 2.9 percent on average over 2025-26, still lagging the pace of other EMDEs by a substantial margin (figure 1.9.E). Despite the decline in sovereign risk spreads, these economies continue to face elevated borrowing costs and high debt burdens, making them susceptible to sudden swings in investor sentiment. Limited capital market access and fiscal vulnerabilities remain a drag on business and consumer confidence; they also reduce the scope for fiscal spending to support activity and undertake productivity-enhancing investments.

More broadly, the recovery from the successive shocks of the past few years remains incomplete in

BOX 1.1 Regional perspectives: Outlook and risks

Emerging market and developing economy regions face varying growth prospects this year. Growth is projected to moderate in East Asia and Pacific, amid weak domestic demand in China, as well as in Europe and Central Asia owing to decelerations in some large economies following strong growth last year. In contrast, a pickup is anticipated in Latin America and the Caribbean, the Middle East and North Africa, South Asia, and Sub-Saharan Africa, partly underpinned by robust domestic demand. In 2026, growth is expected to strengthen in most regions. Risks to the outlook remain tilted to the downside across all regions, centering on adverse shifts in global trade and other economic policies. The possibility of escalating conflict, slower-than-expected growth in China and the United States, higher-than-expected inflation and attendant slower monetary policy easing, and natural disasters pose further downside risks. Conversely, faster-than-expected growth in major economies and lower-than-expected inflation and faster monetary policy easing present key upside risks.

Introduction

Against a backdrop of heightened trade restrictive measures and subdued global growth, emerging market and developing economy (EMDE) regions face varying growth prospects. Although monetary easing has commenced in all regions and is expected to provide some support to domestic demand, the anticipated pace and extent of easing varies across regions. Moreover, against a backdrop of elevated public debt, fiscal consolidation is expected to weigh on activity in some regions. Since global trade growth is expected to remain below pre-pandemic averages, while international tourism has largely returned to pre-pandemic levels, domestic demand will serve as the primary driver of growth across regions. After moderating somewhat last year, global commodity prices are expected to soften further this year, benefiting commodity importers but posing a headwind to some commodity exporters.

Next year, growth is projected to firm in most EMDE regions. However, the forecasts imply that, across regions, growth will be insufficient to achieve consistent progress toward catching up to advanced-economy per capita income levels. Moreover, risks to the outlook remain tilted to the downside. In particular, adverse shifts in global trade and other economic policies, as well as heightened policy uncertainty, could weigh on activity across all regions.

In this context, this box considers two questions:

- What are the cross-regional differences in the outlook for growth?

- What are the key risks to the outlook for EMDE regions?

Note: This box was prepared by Samuel Hill.

Outlook

Growth is set to diverge across EMDE regions this year, falling in EAP and ECA—mainly due to slower growth in large economies weighing on the broader regional outlook—and picking up in LAC, MNA, SAR, and SSA (figure B1.1.1.A). In EAP, the anticipated slowdown reflects a further deceleration in China amid weak domestic demand and a continued property sector slump. Activity is also expected to decelerate in ECA, where the Russian Federation and Türkiye are projected to slow in part reflecting the lagged impact of tight monetary policy.

In contrast, growth is expected to pick up in MNA predicated on the assumption of an unwinding of oil production cuts and associated rising energy production and exports among oil-exporting economies. Growth in oil-importing economies in MNA is also set to firm, supported by moderating inflation and improved sentiment. A more modest acceleration is envisaged in LAC, partly driven by a rebound in Argentina following two consecutive years of contraction. Growth is projected to edge up in SAR—which is set to remain the fastest growing region over the forecast horizon—supported by firming growth in India. Growth is also anticipated to pick up in SSA, where activity will be supported by lower inflation and easing financial conditions.

Compared with the June projections, growth this year has been revised down in ECA, owing chiefly to the delayed effects of tighter-than-expected monetary policy in Türkiye and the assumption of continued active hostilities in Ukraine (figure B1.1.1.B). Growth has also been downgraded in MNA, due to weaker-than-expected oil production, and in LAC, where disinflation is proceeding more slowly than previously assumed in some countries. In contrast, projections have been

BOX 1.1 Regional perspectives: Outlook and risks (*continued*)

FIGURE B1.1.1 Regional outlooks

Growth prospects vary across EMDE regions this year, declining in some regions mainly owing to decelerations in large economies. Projected growth this year has been downgraded in ECA, LAC, and MNA, with the downgrades variously reflecting tighter-than-expected monetary policy, oil production cuts, and the adverse impacts of conflict. The forecasts imply slower catch-up to advanced-economy per capita income levels compared with the pre-pandemic period in EAP and SAR, generally little to no catch-up in ECA, LAC, and MNA, and a further widening of the income gap in SSA.

A. Output growth

B. Growth forecast revisions

C. Differences between per capita income growth in EMDE regions and advanced economies

Source: World Bank.
Note: e = estimate; EAP = East Asia and Pacific; ECA = Europe and Central Asia; EMDEs = emerging market and developing economies; f = forecast; LAC = Latin America and the Caribbean; MNA = Middle East and North Africa; SAR = South Asia; SSA = Sub-Saharan Africa.
A. Aggregate growth rates are calculated using GDP weights at average 2000-19 prices and market exchange rates. "2010-19" refers to the period averages of regional growth rates. Data for 2025 and 2026 are World Bank forecasts.
B. Revisions reflect differences in forecasts presented in the June 2024 edition of the *Global Economic Prospects* report and the current forecasts. Data for 2025 and 2026 are World Bank forecasts.
C. Bars and dashes represent annual average GDP per capita growth in EMDE regions minus the annual average GDP per capita growth in advanced economies, expressed in percentage points.

revised up slightly in EAP, partly reflecting somewhat stronger-than-expected prospects in China, and in SSA, on account of unexpectedly robust growth momentum in some countries.

In the second half of 2024, headline inflation in most EMDE regions settled around central bank targets or continued to decline toward them, supported by slowing demand in some major economies and moderating commodity prices. Price pressures were particularly subdued in EAP, where headline and core inflation are below central bank targets in some countries, including China. In most inflation-targeting countries in SAR, headline inflation was also below or within target ranges. In contrast, inflation generally remained elevated in ECA, partly reflecting strong wage growth, and in some countries in LAC, MNA, and SSA, often driven by food inflation.

Alongside an anticipated further recovery in global goods trade this year, export growth is expected to firm somewhat in most EMDE regions. The projected acceleration is particularly notable in MNA, driven by

an assumed ramp-up in energy production and exports, and to a lesser extent in ECA, partly reflecting spillovers from a modest recovery in euro area activity. In contrast to the expected uptick in goods export growth, tailwinds from the global tourism recovery have largely faded, except in EAP to some extent, where reopening was delayed. Consistent with the global trade outlook, trade growth in some regions is set to remain below pre-pandemic averages.

Given the tepid outlook for trade growth across EMDE regions, solid domestic demand is expected to drive growth, supported by moderating inflation and easing monetary policy, which will bolster household incomes as well as consumer and business confidence. In some regions, including parts of ECA and SAR, consumption will be further supported by remittances sustained by solid labor market conditions in worker destination economies. Consumption growth is anticipated to pick up modestly in LAC and more significantly in SSA, following years of subpar activity. Investment is also set to accelerate in LAC and SSA and remain buoyant in SAR. In contrast, consumption is expected to remain

BOX 1.1 Regional perspectives: Outlook and risks (*continued*)

FIGURE B1.1.2 Regional risks

Risks to the baseline projections for EMDE regions remain tilted to the downside. Amid heightened policy uncertainty and shifting trade policies, escalating trade protectionism could dampen exports and growth across all regions. Heightened conflict and its fallout also pose a major risk to all regions, particularly ECA, MNA, and SSA. Resurgent inflationary pressures could keep interest rates higher for longer, adding to debt-servicing burdens in all regions, while growth in China and the United States could surprise to the downside, weighing especially on regions with close trade linkages to them. More frequent and costly climate-change-related natural disasters pose a further downside risk to all regions.

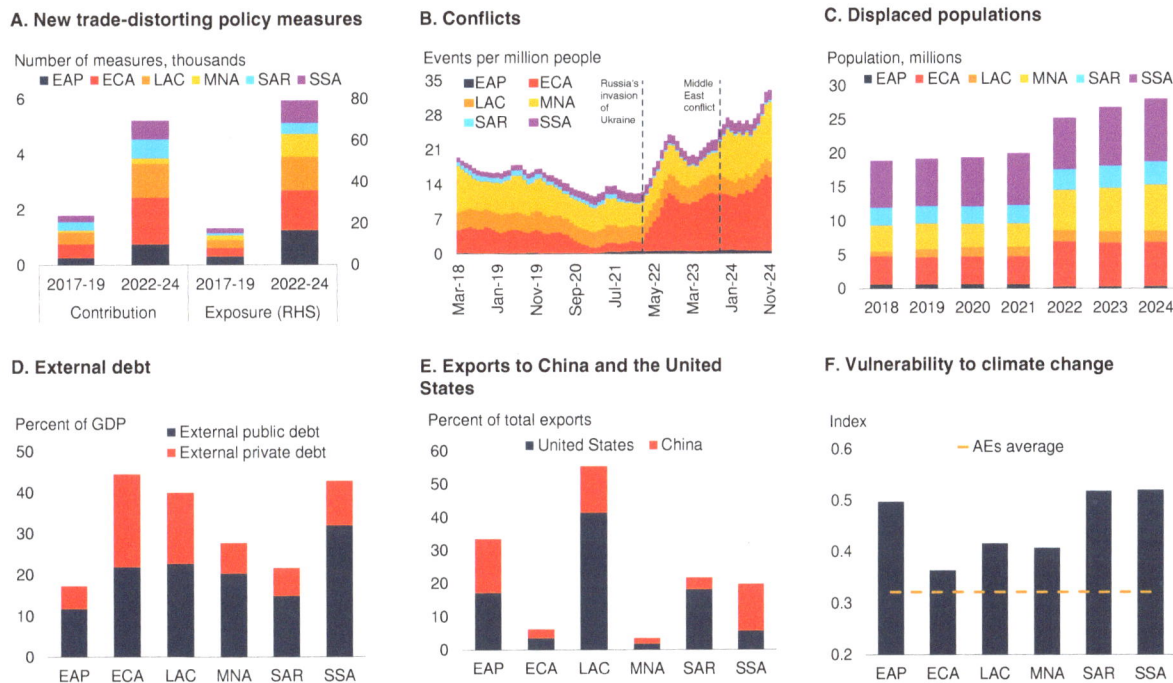

A. New trade-distorting policy measures

B. Conflicts

C. Displaced populations

D. External debt

E. Exports to China and the United States

F. Vulnerability to climate change

Sources: ACLED (database); Global Trade Alert (database); International Monetary Fund; ND-GAIN (database); UN Comtrade (database); UNHCR (database); World Bank.

Note: AEs = advanced economies; EAP = East Asia and Pacific; ECA = Europe and Central Asia; EMDEs = emerging market and developing economies; LAC = Latin America and the Caribbean; MNA = Middle East and North Africa; SAR = South Asia; SSA = Sub-Saharan Africa.

A. The number of harmful trade measures implemented by and affecting different EMDE regions. Harmful trade measures include the sum of "Amber" and "Red" measures classified as harmful in the Global Trade Alert database. Each measure can be implemented by and target multiple countries. Data have been adjusted for reporting lags as of December 19, 2024.

B. Stacked bars show three-month moving averages of the number of reported individual conflict events per million people in each of the six EMDE regions. Major conflicts involve multiple conflict events, including battles, explosions, riots, and violence against civilians. The date of Russia's invasion of Ukraine is February 24, 2022. The date of the Middle East conflict is October 7, 2023. Last observation is end-November 2024.

C. Number of forcibly displaced persons by country of asylum, including refugees under UNHCR's mandate and asylum-seekers.

D. GDP-weighted average of gross external debt as a share of GDP. Annual data as of 2022. Sample includes 105 EMDEs (15 in EAP, 22 in ECA, 23 in LAC, 10 in MNA, 8 in SAR, and 27 in SSA).

E. Percent of gross regional goods exports to China and the United States in 2022. EAP excludes China.

F. Vulnerability measures exposure, sensitivity, and capacity to adapt to the negative effects of climate change. Index ranges from 0 to 1; higher values indicate higher vulnerability. Notre Dame Global Adaptation Initiative measures overall vulnerability by considering six life-supporting dimensions: food, water, health, ecosystem services, human habitats, and infrastructure. Orange line denotes the simple average of indices of advanced economies in 2022. Last observation is 2022.

subdued in EAP, partly reflecting weak consumer confidence and soft labor market conditions in China.

Mostly easing financial conditions, reflecting cuts in interest rates in major advanced economies and across EMDE regions, along with solid global investor risk appetite, are expected to support activity. However, the anticipated pace of monetary policy easing varies considerably across regions. Interest rates are set to fall steadily in regions where easing cycles have more recently begun, including MNA, SSA, and SAR. In contrast, in some parts of ECA and LAC, where signs of elevated inflationary pressures persist, policy easing is expected to proceed gradually and unevenly. In EAP,

BOX 1.1 Regional perspectives: Outlook and risks (*continued*)

interest rates are already low by historical standards in many countries, limiting the scope for large interest rate cuts even with well-contained inflation pressures. To varying degrees, fiscal consolidation is expected to offset some of the support from easing monetary policy in certain regions.

Next year, growth is projected to strengthen in MNA, as oil production and exports accelerate, and in ECA, LAC, and SSA, where further declines in inflation and interest rates are anticipated to boost domestic demand. Elsewhere, growth is expected to soften slightly or remain stable. Overall, the forecasts imply that growth will be insufficient to achieve consistent progress toward narrowing the per capita income gap with advanced economies across EMDE regions (figure B1.1.1.C). For the period 2021-26, catch-up is set to slow compared to the decade preceding the pandemic in the fastest growing regions, EAP and SAR, remain slow in ECA and LAC, and continue to stagnate in MNA. Worse still, despite a projected uptick in growth, per capita income in SSA—the poorest and most poverty-stricken region—is set to fall further behind.

Risks

Risks to the baseline growth projections for EMDE regions remain tilted to the downside. Heightened policy uncertainty, particularly the threat of adverse global policy shifts, including further trade protectionism, poses a major risk to all regions. Escalating conflict also poses downside risks, particularly in regions where active conflicts are situated. Additional downside risks arise from persistently elevated inflation, which could hinder anticipated monetary policy easing, and adverse spillovers from weaker-than-expected growth in China and the United States. Climate-change-related natural disasters pose further downside risks to all regions. On the upside, growth in major economies could exceed expectations, while global disinflation and monetary easing could proceed more quickly than anticipated, with positive consequences for activity in all EMDE regions.

Heightened global policy uncertainty and potential adverse policy shifts, especially regarding trade policies, poses a downside risk across EMDE regions. Against a backdrop of increased global trade fragmentation, all regions have both implemented and been the target of,

new trade restriction measures (figure B1.1.2.A; Aiyar and Ohnsorge 2024). Additional such measures, which would further fragment global trade, could dampen trade growth, depress broader economic activity, and raise prices. Export-oriented regions with significant manufacturing bases are particularly vulnerable to the effects of heightened protectionism and supply chain reorientation, notably EAP, ECA, and LAC.

Amid already heightened global tensions, intensifying conflict poses a downside risk to growth in all EMDE regions (figure B1.1.2.B). Regions experiencing major conflicts, notably ECA, MNA, and SSA, are most exposed to direct costs, including disruptions to production, destruction of physical capital, and the displacement of populations (figure B1.1.2.C; Deininger et al. 2024). However, other regions are also exposed to adverse spillovers. In particular, conflict in the Middle East risks disrupting global oil and natural gas supplies, which could push up global energy prices and inflation, and dampen activity, especially in regions more dependent on imported energy, including EAP and SAR (World Bank 2024a).

Although inflation has been settling toward targets in most advanced economies and EMDEs, resilient activity and robust wage growth could result in more persistent global inflation than projected. In turn, this could prompt central banks in advanced economies and EMDEs to maintain higher policy rates, weighing on activity across EMDE regions. Regions where activity is expected to strengthen and inflation remains somewhat elevated—including LAC and SAR and some parts of ECA, MNA, and SSA—are most vulnerable. In addition, rapid shifts in expectations about policy interest rates could stoke global financial market volatility and increase debt-servicing costs, with particularly adverse consequences for EMDE regions reliant on external debt—including ECA, LAC, and SSA, and parts of MNA and SAR (figure B1.1.2.D).

Growth in the world's two largest economies, the United States and China, could fall short of expectations, generating adverse spillovers, particularly in EMDE regions with substantial trade linkages to them (figure B1.1.2.E; chapter 3). In the United States, following several years of robust job growth, the labor market could cool rapidly, leading to weaker-than-expected consumption. In China, the property slump

BOX 1.1 Regional perspectives: Outlook and risks (*continued*)

could intensify, further eroding confidence, weakening household balance sheets and consumption, and reducing industrial demand. An unexpected slowdown in either economy would weaken external demand across all EMDE regions, especially in EAP and LAC, and weigh on global commodity prices and economic activity in some commodity-exporting regions, particularly in ECA, MNA, and SSA.

Natural disasters, including more severe and frequent climate-change-related events, could dampen both short- and long-term growth in all EMDE regions (figure B1.1.2.F). Many regions are vulnerable to disruptive weather events such as droughts and floods, including ECA, which can intensify pervasive food insecurity, notably in MNA, SAR, and SSA. Moreover, such climate-change-related hazards would tend to exacerbate inequality given that poorer households are disproportionately exposed (Behrer et al. 2024). Small states, spread across all EMDE regions but concentrated in EAP and LAC, are particularly vulnerable to severe

floods and storms that endanger life and economic activity (World Bank 2024b).

On the upside, global disinflation could proceed more quickly than anticipated, paving the way for faster interest rate cuts than assumed. Lower inflation and interest rates would especially boost demand in regions where interest rates remain elevated, including LAC. An additional upside risk is faster-than-expected growth in China, on account of additional policy support measures, or in the United States, where strong household balance sheets could underpin more resilient consumption than assumed in the baseline. Commodity-exporting regions, including MNA and SSA, and to a lesser extent ECA, could benefit from higher prices and increased demand for commodity exports. In addition, regions with the strongest direct trade linkages to China and the United States, including EAP and LAC, could experience notably stronger external demand—though this could be tempered by additional trade protectionism.

many EMDEs. Despite the projected pickup in growth over 2025-26, the level of output for EMDEs excluding China is expected to remain about 4 percent below the pre-pandemic trajectory by 2026 (figure 1.9.F). Many long-term drivers of growth have also come under further pressure, with trade—a key driver of investment and productivity growth in EMDEs—facing headwinds from heightened geopolitical tensions, trade fragmentation, and elevated trade policy uncertainty.

LICs outlook

Growth in LICs is forecast to rebound to an average of 5.8 percent in 2025-26 (box 1.2). The recovery follows much weaker-than-expected growth in 2024, due to renewed violent conflict in Sub-Saharan Africa, particularly Sudan. The projected rebound over the forecast horizon depends on a recovery in LICs facing fragile and conflict-affected situations (FCS LICs), where substantial improvements in security situations are

assumed to take place. Furthermore, the forecast assumes that no new conflicts in LICs emerge, that inflation continues to abate, and that no debt crises occur.

The growth forecasts for LICs in 2025 and 2026 have been upgraded by 0.4 percentage point each, compared to June. The upward revisions are mostly predicated on improved growth prospects for some non-FCS LICs (such as Uganda), and on an end to conflict leading to economic stabilization in a few FCS-LICs (such as Sudan). Even so, the level of output in LICs is expected to remain almost 5 percent below the pre-pandemic trajectory by 2026, suggesting material output losses in many countries where extreme poverty is already pervasive.

Many LICs will continue to face daunting challenges (chapter 4). In some FCS LICs, violent conflict has resulted in the destruction of industrial capacity and significant displacement of the population, which is likely to prevent a near-term recovery in economic activity. For

FIGURE 1.10 Per capita income growth

Per capita GDP in EMDEs excluding China and India peaked relative to advanced economy incomes in the early 2010s, with growth in many EMDEs set to remain tepid over 2021-26. Per capita GDP in LICs is set to fall further behind that of advanced economies overall, with less than one quarter of LICs appearing on course to become middle-income by 2050. In LICs and fragile and conflict-affected economies, per capita income is expected to remain substantially below the pre-pandemic trend. After steady progress in the decades preceding the pandemic, the extreme poverty rate in EMDEs excluding China and India remains higher than in 2019.

A. EMDE per capita GDP relative to advanced economies

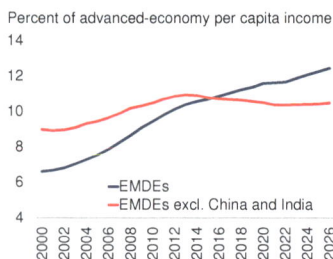

B. Difference between per capita income growth in EMDEs and advanced economies

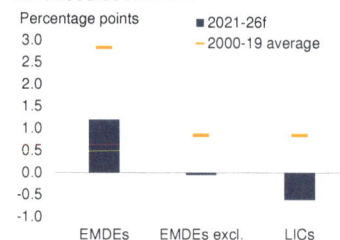

C. Trajectories for graduation to middle-income status in LICs

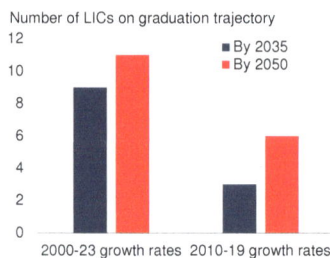

D. Per capita income forecast revisions and output losses among LICs

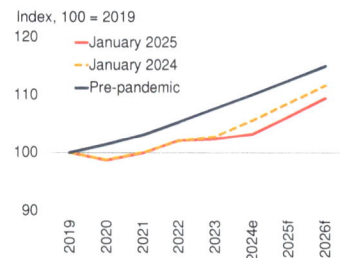

E. Per capita income forecast revisions and output losses among FCS economies

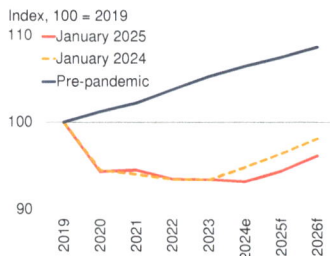

F. Average annual reduction in extreme poverty rates

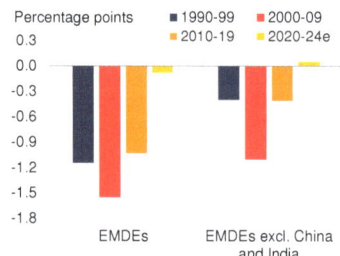

Sources: Mahler, Yonzan, and Lakner (2022); WDI (database); World Bank Poverty and Inequality Platform; World Bank.
Note: EMDEs = emerging market and developing economies; e = estimate; f = forecast; FCS = fragile and conflict-affected situations; LICs = low-income countries. Aggregate GDP per capita is calculated as aggregated GDP divided by the aggregate population. GDP aggregates are calculated using real U.S. dollar GDP weights at average 2010-19 prices and market exchange rates.
B. Bars and markers represent annual average per capita GDP growth for each country group minus the annual average GDP per capita growth in advanced economies. The year 2020 is excluded due to extreme volatility related to the pandemic.
C. Graduation trajectories assume that the threshold for middle-income status increases at the same average pace as over 2000-23. Average growth rates are calculated based on GNI per capita in U.S. dollars (Atlas method), which is the measure used to determine middle-income status.
D.E. Panels show the level of per capita income. "January 2025" and "January 2024" refer to the forecasts presented in the corresponding editions of the *Global Economic Prospects* report. For 2023 and beyond, the pre-pandemic trend is the January 2020 baseline projection extended using the projected growth rate for 2022. Shaded areas indicate the output loss since 2019.
F. Extreme poverty is defined as living below the International Poverty Line of $2.15 per day. Estimates after 2022 are nowcasts.

many highly indebted LICs, slow progress in debt restructuring and limited access to new external financing continue to pose headwinds. More generally, the high cost of debt service in LICs remains a constraint on fiscal resources that could otherwise be used to support vulnerable populations.

Per capita income growth

Against the backdrop of weakening potential growth, elevated government debt, and substantial policy uncertainty, most EMDEs are exiting the first quarter of this century with per capita GDP on a trajectory that implies very slow progress in closing the gap with advanced-economy incomes in the second quarter of the century (World Bank 2024c). The incomplete recovery from the pandemic and successive shocks of the past four years, combined with an escalation of conflict in some economies, has further hindered the pace of poverty reduction and per capita income catch-up across EMDEs. Per capita income growth is estimated to have slowed to 3.1 percent in EMDEs in 2024—1 percentage point below the 2000-19 average. In LICs, per capita income grew 0.8 percent in 2024—considerably weaker than the average pace of 2000-19. Meanwhile, per capita income contracted 0.5 percent in 2024 in FCS, with the greatest declines in economies where violence and conflict have been acute.

Per capita income growth in EMDEs is projected to remain below its 2000-19 average over 2025-26, at 3.1 percent. A longer-term slowdown was already well underway prior to the pandemic, as the boost from international integration and domestic reforms in the 2000s faded in many EMDEs (figure 1.10.A; chapter 3). Excluding China and India—the main sources of EMDE income convergence this century—progress in closing the per capita income gap with advanced economies stalled in the mid-2010s. This trend is so far continuing in the 2020s, with many LICs and FCS falling further behind (figure 1.10.B). Indeed, even assuming average 2010s growth rates—which were somewhat stronger than those of recent years—less than one-quarter of LICs appear on course to graduate to middle-income by 2050, down from close to two-thirds of eligible countries in the last 25 years (chapter 4; figure 1.10.C).

BOX 1.2 Low-income countries: Recent developments and outlook

The number of people struggling with extreme poverty in low-income countries (LICs) remains high. Recent flare-ups of violent conflict have heightened the challenges faced by many of these countries, as have increased debt-service costs and reduced fiscal policy space for many more. This resulted in downward revisions for growth in LICs in 2024, now estimated at 3.6 percent. Growth in these countries is forecast to rise to 5.8 percent a year, on average, in 2025 and 2026—an upward revision from previous projections mainly driven by improvements in the outlook for some fragile and conflict-affected LICs. Per capita income growth is projected to increase to an average of 3 percent in 2025-26 but will remain uneven. Risks to the outlook are tilted to the downside. They include intensifying insecurity and violent conflict, especially in the Middle East and Sudan, which could lead to negative spillovers for many LICs, including increased food insecurity. Other downside risks are lower global growth due to heightened uncertainty and the potential for adverse changes in trade policies, more persistent inflation, increased risk of government debt distress, and more frequent or intense extreme weather events.

Introduction

In low-income countries (LICs), growth remained subdued at 3.6 percent last year. This partly reflected slower-than-expected expansion in major LICs, including the Democratic Republic of Congo and Ethiopia, but also high levels of violent conflict in fragile and conflict-affected situations (FCS), especially Sudan (figure B.1.2.1.A). These developments resulted in a downward revision of nearly 2 percentage points for growth in LICs in 2024 compared to the January forecast last year. In 2025-26, growth in these economies is expected to accelerate, following the easing of overlapping shocks that hit them in the past half decade, including the pandemic, high inflation, and tightening financial conditions.

Although inflation has slowed in many LICs, costs of living remain elevated and the number of people struggling with extreme poverty and food insecurity in these countries remains high. Policy space, which was narrow before the pandemic, has been further depleted by increased debt and interest payments, requiring fiscal tightening and constraining the ability of governments to support the poor in many LICs. Elevated violence has continued to exacerbate poverty and increased the number of displaced people.

Various downside risks cloud LICs' prospects, including further increases in domestic political instability and violent conflict, and more persistent inflation than projected, which could keep monetary policies tighter for longer than assumed. Greater frequency or intensity of adverse weather events could also weigh on economic activity.

Against this backdrop, this box addresses the following questions.

- What have been the main recent economic developments in LICs?

- What is the outlook for LICs?

- What are the risks to the outlook?

Recent developments

Despite some improvement, growth in LICs remained subdued at an estimated 3.6 percent in 2024. The estimate reflects a further 15 percent GDP contraction in Sudan, which took the country's output to levels more than one-third lower than before the start of the current conflict. The pickup in growth last year was partly driven by accelerated activity in agriculture-exporting LICs, amid solid investment growth in Uganda. Part of the improvement in growth also reflects a less pronounced drag from the slower contraction of Sudan's economy than in 2023.

At the country level, growth estimates for more than 40 percent of LICs in 2024 have been revised down from June projections. Most of these downgrades pertain to FCS LICs, with growth estimates lowered in more than half of these countries, most pronouncedly in Sudan and South Sudan. This resulted in a downward revision of 1.4 percentage points for LIC growth in 2024 compared to the June forecast, on top of a 0.5-percentage-point downgrade already incorporated in the June forecast.

Highlighting the economic and humanitarian costs of violent conflict in LICs, output growth differed significantly between FCS and non-FCS LICs in 2024.

Note: This box was prepared by Dominik Peschel.

BOX 1.2 Low-income countries: Recent developments and outlook (*continued*)

FIGURE B1.2.1 LICs: Recent developments

The incidence of violence has remained high in LICs, mainly reflecting violent conflicts in the Sahel and East Africa. Consequently, the number of displaced people has increased in recent years. While median consumer price inflation in LICs has moderated since late 2022, food price inflation rose in 2024, posing a significant challenge in many of these countries.

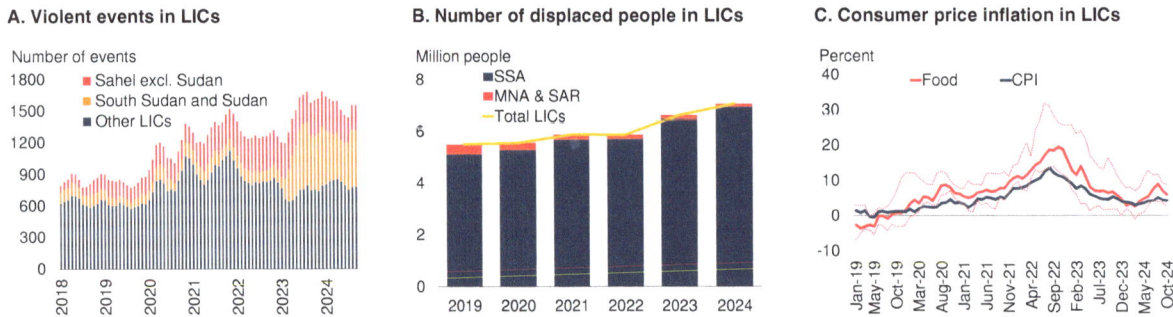

A. Violent events in LICs

B. Number of displaced people in LICs

C. Consumer price inflation in LICs

Sources: ACLED (database); Haver Analytics; United Nations High Commissioner for Refugees (UNHCR) Refugee Population Statistics Database; World Bank.
Note: excl. = excluding; LICs = low-income countries.
A. Three-month moving average. Violent events include battles, explosions, violence against civilians, and riots. Last observation is November 2024.
B. MNA = Middle East and North Africa, SAR = South Asia, SSA = Sub-Saharan Africa. Statistic covers forcibly displaced persons by country of asylum comprising of refugees under UNHCR's mandate and asylum-seekers; excludes internally displaced persons. Sample includes 25 countries, of which at least 22 are in Sub-Saharan Africa.
C. Change in prices from 12 months earlier. Dotted lines refer to the interquartile range of food price inflation. Median for the sample of eight LICs. Last observation is October 2024.

Output growth in non-FCS LICs edged up to an estimated 5.6 percent, mainly driven by improvements in both Uganda, which benefited from an oil-related infrastructure boom, and Madagascar, where ongoing structural reforms boosted growth. However, in FCS LICs, excluding the Democratic Republic of Congo and Ethiopia, output contracted by 1.3 percent, mostly on account of the conflict-related contraction in Sudan. The conflict in Sudan has led to the internal displacement of about 10 million people, and more than 2 million have fled the country (figure B.1.2.1.B). Sudan's government institutions have collapsed, and population displacements, along with reduced economic activity, have contributed to a sharp decline in government revenues.

In the Democratic Republic of Congo, growth slowed to 4.9 percent in 2024, as violent conflict in the eastern part of the country disrupted mining operations and resulted in the internal displacement of several million people. In Ethiopia, growth moderated to 6.1 percent following foreign exchange market reforms and tighter monetary policy.

While annual consumer price inflation in the median LIC has declined from its mid-2022 peaks, food prices picked up in 2024 in many LICs (figure B.1.2.1.C). Some LICs in the Sahel and East Africa were hit by severe floods in 2024 (Burkina Faso, Chad, Mali, Central African Republic, Niger, South Sudan), while LICs in Southern Africa experienced El Niño-related droughts (Malawi, Mozambique), which adversely affected harvests and raised local food prices. Moreover, in some countries, food price inflation remained persistently high (Ethiopia, Malawi, Sierra Leone), while in others, it was driven by conflict (South Sudan).

Outlook

Growth in LICs is projected to firm from 3.6 percent in 2024 to an average of 5.8 percent a year in 2025-26 (table B.1.2.1). At the same time, this growth rate, though substantially higher than in the past two years, will not make up for the lost ground that the overlapping shocks of the past half decade have caused. At the end of 2026, LICs will still face output losses of nearly 5 percent compared to their pre-pandemic baseline, with worse results for FCS LICs that were also hit by a wave of political instability and violent conflict in recent years. LICs also continue to face multiple challenges, including high debt and limited access to financing.

BOX 1.2 Low-income countries: Recent developments and outlook (*continued*)

FIGURE B1.2.2 LICs: Outlook and risks

Growth estimates in LICs for 2024 have been revised sharply downward, mainly as a result of delays in stabilization as violent conflict in East Africa continues. Meanwhile, upward revisions in the forecasts for non-FCS LICs result in a slightly higher growth forecast for LICs in 2025-26. Fragile and conflict-affected LICs, excluding the Democratic Republic of Congo and Ethiopia, are projected to merely stabilize their capita income losses in 2025-26 relative to the pre-pandemic trend. Despite their projected high growth, LICs will not be able to close the gap. Government debt-to-GDP ratios in LICs are expected to decline in the forecast period, and interest payments as a percentage of GDP are expected to moderate somewhat.

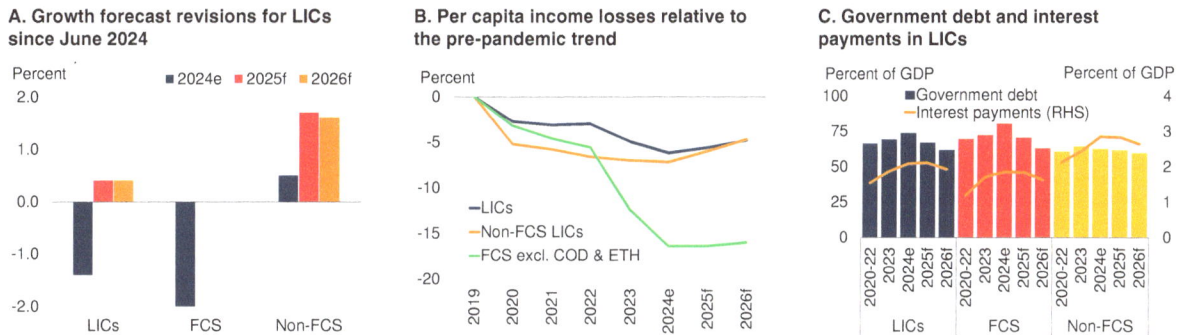

A. Growth forecast revisions for LICs since June 2024

B. Per capita income losses relative to the pre-pandemic trend

C. Government debt and interest payments in LICs

Sources: International Monetary Fund; World Bank.
Note: e = estimate; f = forecast; excl. = excluding; COD = Democratic Republic of Congo; ETH = Ethiopia; FCS = fragile and conflict-affected situations; GDP = gross domestic product; LICs = low-income countries.
A. Revisions relative to forecast published in the June 2024 edition of the *Global Economic Prospects* report. Sample comprises 21 LICs.
B. Panel shows percent deviation from the 2020 January *Global Economic Prospects* baseline projections for GDP per capita.
C. Simple averages of country groupings. Sample includes 21 LIC countries.

The forecast assumes that the security situation in a number of LICs improves substantially and that no new violent conflicts break out, that inflation continues to abate, that no debt crises emerge, and that no unusually adverse weather events take place. That said, the growth forecast has been upgraded by 0.4 percentage point a year compared to June, on account of an upward revision for non-FCS LICs that mainly reflects a sharp upward revision to growth in Uganda, where oil production is expected to commence during the forecast horizon (figure B.1.2.2.A). At the country level, there are as many forecast downgrades as upgrades for LICs in 2025.

Anticipating improvements in the security situation in some countries, growth in FCS LICs is forecast to increase from 2.8 percent in 2024 to about 5.2 percent a year in 2025-26. The pickup largely reflects a projected return to growth in Sudan, based on the assumption of a ceasefire in the ongoing conflict—which has already heavily damaged the country's industrial base along with education and health facilities. Moreover, the outlook for the two largest economies in this group—Ethiopia and the Democratic Republic of Congo—diverges. In Ethiopia, growth is

expected to benefit from last year's macroeconomic reforms and is projected to strengthen. In contrast, growth in the Democratic Republic of Congo is forecast to soften toward the end of the forecast period amid fiscal consolidation efforts—a downward revision of 1 percentage point a year, on average, compared to the June forecast.

Growth in non-FCS LICs, a small set of countries, is forecast to strengthen from 5.6 percent in 2024 to an average of 7.3 percent a year in 2025-26. However, the upward revision in growth projections is mainly driven by stronger growth in Uganda. Moreover, economic activity in Rwanda is expected to continue benefiting from solid private investment and favorable agricultural conditions. In Madagascar, growth is forecast to edge up further as ongoing structural reforms in key sectors take effect.

Per capita income growth in LICs is expected to increase from a subdued 0.8 percent in 2024 to an average of 3.0 percent a year in 2025-26. However, compared to the pre-pandemic trend, the level of per capita income in LICs is expected to be nearly 5 percent lower by the end of 2026, and nearly 16 percent lower

BOX 1.2 Low-income countries: Recent developments and outlook (*continued*)

TABLE B1.2.1 Low-income country forecasts[a]
(Real GDP growth at market prices in percent, unless indicated otherwise)

Percentage-point differences from June 2024 projections

	2022	2023	2024e	2025f	2026f	2024e	2025f	2026f
Low-Income Countries, GDP [b]	**5.1**	**3.0**	**3.6**	**5.7**	**5.9**	**-1.4**	**0.4**	**0.4**
GDP per capita (U.S. dollars)	2.2	0.2	0.8	2.9	3.1	-1.4	0.4	0.4
Afghanistan[c]	-6.2	2.7	..	..	..	..	..	..
Burkina Faso	1.5	3.0	3.7	3.9	4.1	0.0	0.1	-0.1
Burundi	1.8	2.7	2.2	3.5	4.2	-1.6	-0.9	-0.6
Central African Republic	0.5	0.7	0.7	1.1	2.0	-0.6	-0.6	0.1
Chad	2.8	4.2	3.0	2.1	3.5	0.3	-1.2	0.6
Congo, Dem. Rep.	8.9	8.4	4.9	5.0	4.6	-1.1	-0.9	-1.1
Eritrea	2.5	2.6	2.8	3.0	3.3	0.0	0.0	0.0
Ethiopia[d]	6.4	7.2	6.1	6.5	7.1	-0.9	-0.5	0.1
Gambia, The	4.9	5.3	5.6	5.8	5.4	0.1	0.0	0.0
Guinea-Bissau	4.2	5.2	5.0	5.0	5.0	0.3	0.2	0.1
Liberia	4.8	4.7	5.3	5.7	5.8	0.0	-0.5	-0.5
Madagascar	4.0	3.8	4.5	4.6	4.7	0.0	0.0	0.0
Malawi	0.9	1.6	1.8	4.2	3.3	-0.2	0.3	-0.8
Mali	3.5	3.5	3.7	4.0	4.5	0.6	0.5	0.0
Mozambique	4.4	5.4	4.0	4.0	4.0	-1.0	-1.0	-0.4
Niger	11.5	2.0	5.7	8.5	4.6	-3.4	2.3	-0.5
Rwanda	8.2	8.2	7.6	7.8	7.5	0.0	0.0	0.0
Sierra Leone	5.3	5.7	4.3	4.7	4.7	0.8	0.7	0.4
Somalia	2.7	4.2	4.4	4.5	4.5	0.7	0.6	0.5
South Sudan[d]	-2.3	-1.3	-7.8	-11.4	6.1	-9.8	-15.2	2.1
Sudan	-1.0	-20.1	-15.1	1.3	2.9	-11.6	2.0	1.7
Syrian Arab Republic[c]	0.7	-1.2	-1.5	-1.0	..	0.0	..	..
Togo	5.8	6.4	5.3	5.4	5.8	0.2	0.0	0.2
Uganda[d]	4.7	5.3	6.0	6.2	10.8	0.0	0.0	4.2
Yemen, Rep.[c]	1.5	-2.0	-1.0	1.5	..	0.0	0.0	..

Source: World Bank.

Note: e = estimate; f = forecast. World Bank forecasts are frequently updated based on new information and changing (global) circumstances. Consequently, projections presented here may differ from those contained in other Bank documents, even if basic assessments of countries' prospects do not significantly differ at any given moment in time.

a. The Democratic People's Republic of Korea is not projected on account of data limitations.

b. Aggregate growth rates are calculated using GDP weights at average 2010-19 prices and market exchange rates.

c. Forecasts for Afghanistan (beyond 2023), the Syrian Arab Republic (beyond 2025), and the Republic of Yemen (beyond 2025) are excluded because of a high degree of uncertainty.

d. GDP growth rates are on a fiscal year basis. For example, the column for 2022 refers to FY2021/22.

for FCS LICs, excluding the two major economies in this group—the Democratic Republic of Congo and Ethiopia (figure B.1.2.2.B). Per capita income growth is primarily driven by strong expansion in non-FCS LICs and the two major FCS LICs. In the remaining LICs, growth is forecast at a mere 1 percent, keeping average per capita income well below its pre-pandemic level. At the country level, per capita income in nearly half of FCS LICs is expected to remain below pre-pandemic levels by the end of 2026.

Progress in poverty reduction in many LICs is thus expected to remain limited (chapter 4). Per capita income growth rates are largely insufficient to raise living standards significantly. Moreover, several populations continue to experience negative spillovers from violent conflicts and political instability, such as displacement and food shortages, exacerbating the situation in those countries, especially in East Africa and the Sahel region.

BOX 1.2 Low-income countries: Recent developments and outlook (*continued*)

Risks

Risks to the outlook remain tilted to the downside, especially for FCS LICs. These countries suffer from fragility stemming from persistent poverty, as well as ongoing violence and conflict, especially those in East Africa and the Sahel (Burkina Faso, Democratic Republic of Congo, Mali, Somalia, South Sudan, Sudan). An escalation of conflict in East Africa could lead to extended humanitarian crises in LICs and further destruction of infrastructure, and exacerbate already-severe food insecurity across LICs in the region, as many of these countries rely heavily on food imports. Similarly, intensified conflict in the Middle East could lead to sharply higher oil prices, triggering a renewed pickup in inflation across LICs. A conflict-induced oil price spike could also raise global food prices by driving up transportation and production costs, as many fertilizers are byproducts of the oil and gas industry.

Global growth could be lower than projected. Unexpected adverse changes in trade policies could result in further trade fragmentation and dampen global activity. A potential intensification of protectionist measures could lead to further trade barriers and retaliation between trading blocs that, in addition to their potential inflationary effects, could adversely affect economic prospects. Such adverse developments could also affect the outlook for LICs.

If global inflation proves more persistent than expected, major central banks may need to slow the pace of their monetary policy easing, resulting in a slower-than-expected improvement in financial conditions for LICs. While high debt-service costs remain a burden for many LICs, liquidity concerns and financing conditions have become pressing challenges (IMF 2024a). This is particularly relevant as access to external financing at favorable interest rates has dwindled in recent years (Mawejje 2024).

A deterioration in financing conditions facing LICs could further heighten the risk of government debt distress in some of these countries—especially as public debt restructuring has become more complicated in recent years amid a more diverse set of creditors (Chrimes et al. 2024). Furthermore, sizable primary deficits have driven the debt buildup in LICs, reflecting expenditure pressures amid persistent revenue weakness (Mawejje 2024). As a result, nearly half of LICs (12 out of 26) were in or at high risk of government debt distress at the end of October 2024 (IMF 2024b). Government debt-to-GDP ratios in LICs are expected to gradually decline from recent high levels, but still stand at 61.5 percent, on average, at the end of 2026. Though easing somewhat, interest payments are expected to remain elevated across LICs, averaging 2 percent of GDP over the forecast period, and be higher for non-FCS LICs (figure B.1.2.2.C).

Economic growth and the pace of poverty reduction could slow markedly in LICs if the adverse effects of climate change intensify. Extreme weather events, such as droughts and floods, have frequently had catastrophic consequences in LICs, especially in the Sahel region (Silvestre et al. 2024). These countries generally have limited capacity—both institutionally and in terms of infrastructure—to cope with natural disasters. The number of people facing extreme hunger remains high, especially across East Africa, where malnutrition is exacerbated by violent conflict and the displacement of people. The number of people in LICs facing a food crisis or worse conditions reached about 147 million people in 2024 (GRFC database). This figure could rise if extreme weather events occur.

The erosion in per capita incomes since 2020 in the most vulnerable economies reflects myriad factors, including intensifying conflict and violence, political instability, food and energy price shocks, limited access to financing, and elevated debt. Following successive negative growth surprises, FCS and LICs are now projected to experience weaker recoveries in per capita incomes than previously assumed. Compared to the pre-pandemic trend, the level of per capita income in LICs and FCS is on track to be nearly 5 and 12 percent lower, respectively, by the end of 2026 (figures 1.10.D and 1.10.E). Losses relative to trend exceed 20 percent in some economies afflicted with widespread fragility, violence, and conflict (for example, Central African Republic,

Niger, Sudan, Ukraine, and West Bank and Gaza).

After notable progress in reducing extreme poverty rates in the decades before the pandemic, progress has slowed and narrowed, with the extreme poverty rate in EMDEs excluding China and India still higher last year than before the pandemic (figure 1.10.F; Mahler, Yonzan, and Lakner 2022). While some regions have seen renewed reductions in extreme poverty— particularly SAR, owing to notable declines in India and Bangladesh—others have experienced significant increases, mainly due to conflict. In MNA, the population living in extreme poverty has risen by almost 60 percent since 2019, while it has increased by 13 percent in SSA (World Bank 2024d). In addition, the challenge of reducing poverty globally has been made more severe by the narrowing of fiscal space in many EMDEs, curbing the scope for productivity-enhancing public investment, and by pandemic-related damage to human capital, which has likely reduced future earnings (Schady et al. 2023).

Global outlook and risks

Summary of global outlook

Global growth is projected to stabilize at an average of 2.7 percent in 2025-26, broadly in line with the June forecasts but below the pre-pandemic decade average pace of 3.1 percent (figure 1.11.A). Growth is expected to be supported by an improvement in real income growth as inflation continues to moderate, aided by lower commodity prices, as well as by the easing of policy rates globally. However, advanced-economy policy rates in 2025 are expected to remain much higher than the unusually low levels registered for most of the 2010s (figure 1.11.B).

This outlook entails diverging dynamics across advanced economies and EMDEs. Growth in advanced economies is expected to edge up in 2025-26, mainly reflecting a recovery in the euro area and Japan, which is partly offset by an expected deceleration in U.S. activity on the back of moderating consumption. In China, longer-term structural trends combined with continuing challenges in the property sector are expected to

weigh further on activity. In contrast, aggregate growth in other EMDEs is projected to firm over the forecast horizon, supported by easier financing conditions, recovering real incomes, and improving industrial activity and external demand.

The subdued pace of global growth reflects both the scarring effects of the adverse shocks of the past few years and a secular deceleration of potential growth in major economies. The restrained outlook for growth in EMDEs will make it more challenging to further reduce poverty and to close per-capita income gaps with advanced economies, even absent further headwinds emanating from adverse policy shifts, weaker growth in major economies, and persistently higher benchmark interest rates than in the pre-pandemic decade.

Risks to the outlook

The balance of risks to the outlook continues to be tilted to the downside, despite the presence of some important upside risks. Global growth could be lower than projected due to heightened uncertainty and the potential for substantial adverse policy shifts, particularly relating to trade policies. The latter could result in further trade fragmentation and dampen activity, particularly in export-oriented EMDEs. Global economic activity could also be adversely affected by a growing severity or incidence of conflict, such as a prolonged escalation of the conflict in the Middle East, which could substantially disrupt oil and natural gas supplies.

Other downside risks to global growth include a resurgence of inflationary pressures, even beyond the potential inflationary effects of heightened trade protectionism and conflict-related shocks. This could be driven, for instance, by persistently elevated services price inflation, which could require many central banks to slow the pace of monetary policy easing and keep policy rates higher for longer. In addition, growth in major economies could surprise on the downside. In the United States, significant trade policy shifts and faster cooling of the labor market could reduce growth relative to the baseline. Meanwhile, growth in China could be weaker than expected owing to a deeper or more prolonged property sector downturn or persistent weakness in consumption. More severe and frequent climate events could reduce activity in the near term while amplifying the slowdown in the fundamental drivers of growth over the longer term.

On the upside, faster-than-anticipated global disinflation could result from greater progress on goods deflation arising from lower commodity prices or from stronger productivity gains, possibly linked to artificial intelligence (AI). This could enable central banks to cut policy rates faster than expected in the baseline. Additionally, growth in major economies could be stronger than anticipated. In the United States, more expansionary fiscal policy and resilient consumption—bolstered, for example, by strong household balance sheets—could push near-term growth above expectations. In China, expanded policy support could lead to upside surprises in near-term growth.

Downside risks

Heightened policy uncertainty and unexpected trade policy shifts

Over the past year, elections in economies representing nearly 60 percent of global GDP were accompanied by unusually high levels of economic policy uncertainty and heightened risks of substantial policy shifts in the post-election period. Heightened uncertainty about the direction and scope of policies—including trade, fiscal, monetary, and regulatory policies—tends to weigh on sentiment, causing firms and consumers to delay spending and lenders to raise the cost of finance, thereby dampening growth. For example, estimates suggest that a sustained increase in global policy uncertainty is associated with slower global and EMDE growth (figure 1.12.A).[3]

Trade policy uncertainty has been a key feature of the recent economic environment. In the first 11 months of 2024, trade policy uncertainty was, on average, more than double that of previous major global election years in recent history, reaching its highest level on record in November 2024. Meanwhile, the number of new trade restrictions

---

[3] Specifically, a 10-percent increase in global economic policy uncertainty is associated with about a 0.2-percentage-point decline in EMDE growth after one year.

FIGURE 1.11 Global outlook

Global growth is projected to stabilize at an average of 2.7 percent in 2025-26 yet remain below the average pace of 3.1 percent in the pre-pandemic decade. Monetary policy easing in both advanced economies and EMDEs, along with moderating inflation, is expected to support growth. Nevertheless, policy rates in advanced economies in 2025 are projected to remain much higher than during most of the 2010s.

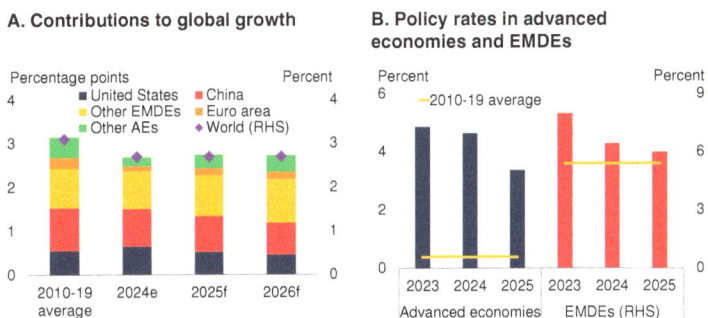

A. Contributions to global growth

B. Policy rates in advanced economies and EMDEs

Sources: Bloomberg; Consensus Economics; Haver Analytics; World Bank.
Note: AEs = advanced economies; e = estimate; EMDEs = emerging market and developing economies; f = forecast; RHS = right-hand scale.
A. Aggregates are calculated using real U.S. dollar GDP weights at average 2010-19 prices and market exchange rates.
B. Blue bars represent GDP-weighted averages of policy rates for 2023-24 and policy rate expectations for 2025 for the United States, the euro area, and the United Kingdom. Policy rate expectations are derived from futures curves observed on December 23, 2024. The red bars represent the median 3-month government bond yields for 2023-24 and the median Consensus Economics forecasts for 1-year-ahead yields (or policy rates) for 2025. Sample includes 16 EMDEs and is based on December 2024 surveys.

---

introduced annually has surged to about five times the 2010-19 average. The continuation and potential intensification of protectionist measures could lead to retaliation between trading blocs, worsening economic prospects broadly.

In particular, a substantial increase in tariffs by the United States could have adverse effects not only on trading partners but also on domestic consumers and producers. While the ultimate impact of tariffs on domestic prices and economic growth depends on market structure and the availability of domestic substitutes, it is likely that sizable U.S. tariff increases would push prices of imported goods higher and require parts of supply chains to adjust to higher costs and regulatory uncertainty.[4] The introduction of significant

---

[4] There is a debate in the literature on the appropriate response of monetary policy to tariff shocks. On the one hand, the inflationary impact of a rise in tariffs could warrant tighter monetary policy, with the degree of tightening depending on the magnitude and persistence of the rise in inflation and the impact on inflation expectations (Barattieri, Cacciatore, and Ghironi 2021). On the other, tariff increases may render the monetary policy response more complex, as their similarity to a contractionary demand shock may require monetary easing despite an initial increase in inflation (Bergin and Corsetti 2023).

FIGURE 1.12 Downside risks

Global growth could be weaker than expected due to elevated policy uncertainty and adverse trade policy shifts. A sustained increase in global policy uncertainty could notably hurt global and EMDE growth. Illustrative simulations suggest that an increase in U.S. tariffs would have adverse effects on global and EMDE growth, which would be amplified by retaliatory action from U.S. trading partners. In China, the real estate market slump could deepen, with property prices falling further and weighing on consumption and investment. The disruptive effects of climate change, which are becoming increasingly evident amid record-high average temperatures, could become larger and more frequent.

A. Cumulative impact of a 10 percent rise in global economic policy uncertainty on output growth

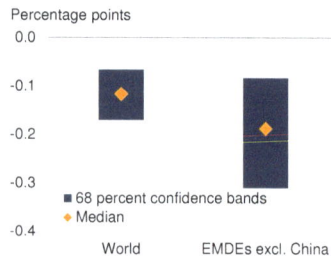

B. Impact of a 10-percentage-point increase in U.S. tariffs on global and EMDE growth

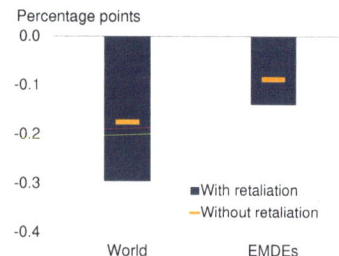

C. Change in property prices during real estate slumps in major economies

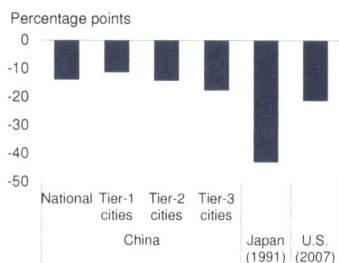

D. July temperature anomalies relative to 1901-2000 average

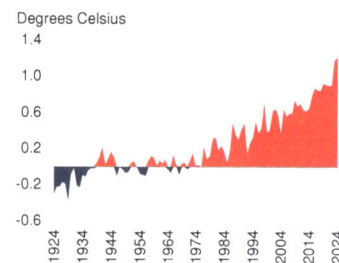

Sources: Haver Analytics; National Oceanic and Atmospheric Administration; OECD; Oxford Economics; World Bank.
Note: AEs = advanced economies; EMDEs = emerging market and developing economies.
A. Panel shows the cumulative responses of output growth after one year to a 10 percent increase in global economic policy uncertainty. Three types of Bayesian vector autoregressions are estimated over 1998Q1-2023Q4, with four lags. Aggregates are based on the GDP-weighted averages of 32 advanced economies and 39 EMDEs excluding China.
B. Impact on annual growth in 2025 relative to the baseline in the case of a 10-percentage-point increase in U.S. tariffs, with and without global retaliation.
C. "Japan" and "U.S." denote the peak-to-trough percentage decline in property prices during major real estate market slumps between 1991Q1 and 2006Q3 in Japan, and between 2007Q1 and 2011Q2 in the United States. "China" denotes the percentage decline in national property prices, and by city tier since the national peak in August 2021. City tier refers to groups of cities based on size and affluence, with tier-1 cities generally the largest and most affluent. Last observation is November 2024.
D. The temperature anomaly measures the difference between the preceding 12-month average global land and ocean temperature for each month and the long-term average temperature (1901-2000). Last observation is August 2024.

additional restrictions on manufacturing exports of China and other large trading partners would negatively impact exporting firms in these countries, as well as their global suppliers. Moreover, retaliatory actions from trading partners could further disrupt global supply

chains, adding to production costs and stoking even greater uncertainty.[5]

A global macroeconomic model is used to calibrate the possible implications of rising U.S. tariffs.[6] Simulations suggest that a 10-percentage-point increase in U.S. tariffs on all trading partners in 2025, without retaliatory tariffs being imposed in response, would reduce global growth by 0.2 percentage point for the year, relative to the baseline (figure 1.12.B). Additionally, growth in EMDEs would be weaker by 0.1 percentage point. In the presence of proportional retaliatory tariffs by trading partners, the negative effects on global and EMDE growth relative to the baseline would increase to a total of about 0.3 and 0.2 percentage point, respectively. These impacts could be further amplified if this global rise in trade protectionism were accompanied by heightened policy uncertainty.

These simulation results are consistent with other studies that analyze the impact of a comparable increase in U.S. tariffs. Without retaliation from trading partners, higher tariffs are found to have a proportionally larger effect on U.S. growth, with a doubling in U.S. universal tariffs estimated to nearly double the negative impact on U.S. GDP (The Budget Lab 2024). Some studies also suggest that retaliation by trading partners would amplify these negative impacts on U.S. output. For instance, some estimates indicate that a 10-percentage-point increase in U.S. tariffs would reduce the level of U.S. GDP by 0.4 percent, while retaliation from trading partners would increase the total negative impact to 0.9 percent (McKibbin, Hogan, and Noland 2024).

Escalation of armed conflicts and geopolitical tensions

By some measures, the number of armed conflicts over the last couple of years—including both

---

[5] Recent studies suggest that the 2018-19 U.S. tariff increases were fully passed on to consumers and firms, with limited positive effects on the trade balance and employment (Autor et al. 2024; Barattieri, Cacciatore, and Ghironi 2021; Cavallo et al. 2021). Higher prices, in turn, led to a reduction in real income in the United States (Amiti et al. 2021).

[6] The simulations here and in subsequent sections are conducted using the Oxford Economics Global Economic Model, a semi-structural macroeconomic projection model that includes 188 individual country blocks in its extended version, available at quarterly or annual frequencies (Oxford Economics 2019).

interstate and intrastate conflicts—was the highest since World War II (UCDP 2024). A major escalation in the intensity or incidence of conflicts and geopolitical tensions represents a substantial downside risk to global economic activity and would likely also set back progress considerably on a range of broader development goals. At the global level, a prolonged intensification of the conflict in the Middle East could substantially disrupt oil and natural gas supplies, causing energy prices to rise sharply, with adverse implications for inflation and global activity. Uncertainty around Russia's ongoing invasion of Ukraine also poses continued risks to commodity markets and regional security. At the same time, the dissipation of conflict could help mitigate headwinds to growth from such events. In particular, receding conflict in Europe could improve confidence and thus lift domestic demand, particularly investment, which has been a source of weakness in recent years.

More broadly, both interstate and civil armed conflicts result in the destruction of physical and human capital in directly affected locales, often culminating in deep recessions and persistent output losses (Federle et al. 2024). Intense conflicts are especially prevalent in LICs, with estimates indicating that the onset of conflict tends to lower GDP per capita by about 15 percent after five years (chapter 4). Risks to life and property forestall private investment and disrupt patterns of production and the provision of public services (Collier et al. 2003; Gates et al. 2012). Elevated military expenditure can squeeze out productive spending, including on education, health, and infrastructure. At the same time, declines in productive capacity caused by conflict reduce future expected incomes, raising risk premia and increasing the chances of debt default (Rexer, Kapstein, and Rivera 2023). Moreover, conflicts often have severe adverse spillovers, leading, for instance, to weaker trade and private investment and greater susceptibility to conflict in neighboring countries.

Beyond violent conflicts, an array of geopolitical pressures has been building, marked by increasing fragmentation, the growing prominence of populism in many countries, and a seemingly reduced appetite for international cooperation. Escalating geopolitical tensions can impact global economic activity through disruptions in trade and financial linkages and commodity markets, as well as heightened uncertainty. EMDEs are particularly vulnerable to the indirect effects of escalating geopolitical tensions, such as the impacts on trade from restrictive measures or the effects on capital flows from weak global investor confidence.

Heightened geopolitical tensions amid the growing digitalization of critical infrastructure have been accompanied by the emergence of new threats, notably the increasing risk of cyberattacks. From 2014 to 2023, disclosed cyber incidents globally grew at an average annual rate of 21 percent, with upper-middle-income countries registering the highest increase in the number of incidents, at 37 percent (Vergara Cobos 2024). The escalating frequency and costs of cyber incidents are likely to result in economic losses. Moreover, the potentially systemic nature of cyber risks could lead to adverse scenarios of national or international significance, such as "cyber runs"—runs on financial institutions prompted by cyberattacks—or the sabotage of key energy or transport networks.

Higher-than-expected inflation

The decline in global headline inflation over the past year has not been smooth, with bouts of re-emerging inflationary pressures interrupting progress. Whereas food and energy prices generally stabilized or declined last year, core inflation remained elevated, largely due to services prices. While trade policy shifts leading to higher global tariffs, as well as heightened conflict, could add to price pressures, inflation could also be higher on account of resilient activity in the services sector. Additionally, the robust wage growth observed in recent years globally could endure as real wages continue to recover, feeding inflationary pressures with a lag, even as labor markets begin to cool (Michelis et al. 2024).

Furthermore, while the baseline envisions broadly moderating commodity prices, commodity-specific supply concerns have caused price surges at various points over the last year, including those resulting from mine closures (copper), trade restrictions (rice), weather-related events (beverages), and geopolitical risk (crude oil and European natural gas). An increased prevalence of these supply shocks, especially if they affect food or energy, could impede the anticipated softening of commodity prices, putting upward pressure on inflation relative to expectations.

More persistent inflationary pressures could require central banks to slow the pace of easing—or even tighten policy if necessary—keeping policy rates higher for longer. This, in turn, would weigh on consumption and investment spending, and lead to higher interest payments on government debt. Rapid changes in policy rate expectations, particularly if driven by inflation concerns, could lead to sharp asset repricing and weaker risk appetite. This could further weigh on growth in both advanced economies and EMDEs, and trigger capital outflows from more vulnerable EMDEs.

Weaker-than-expected growth in major economies

The outlook for major economies, notably the United States and China, is subject to additional downside risks beyond those that might arise from escalating trade tensions. The realization of downside risks in either economy could have a range of global repercussions. In the United States, recent labor market indicators suggest that the expansion of the labor supply has begun to weaken, while consumer spending is showing signs of easing in line with slowing disposable income growth. It is possible that the gradual moderation in U.S. growth expected in the baseline may, in fact, occur more quickly and be more pronounced. This could result from abrupt shifts in trade policies—in particular, large increases in tariffs—which could dampen consumer and business spending. Lower spending, in turn, could lead to a more abrupt cooling in the labor market and reduce the pace of labor income growth if businesses pull back sharply on hiring and accelerate layoffs. Household spending may be particularly vulnerable to slowing disposable income since the pandemic-related savings cushion has likely been largely depleted.

Negative growth spillovers from weaker U.S. demand would be felt globally. Softer U.S. goods imports, second in size only to China's, would weigh on industrial activity in export-oriented EMDEs. Weaker U.S. demand would also have repercussions for commodity markets, potentially prompting commodity prices to decline more than in the baseline and pushing growth lower in commodity exporters. Finally, the dominant position of the United States in the global financial system would likely mean that softer investor sentiment would reverberate globally, with reduced risk appetite tightening financial conditions in EMDEs—particularly those with weak credit ratings.

In China, in addition to the effects of potentially higher tariffs, an intensification of the property sector correction, marked by further falls in real estate investment, presents a key downside risk. This would have broad adverse knock-on effects on domestic and global activity, reducing demand for some commodities, especially metals. More protracted and larger declines in property prices—which have, on average, fallen by about 14 percent from their peak in late 2021—could further weaken household balance sheets and have broader financial fallout, with adverse implications for heavily exposed lenders, notably smaller commercial banks (figure 1.12.C). Mounting adverse wealth effects amid subdued consumer confidence and soft labor market conditions would put further downward pressure on already-weak demand for household goods and services activity, including outbound tourism to key destinations in EAP.

More frequent and severe climate-change-related disasters

The cascading effects of climate change are becoming increasingly evident in the form of a range of environmental shifts, including more frequent and severe weather events, rising sea levels, and higher average temperatures. For instance, average temperatures reached record-breaking levels in the summer of last year—the global average temperature in July was over 1°C higher than the twentieth century average July temperature, slightly exceeding the record set in

July 2023 (figure 1.12.D). Gradual warming and the increasing frequency of natural disasters will have adverse economic effects. In the short run, the direct impacts of climate change can take the form of macroeconomic shocks associated with infrastructure damage, agricultural losses, and commodity price spikes caused by droughts, floods, and storms (Debelle 2019; Zaveri, Damania, and Engle 2023).

In the longer run, the adverse effects of climate change may include increased uncertainty, reduced investment, and weaker trend productivity growth (Angeli et al. 2022). Moreover, the negative economic impacts from gradual temperature rises have grown since the 2000s and may increase in a nonlinear manner as temperature deviations from historical norms expand (Burke, Hsiang, and Miguel 2015; Felbermayr et al. 2014; WMO 2024). Estimates suggest that a 1° C temperature shock could potentially lead to a peak medium-run decline in global GDP as large as 12 percent (Bilal and Kanzig 2024; Nath, Ramey, and Klenow 2024). Climate-related shocks can have substantial and long-lasting impacts on vulnerable households, with extreme droughts and floods setting back human capital development (Zhang and Borja-Vega 2024).

Climate change is also becoming increasingly relevant for monetary policy (Lagarde 2024). Financial risks from climate change could manifest in higher borrowing costs, potential bank loan losses due to interruptions and bankruptcies caused by severe weather events, greater precautionary saving, and, in extreme circumstances, financial crises (Rudebusch 2019). Headwinds to growth from weather events may be amplified in many EMDEs by a lack of fiscal space to respond effectively and could be further exacerbated by damage to public sector assets, with disproportionate effects on poor households (Hallegatte et al. 2016; Milivojevic 2023).

Upside risks

Lower global inflation and faster monetary easing

The baseline outlook entails a further gradual decline in inflation, reaching close to target or pre-

FIGURE 1.13 Upside risks

Expanding manufacturing production in some regions could put downward pressure on import price inflation in many economies. Stronger-than-expected growth in China and the United States could boost activity elsewhere. Recent estimates suggest that a 1-percentage-point positive shock to growth in China or the United States would lead to a 1.8 percent or 2.9 percent cumulative increase, respectively, in output across other EMDEs after three years.

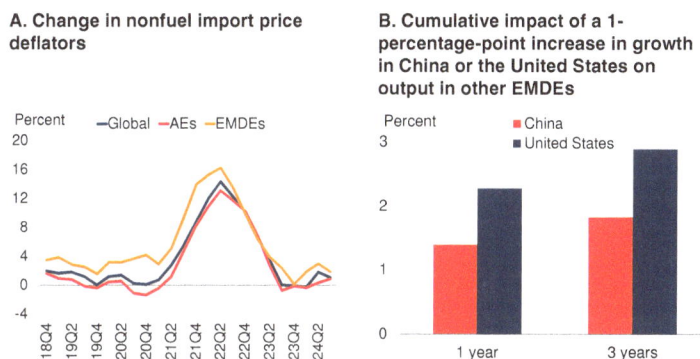

A. Change in nonfuel import price deflators

B. Cumulative impact of a 1-percentage-point increase in growth in China or the United States on output in other EMDEs

Sources: Oxford Economics; World Bank.
Note: AEs = advanced economies; EMDEs = emerging market and developing economies.
A. Median year on year percentage changes in the nonfuel import price deflator by economy group.
B. Cumulative impulse responses of output in EMDEs excluding Brazil, China, and India to a 1-percentage-point increase in output growth in China and the United States. Annex 3.2 contains further methodological information.

pandemic levels toward the end of this year in most economies. However, a faster decline could occur if energy- and food-driven disinflation seen over the past couple of years were to continue. For example, price declines for energy over the forecast horizon could prove larger than anticipated due to decelerating global oil demand and solid increases in production generating potentially sizable excess global oil supply (World Bank 2024e). This, in turn, could result in reduced transportation costs and weaker demand for energy feedstocks—such as maize, sugar, and various food oils—and thus lower prices for these commodities, reducing overall food commodity prices. Together, these trends could give rise to lower-than-expected headline and core inflation and stronger real income growth for households, as well as feed lower inflation expectations.

In addition, stabilization in freight costs and expanding manufacturing production in some regions could exert further downward pressure on import price inflation (figure 1.13.A). Weaker import price inflation could also support a faster slowdown in core and headline inflation over

2025-26 than assumed in the baseline. Finally, the recent pickup in productivity growth, in the context of increasing usage of new technologies such as AI, may prove enduring and could reduce inflation further, even while supporting growth. A faster-than-projected decline in inflation might prompt central banks to ease monetary policy more than assumed in the baseline, further bolstering global demand. That said, the medium-term boost to growth prospects from the adoption of new technologies could be tempered by adverse distributional impacts.

Stronger growth in major economies

Compared to the baseline, stronger global growth could result if growth in major economies surprises on the upside. In the United States, fiscal policy may prove expansionary over the forecast horizon, compared to the slightly contractionary stance assumed in the baseline. For example, the renewal of expiring individual and business tax provisions of the Tax Cuts and Jobs Act (TCJA) could fuel further strong U.S. consumption growth in the near term by reducing taxes paid by households and boosting disposable incomes, even if it leads to a widening of the U.S. fiscal deficit starting in 2026. In general, the impact of such tax changes could result in stronger private consumption than in the baseline and feed through to higher corporate investment over time (Mertens and Ravn 2013; Romer and Romer 2010).

Simulation results suggest that extending TCJA provisions expiring at the end of this year would raise U.S. growth by 0.4 percentage point in 2026. Effects of this magnitude are consistent with other studies on the topic, which find U.S. growth impacts in 2026 of between 0.2 and 0.4 percentage point (Bryson and Pugliese 2024). The boost to U.S. domestic demand is somewhat attenuated by the distributional aspects of extended personal tax measures, with income gains accruing mainly to the top quintile of the income distribution, which has a comparatively low marginal propensity to consume. Global spillovers are small partly because modestly higher U.S. inflation results in tighter U.S. monetary policy and more restrictive global financial conditions.

Independent of potential tax reforms, there may be further room for resilient consumption growth

in the United States. Globally, higher U.S. domestic demand for imported goods and stronger risk appetite in financial markets would then have positive spillovers for economic activity, albeit partially offset by higher U.S. policy interest rates than in the baseline. Overall, estimates suggest that a 1-percentage-point increase in U.S. growth could, after three years, lead to a cumulative 2.9 percent rise in GDP across other EMDEs (figure 1.13.B; chapter 3).

Growth could also surprise on the upside in China. Recent fiscal, monetary, and regulatory policy measures represented a relatively restrained stimulus. Policy makers could choose to implement more concerted and aggressive efforts to boost private consumption and increase spending on public goods and services. Additionally, expanded policy support for the property sector could stabilize real estate activity sooner than assumed, removing a key drag on domestic activity. In particular, measures to boost property demand and address the property supply overhang could prop up real estate prices and sales, supporting property investment. Such measures could help buoy consumer and business confidence, lifting private consumption and business sentiment. A faster-than-assumed recovery in China's property sector would likely result in significant positive spillovers to China's trade partners, especially EMDE metals exporters. Recent estimates suggest that a 1-percentage-point growth shock in China could lead to a 0.8 percent cumulative increase in global GDP over three years, with larger impacts for countries that trade closely with China and are highly integrated into global value chains (chapter 3).

Policy challenges

As the world exits the first quarter of the twenty-first century, the primary challenge for policy makers is to realign development goals that have been derailed by large negative shocks since 2020, which came on the heels of a decade of slowing progress. In an environment of elevated policy uncertainty, including relating to possible post-election policy shifts in many countries, EMDEs need to calibrate their policies to mitigate the growth-dampening effects of uncertainty. This will require navigating a difficult external environment and a comprehensive set of reforms to sustainably boost EMDE growth along several dimensions. The global community has a crucial role to play in tackling trade fragmentation and limiting its damages—if trade disputes occur, high priority should be placed on reaching orderly, de-escalatory outcomes. Maintaining international cooperation is also essential for mitigating EMDE debt vulnerabilities and addressing the looming climate crisis.

At the national level, where inflation is proving more persistent, monetary policies need to remain focused on price stability. In addition, close supervision of bank credit quality and capital levels can help safeguard financial stability. High debt burdens will require policy makers to balance sizable investment needs with fiscal sustainability. More generally, structural reforms are needed to foster potential growth and put a wide range of development goals on track. These include measures to lessen conflict risks, boost human capital, bolster labor force inclusion, and address food insecurity.

Key global challenges

Trade fragmentation

Boosting international trade is a key priority. Trade, spurred by a rules-based and predictable multilateral trading system, has been crucial in reducing poverty and lowering inequality between countries. Estimates indicate that reductions in trade costs between 1995 and 2020 boosted global real GDP over the period by nearly 7 percent and by over 30 percent in low-income countries, in turn helping accelerate income catch-up for these countries (WTO 2024).

Proliferating trade restrictions, disruptions to global value chains, and a further weakening of the multilateral trading system could lead to sizable global welfare losses. These effects will impact all economies but could be particularly adverse for EMDEs, where trade exposure has created—directly and indirectly—high-quality, productive, and well-paying jobs (Maliszewska and Winkler 2024). Advanced economies accounted for 70 percent of new trade-restrictive policy measures

FIGURE 1.14 **Global policy challenges**

Advanced economies have been the main contributors to new trade-distorting policy measures, which have disproportionately affected EMDEs. Weaker fiscal positions and higher levels of debt across many EMDEs, notably LICs, highlight the need for global policy action to prevent costly debt crises. Indeed, the wave of EMDE debt buildup that began in 2010 has been the broadest and fastest among the waves of debt accumulation since 1970. Climate change is a major longer-term challenge to global development, necessitating large investments in adaptation, notably in LICs.

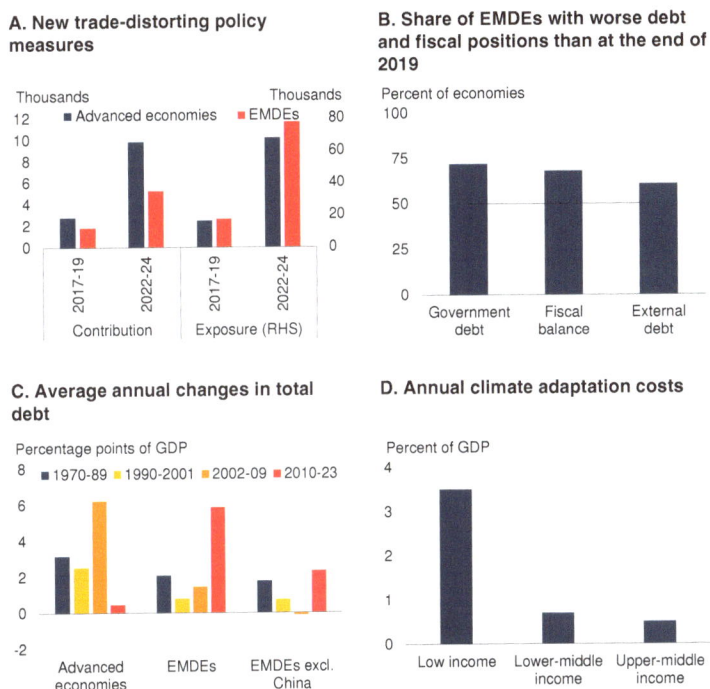

A. New trade-distorting policy measures

B. Share of EMDEs with worse debt and fiscal positions than at the end of 2019

C. Average annual changes in total debt

D. Annual climate adaptation costs

Sources: Global Trade Alert (database); Haver Analytics; Kose et al. (2021); United Nations Environment Programme (2023); World Bank.

Note: EMDEs = emerging market and developing economies; LICs = low-income countries; RHS = right-hand scale.

A. Panel shows implemented interventions by countries that discriminate against foreign interests. "Contribution" represents the number of measures implemented by each country group. "Exposure" represents the number of measures affecting each country group. Each measure can be implemented by and target multiple countries. Adjusted data (for reporting lags) as of December 19, 2024.

B. Panel shows the share of EMDEs with higher government or total external debt or with worse fiscal balances (all as a percent of GDP) in the latest quarter with data than in 2019Q4. Fiscal balances are a four-quarter moving sum. Debt and fiscal data are for central governments in some countries. Sample includes 59, 68, and 62 EMDEs for government debt, fiscal balance, and external debt, respectively. Horizonal line indicates 50 percent.

C. Total debt is the sum of government and private debt. Rates of change are calculated as changes in total debt-to-GDP ratios over the duration of waves, divided by the number of years in each wave. As identified in Kose et al. (2021), there are four waves of global debt: 1970-89, 1990-2001, 2002-09, and 2010-23. Aggregates are computed using current GDP in U.S. dollars.

D. Undiscounted annual costs of adaptation for the period up to 2030, based on modeled estimates for coastal zones, river floods, infrastructure, agriculture, fisheries, aquaculture, and marine ecosystems, health, early warning and social protection, and terrestrial biodiversity and ecosystem services. Qualitative assessments for cooling demand and labor productivity, business and industry, capacity-building, and socially contingent effects are also considered.

implemented over the 2022-24 period, which disproportionately affected EMDEs (figure 1.14.A). Discriminatory policies aimed at reducing imports and bolstering domestic production are likely to create relatively few jobs at a high cost (Barattieri and Cacciatore 2023; Bombardini et al. 2024).

International cooperation is needed to mitigate the adverse effects of geopolitical tensions on trade networks, foster a level playing field for international commerce, reduce trade policy uncertainty, and enhance transparency regarding trade policies and practices. When trade disputes emerge, affected parties should prioritize finding swift, orderly, and sustainable resolutions to minimize associated uncertainty and adverse spillovers to third parties. In addition, legal and judicial frameworks governing trade may need to evolve to address challenges related to mounting subsidies that can distort global markets (Rotunno and Ruta 2024). These subsidies—often motivated by legitimate objectives such as industrial development, supply chain resilience, and national security considerations—frequently lack transparency and are inadequately regulated by existing international rules.

To actively foster trade-related benefits, countries can pursue new deep trade agreements—those that address nontariff barriers—which can stimulate trade and mitigate the negative effects of trade-distorting policies (Barattieri, Mattoo, and Taglioni 2024; Mattoo, Mulabdic, and Ruta 2022). At the national level, to ensure that the gains from trade are widely shared, governments can implement complementary domestic policies, such as labor, education, and taxation reforms that support potentially displaced workers and facilitate their transition to expanding industries (WTO 2024).

Debt vulnerabilities

Many EMDEs are vulnerable to debt distress, especially following the sharp rises in debt levels and borrowing costs in recent years. Relative to 2019 levels, government debt is higher in nearly three-quarters of EMDEs, and more than half of EMDEs face weaker fiscal positions and higher levels of external debt (figure 1.14.B). Moreover, looking at the major waves of debt accumulation in EMDEs since the 1970s, the fourth wave—which began in 2010—has been the largest, broadest, and fastest-growing compared to the

previous three (figure 1.14.C; Kose et al. 2021). This debt buildup raises concerns about its potential consequences for macroeconomic and financial stability. Sovereign debt defaults are typically associated with large output losses, sharp increases in borrowing costs, exclusion from international capital markets, and trade and financial system disruptions. Besides these direct economic costs, debt defaults can inflict substantial social costs, including those related to the incidence of poverty, life expectancy, infant mortality, and malnutrition. For instance, evidence suggests that, following a debt default, the number of households in poverty increases by roughly 6 percent after five years and by 10 percent after a decade (Farah-Yacoub, von Luckner, and Reinhart 2024). Similarly, progress on reducing infant mortality slows following aggregate income shocks resulting from sovereign defaults.

Decisive policy action is needed to address developing risks and avoid debt crises, which bring sizable economic and social costs. Absent such action, potential debt defaults in countries at high risk could severely undermine progress on development goals and the green transition, with major global implications (Diwan et al. 2024). In the case of LICs, it is critical for the global community to boost concessional financing—grants have declined sharply (relative to gross national income) since 2020 despite a substantial increase in International Development Association (IDA) resources allocated to LICs (Mawejje 2024).

For EMDEs in debt distress, or on the brink of it, debt restructuring is critical for reducing the costs of debt crises. The G20 Common Framework has begun to improve the efficiency of the sovereign debt resolution processes. In addition, the Global Sovereign Debt Roundtable has proved helpful as a platform for key international stakeholders to develop a greater common understanding of critical issues related to debt restructurings (IMF 2024c). Further progress is needed to improve the efficiency of restructurings under the Common Framework, which needs to be adapted to manage the increasingly complex sovereign debt landscape characterized by more diverse creditors and sophisticated debt instruments. Moreover, it is essential to improve creditor coordination in cases that are not eligible for treatment under the Common Framework. Alongside these efforts, domestic policy actions to improve fiscal space and strengthen institutions and governance frameworks need to be prioritized.

Climate change and biodiversity loss

In addition to representing a key risk to near-term growth prospects, climate change is one of the biggest longer-term challenges to global development. This underscores the need for substantial investments to address climate change mitigation and adaptation, with the poorest countries facing particularly large needs and high adaption costs (figure 1.14.D; World Bank 2023a). Yet current global commitments remain insufficient to reach net zero by 2050. Through the increasing manifestation of physical and transition risks, the costs of policy inaction would substantially outweigh those of a timely and orderly climate transition, with EMDEs being particularly vulnerable to these risks (NGFS 2023).

Moreover, climate change is a direct driver of biodiversity loss. Even under a 1.5°C to 2°C global warming scenario, the geographic areas suitable for most terrestrial species are projected to shrink markedly (IPBES 2019). Conversely, there is abundant evidence that the loss of nature exacerbates climate change (Johnson et al. 2021). Although biodiversity loss in low- and middle-income countries may not substantially reduce economic output today, given the abundance of "ecosystem services" (such as marine fisheries and timber from native forests) relative to physical capital, it still imposes substantial economic costs by reducing future growth opportunities (Giglio et al. 2024). Hence, policy makers need to take better account of the longer-term costs of biodiversity loss, and take mitigating steps, even if its near-term economic impacts appear modest.

Well-designed and coordinated policies—particularly those supporting innovation—that address biodiversity loss can also support climate change mitigation and adaptation efforts (World

Bank 2021). Global priorities to set economies on a more sustainable growth path include engaging economic and financial decision-makers to address the drivers of biodiversity loss by integrating nature considerations into financial decisions, national strategies, and economic and trade policies (World Bank 2021). Unlocking investment in nature conservation, restoration, and the sustainable use of nature is another priority. Subsidy reform and carbon pricing, as integral parts of the policy mix, can help contribute toward these investments, mobilize domestic resources, and help align incentives. For example, the introduction of carbon taxes, combined with the elimination of fossil fuel subsidies, can incentivize investment in energy-efficient technologies (World Bank 2023b). Moreover, fewer trade and investment restrictions on green technologies will also help boost green investments in EMDEs along with knowledge spillovers toward these economies.

EMDE monetary and financial policy challenges

In many EMDEs, risks to core inflation persist. Central banks need to be vigilant about upside risks to inflation, particularly in economies where it remains above target, standing ready to reduce the pace of monetary easing—and even tighten policy, if necessary. Communicating monetary policy decisions clearly, leveraging credible monetary frameworks, and safeguarding central bank independence will help EMDEs anchor inflation expectations and reduce financial market volatility.

Policy interest rate differentials between EMDEs and key advanced economies widened in the second half of 2024 as the U.S. Federal Reserve joined other advanced economies in easing monetary policy (figure 1.15.A). An upswing in capital flows to EMDEs generally coincided with the initial easing of U.S. interest rates, but those flows reversed in the fourth quarter amid higher U.S. yields and heightened policy uncertainty, including concerning potential trade tensions (figure 1.15.B). Against the backdrop of a stronger U.S. dollar, rising government debt in some advanced economies, and inflation risks, adverse

FIGURE 1.15 EMDE monetary and financial policy challenges

Policy interest rate differentials between EMDEs and major advanced economies widened in the second half of 2024 with the onset of monetary easing in the United States. Alongside this, net portfolio capital inflows to EMDEs slowed, and the U.S. dollar strengthened against EMDE currencies—a trend that, if sustained, could pose inflation and financial stability challenges in EMDEs. As the size of impaired assets has grown in LICs, improving oversight, underwriting, and risk management practices can attenuate risks. With cyber-attacks on the rise, action needs to be taken to protect critical digital and market infrastructure.

A. Interest rate differentials between EMDEs excluding China and the United States

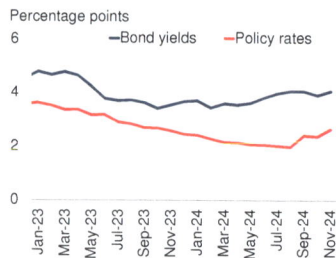

B. Capital flows to EMDEs

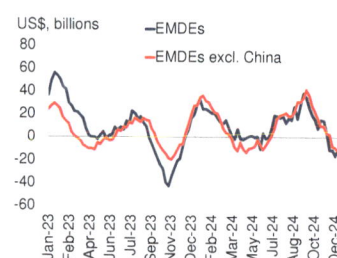

C. Nonperforming loans by banks

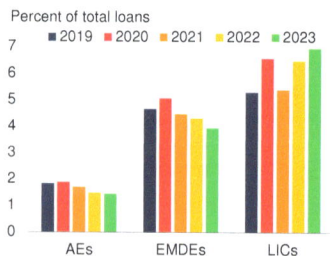

D. Frequency of cyber events in the financial and insurance sector

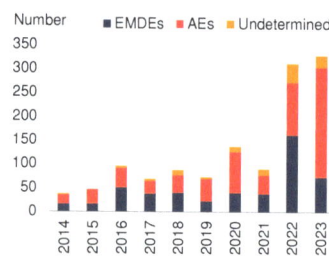

Sources: Bloomberg; Harry and Gallagher (2018); Haver Analytics; Institute of International Finance (database); World Development Indicators (database); World Bank.
Note: AEs = advanced economies; EMDEs = emerging market and developing economies; LICs = low-income countries.
A. Red line indicates the differential between the U.S. federal funds rate and the GDP-weighted average of policy rates for up to 18 EMDE central banks. Blue line indicates the differential between the U.S. 10-year government bond yield and the GDP-weighted average of 10-year government bond yields for up to 14 EMDEs. Last observation is November 2024.
B. Net nonresident debt and equity flows to EMDEs. Cumulative total using weekly data. Sample includes 17 EMDEs for equity flows and 10 EMDEs for debt flows. Last observation is December 13, 2024.
C. Panel shows median nonperforming loans for country groups. Based on a consistent sample of 36 advanced economies and 89 EMDEs, of which 8 are LICs. Bars for 2019-22 show annual figures. Bars for 2023 show data available up to 2023Q2.
D. Panel shows the frequency of disruptive or exploitative cyberattacks focused on the financial and insurance industry across advanced economies, EMDEs, and undetermined locations by year. Last observation is 2023.

shifts in investor sentiment in the coming months could trigger episodes of market volatility and result in sizeable net capital outflows from EMDEs.

In addition to fostering sound macrofinancial policy frameworks, policy makers and regulators in EMDEs need to be prepared to deploy policy tools to contain risks to financial stability. Precautionary steps can include comprehensive stress tests for financial institutions and measures to preserve or replenish foreign currency reserves. These strategies may involve implementing policies that boost investor confidence and attract foreign capital, while reducing dependence on volatile sources of funding. When outflows occur, targeted interventions to manage capital flows and exchange rate and financial volatility could become appropriate in limited circumstances.

Nonperforming loans have edged down in EMDEs as a whole in recent years but have crept up in LICs (figure 1.15.C). In banking sectors where credit growth has risen, regulators need to prioritize measures to preserve financial stability. This includes strengthening supervisory oversight and requiring banks and nonbank financial institutions to apply stricter underwriting standards and risk management systems (IMF 2019). Regulators could also consider requiring complex banking institutions to develop or enhance rapid and orderly resolution plans to mitigate the potential for financial market turmoil and contagion across the financial system in the event of a systemic failure.

In recent years, the frequency of cyberattacks on the financial sector has increased, coinciding with the ongoing digitalization of financial architecture and products (figure 1.15.D; Harry and Gallagher 2018). Policy makers need to consider measures aimed at addressing associated threats to financial stability and take steps toward protecting critical digital and market infrastructure. This includes addressing cyber and operational risks associated with the functioning of mobile money or payment services, money laundering, and data privacy (Feyen et al. 2023).

EMDE fiscal policy challenges

EMDEs require considerable fiscal resources to tackle development challenges, including growth-enhancing investments, developing climate-resilient infrastructure, and providing targeted support to vulnerable populations. Mobilizing additional resources in an environment of growing debt-servicing costs while safeguarding fiscal sustainability constitutes a delicate balancing act, especially for LICs (figure 1.16.A).

Progress in mobilizing tax revenue in EMDEs has halted since the global financial crisis. Although the average tax-to-GDP ratio in EMDEs has increased by 3.5 to 5 percentage points since the early 1990s, almost all this progress took place before 2008 (Benitez et al. 2024). In LICs, the need to mobilize revenues, including from taxes, remains acute given large development needs. Over 2011-23, LICs mobilized total revenues amounting to about 18 percent of GDP—11 percentage points lower than in other EMDEs, with this difference largely explained by weaker tax revenue collection. LICs have collected, on average, less than two-thirds of their potential tax revenue—well below the estimate for other EMDEs (figure 1.16.B). The ability of LICs to raise tax revenues is impeded by several structural factors, including weak institutions, underdeveloped financial sectors, limited use of information technology, and high levels of informality (Mawejje 2024). At the same time, other sources of revenue in LICs have been shrinking, with net overseas development assistance declining by 5 percentage points of GDP over 2020-22, to 7 percent of GDP in 2022—its lowest level in two decades.

Priority should be placed on broadening tax bases, which tends to be more supportive of growth than raising statutory tax rates (Dabla-Norris and Lima 2023). This could be achieved, for instance, by eliminating costly tax exemptions and deductions. EMDEs also have significant scope to improve compliance by strengthening their revenue administrations, including by better leveraging digital technologies. Additionally, many EMDEs, particularly those with limited fiscal space, need to redouble efforts to rationalize large government wage bills and reform social safety nets to provide targeted support to vulnerable populations. Well-implemented digitalization can further support the efficiency of social spending (Amaglobeli et al. 2023). Moreover, the share of EMDEs with debt on a rising trajectory has risen in recent years, despite some improvement since the pandemic-induced recession of 2020 (figure 1.16.C).

FIGURE 1.16 EMDE fiscal policy challenges

EMDEs, especially LICs, require considerable fiscal resources to meet development needs in an environment of higher debt-servicing costs. Tax revenues fall short of potential across EMDEs, particularly in LICs. More broadly, the share of EMDEs with debt on a rising trajectory has increased in recent years, despite some improvement since the pandemic, underscoring the need to reduce debt vulnerabilities and rebuild fiscal space. Elevated debt levels pose severe challenges in LICs, with not a single LIC at low risk of debt distress.

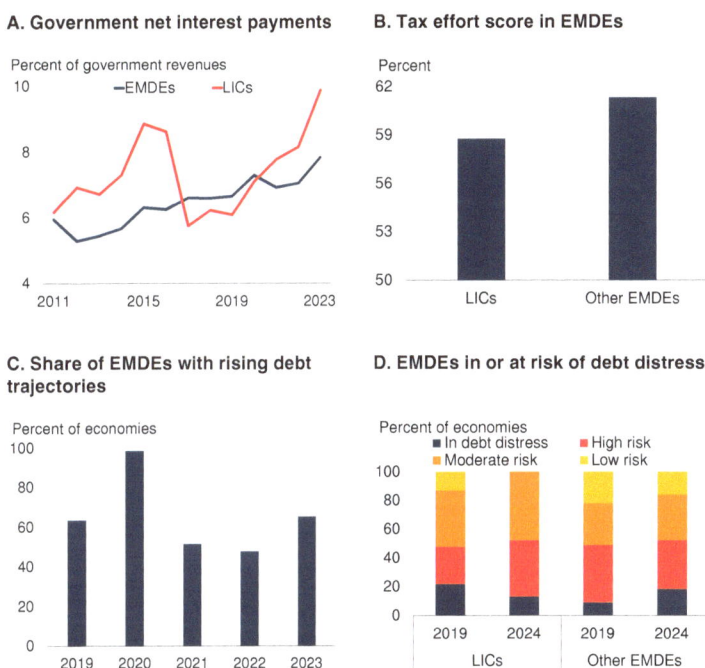

A. Government net interest payments

B. Tax effort score in EMDEs

C. Share of EMDEs with rising debt trajectories

D. EMDEs in or at risk of debt distress

Sources: Kose et al. (2022); Mawejje (2024); McNabb, Danquah, and Tagem (2021); World Development Indicators (database); World Bank-IMF Debt Sustainability Framework; World Bank.
Note: EMDEs = emerging market and developing economies; LICs = low-income countries.
A. Net interest payments are the difference between primary balances and overall fiscal balances. Aggregates are computed with government revenues in U.S. dollars as weights, based on 150 EMDEs, including 24 LICs.
B. Tax effort is a proxy for domestic revenue capacity and measures the ratio of actual tax collected to tax potential (maximum revenues given the structure of the economy and economic environment, and assuming efficient tax policy design and perfect collection). Tax potential estimates are the latest available data points for each country, based on the pooled estimates reported in McNabb, Danquah, and Tagem (2021). Based on 126 EMDEs, of which 19 are LICs.
C. Bars show the share of countries in which primary balance sustainability gaps are negative (that is, debt is on a rising trajectory or is associated with debt-increasing fiscal positions).
D. Share of LICs and other EMDEs in overall debt distress or at risk of debt distress, based on the joint World Bank-IMF Debt Sustainability Framework for Low-Income Countries (LIC-DSF). Sample includes 24 LICs and 46 other EMDEs.

Implementing sound fiscal frameworks can help guide the process of rebuilding fiscal space and reducing debt vulnerabilities.

Additionally, unexpected shifts in EMDE fiscal policy, particularly in the context of elections in numerous countries last year, pose a risk to fiscal sustainability by potentially interrupting ongoing or reversing earlier fiscal consolidation efforts. Fiscal policy tends to be looser, with larger slippages, during election years. In EMDEs, the deterioration in primary deficits is generally not unwound after elections, while the deterioration in primary spending is only partially unwound, mainly through cuts in capital spending (de Haan, Ohnsorge, and Yu 2023). It is, therefore, critical for countries to avoid fiscal slippages and enhance transparency of public finances to safeguard medium-term fiscal sustainability.

Coordinated efforts are needed to improve fiscal policy management in EMDEs, particularly LICs—no LIC is judged to be at low risk of debt distress (figure 1.16.D). Global policy action can support LICs' efforts to address their debt challenges and prevent a further worsening of debt stress through external debt relief and concessional financing, as well as fiscal policy advice and technical assistance.

EMDE structural policy challenges

EMDEs face the pressing challenge of closing significant development gaps in an environment of subdued growth prospects and limited fiscal space. Decisive efforts are needed to tackle humanitarian crises stemming from conflicts. Structural reforms are essential to promote investments in human capital and enhance labor force inclusion, helping to reverse the scarring effects of the pandemic and foster potential growth. Shoring up food security is also vital, especially given ongoing conflicts and growing trade restrictions.

Tackling the rise in conflicts and associated damage

Irrespective of wider development trends, EMDEs experiencing conflict—either domestic or inter-state—have little chance of improving long-term living standards (chapter 4). The roots of armed conflicts and instability are complex, but the high incidence of these events—particularly among LICs—calls for increased focus on reducing susceptibility to conflict and on rebuilding in its aftermath (figure 1.17.A).

Reducing the incidence of conflict and violence extends far beyond economic policy and may require significant reforms of socio-political structures and public institutions. Moreover, even comprehensive efforts to foster peaceful and stable societies may prove insufficient to avoid some interstate conflicts. Nevertheless, with respect to

domestic instability and violence, reducing inequality, food insecurity, and competition over resources—including natural resources—can lower conflict risks (Blattman and Miguel 2010; Vesco et al. 2020). More generally, lower per capita GDP is correlated with increased conflict risks, possibly reflecting the lower opportunity cost of engaging in armed rebellion in societies with severely limited economic opportunities (Jakobsen, De Soysa, and Jakobsen 2013). To this extent, policies enabling sustainable growth can be conflict-reducing, especially those that foster structural transformation by transitioning workers out of traditional subsistence occupations into higher-productivity sectors (Vestby, Buhaug, and von Uexkull 2021).

In addition, evidence that climate-change-related shocks are more likely to generate conflict in poorer societies suggests that adaptation to climate change—alongside many other benefits—can lessen conflict risks (Burke et al. 2024a, 2024b). At a more localized level, targeted employment programs—such as access to vocational training and complementary capital inputs—may help reduce the chances of former fighters returning to armed groups (Blattman and Annan 2015).

In resource-dependent economies, the effective management of natural resources can help lessen conflict risks. On the one hand, resource extraction can generate wealth that can be channeled into building human and physical capital. On the other hand, especially in settings with weak governance, natural resource dependence can lead to rent seeking, potentially with socially destabilizing consequences (Berman et al. 2017). Therefore, countries pursuing resource-led development need to prioritize raising governance standards, reducing corruption, and transparently channeling resource rents into public goods such as education and infrastructure, which, in turn, may enable future diversification. The international community also has an important role to play in bolstering surveillance of and combating illegal commodity trade.

Lifting human capital and bolstering labor force inclusion

Human capital accounts for at least one-third of the variation in labor earnings within countries, and at least one-half of the variation in earnings per worker across countries (Deming 2022). Lifting human capital is essential for EMDEs to support sustainable and inclusive growth, reduce poverty, attain critical development goals, and reverse the decline in potential growth (IMF 2024c; World Bank 2024b). Estimates suggest that workers in EMDEs are only slightly more than half as productive as they could be if they achieved their full health and education potential (defined as no stunting, survival to at least age 60, and 14 years of high-quality school by age 18, respectively). Moreover, only about one-third of human capital potential is utilized in the labor market, with the remaining two-thirds either unemployed, underemployed, or not participating in productive work (World Bank 2024f). Thus, improving the quality of, and access to, education, healthcare, and employment opportunities remains a key challenge.

Policies focused on the quality of labor supply and the allocation of labor can be broad-based, aiming to lift levels across the working-age population as a whole, or can be targeted to specific groups. Improving general education levels, especially the quality of education and learning-adjusted years of schooling outcomes, is a cost-effective and efficient way to boost both growth and employment, fostering a better-skilled and more adaptable and engaged labor force (Angrist et al. 2025). Each additional year of schooling is estimated to boost hourly earnings by 9 percent (Psacharopoulos and Patrinos 2018). Active labor market policies can also include specific training or retraining programs to reverse pandemic-related scarring, help lagging segments of the labor force find employment, and address persistently high informality and labor market segmentation.

In the coming decades, EMDEs will face substantial and varied demographic shifts, creating both opportunities and challenges. For instance, the working-age population in Sub-Saharan Africa (SSA) and SAR is projected to increase substantially by 2050, while that in EAP is projected to decline (figure 1.17.B). Additionally, many EMDEs continue to contend with substantial gender gaps in labor force participation and labor income, despite progress over the past three

FIGURE 1.17 EMDE structural policy challenges

Tackling the high incidence of conflict and its associated impacts, particularly in LICs, is crucial for raising living standards and addressing development challenges. EMDEs are set to face large shifts in the working-age population over the coming decades, presenting both opportunities and challenges. Substantial gender gaps in labor force participation remain, despite progress in recent decades in some regions. Acute food insecurity in EMDEs has risen steadily in recent years, with conflict as a key driver.

A. Economies experiencing intense conflict

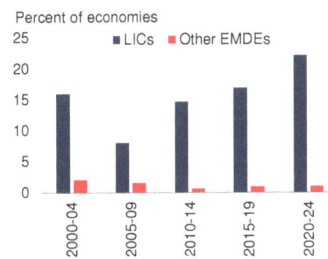

B. Projected change in the working-age population between 2024 and 2050

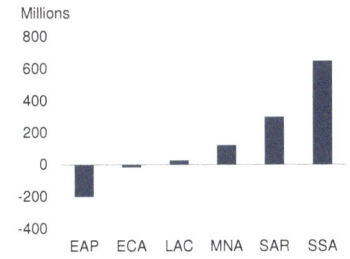

C. Ratio of female to male labor force participation

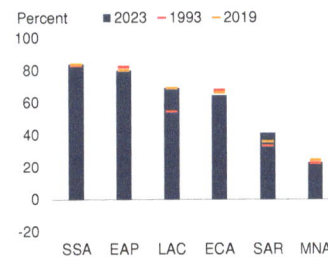

D. Primary drivers of acute food insecurity in EMDEs

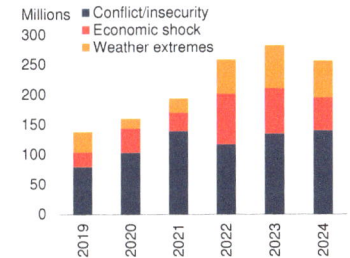

Sources: Food Security Information Network; ILO Modelled Estimates (database); UN Population Prospects (database); Uppsala Conflict Data Program; World Development Indicators (database); World Bank.

Note: EAP = East Asia and Pacific; ECA = Europe and Central Asia; EMDEs = emerging market and developing economies; LAC = Latin America and the Caribbean; LICs = low-income countries; MNA = Middle East and North Africa; SAR = South Asia; SSA = Sub-Saharan Africa.

A. Intense conflict is defined as a situation resulting in more than 50 battle-related deaths per million people.

B. Bars show the change in the total working-age population (defined as individuals aged 15-64 years) across EMDE regions between 2024 and 2050.

C. Panel shows the ratio of female to male labor force participation over the indicated periods for comparison.

D. Number of people with acute food insecurity caused by conflict and poor security situations, economic shocks, and weather extremes. Data for 2024 is up to August.

decades in some regions (figure 1.17.C). Moreover, the impact of COVID-19 on work stoppages was generally greater for women than men, partially reversing hard-won progress over the past decades (ILO 2024). Barriers to female labor force participation can include limited access to child or elderly care; mismatches in education and skills; discrimination in hiring and retention; and restrictive policies, laws, and sociocultural norms (Halim et al. 2023).

Policies to support women and girls through education and skills development have borne some fruit globally, though there is still significant scope for further progress. Further reducing gender gaps in terms of educational attainment, in particular in SSA where such gaps remain sizable for women, is an important challenge (World Bank 2024g). In contrast, in some regions, such as Latin America and the Caribbean (LAC), males are increasingly at risk of lower education outcomes compared to females. Countries can consider a range of measures to enhance childcare options, including policies that prioritize expanding coverage for the most vulnerable households (Devercelli and Beaton-Day 2020). Strengthening social protection and safety nets, broader employment incentives, and public-works initiatives have helped boost the inclusion of women and other disadvantaged groups in the labor force of EMDEs (Peterman et al. 2024).

Structural shifts, such as technological innovation, present both challenges and opportunities for workers, including in EMDEs. Automation and digital technologies have the potential to boost labor productivity and incomes. At the same time, they can lead to labor market disruptions, and the implications for aggregate employment are unclear. Should large productivity gains materialize from AI, they could enhance incomes broadly, though individuals with higher levels of education are more likely to benefit (Cazzaniga et al. 2024). The extent to which such innovations entail a structural shift in employment and bolster growth in an inclusive and equitable manner ultimately depends on institutional arrangements, the regulatory regime, the ability to improve educational outcomes, and associated policies, such as social security and retraining opportunities for affected workers.

Confronting food insecurity

Food insecurity in EMDEs has risen markedly since the pandemic, with the number of people facing acute food insecurity by mid-2024 more than twice that in 2019. Moreover, acute food insecurity is likely to have worsened in hunger hotspots across SSA, MNA, EAP, and LAC regions by the end of 2024 (FAO 2024). Conflict is a key driver of acute food insecurity, affecting about twice as many people as extreme weather events and economic shocks (figure 1.17.D; World Bank 2024f). Increasing and sustained hostilities limit humanitarian access, preventing the delivery of food assistance and other resources needed to support livelihoods.

The impact of climate-change-related weather events and natural disasters on food insecurity has also become substantially more pronounced in recent years. Climate-driven food insecurity and supply instability are projected to increase further with global warming, interacting with non-climate-change-related drivers such as conflict (IPCC 2023). These issues could be compounded in EMDEs facing pre-existing vulnerabilities or those EMDEs who are at high risk of debt distress, with limited resources to support vulnerable populations.

To address escalating food insecurity, a multi-pronged approach is needed to support production and producers, facilitate increased trade in food and production inputs, support vulnerable households, and invest in sustainable food security. It is important to invest in integrated solutions that go beyond emergency responses to address the drivers of food insecurity, improving resilience and stability in affected regions. Key measures include enhancing financial support and technical assistance for farmers, improving supply chains to reduce post-harvest food losses, improving hygiene in food distribution channels, and strengthening links between production and consumption centers. Promoting agricultural practices that are more climate-smart and produce a more diverse mix of foods can improve food systems' resilience, increase farm incomes, improve climate change resilience, and enhance the availability and affordability of nutrient-dense foods. In addition, governments of food-exporting countries can improve global food security by limiting export bans and food stockpiling.

TABLE 1.2 Emerging market and developing economies[1]

Commodity exporters[2]		Commodity importers[3]	
Algeria*	Kyrgyz Republic	Afghanistan	Samoa
Angola*	Lao PDR	Albania	Serbia
Argentina	Liberia	Antigua and Barbuda	Somalia
Armenia	Libya*	Bahamas, The	Sri Lanka
Azerbaijan*	Madagascar	Bangladesh	St. Kitts and Nevis
Bahrain*	Malawi	Barbados	St. Lucia
Belize	Mali	Belarus	St. Vincent and the Grenadines
Benin	Mauritania	Bosnia and Herzegovina	Syrian Arab Republic
Bhutan*	Mongolia	Bulgaria	Thailand
Bolivia*	Mozambique	Cambodia	Tonga
Botswana	Myanmar*	China	Tunisia
Brazil	Namibia	Djibouti	Türkiye
Burkina Faso	Nicaragua	Dominica	Tuvalu
Burundi	Niger	Dominican Republic	Vanuatu
Cabo Verde	Nigeria*	Egypt, Arab Rep.	Viet Nam
Cameroon*	Oman*	El Salvador	
Central African Republic	Papua New Guinea	Eswatini	
Chad*	Paraguay	Georgia	
Chile	Peru	Grenada	
Colombia*	Qatar*	Haiti	
Comoros	Russian Federation*	Hungary	
Congo, Dem. Rep.	Rwanda	India	
Congo, Rep.*	São Tomé and Príncipe	Jamaica	
Costa Rica	Saudi Arabia*	Jordan	
Côte d'Ivoire	Senegal	Kiribati	
Ecuador*	Seychelles	Lebanon	
Equatorial Guinea*	Sierra Leone	Lesotho	
Eritrea	Solomon Islands	Malaysia	
Ethiopia	South Africa	Maldives	
Fiji	South Sudan*	Marshall Islands	
Gabon*	Sudan	Mauritius	
Gambia, The	Suriname	Mexico	
Ghana*	Tajikistan	Micronesia, Fed. Sts.	
Guatemala	Tanzania	Moldova	
Guinea	Timor-Leste*	Montenegro	
Guinea-Bissau	Togo	Morocco	
Guyana*	Uganda	Nauru	
Honduras	Ukraine	Nepal	
Indonesia*	United Arab Emirates*	North Macedonia	
Iran, Islamic Rep.*	Uruguay	Pakistan	
Iraq*	Uzbekistan	Palau	
Kazakhstan*	West Bank and Gaza	Panama	
Kenya	Yemen, Rep.*	Philippines	
Kosovo	Zambia	Poland	
Kuwait*	Zimbabwe	Romania	

* Energy exporters.

1. Emerging market and developing economies (EMDEs) include all those that are not classified as advanced economies and for which a forecast is published for this report. Dependent territories are excluded. Advanced economies include Australia; Austria; Belgium; Canada; Cyprus; Czechia; Denmark; Estonia; Finland; France; Germany; Greece; Hong Kong SAR, China; Iceland; Ireland; Israel; Italy; Japan; the Republic of Korea; Latvia; Lithuania; Luxembourg; Malta; the Netherlands; New Zealand; Norway; Portugal; Singapore; the Slovak Republic; Slovenia; Spain; Sweden; Switzerland; the United Kingdom; and the United States. Since Croatia became a member of the euro area on January 1, 2023, it has been removed from the list of EMDEs, and related growth aggregates, to avoid double counting.

2. An economy is defined as commodity exporter when, on average in 2017-19, either (1) total commodities exports accounted for 30 percent or more of total exports or (2) exports of any single commodity accounted for 20 percent or more of total exports. Economies for which these thresholds were met as a result of re-exports were excluded. When data were not available, judgment was used. This taxonomy results in the classification of some well-diversified economies as importers, even if they are exporters of certain commodities (for example, Mexico).

3. Commodity importers are EMDEs not classified as commodity exporters.

References

ACLED (Armed Conflict Location & Event Data Project) database. Accessed on November 25, 2024. https://acleddata.com/data-export-tool/.

Aiyar, S., D. Malacrino, and A. F. Presbitero. 2024. "Investing in Friends: The Role of Geopolitical Alignment in FDI Flows." *European Journal of Political Economy* 83 (June): 102508.

Aiyar, S., and F. Ohnsorge. 2024. "Geoeconomic Fragmentation and "Connector" Countries." CAMA Working Paper 53/2024, Centre for Applied Macroeconomic Analysis, Australian National University, Canberra, Australia.

Amaglobeli, D., R. de Mooij, A. Mengistu, M. Manabu Nose, et al. 2023. "Transforming Public Finance Through GovTech." IMF Staff Discussion Note 2023/04, International Monetary Fund, Washington, DC.

Amiti, M., M. Gomez, S. H. Kong, and D. Weinstein. 2024. "Trade Protection, Stock-Market Returns, and Welfare." NBER Working Paper 28758, National Bureau of Economic Research, Cambridge, MA.

Angeli M., C. Archer, S. Batten, A. Cesa-Bianchi, L. D'Aguanno, A. Haberis, T. Löber, et al. 2022. "Climate Change: Possible Macroeconomic Implications." Quarterly Bulletin 2022, Q4, Bank of England, London.

Angrist, N., D. K. Evans, D. Filmer, R. Glennerster, F. H. Rogers, and S. Sabarwal. 2025. "How to Improve Education Outcomes Most Efficiently? A Review of the Evidence Using a Unified Metric." *Journal of Development Economics* 172 (January): 103382.

Autor, D., A. Beck, D. Dorn, and G. H. Hanson. 2024. "Help for the Heartland? The Employment and Electoral Effects of the Trump Tariffs in the United States." NBER Working Paper 32082, National Bureau of Economic Research, Cambridge, MA.

Bailey, M. A., A. Strezhnev, and E. Voeten. 2017. "Estimating Dynamic State Preferences from United Nations Voting Data." *Journal of Conflict Resolution* 61 (2): 430-56.

Barattieri, A., and M. Cacciatore. 2023. "Self-Harming Trade Policy? Protectionism and Production Networks." *American Economic Journal: Macroeconomics* 15 (2): 97-128.

Barattieri, A., M. Cacciatore, and F. Ghironi. 2021. "Protectionism and the Business Cycle." *Journal of International Economics* 129 (March): 103417.

Barattieri, A., A. Mattoo, and D. Taglioni. 2024. "Trade Effects of Industrial Policies: Are Preferential Agreements a Shield?" Policy Research Working Paper 10806, World Bank, Washington, DC.

Behrer, P., J. Rexer, S. Sharma, and M. Triyana. 2024. "Household and Firm Exposure to Heat and Floods in South Asia." Policy Research Working Paper 10947, World Bank, Washington, DC.

Benitez, J. C., M. Mansour, M. Pecho, and C. Vellutini. 2024. "Building Tax Capacity in Developing Countries." IMF Staff Discussion Note 2023/006, International Monetary Fund, Washington, DC.

Bergin, P., and G. Corsetti. 2023. "The Macroeconomic Stabilization of Tariff Shocks: What is the Optimal Monetary Response?" *Journal of International Economics* 143 (July): 103758.

Berman, N., M. Couttenier, D. Rohner, and M. Thoenig. 2017. "This Mine is Mine! How Minerals Fuel Conflicts in Africa." *American Economic Review* 107 (6): 1564-610.

Bilal, A., and D. R. Känzig. 2024. "The Macroeconomic Impact of Climate Change: Global vs. Local Temperature." NBER Working Paper 32450, National Bureau of Economic Research, Cambridge, MA.

Blattman, C., and J. Annan. 2015. "Can Employment Reduce Lawlessness and Rebellion? A Field Experiment with High-Risk Men in a Fragile State." NBER Working Paper 21289, National Bureau of Economic Research, Cambridge, MA.

Blattman, C., and E. Miguel. 2010. "Civil War." *Journal of Economic Literature* 48 (1): 3-57.

Bombardini, M., A. Gonzalez-Lira, B. Li, and C. Motta. 2024. "The Increasing Cost of Buying American." NBER Working Paper 32953, National Bureau of Economic Research, Cambridge, MA.

Bryson, J. H., and M. Pugliese. 2024. "The 2024 U.S. Elections: Economic Implications." *Wells Fargo Economics* (Special Commentary). November 6, 2024. https://wellsfargo.bluematrix.com/links2/html/5fd9397 7-359f-4bff-8db1-42935f3e8f45.

Burke, M., J. Ferguson, S. Hsiang, and E. Miguel. 2024a. "Will Wealth Weaken Weather Wars?" *AEA Papers and Proceedings* 114 (May): 65-69.

Burke, M., J. Ferguson, S. M. Hsiang, and E. Miguel. 2024b. "New Evidence on the Economics of Climate and Conflict." NBER Working Paper 33040, National Bureau of Economic Research, Cambridge, MA.

Burke, M., S. M. Hsiang, and E. Miguel. 2015. "Global Non-linear Effect of Temperature on Economic Production." *Nature* 527: 235-39.

Cavallo, A., G. Gopinath, B. Neiman, and J. Tang. 2021. "Tariff Pass-Through at the Border and at the Store: Evidence from U.S Trade Policy." *American Economic Review: Insights* 3 (1): 19-34.

Cazzaniga, M., F. Jaumotte, L. Li, G. Melina, A. Panton, C. Pizzinelli, E. Rockall, and M. M. Tavares. 2024. "Gen-AI: Artificial Intelligence and the Future of Work." Staff Discussion Note 2024/001, International Monetary Fund, Washington, DC.

Chrimes, T., B. Gootjes, M. A. Kose, and C. Wheeler. 2024. *The Great Reversal: Prospects, Risks, and Policies in International Development Association (IDA) Countries.* Washington, DC: World Bank.

Collier, P., V. L. Elliot, H. Hegre, A. Hoeffler, M. Reynal-Querol, and N. Sambanis. 2003. *Breaking the Conflict Trap: Civil War and Development Policy.* Washington, DC: World Bank; New York: Oxford University Press.

Dabla-Norris, E., and F. Lima. 2023. "Macroeconomic Effects of Tax Rate and Base Changes: Evidence from Fiscal Consolidations." *European Economic Review* 153 (April): 104399.

De Haan, J., F. Ohnsorge, and S. Yu. 2023. "Election-Induced Fiscal Policy Cycles in Emerging Market and Developing Economies." CEPR Discussion Paper 18708, Centre for Economic Policy Research, London.

Debelle, G. 2019. "Climate Change and the Economy." Speech, Centre for Policy Development, Sydney, Australia.

Deininger, K. W., D. W. Ali, N. Kussul, G. Lemoine, and A. Shelestov. 2024. "Micro-Level Impacts of the War on Ukraine's Agriculture Sector: Distinguishing Local and National Effects over Time." Policy Research Working Paper 10869, World Bank, Washington, DC.

Deming, D. J. 2022. "Four Facts about Human Capital." *Journal of Economic Perspectives* 36 (3): 75-102.

Devercelli, E. A., and F. Beaton-Day. 2020. *Better Jobs and Brighter Futures: Investing in Childcare to Build Human Capital.* Washington, DC: World Bank.

Diwan, I., M. Guzman, M. Kessler, V. Songwe, and J. E. Stiglitz. 2024. "An Updated Bridge Proposal: Towards A Solution to the Current Sovereign Debt Crises and to Restore Growth." Policy Note, Finance for Development Lab and Initiative for Policy Dialogue, Paris.

Fang, X., S. Kothari, C. McLoughlin, and M. Yenice. 2020. "The Economic Consequences of Conflict in Sub-Saharan Africa." IMF Working Paper 2020/221, International Monetary Fund, Washington, DC.

FAO (Food and Agriculture Organization) and WFP (World Food Programme). 2024. *Hunger Hotspots: FAO-WFP Early Warnings on Acute Food Insecurity, June to October 2024 Outlook.* Rome, Italy.

Farah-Yacoubm J. P., C. M. G. von Luckner, and C. M. Reinhart. 2024. "The Social Costs of Sovereign Default." NBER Working Paper 32600, National Bureau of Economic Research, Cambridge, MA.

Federle, J., A. Meier, G. Müller, W. Mutschler, and M. Schularick. 2024. "The Price of War." CEPR Discussion Paper 18834, Center for Economic and Policy Research, Washington, DC.

Felbermayr, G., and J. Gröschl. 2014. "Naturally Negative: The Growth Effects of Natural Disasters." *Journal of Development Economics* 111 (C): 92-106.

Feyen, E., H. Natarajan, and M. Saal. 2023. *Fintech and the Future of Finance: Market and Policy Implications.* Washington, DC: World Bank.

Gates, S., H. Hegre, H. M. Nygard, and H. Strand. 2012. "Development Consequences of Armed Conflict." *World Development* 40 (9): 1713-22.

Giglio, S., T. Kuchler, J. Stroebel, and O. Wang. 2024. "The Economics of Biodiversity Loss." NBER Working Paper 32678, National Bureau of Economic Research, Cambridge, MA.

Global Trade Alert (database). Accessed on December 18, 2024. https://globaltradealert.org/data_extraction.

GRFC (Global Report on Food Crises) database. Food Security Information Network. Accessed on September 27, 2024. https://fsinplatform.org/global-report-food-crises-2024-mid-year-update.

Halim, D., B. M. O'Sullivan, and A. Sahay. 2023. *Increasing Female Labor Force Participation.* Gender Thematic Policy Notes Series. January. Washington, DC: World Bank.

Hallegatte, S., M. Bangalore, L. Bonzanigo, M. Fay, T. Kane, U. Narloch, J. Rozenberg, et al. 2016. *Shock*

Waves: Managing the Impacts of Climate Change on Poverty. Washington, DC: World Bank.

Harry, C., and N. Gallagher, 2018. "Classifying Cyber Events: A Proposed Taxonomy." *Journal of Information Warfare* 17 (3): 17-31.

Holston, K., T. Laubach, and J. Williams. 2023. "Measuring the Natural Rate of Interest after COVID-19." Federal Reserve Bank of New York Staff Reports No. 1063, June.

Hördahl, P., and O. Tristani. 2014. "Inflation Risk Premia in the Euro Area and the United States." *International Journal of Central Banking* 10 (3): 1-47.

ILO (International Labour Organization). 2024. *World Employment and Social Outlook: September 2024.* September. Geneva: International Labour Organization.

ILO Modelled Estimates (database), International Labour Organization, Geneva. Accessed on September 27, 2024. https://ilostat.ilo.org/methods/concepts-and-definitions/ilo-modelled-estimates/.

IMF (International Monetary Fund). 2019. *Global Financial Stability Report: Vulnerabilities in a Maturing Credit Cycle.* Washington, DC: International Monetary Fund.

IMF (International Monetary Fund). 2024a. Macroeconomic Developments and Prospects for Low-Income Countries—2024. International Monetary Fund, Washington, DC.

IMF (International Monetary Fund). 2024b. List of LIC DSAs for PRGT Eligible Countries (as of October 31, 2024). International Monetary Fund, Washington, DC.

IMF (International Monetary Fund). 2024c. *World Economic Outlook: Steady but Slow: Resilience amid Divergence.* Washington, DC: International Monetary Fund.

Institute of International Finance (database). Accessed on December 18, 2024. https://iif.com/.

International Debt Statistics (database), World Bank, Washington, DC. Accessed on December 18, 2024. https://worldbank.org/en/programs/debt-statistics/ids.

IPBES (Intergovernmental Science-Policy Platform on Biodiversity and Ecosystem Services). 2019. *Global Assessment Report on Biodiversity and Ecosystem Services of the Intergovernmental Science-Policy Platform on Biodiversity and Ecosystem Services*, edited by E. S.

Brondizio, J. Settele, S. Díaz, and H. T. Ngo. Bonn, Germany: IPBES Secretariat.

IPCC (Intergovernmental Panel on Climate Change). 2023. *Climate Change 2023 Synthesis Report Summary for Policymakers.* Geneva: IPCC.

Jakobsen, T. G., I. De Soysa, and J. Jakobsen. 2013. "Why Do Poor Countries Suffer Costly Conflict? Unpacking Per Capita Income and the Onset of Civil War." *Conflict Management and Peace Science* 30 (2): 140-60.

Johnson, J. A., G. Ruta, U. Baldos, R. Cervigni, S. Chonabayashi, E. Corong, O. Gavryliuk, et al. 2021. *The Economic Case for Nature: A Global Earth-Economy Model to Assess Development Policy Pathways.* Washington, DC: World Bank.

Kose, M. A., S. Kurlat, F. Ohnsorge, and N. Sugawara. 2022. "A Cross-Country Database of Fiscal Space." *Journal of International Money and Finance* 128 (November): 102682.

Lagarde, C. 2024. "Central banks in a Changing World: The Role of the ECB in the Face of Climate and Environmental Risks." Speech, European Central Bank, Frankfurt.

Laubach, T., and J. C. Williams. 2003. "Measuring the Natural Rate of Interest." *The Review of Economics and Statistics* 85 (4): 1063-70.

Lubik, T., and C. Matthes. 2023. "The Stars Our Destination: An Update for Our R* Model." Economic Brief 23-32, Federal Reserve Bank of Richmond, Richmond.

Mahler, D. G., N. Yonzan, and C. Lakner. 2022. "The Impact of COVID-19 on Global Inequality and Poverty." Policy Research Working Paper 10198, World Bank, Washington, DC.

Maliszewska, M., and D. Winkler. 2024. *Leveraging Trade for More and Better Jobs.* Prosperity Insight Series. September. Washington, DC: World Bank.

Mattoo, A., A. Mulabdic, and M. Ruta. 2022. "Trade Creation and Trade Diversion in Deep Agreements." *Canadian Journal of Economics* 55 (3): 1598-637.

Mawejje, J. 2024. *Fiscal Vulnerabilities in Low-Income Countries: Evolution, Drivers, and Policies.* Washington, DC: World Bank.

McKibbin, W. J., M. Hogan, M. Noland. 2024. "The International Economic Implications of a Second Trump Presidency." Working Papers 24-20, Peterson

Institute for International Economics, Washington, DC.

McNabb, K., M. Danquah, and A. Tagem. 2021. "Tax Effort Revisited: New Estimates from The Government Revenue Dataset." WIDER Working Paper 170, United Nations University World Institute for Development Economics Research, Helsinki.

Mertens, K., and M. O. Ravn. 2013. "The Dynamic Effects of Personal and Corporate Income Tax Changes in the United States." *American Economic Review* 103 (4): 1212-47.

Michelis, A. D., G. Lofstrom, M. McHenry, M. Orak, A. Queralto, and M. Scaramucci. 2024. "Has the Inflation Process Become More Persistent? Evidence from Major Advanced Economies." FEDS Notes, Board of Governors of the Federal Reserve System, Washington, DC.

Milivojevic, L. 2023. "Natural Disasters and Fiscal Drought." Policy Research Working Paper 10298, World Bank, Washington, DC.

Nath, I. B., V. A. Ramey, and P. J. Klenow. 2024. "How Much will Global Warming Cool Global Growth?" NBER Working Paper 32761, National Bureau of Economic Research, Cambridge, MA.

ND-GAIN (Notre Dame Global Adaptation Initiative Country Index) database. Accessed on November 8, 2024. https://gain.nd.edu/our-work/country-index/download-data/.

NGFS (Network for Greening the Financial System). 2023. "NGFS Climate Scenarios for Central Banks and Supervisors." https://ngfs.net/en/ngfs-climate-scenarios-phase-iv-november-2023.

Novta, N., and Pugacheva, E. 2021. "The Macroeconomic Costs of Conflict." *Journal of Macroeconomics* 68: 103286.

Ohnsorge, F., M. Stocker, and M. Y. Some. 2016. "Quantifying Uncertainties in Global Growth Forecasts." Policy Research Working Paper 7770, World Bank, Washington, DC.

Oxford Economics. 2019. "Global Economic Model." July. Oxford Economics, Oxford, U.K.

Peterman, A., J. Wang, K. K. Sonke, and J. Steinert. 2024. "Social Safety Nets, Women's Economic Achievements and Agency: A Systematic Review and Meta-analysis." CGD Working Paper 684, Center for Global Development, Washington, DC.

Psacharopoulos, G., and H. A. Patrinos. 2018. "Returns to Investment in Education: A Decennial Review of the Global Literature." Policy Research Working Paper 8402, World Bank, Washington, DC.

Rexer, J. M., E. B. Kapstein, and A. F. Rivera. 2022. "Pricing Conflict Risk: Evidence from Sovereign Bonds." ESOC Working Paper 33, Empirical Studies of Conflict Project, Princeton, NJ.

Romer, C. D., and D. H. Romer. 2010. "The Macroeconomic Effects of Tax Changes: Estimates Based on a New Measure of Fiscal Shocks." *American Economic Review* 100 (3): 763-801.

Rotunno, L., and M. Ruta. 2024. "Trade Spillovers of Domestic Subsidies." IMF Working Paper 2024/041, International Monetary Fund, Washington, DC.

Rudebusch, G. D. 2019. "Climate Change and the Federal Reserve." FRBSF Economic Letter 2019-09, Federal Reserve Bank of San Francisco.

The Budget Lab. 2024. "Fiscal, Macroeconomic, and Price Estimates of Tariffs Under Both Non-retaliation and Retaliation Scenarios." The Budget Lab at Yale, New Haven.

Sylvestre, F., A. Mahamat-Nour, T. Naradoum, M. Alcoba, L. Gal, A. Paris, J. F. Cretaux, et al. 2024. "Strengthening of the Hydrological Cycle in the Lake Chad Basin Under Current Climate Change." *Nature Scientific Reports* (2024) 14:24639.

UCDP (Uppsala Universitet). 2024. "Record Number of Armed Conflicts in the World–Press Release." Uppsala Universitet, Uppsala, Sweden.

UN (United Nations). 2024. 2024 Revision of World Population Prospects (database). New York: UN.

UN Comtrade (United Nations) database. "UN Comtrade." Accessed on December 18, 2023. https://comtradeplus.un.org/.

UNEP (United Nations Environment Programme). 2023. "Adaptation Gap Report 2023." United Nations Environment Programme, Nairobi.

UNHCR (United Nations High Commissioner for Refugees) Refugee Population Statistics Database. Accessed on December 18, 2024. https://unhcr.org/refugee-statistics/download/?url=IAr67y.

Vergara Cobos, E. 2024. *Cybersecurity Economics for Emerging Markets*. Washington, DC: World Bank.

Vesco, P., S. Dasgupta, E. De Cian, and C. Carraro. 2020. "Natural Resources and Conflict: A Meta-analysis of the Empirical Literature." *Ecological Economics* 172 (June): 106633.

Vestby, J., H. Buhaug, and N. Von Uexkull. 2021. "Why Do Some Poor Countries See Armed Conflict While Others Do Not? A Dual Sector Approach." *World Development* 138 (February): 105273.

WMO (World Meteorological Organization). 2024. "State of the Global Climate 2023." World Meteorological Organization, Geneva.

World Bank. 2021. *Unlocking Nature-Smart Development: An Approach Paper on Biodiversity and Ecosystem Services.* Washington, DC: World Bank.

World Bank. 2023a. *Scaling Up to Phase Down: Financing Energy Transitions in the Power Sector.* Washington, DC: World Bank.

World Bank. 2023b. *South Asia Development Update: Toward Faster, Cleaner Growth.* Washington, DC: World Bank.

World Bank. 2024a. *Commodity Markets Outlook.* October. Washington, DC: World Bank.

World Bank. 2024b. *Global Economic Prospects.* June. Washington, DC: World Bank.

World Bank. 2024c. *World Development Report 2024: The Middle-Income Trap.* Washington, DC: World Bank.

World Bank. 2024d. *Poverty, Prosperity, and Planet Report 2024: Pathways out of the Polycrisis.* Washington, DC: World Bank.

World Bank. 2024e. *Commodity Markets Outlook.* April. Washington, DC: World Bank.

World Bank. 2024f. "Human Capital Project: A Project for the World." Human Capital Project Factsheet. April. https://thedocs.worldbank.org/en/doc/6e16262c 5f430d37e72f103e764c2721-0140052024/original/ HCP-Fact-Sheet-April-2024.pdf.

World Bank. 2024g. "Gender Data Portal: Lower Secondary Completion Rate." World Bank, Washington, DC.

World Bank-WDI (World Development Indicators) database. "World Development Indicators." Accessed on December 18, 2024. https://databank.world bank.org/source/world-development-indicators.

WTO (World Trade Organization). 2024. *World Trade Report 2024: Trade and Inclusiveness. How to Make Trade Work for All.* September. Geneva: World Trade Organization.

Zaveri, E., R. Damania, and N. Engle. 2023. "Droughts and Deficits: Summary Evidence of the Global Impact on Economic Growth." Water Global Practice Working Paper, World Bank, Washington, DC.

Zhang, F., and C. Borja-Vega. 2024. *Water for Shared Prosperity.* Washington, DC: World Bank.

CHAPTER 2

REGIONAL OUTLOOKS

EAST ASIA and PACIFIC

Growth in the East Asia and Pacific (EAP) region is projected to slow to 4.6 percent in 2025 and 4.1 percent in 2026, down from an estimated 4.9 percent in 2024, reflecting a further deceleration in China. In China, growth is expected to decline from 4.9 percent in 2024 to 4.5 percent in 2025 and 4.0 percent in 2026, amid broad-based weakness in domestic demand. Elsewhere in the region, growth is projected to edge up to 4.9 percent in 2025 before settling at 4.7 percent in 2026, anchored by solid domestic demand. Risks to the outlook remain tilted to the downside and center on adverse global policy shifts, particularly relating to trade policies, and a sharper slowdown in China. Further downside risks include spillovers from an intensification of conflict, notably in the Middle East, and climate-change-related natural disasters. Prospects for U.S. growth, global inflation, and monetary policies remain uncertain and present both upside and downside risks to the region.

Recent developments

Growth in EAP moderated to an estimated 4.9 percent in 2024—marginally stronger than envisaged in June—from 5.1 percent in 2023, primarily reflecting a deceleration in China. In China, growth slowed to an estimated 4.9 percent in 2024, as domestic activity softened amid subdued consumer confidence and weakening consumption (figures 2.1.1.A and 2.1.1.B). The ongoing property sector slump further dampened growth, with property prices experiencing widespread declines (figure 2.1.1.C). Overall investment growth remained tepid, as solid infrastructure and manufacturing sector investment offset further declines in real estate investment (figure 2.1.1.D). Industrial activity benefited from strengthening external demand, with exports rebounding in 2024, driven by a further recovery in global trade. Meanwhile, weak domestic demand weighed on import growth.

In response to subdued activity, China's authorities announced a series of policy measures to support demand in late 2024, building on earlier efforts. The People's Bank of China cut policy interest rates and lowered the reserve requirement ratio. Additional measures were implemented to support the property market, including increased liquidity provision for developers, an expanded scheme for local governments and state-owned enterprises to purchase newly completed properties, reductions in interest rates for existing mortgages, and reduced minimum required downpayment ratios. Government special bond issuance was also expanded to support spending alongside steps to bring local government off-balance sheet debt onto budgets—and refinance it at lower rates—with the aim of reducing fiscal risks.

In EAP excluding China, growth rose to an estimated 4.8 percent in 2024 from 4.3 percent in 2023, supported by the rebound in global goods trade, continued recovery in inbound tourism, and buoyant domestic demand (figures 2.1.2.A and 2.1.2.B). This was slightly higher than June forecasts, partly reflecting stronger-than-expected economic momentum. The acceleration in activity was broad-based, with growth picking up in most economies, including many of the larger export-oriented ones, notably Malaysia and Viet Nam. Growth also increased in the Pacific Island subregion, reaching an estimated 4.3 percent, led by a marked acceleration in Papua New Guinea underpinned by an uptick in mining activity.

Across the region's major economies, including China, Indonesia, and Thailand, both headline

Note: This section was prepared by Samuel Hill.

FIGURE 2.1.1 **China: Recent developments**

After a solid start to 2024, growth in China moderated. Consumption growth was tepid, partly reflecting soft labor market conditions and weak consumer confidence. Activity was also dampened by a continued property sector slump, with further widespread declines in property prices. Real estate investment contracted further but was offset by expanding infrastructure and manufacturing investment.

A. China: Growth

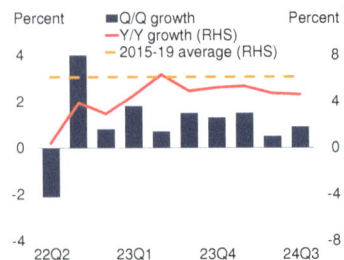

B. China: Consumer confidence

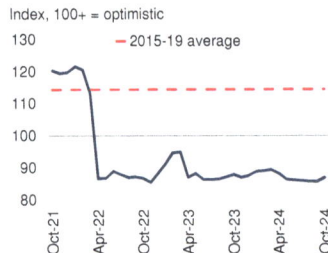

C. China: Property prices

D. China: Fixed-asset investment growth

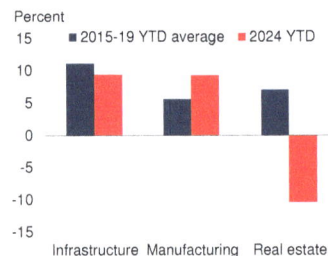

Sources: Haver Analytics; National Bureau of Statistics of China; World Bank.
Note: YTD = year-to-date.
A. Quarter-on-quarter (Q/Q) and year-on-year (Y/Y) real GDP growth. 2015-19 average denotes the period average of year-on-year growth. Last observation is 2024Q3.
B. Consumer confidence on a scale of 0 to 200, where 200 indicates extreme optimism, 0 indicates extreme pessimism, and 100 indicates neutrality. Last observation is October 2024.
C. Orange line denotes price index of existing residential buildings. Blue bars denote share of cities with falling year-on-year existing residential building prices. Sample includes 70 major cities. Last observation is November 2024.
D. Blue bars denote the simple average of 2015-19 year-on-year growth of year-to-date nominal fixed-asset investment subcomponents from January to November. Red bars denote year-on-year growth of year-to-date nominal fixed-asset investment subcomponents from January to November 2024.

and core consumer price inflation sat within or below central bank targets toward the end of 2024 (figure 2.1.2.C). Elevated inflation was mostly confined to the Lao People's Democratic Republic and Myanmar, reflecting significant currency depreciations and, in Myanmar's case, supply disruptions caused by widespread armed conflict. In China, weak domestic demand and economic slack continued to suppress consumer and producer price pressures. In recent months, both headline and core consumer price inflation hovered close to zero, while producer price inflation remained negative.

In the second half of 2024, financial conditions were generally more supportive across the region, reflecting domestic and global factors. These included declining interest rates in major advanced economies, notably the United States, expectations of further monetary policy easing in these economies, and solid global investor risk appetite. Stock markets in China also initially rallied in response to policy support measures. Although net portfolio capital inflows to China and other major EAP economies were mostly positive, they turned negative toward the end of the year, and exchange rates weakened for some EAP economies (figure 2.1.2.D). With inflation contained, official interest rates were cut in most large EAP economies.

Outlook

Growth in EAP is projected to slow to 4.6 percent in 2025 and 4.1 percent in 2026, mainly owing to a further deceleration in China (figure 2.1.3.A; table 2.1.1). In contrast, growth in EAP excluding China is expected to edge up to 4.9 percent in 2025 before settling at 4.7 percent in 2026, reflecting buoyant growth in many major economies (figure 2.1.3.B). In the Pacific Island economies, growth is anticipated to hold at 4.3 percent in 2025 before easing to around long-term averages, reaching 3.4 percent in 2026. Compared with June projections, growth in EAP is expected to be 0.4 percentage point higher in 2025, partly reflecting policy support in China as well as surprisingly strong economic momentum in some major economies.

In China, growth is projected to slow further to 4.5 percent this year—0.4 percentage point higher than the June forecast, reflecting a boost to domestic demand from recent additional policy support measures and strong export momentum in late 2024. The forecast implies that outside the pandemic-affected years, 2025 will be the first year in over three decades that China's growth falls short of that in the rest of the region. Consumption growth will remain weak against a backdrop of subdued consumer confidence, soft labor market conditions, and adverse wealth effects from declining property prices. With leading indicators of property activity—notably construction starts and mortgage lending—remaining weak in the second half of 2024, a broad-based stabilization of the property sector is only expected later this year, dragging on overall investment growth (figure 2.1.3.C). In 2026, growth is projected to edge down to 4 percent, in line with moderating potential growth. Consumption and investment are set to remain lackluster amid a continued population decline, a further buildup of public and corporate debt, and slowing productivity growth.

Elsewhere in EAP, solid domestic demand is expected to underpin growth over the forecast horizon. Private consumption is set to remain firm, supported by low inflation and robust labor market conditions that will bolster household incomes. In some Pacific Island economies, spending will also be boosted by buoyant remittances supported by expanded temporary migration schemes (World Bank 2024a). With monetary policy easing lowering borrowing costs across many EAP economies, generally supportive financial conditions are also anticipated to buoy domestic demand. However, elevated debt will exert some headwinds to private investment, while the outlook for public investment across the region is mixed (World Bank 2024b). In some countries, the step-up in government debt during the pandemic and still-elevated fiscal deficits will constrain spending. In all, investment growth is expected to pick up somewhat, but fall short of pre-pandemic averages.

Following the rebound in goods exports in several EAP economies last year, coupled with the continuing recovery in services exports in some tourism-dependent economies, trade growth is projected to settle below pre-pandemic rates over the forecast horizon—in line with the global outlook. In China, amid heightened global trade policy uncertainty and following last year's rebound, export growth is set to ease, while imports growth will remain muted amid weak domestic demand. Alongside decelerating activity in China, elsewhere in the region export growth is likely to slow most in countries that experienced the strongest rebounds—particularly in highly export-oriented economies such as Malaysia. In contrast, where trade growth was slower last year

FIGURE 2.1.2 EAP excluding China: Recent developments

In East Asia and Pacific excluding China, growth strengthened in some economies in 2024, supported by a rebound in global trade. Major economies in the region experienced stronger goods exports, while tourism also continued to recover. Across the region, headline inflation generally remained within or below targets and close to zero in China amid weak domestic demand. Although net capital inflows to the region were generally positive in 2024, they turned negative toward the end of the year.

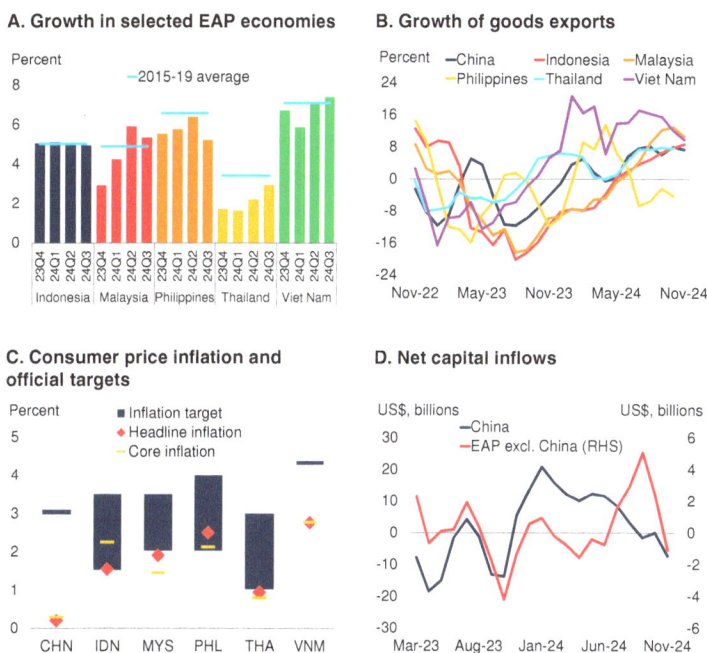

A. Growth in selected EAP economies

B. Growth of goods exports

C. Consumer price inflation and official targets

D. Net capital inflows

Sources: Haver Analytics; Institute of International Finance (database); World Bank.
Note: CHN = China; EAP = East Asia and Pacific; IDN = Indonesia; MYS = Malaysia; PHL = the Philippines; THA = Thailand; VNM = Viet Nam.
A. Year-on-year real GDP growth. Last observation is 2024Q3.
B. Value of goods exports in U.S. dollars. Three-month moving average of year-on-year change. Last observation is November 2024 for China, Indonesia, Malaysia, and Viet Nam. Last observation is October 2024 for the Philippines and Thailand.
C. Year-on-year core and headline consumer price inflation. Last observation is November 2024 for China, Indonesia, the Philippines, Thailand and Viet Nam. Last observation is October 2024 for Malaysia.
D. Three-month moving average of net portfolio (debt and equity) inflows. Last observation is November 2024.

and economic activity relies more on domestic demand, including in Indonesia, steadier trade growth is expected over the forecast horizon.

With growth set to converge toward potential growth rates across EAP, and global commodity prices projected to edge down this year and next, inflation is generally expected to hover around or below central bank targets in the region's major economies. In China, consumer price inflation is anticipated to edge up from its recent low levels, as food price deflation ends, alongside a normaliza-

FIGURE 2.1.3 EAP: Outlook

Growth in EAP is projected to slow from an estimated 4.9 percent in 2024, to 4.6 percent in 2025, and 4.1 percent in 2026, mainly reflecting decelerating activity in China. Elsewhere in East Asia, growth will be broadly stable—anchored by solid domestic demand—but slow over the projection horizon in Pacific Island economies. The projected slowdown in China partly reflects anticipated continued weakness in the property sector amid further falls in construction starts. Across the region, monetary policy easing is expected to provide modest support to growth.

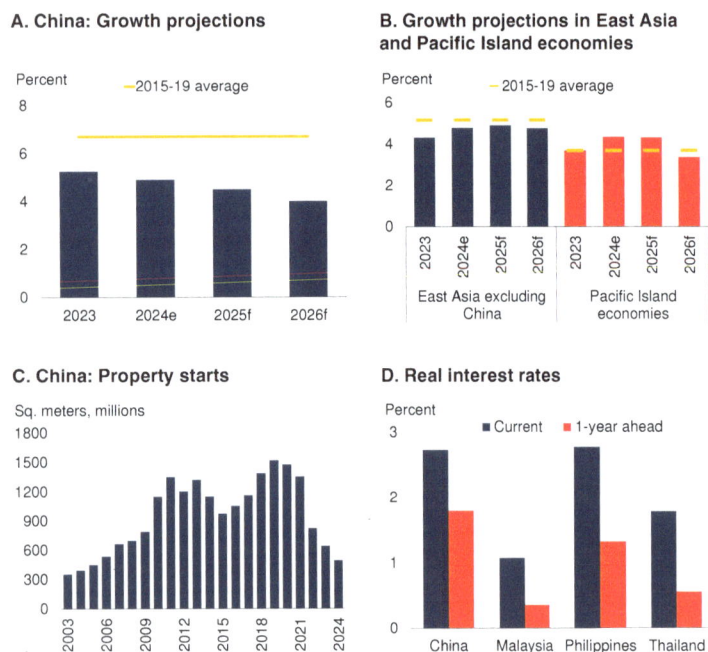

A. China: Growth projections

B. Growth projections in East Asia and Pacific Island economies

C. China: Property starts

D. Real interest rates

Sources: Bloomberg; Consensus Economics; Haver Analytics; World Bank.

Note: e = estimate; EAP = East Asia and Pacific; f = forecast.

A. Annual real GDP growth. Projections for 2025 and 2026 are by the World Bank.

B. Annual real GDP growth. Projections for 2025 and 2026 are by the World Bank. Aggregate growth rates are calculated using average 2015-19 GDP weights and market exchange rates.

C. Year-to-date volume of residential building floor space construction commenced between January and September. Last observation is November 2024.

D. Current real rate is the current policy rate minus the Consensus Economics 2024 inflation forecast; "1-year ahead" is the 30-day rolling average of the one-year-ahead market-implied policy rate minus the Consensus Economics 2025 inflation forecast. Last observation is December 18, 2024.

tion of domestic food market conditions. However, subdued domestic demand and economic slack will continue to weigh on prices, with supply-demand imbalances in some industrial sectors putting downward pressure on producer prices (World Bank 2024c). As a result, consumer price inflation is expected to remain well below its pre-pandemic average as well as the target of around 3 percent.

Easing financial conditions will provide a modest tailwind to activity in EAP over the forecast horizon. Against the generally benign backdrop

for regional inflation and with interest rates set to continue declining in many advanced economies, monetary policy is expected to ease further across EAP (figure 2.1.3.D). However, in many cases, interest rates are already low by historical standards; hence, expected rate cuts and the subsequent positive impulse on activity are anticipated to be modest. Moreover, in China, the impact of lower interest rates will be muted by weak private credit demand, compressed bank profit margins, and subdued business and consumer sentiment.

Fiscal policy is set to exert a more mixed impact on activity across the region. In some EAP economies, including Cambodia, Malaysia, and Viet Nam, modest fiscal consolidation is anticipated, partly supported by buoyant revenues. In China, increased government debt issuance will enable continued solid public spending, including on infrastructure, and help free up some fiscal space for local governments. Elsewhere, new policy commitments and planned accelerations in budget execution, including in Thailand, are expected to result in a supportive fiscal policy stance.

Risks

Risks to the EAP outlook remain tilted to the downside and centered on adverse global policy shifts, especially trade policies, and weaker-than-expected growth in China, with spillovers to other countries in the region. Heightened uncertainty about trade policies around the world poses a particularly significant threat given the importance of export-oriented activity linked to global value chains in many EAP economies. Rising conflict and more frequent climate-change-related natural disasters present further downside risks. Prospects for U.S. growth, global inflation, and monetary policy remain uncertain and subject to both upside and downside risks, the materialization of which could boost or dampen EAP activity.

Heightened global policy uncertainty, particularly relating to trade policies, poses a key downside risk for the region. Recent years have seen a proliferation of trade policy restrictions enacted by and targeting EAP economies (figure 2.1.4.A). These include restrictions on a variety of goods imported from China—including electric vehicles, steel, and textiles. Further trade policy restriction measures affecting China and the broader region would raise production costs, increase prices for consumers, weigh on economic activity, and may provoke retaliatory actions (chapter 1). Heightened trade policy uncertainty could also cause investment delays, particularly related to global production networks that rely on open trade policies, dampening employment and household incomes.

In addition, China's growth outlook faces significant downside risks, with implications for other EAP economies (chapter 3). Amid slowing urban population growth, a worsening property sector slump could negatively impact domestic activity through various channels, notably by further depressing consumer confidence and spending while reducing demand for construction materials (figure 2.1.4.B). Reduced discretionary household spending could reduce tourism activity across EAP, while weaker industrial activity could dampen prices for key commodity exports, including metals. The financial fallout from the property downturn could intensify, further weighing on smaller commercial banks and local governments reliant on land sales, worsening fiscal pressures and curtailing public spending.

With core inflation low by historical standards, deflation in China poses a further downside risk. Falling prices could cause consumers to delay spending and businesses to shelve investment plans. However, on the upside, the possibility of increased policy support, particularly central government-funded fiscal measures, could lift domestic growth and boost demand across EAP economies. Additional targeted support for the property sector could help stabilize real estate activity sooner than expected.

The outlook for the U.S. economy is subject to both upside and downside risks, which could have significant consequences for EAP economies if realized. On the downside, a faster-than-expected cooling in the U.S. labor market and slowing consumption growth could weaken demand for EAP exports, with adverse spillovers to broader activity, including employment and household

FIGURE 2.1.4 EAP: Risks

A further ratcheting up of trade protection measures could increase uncertainty and dampen trade and growth across the region. In China, amid slowing urban population growth, the downturn in the property sector could worsen, further weighing on domestic activity. Climate-change-related natural disasters, notably damaging floods and storms, pose a downside risk, especially in the region's numerous small states. A resurgence in global inflation could also keep interest rates higher for longer, adding to the burden of servicing rising debt across the region.

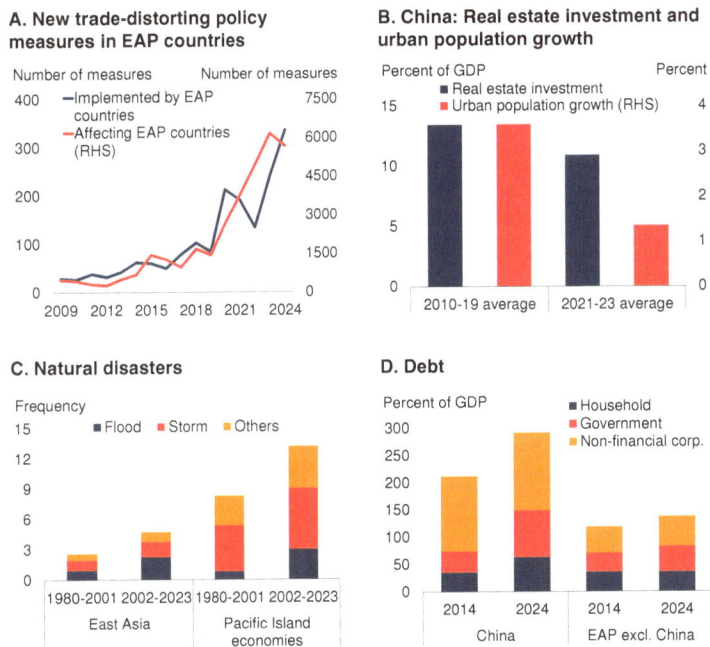

A. New trade-distorting policy measures in EAP countries

B. China: Real estate investment and urban population growth

C. Natural disasters

D. Debt

Sources: EM-DAT (database); Global Trade Alert (database); Haver Analytics; Institute of International Finance (database); World Bank.
Note: corp. = corporation; EAP = East Asia and Pacific.
A. Lines show the number of harmful trade measures implemented by and affecting EAP. Harmful trade measures include the sum of "Amber" and "Red" measures classified as harmful in the Global Trade Alert database. Each measure can be implemented by and target multiple countries. Data have been adjusted for reporting lags as of December 19, 2024.
B. Blue columns denote average annual completed real estate investment as a share of GDP. Red columns denote average annual growth in the urban population. Last observation is end-2023.
C. Frequency is calculated based on the annual number of natural disasters per one million square kilometers of land area. Natural disasters include droughts, earthquakes, extreme temperatures, floods, storms, volcanic activities, and wildfires. Last observation is end-2023.
D. Aggregates are calculated as a GDP-weighted average. 2014 refers to 2014Q2 and 2024 refers to 2024Q2. EAP excluding China includes Indonesia, Lao PDR, Malaysia, Mongolia, Papua New Guinea, the Philippines, Thailand, and Viet Nam. Last observation is 2024Q2.

consumption. Weaker demand from the United States could also dampen sentiment in the region and weigh on investment. In contrast, unexpectedly strong U.S. growth could lift EAP exports, buoy sentiment, and boost growth.

Escalating conflict in various parts of the world, particularly the Middle East, could have adverse consequences for EAP economies. Disruptions in global commodity supplies, particularly oil and natural gas, could raise consumer and producer prices, stoke inflation, and reduce disposable household incomes and consumption (World Bank 2024d). Moreover, within EAP, further escalation of the already-severe conflict poses a key downside risk to activity in Myanmar, with the possibility of adverse spillovers to neighboring countries, including relating to refugee flows (World Bank 2024e).

More frequent climate-change-related natural disasters, notably damaging floods and storms, present a downside risk to both the near-term outlook and long-term growth prospects. Downside risks are particularly pronounced in EAP's many small states, which endure some of the most costly and frequent natural disasters among all emerging market and developing economies (figure 2.1.4.C; World Bank 2024f). However, as evidenced by typhoon Yagi—which in September 2024 caused death and destruction

across several EAP economies, including Thailand and Viet Nam—larger countries are also exposed.

Global disinflation could proceed more slowly or more rapidly than expected. This could, in turn, result in higher- or lower-than-expected interest rates, affecting EAP. Global inflation could prove more persistent than assumed, including in sectors experiencing strong demand, notably services. Attendant higher global interest rates would weigh on global demand, including for EAP exports, and potentially dampen capital inflow to the region. It would also limit EAP central banks' ability to cut interest rates and add to the cost of servicing growing public and private debt (figure 2.1.4.D). Conversely, faster-than-expected global disinflation could allow some central banks to ease monetary policy more quickly, bolstering demand and sentiment in EAP economies.

TABLE 2.1.1 East Asia and Pacific forecast summary

(Real GDP growth at market prices in percent, unless indicated otherwise)

Percentage-point differences from June 2024 projections

	2022	2023	2024e	2025f	2026f	2024e	2025f	2026f
EMDE EAP, GDP [1]	**3.4**	**5.1**	**4.9**	**4.6**	**4.1**	**0.1**	**0.4**	**0.0**
GDP per capita (U.S. dollars)	3.2	5.0	4.8	4.5	4.0	0.1	0.4	0.0
(Average including countries that report expenditure components in national accounts)[2]								
EMDE EAP, GDP [2]	3.4	5.1	4.9	4.6	4.1	0.1	0.4	0.0
PPP GDP	3.6	5.1	4.9	4.6	4.2	0.1	0.3	0.0
Private consumption	2.3	7.9	5.2	5.1	5.3	-1.0	-0.4	0.0
Public consumption	4.1	6.0	3.0	3.3	3.3	-0.4	0.4	0.4
Fixed investment	3.4	4.8	3.6	3.8	3.8	-0.4	-0.1	-0.1
Exports, GNFS [3]	1.5	0.6	7.2	4.6	3.0	3.6	1.8	0.1
Imports, GNFS [3]	-0.3	2.5	4.0	3.5	3.7	0.6	0.1	0.1
Net exports, contribution to growth	0.4	-0.3	0.8	0.4	0.0	0.7	0.4	0.0
Memo items: GDP								
China	3.0	5.2	4.9	4.5	4.0	0.1	0.4	0.0
East Asia and Pacific excluding China	5.9	4.3	4.8	4.9	4.7	0.2	0.2	-0.1
Indonesia	5.3	5.0	5.0	5.1	5.1	0.0	0.0	0.0
Thailand	2.5	1.9	2.6	2.9	2.7	0.2	0.1	-0.2
Commodity exporters	5.3	4.8	4.7	4.9	4.8	-0.1	0.1	0.0
Commodity importers excluding China	6.4	3.8	4.8	4.9	4.7	0.4	0.2	-0.1
Pacific Island Economies [4]	6.7	3.7	4.3	4.3	3.4	-0.2	1.1	0.4

Source: World Bank.

Note: e = estimate; f = forecast; PPP = purchasing power parity; EMDE = emerging market and developing economy. World Bank forecasts are frequently updated based on new information and changing (global) circumstances. Consequently, projections presented here may differ from those contained in other Bank documents, even if basic assessments of countries' prospects do not differ at any given moment in time.

1. GDP and expenditure components are measured in average 2010-19 prices and market exchange rates. Excludes the Democratic People's Republic of Korea and dependent territories.
2. Subregion aggregate excludes the Democratic People's Republic of Korea, dependent territories, Fiji, Kiribati, the Marshall Islands, the Federated States of Micronesia, Myanmar, Palau, Papua New Guinea, Samoa, Timor-Leste, Tonga, Tuvalu, and Vanuatu, for which data limitations prevent the forecasting of GDP components.
3. Exports and imports of goods and nonfactor services (GNFS).
4. Includes Fiji, Kiribati, the Marshall Islands, the Federated States of Micronesia, Nauru, Palau, Papua New Guinea, Samoa, the Solomon Islands, Tonga, Tuvalu, and Vanuatu.

TABLE 2.1.2 East Asia and Pacific country forecasts [1]

(Real GDP growth at market prices in percent, unless indicated otherwise)

Percentage-point differences from June 2024 projections

	2022	2023	2024e	2025f	2026f	2024e	2025f	2026f
Cambodia	5.1	5.0	5.3	5.5	5.5	-0.5	-0.6	-0.9
China	3.0	5.2	4.9	4.5	4.0	0.1	0.4	0.0
Fiji	19.8	7.5	4.0	3.6	3.3	0.5	0.3	0.0
Indonesia	5.3	5.0	5.0	5.1	5.1	0.0	0.0	0.0
Kiribati	3.9	4.2	5.8	4.1	3.3	0.2	2.1	1.2
Lao PDR	2.7	3.7	4.1	3.7	3.7	0.1	-0.4	-0.4
Malaysia	8.9	3.6	4.9	4.5	4.3	0.6	0.1	0.0
Marshall Islands [2]	-0.6	3.0	3.4	4.0	3.2	0.4	2.0	1.7
Micronesia, Fed. Sts. [2]	-1.4	0.4	1.1	1.7	1.1	0.0	0.0	0.0
Mongolia	5.0	7.2	5.3	6.5	6.1	0.5	-0.1	-0.2
Myanmar [2][3]	4.0	1.0	-1.0	2.0	..	-2.0	..	..
Nauru [2]	2.8	0.6	1.8	2.0	1.9	0.4	0.8	0.9
Palau [2]	0.0	0.2	12.0	11.0	3.5	-0.4	-0.9	0.0
Papua New Guinea	5.7	3.0	4.5	4.6	3.5	-0.3	1.5	0.5
Philippines	7.6	5.5	5.9	6.1	6.0	0.1	0.2	0.1
Samoa [2]	-5.4	9.2	9.4	5.5	2.8	3.9	2.0	0.1
Solomon Islands	2.3	3.0	2.5	2.9	2.9	-0.3	-0.2	-0.1
Thailand	2.5	1.9	2.6	2.9	2.7	0.2	0.1	-0.2
Timor-Leste	4.0	2.3	3.5	3.4	3.6	0.1	-0.6	-0.2
Tonga [2]	0.1	2.0	1.8	2.4	2.0	-0.7	0.2	0.4
Tuvalu	0.4	3.9	3.5	3.0	2.5	0.0	0.6	0.3
Vanuatu	1.9	2.2	0.9	1.5	2.1	-2.8	-2.0	-1.0
Viet Nam	8.1	5.0	6.8	6.6	6.3	1.3	0.6	-0.2

Source: World Bank.

Note: e = estimate; f = forecast. World Bank forecasts are frequently updated based on new information and changing (global) circumstances. Consequently, projections presented here may differ from those contained in other Bank documents, even if basic assessments of countries' prospects do not significantly differ at any given moment in time.

1. Data are based on GDP measured in average 2010-19 prices and market exchange rates.

2. Values for Timor-Leste represent non-oil GDP. For the following countries, values correspond to the fiscal year: the Marshall Islands, the Federated States of Micronesia, and Palau (October 1-September 30); Myanmar (April 1-March 31); Nauru, Samoa, and Tonga (July 1-June 30).

3. Data for Myanmar beyond 2025 (which corresponds to the year ending March 2026) are excluded because of a high degree of uncertainty.

EUROPE and CENTRAL ASIA

Growth in Europe and Central Asia (ECA) is projected to moderate to 2.5 percent this year before picking up to 2.7 percent in 2026. The slowdown in 2025 primarily reflects softer activity in the Russian Federation and Türkiye. Excluding these economies and Ukraine, growth is forecast to strengthen to an average of 3.3 percent in 2025-26. Private consumption and investment are expected to be the main growth drivers amid less restrictive monetary policies and easing inflationary pressures. A key downside risk to the outlook is the potential for heightened global policy uncertainty and adverse trade policy shifts, which could weigh on trade, capital flows, and growth prospects across the region. Other risks include escalating geopolitical tensions, particularly those related to Russia's invasion of Ukraine, and higher-than-expected regional inflation.

Recent developments

Growth in Europe and Central Asia (ECA) is estimated to have slowed to 3.2 percent in 2024, primarily due to weaker expansions in the Russian Federation and Türkiye, partly reflecting the impact of tighter monetary policy. Manufacturing PMIs in Russia and Türkiye suggest moderating activity, with Türkiye's PMI remaining in contractionary territory. Although still below the threshold of 50, Poland's PMI has steadily gained momentum in recent quarters (figure 2.2.1.A). Russia's invasion of Ukraine continues to weigh on regional activity. ECA currencies have been somewhat volatile, with several depreciating against the U.S. dollar. Amid heightened geopolitical uncertainty and macroeconomic risks, central banks in Poland and Türkiye have substantially increased gold purchases since mid-2023, likely as a hedge against economic volatility (figure 2.2.1.B).

In Russia, growth is estimated to have moderated to 3.4 percent in 2024, primarily due to weaker private consumption amid tight monetary policy and elevated inflation. However, the 0.5 percentage point upward revision from the June forecast reflects stronger-than-expected consumption earlier in the year, supported by rising wages

amid a tight labor market. Ongoing fiscal expansion, driven by military spending and import substitution efforts, has also supported consumption. After cuts in early 2024, crude oil production is expected to have stabilized at about 9.2 mb/d in the fourth quarter, slightly above the OPEC+ target (IEA 2024).

In Türkiye, growth softened to an estimated 3.2 percent in 2024, as private demand moderated amid a monetary policy tightening cycle that began in mid-2023. The economy fell into recession in the third quarter as activity was slower than expected. Headline inflation, which peaked at 75.5 percent (year-on-year) in May 2024, declined to 49.4 percent in September—below the nominal policy interest rate for the first time in three years—and edged further down to 47.1 percent by November. Inflation expectations have also shown signs of easing. Türkiye's external imbalances have improved, with a sharply narrowing current account deficit, rising international reserves, and a declining risk premium contributing to a significant reduction in sovereign spreads (figure 2.2.1.C).

Growth in Ukraine is estimated to have slowed to 3.2 percent in 2024, reflecting challenges such as reduced energy capacity and winter power outages, which constrained trade and industrial output gains. Despite these obstacles and continued attacks on infrastructure, the economy has shown

Note: This section was prepared by Marie Albert.

FIGURE 2.2.1 ECA: Recent developments

High-frequency indicators in the Russian Federation and Türkiye point to a slowdown in economic activity. Several central banks in the region have been accumulating gold reserves, partly in response to geopolitical tensions. External financing conditions have improved in some economies, particularly Türkiye. Stalled progress in reducing regional inflation to some degree reflects elevated wage growth.

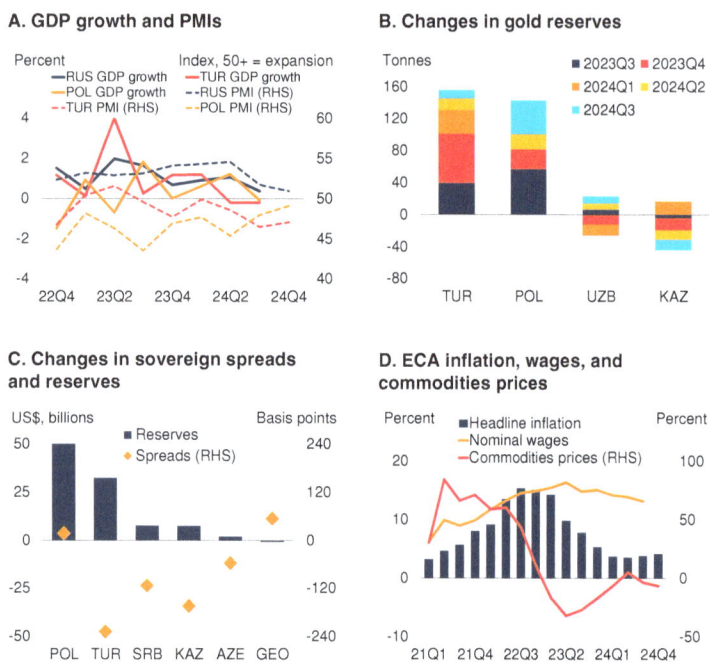

A. GDP growth and PMIs

B. Changes in gold reserves

C. Changes in sovereign spreads and reserves

D. ECA inflation, wages, and commodities prices

Sources: Haver Analytics; IMF, International Financial Statistics; J.P. Morgan; World Bank; World Gold Council.

Note: AZE = Azerbaijan; GEO = Georgia; KAZ = Kazakhstan; PMI = purchasing managers' index; POL = Poland; RUS = Russian Federation; SRB = Serbia; TUR = Türkiye; UZB = Uzbekistan.

A. PMI readings above (below) 50 indicate expansion (contraction). Last observations are respectively 2024Q3 for GDP growth and 2024Q4 for PMIs. Data for 2024Q4 include October and November 2024.

B. Bars show the accumulation of quarterly changes in central bank gold reserves for economies with significant changes, starting from 2023Q3.

C. Diamonds represent changes in J.P. Morgan Emerging Market Bond Index spreads, while bars depict changes in international reserves. The changes are calculated as the difference in values between November 2024 and January 2023.

D. Lines show year-on-year trends in commodities prices and ECA median nominal wages. Bars show year-on-year trends in ECA median headline inflation. Last observations are 2024Q4 for headline inflation and commodities prices, and 2024Q3 for nominal wages. Data for 2024Q4 include October and November 2024.

significant resilience. In September, approximately $20 billion of outstanding commercial debt through Eurobonds was restructured, with Eurobond amortization and interest payments expected to fall by $7.6 billion between 2025 and 2027 compared to pre-restructuring obligations. The opening of European Union (EU) accession talks and the Ukraine Plan under the EU financing facility (financial support over the 2024-27 period) serve as significant anchors for EU alignment.

The process of disinflation stalled in ECA, with median headline inflation at 4.3 percent in November (year-on-year), and core inflation at 5.6 percent—twice as high as pre-pandemic levels. Declining commodity prices offered some relief, yet wage pressures from tight labor markets, especially in services, remain elevated (figure 2.2.1.D). Most ECA central banks have consequently paused easing monetary policy. Since April, Russia's central bank has raised its benchmark rate three times, reaching a record 21 percent in October —the highest level since 2003.

The region continues to face various external challenges. Weak demand from key trading partners, particularly in the European Union, has hindered export recoveries in Central Europe and the Western Balkans, where economies remain heavily integrated into European automobile supply chains. However, tourism activity—now surpassing pre-pandemic levels—continues to support growth in these subregions, notably benefiting Albania and Montenegro. While remittance inflows have moderated, they remain above pre-invasion levels in several South Caucasus countries. Meanwhile, remittances in Central Asia, particularly Tajikistan, remain robust, sustaining private consumption (World Bank 2024g).

Outlook

Growth in ECA is forecast to moderate to 2.5 percent in 2025 before firming to 2.7 percent in 2026. The slowdown in 2025 is primarily attributed to softer growth in Russia and Türkiye. The 0.4 percentage point downward revision to regional growth in 2025 since the June forecast reflects weaker projections for Türkiye due to delayed monetary tightening effects and for Ukraine due to the ongoing invasion. In 2026, private consumption and investment are expected to drive growth, supported by a gradual disinflation process and monetary policy easing. Excluding Russia, Türkiye, and Ukraine, regional growth is expected to strengthen to 3.3 percent in 2025-26, led by Poland (figure 2.2.2.A; table 2.2.1).

Inflation is expected to decline gradually, supported by moderating commodity prices and easing labor market pressures (World Bank 2024d). This slow disinflation is likely to lead to a cautious approach to monetary policy easing. Given the limited scope for fiscal consolidation, fiscal policy is expected to have a modest impact on growth (figure 2.2.2.B). Government debt is anticipated to rise in half of ECA's economies in 2025.

In Russia, growth is projected to soften to 1.6 percent in 2025 and 1.1 percent in 2026 (table 2.2.2). The expansion of private consumption and investment is expected to moderate due to decelerating wage growth and tighter monetary policy. Fiscal stimulus is expected to subside, as increased military expenditures, which remain substantially above pre-invasion levels, will be offset by higher taxation. Energy export volumes are expected to recover gradually. Over the longer term, constraints on productive capacity, including labor resources, are expected to weigh on potential growth.

In Türkiye, growth is forecast to decelerate to 2.6 percent in 2025, its slowest pace since 2020, before rebounding to 3.8 percent in 2026. The lagged effects of tight monetary policy are expected to weigh on growth this year before fading in 2026. Meanwhile, inflation (year-on-year average) is projected to decrease by 42 percentage points from 2024, reaching 15.9 percent in 2026. Rebalancing in growth is expected to continue in 2025, driven by a larger contribution from net exports as consumption and imports moderate.

Ukraine's growth is projected to moderate to 2 percent in 2025, assuming active hostilities continue throughout the year. A robust recovery of 7 percent is anticipated in 2026, contingent on the cessation of active hostilities, supported by consumption and reconstruction investments. The outlook remains conditional on assumptions about the timing and quantity of external assistance receipts and the duration of Russia's invasion.

Growth in Central Europe is forecast to rebound to 2.8 percent in 2025 and 3 percent in 2026, driven by robust private demand. Investment,

FIGURE 2.2.2 ECA: Outlook

Growth in ECA is projected to weaken to 2.5 percent in 2025 before recovering slightly to 2.7 percent in 2026. Fiscal consolidation efforts are expected to remain limited. Economic activity in Central Europe is likely to continue benefiting from the gradual disbursement of RRF funds. Potential growth in 2022-30 is expected to be lower than in the past two decades, partly due to significant declines in the working-age population.

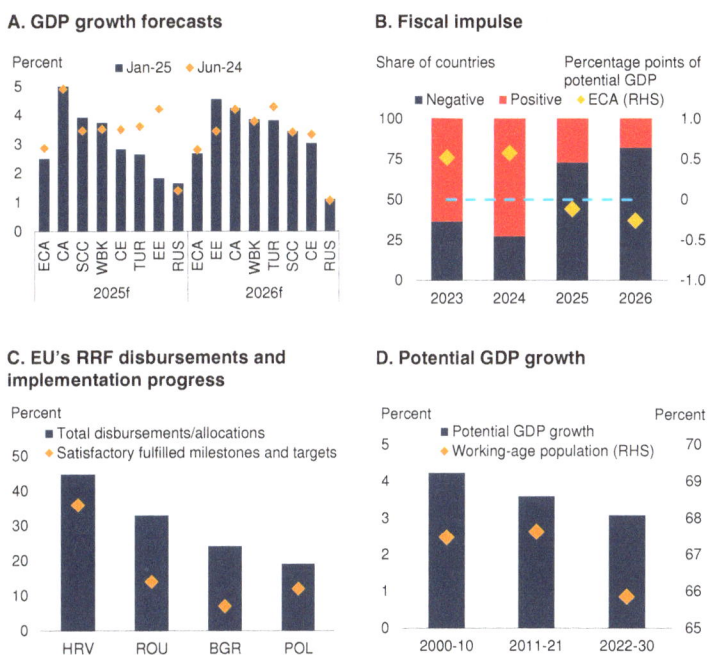

A. GDP growth forecasts

B. Fiscal impulse

C. EU's RRF disbursements and implementation progress

D. Potential GDP growth

Sources: European Commission; IMF *World Economic Outlook* (database); Kose and Ohnsorge (2023); UN Population Prospects (database); World Bank.
Note: BGR = Bulgaria; CA = Central Asia; CE = Central Europe; ECA = Europe and Central Asia; EE = Eastern Europe; f = forecast; HRV = Croatia; POL = Poland; ROU = Romania; RRF = Recovery and Resilience Facility; RUS = Russian Federation; SCC = South Caucasus; TUR = Türkiye; WBK = Western Balkans.
A. Bars and diamonds represent GDP growth forecasts for 2025 and 2026, as reported in the June 2024 and January 2025 editions of *Global Economic Prospects*.
B. Bars show the percentage of ECA economies (sample of 11 countries) with either a positive or negative fiscal impulse. Diamonds indicate the ECA median fiscal impulse as a percentage point of potential GDP across the region. Dashed blue line indicate the 50 percent threshold on the left-hand scale and zero on the right-hand scale. Diamonds above this line indicate a median positive fiscal impulse (fiscal stimulus), while those below reflect a median negative fiscal impulse (fiscal consolidation).
C. Bars show the share of total EU's RRF disbursements relative to allocations, while diamonds indicate the percentage of satisfactory fulfilled milestones and targets. Data reflect the status as of December 20, 2024.
D. Bars show the trends in the average of the working-age population and the average potential economic growth over three decades.

particularly in Poland and Romania, is projected to gain traction from structural reforms and delayed EU funding (Europe Court of Auditors 2024). These countries have disbursed 19 and 33 percent, respectively, of their Recovery and Resilience Facility allocations, with approximately 13 percent of milestones achieved and positively assessed (figure 2.2.2.C). Despite the inflow of EU funding, recently announced fiscal consolidation measures have contributed to notable downward revisions to Romania's outlook since June. Export growth from Central Europe is expected to remain modest due to subdued growth in the euro area.

Activity in the Western Balkans is projected to accelerate to 3.7 percent in 2025 and 3.9 percent in 2026. Private consumption and investment are expected to play a major role, especially in Kosovo, Montenegro, North Macedonia, and Serbia. At the same time, the euro area's sluggish growth is anticipated to provide only limited support for exports. The European Commission's Growth Plan for the Western Balkans could double the size of the region's economy within a decade, supporting EU accession and enhancing infrastructure financing and market integration through the Single Euro Payment Area initiative (World Bank 2024h).

Growth in the South Caucasus is projected to weaken to 3.9 percent in 2025 and 3.4 percent in 2026. Azerbaijan's oil production is expected to decline. Growth in Armenia and Georgia is forecast to converge to potential rates as factors such as re-exports, visitor inflows, and real wage increases that supported growth in 2024 normalize.

In Central Asia, growth is expected to firm to 5 percent in 2025 before easing to 4.2 percent in 2026. An increase in Kazakhstan's growth, supported by higher oil output, is expected to boost the recovery. Remittances inflows to the Kyrgyz Republic and Tajikistan are anticipated to support activity and improve current account balances. Financial institutions in some recipient countries have restricted transfers from Russia due to potential international sanctions, likely redirecting remittance flows through informal channels (World Bank 2024g).

ECA's potential growth is projected to slow to 3.0 percent annually in 2022-30, down from 3.6 percent in 2011-21. Labor supply constraints due to low labor-force participation, especially among women, and shrinking working-age populations driven by aging are expected to limit growth (figure 2.2.2.D; Kose and Ohnsorge 2023). While ECA's educational systems are more robust

compared to those in many other EMDEs, declining quality, particularly in higher education, and significant emigration—especially from the Western Balkans—have impeded human capital development and growth. Further progress in revamping education systems would support convergence with high-income countries (World Bank 2024i).

Risks

Risks to the outlook remain tilted to the downside. Global policy uncertainty persists due to potential adverse policy shifts, especially regarding global trade. Substantial uncertainty around the evolution of Russia's invasion of Ukraine remains a key risk, while elevated regional inflation and severe climate events could further weigh on growth prospects.

The potential for heightened global policy uncertainty and adverse trade policy shifts remains the most significant risk to the region's growth. The rise in global policy uncertainty could dampen the region's trade, capital flows, and growth prospects. Despite the region's high level of trade openness, trade restrictions have surged in recent years in the context of heightened geopolitical tensions. Since early 2024, more than 585 restrictive measures have been introduced by ECA economies (figure 2.2.3.A). Additional protectionist measures from third countries amid increased trade uncertainty would further reduce trade and growth relative to the baseline (chapter 3).

Geopolitical tensions continue to pose a critical risk. The invasion of Ukraine remains a significant factor in shaping the regional outlook. Any further escalation could lead to greater economic disruption across the region. Over the past year, the conflict has directly affected 41 percent of Ukraine's population,[1] underscoring the severe human and economic toll. Military expenditures surged across the region, rising to 4 percent of

---

[1] Estimate from the Armed Conflict Location & Event Data Project (ACLED). ACLED defines "conflict exposure" as the number of people living close to a conflict incident or demonstration, defined as an area of active disorder or unrest.

GDP in 2023—double the average for 2010-21. The increase was particularly pronounced in Ukraine, where defense expenditures accounted for about a third of its GDP in 2023, and in Russia (figure 2.2.3.B).

The disinflation process could slow further in the region, leading to higher-for-longer interest rates that would likely constrain growth. Progress toward central bank inflation targets is expected to be sluggish (figure 2.2.3.C). Tighter-than-expected labor markets, alongside higher wage growth, could intensify inflationary pressures in Central Europe and the Western Balkans. In many economies, inflation remains elevated due to rising service costs and past reliance on Russian energy. High energy intensity leaves many ECA economies vulnerable to supply disruptions (ECB 2024).

Weaker-than-expected growth in Russia have a significant impact on Central Asia and the South Caucasus, primarily through reduced remittance inflows. For example, in Tajikistan, remittances account for nearly 40 percent of GDP—one of the highest ratios in the world, with most inflows originating from Russia (figure 2.2.3.D). A 10-percentage-point increase in the growth of remittances from Russia is associated with a 0.2 to 0.6 percentage point rise in GDP growth in the Commonwealth of Independent States[2] (Arzoumanian 2023).

Delays in implementing structural reforms could hinder the disbursement of EU funds to Central Europe and the Western Balkans and postpone EU accession prospects for current candidate countries. Moreover, some economies may encounter additional challenges in executing large-scale EU-funded infrastructure projects.

Climate-change-related risks remain a significant challenge for ECA, with approximately 21 percent of the region's population exposed to droughts—

---

[2] According to Arzoumanian (2023), Commonwealth of Independent States (CIS) countries covered in the sample include Armenia, Azerbaijan, Belarus, Kazakhstan, Moldova, and Tajikistan. Georgia and Ukraine are not members of the CIS but are included in the sample due to their geographic proximity and large economic ties to Russia.

FIGURE 2.2.3 ECA: Risks

Risks to the outlook remain tilted to the downside. Increased global policy uncertainty and new trade restrictions could further impede trade growth. Military spending in ECA has risen, reflecting heightened geopolitical tensions, mainly due to Russia's invasion of Ukraine. Progress toward central bank targets is expected to proceed at a slow pace. Weaker-than-expected growth in Russia would negatively affect Central Asia and the South Caucasus, notably through reduced remittance inflows.

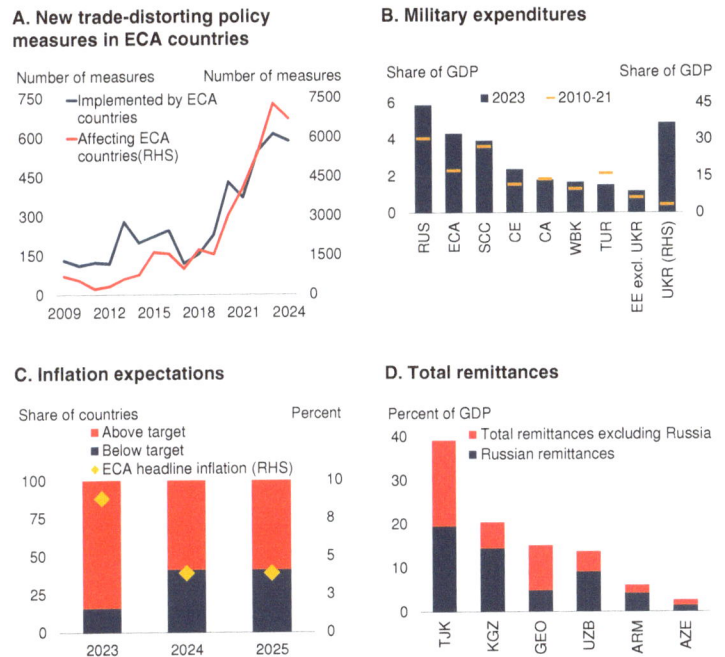

A. New trade-distorting policy measures in ECA countries

B. Military expenditures

C. Inflation expectations

D. Total remittances

Sources: Consensus Economics; Global Trade Alert (database); Haver Analytics; IMF *World Economic Outlook* (database); KNOMAD (database); Stockholm International Peace Research Institute; World Bank.
Note: ARM = Armenia; AZE = Azerbaijan; CA = Central Asia; CE = Central Europe; ECA = Europe and Central Asia; EE = Eastern Europe; GEO = Georgia; KGZ = Kyrgyzstan; RUS = Russian Federation; SCC = South Caucasus; TJK = Tajikistan; TUR = Türkiye; UKR = Ukraine; UZB = Uzbekistan; WBK = Western Balkans.
A. Lines show the number of harmful trade measures implemented by and affecting ECA. Harmful trade measures include the sum of "Amber" and "Red" measures classified as harmful in the Global Trade Alert database. Each measure can be implemented by and target multiple countries. Data have been adjusted for reporting lags as of December 19, 2024.
B. Bars show the average level of military expenditures as a share of GDP in 2023, while orange dashes indicate the average level of military expenditures as a share of GDP during the 2010-21 period (prior to Russia's invasion of Ukraine).
C. Blue bars show the share of ECA economies with inflation below target, while red bars indicate inflation above target. For countries with a target range, the target is defined as the upper bound of that range. Diamonds indicate ECA median headline inflation. Data for 2024 and 2025 reflect Consensus expectations.
D. Red bars show total remittances in percent of GDP, while blue bars show the share of remittances from the Russian Federation in percent of GDP. Data for 2023 (except Russian remittances for 2021).

---

one of the highest rates in the world (World Bank 2024j). In Western Balkans, Bosnia and Herzegovina and Serbia are projected to be disproportionately affected by climate change. These countries face heightened risks through the impact of riverine floods, droughts affecting maize and wheat production, and increased labor heat stress due to rising temperatures (World Bank 2024h).

TABLE 2.2.1 Europe and Central Asia forecast summary

(Real GDP growth at market prices in percent, unless indicated otherwise)

Percentage-point differences from
June 2024 projections

	2022	2023	2024e	2025f	2026f	2024e	2025f	2026f
EMDE ECA, GDP[1]	1.6	3.4	3.2	2.5	2.7	0.2	-0.4	-0.1
GDP per capita (U.S. dollars)	2.0	3.7	3.1	2.3	2.5	0.2	-0.3	-0.1
EMDE ECA excluding Russian Federation, Türkiye, and Ukraine, GDP	4.3	1.9	3.0	3.3	3.3	-0.1	-0.4	-0.1
EMDE ECA excluding Russian Federation and Ukraine, GDP	4.8	3.2	3.1	3.0	3.5	0.0	-0.6	-0.3
EMDE ECA excluding Türkiye, GDP	0.4	2.8	3.2	2.5	2.3	0.2	-0.1	0.0
(Average including countries that report expenditure components in national accounts)[2]								
EMDE ECA, GDP[2]	1.3	3.2	3.1	2.3	2.5	0.1	-0.4	-0.2
PPP GDP	0.7	3.4	3.1	2.3	2.6	0.1	-0.5	-0.1
Private consumption	4.7	6.7	3.3	2.4	2.8	0.6	-0.5	-0.2
Public consumption	3.5	3.8	3.4	2.6	1.8	0.0	-0.2	-0.5
Fixed investment	2.8	10.3	2.8	3.3	3.6	-0.9	-0.8	-0.6
Exports, GNFS[3]	-0.3	-1.2	1.3	2.6	3.3	-1.4	-2.0	-1.1
Imports, GNFS[3]	2.3	5.8	1.4	3.8	4.1	-2.7	-1.6	-1.0
Net exports, contribution to growth	-0.9	-2.5	0.0	-0.4	-0.3	0.5	-0.1	0.0
Memo items: GDP								
Commodity exporters[4]	-1.8	3.9	3.6	2.2	1.9	0.5	0.0	0.1
Commodity exporters excl. Russian Federation and Ukraine	4.6	5.0	4.6	4.7	4.0	0.7	0.2	0.0
Commodity importers[5]	4.8	2.9	2.9	2.8	3.4	-0.1	-0.7	-0.4
Central Europe[6]	4.8	0.5	2.3	2.8	3.0	-0.7	-0.7	-0.3
Western Balkans[7]	3.6	3.4	3.5	3.7	3.9	0.3	0.2	0.1
Eastern Europe[8]	-20.0	4.5	3.5	1.8	4.6	1.1	-2.4	1.2
South Caucasus[9]	7.3	3.7	5.5	3.9	3.4	2.0	0.4	0.0
Central Asia[10]	4.3	5.6	4.7	5.0	4.2	0.6	0.1	0.0
Russian Federation	-1.2	3.6	3.4	1.6	1.1	0.5	0.2	0.0
Türkiye	5.5	5.1	3.2	2.6	3.8	0.2	-1.0	-0.5
Poland	5.3	0.1	3.0	3.4	3.2	0.0	0.0	0.0

Source: World Bank.

Note: e = estimate; f = forecast; PPP = purchasing power parity; EMDE = emerging market and developing economy. World Bank forecasts are frequently updated based on new information and changing (global) circumstances. Consequently, projections presented here may differ from those contained in other Bank documents, even if basic assessments of countries' prospects do not differ at any given moment in time. The World Bank is currently not publishing economic output, income, or growth data for Turkmenistan owing to a lack of reliable data of adequate quality. Turkmenistan is excluded from cross-country macroeconomic aggregates. Since Croatia became a member of the euro area on January 1, 2023, it has been added to the euro area aggregate and removed from the ECA aggregate in all tables to avoid double counting.

1. GDP and expenditure components are measured in average 2010-19 prices and market exchange rates, thus aggregates presented here may differ from other World Bank documents.
2. Aggregates presented here exclude Azerbaijan, Bosnia and Herzegovina, Kazakhstan, Kosovo, the Kyrgyz Republic, Montenegro, Serbia, Tajikistan, and Uzbekistan.
3. Exports and imports of goods and nonfactor services (GNFS).
4. Includes Armenia, Azerbaijan, Kazakhstan, the Kyrgyz Republic, Kosovo, the Russian Federation, Tajikistan, Ukraine, and Uzbekistan.
5. Includes Albania, Belarus, Bosnia and Herzegovina, Bulgaria, Georgia, Hungary, Moldova, Montenegro, North Macedonia, Poland, Romania, Serbia, and Türkiye.
6. Includes Bulgaria, Hungary, Poland, and Romania.
7. Includes Albania, Bosnia and Herzegovina, Kosovo, Montenegro, North Macedonia, and Serbia.
8. Includes Belarus, Moldova, and Ukraine.
9. Includes Armenia, Azerbaijan, and Georgia.
10. Includes Kazakhstan, the Kyrgyz Republic, Tajikistan, and Uzbekistan.

TABLE 2.2.2 Europe and Central Asia country forecasts [1]

(Real GDP growth at market prices in percent, unless indicated otherwise)

Percentage-point differences from
June 2024 projections

	2022	2023	2024e	2025f	2026f	2024e	2025f	2026f
Albania	4.8	3.9	3.7	3.5	3.3	0.4	0.1	-0.2
Armenia	12.6	8.3	5.5	5.0	4.6	0.0	0.1	0.1
Azerbaijan	4.6	1.1	4.0	2.7	2.4	1.7	0.3	0.0
Belarus	-4.7	3.9	4.0	1.2	0.8	2.8	0.5	0.3
Bosnia and Herzegovina [2]	4.2	2.1	2.8	3.2	3.9	0.2	-0.1	-0.1
Bulgaria	4.0	1.9	2.2	2.8	2.7	0.1	-0.3	0.0
Croatia	7.3	3.3	3.5	3.0	2.8	0.5	0.2	0.1
Georgia	11.0	7.5	9.0	6.0	5.0	3.8	1.0	0.0
Kazakhstan	3.2	5.1	4.0	4.7	3.5	0.6	0.0	-0.1
Kosovo	4.3	3.3	3.8	3.9	4.0	0.1	0.0	0.1
Kyrgyz Republic	9.0	6.2	5.8	4.5	4.5	1.3	0.3	0.5
Moldova	-4.6	0.7	2.8	3.9	4.5	0.6	0.0	0.0
Montenegro	6.4	6.3	3.4	3.5	3.2	0.0	0.7	0.2
North Macedonia	2.8	2.1	2.4	3.0	3.2	-0.1	0.1	0.2
Poland	5.3	0.1	3.0	3.4	3.2	0.0	0.0	0.0
Romania	4.0	2.4	1.3	2.1	2.6	-2.0	-1.7	-1.2
Russian Federation	-1.2	3.6	3.4	1.6	1.1	0.5	0.2	0.0
Serbia	2.6	3.8	3.9	4.2	4.2	0.4	0.4	0.2
Tajikistan	8.0	8.3	8.0	6.0	5.0	1.5	1.5	0.5
Türkiye	5.5	5.1	3.2	2.6	3.8	0.2	-1.0	-0.5
Ukraine	-28.8	5.3	3.2	2.0	7.0	0.0	-4.5	1.9
Uzbekistan	6.0	6.3	6.0	5.8	5.9	0.7	0.3	0.2

Source: World Bank.

Note: e = estimate; f = forecast. World Bank forecasts are frequently updated based on new information and changing (global) circumstances. Consequently, projections presented here may differ from those contained in other Bank documents, even if basic assessments of countries' prospects do not significantly differ at any given moment in time. The World Bank is currently not publishing economic output, income, or growth data for Turkmenistan owing to a lack of reliable data of adequate quality. Turkmenistan is excluded from cross-country macroeconomic aggregates.

1. Data are based on GDP measured in average 2010-19 prices and market exchange rates, unless indicated otherwise.

2. GDP growth rate at constant prices is based on production approach.

LATIN AMERICA and THE CARIBBEAN

Growth in Latin America and the Caribbean (LAC) is forecast to increase from 2.2 percent last year to an average of 2.5 percent in 2025-26. This improvement is partly driven by Argentina's expected recovery following two consecutive years of contraction. Most central banks in LAC are anticipated to resume interest rate cuts in 2025 after pausing in the second half of 2024 due to renewed price pressures. A projected softening in commodity prices is expected to weigh on growth only moderately in a few countries. Risks to the outlook remain tilted to the downside. Heightened policy uncertainty and adverse trade policy shifts in the United States could negatively affect the region's exports. A tightening of global financial conditions would raise debt-servicing costs and could prompt faster fiscal consolidation across the region. A sharper-than-expected weakening of growth in China could adversely affect the region's exports. Climate-change-related extreme weather events pose an additional key risk.

Recent developments

Growth in LAC edged downward in 2024 to an estimated 2.2 percent amid weaker public and private consumption. Argentina's economy began to recover in the second half of the year, following a sharp contraction in the first half (figure 2.3.1.A). Last year, growth in Brazil remained elevated because of strong consumption. In contrast, Mexico experienced a marked decline in growth amid weaker export growth. However, in the region's other major economies—Chile, Colombia, and Peru—growth picked up compared to the previous year, driven by exports and investment.

Recent high-frequency indicators have presented a mixed picture (see figures 2.3.1.B and 2.3.1.C). Brazil's composite Purchasing Managers' Index (PMI) has consistently indicated solid growth. In contrast, the manufacturing PMIs for Colombia and Mexico have been volatile, falling into contraction during the third quarter but recovering toward the end of 2024. Monthly activity indicators for Chile have shown mixed results, while those for Peru have been positive. Argentina has seen significant improvements in

Note: This section was prepared by Francisco Arroyo Marioli.

activity in commodity-related sectors, including agriculture, energy, and mining.

Inflation has proven to be more persistent than expected, with progress in several countries stalling during the latter half of 2024. Food inflation rebounded in early to mid-2024, although it remained significantly lower than in 2022. Core inflation also stopped declining in mid-2024 and even experienced a slight increase throughout the second half of the year. In Brazil and Mexico, inflation hovered near the upper limits of the central banks' target ranges. In contrast, Argentina has been an outlier, with its 12-month consumer price inflation rate peaking at nearly 300 percent early last year. Although it has since decreased significantly, cumulative inflation in Argentina remained above 100 percent by the end of the year, partly as a result of sharp currency depreciation and adjustments to regulated prices.

Interest rates fell across the region in 2024, although some central banks slowed their rate cuts in the second half of the year because of persistent core inflation (figure 2.3.1.D). For instance, Brazil's central bank, after a series of cuts beginning in July 2023, raised its benchmark rate in September to address elevated core inflation and robust economic activity. In contrast, the central banks of Chile, Colombia, and Peru

FIGURE 2.3.1 LAC: Recent developments

Differences between actual and potential growth rates in 2024 varied across the region, with Argentina experiencing the largest gap. Business confidence has been high in Mexico and rebounded significantly in Argentina in the last months of 2024. Purchasing managers' indexes have also diverged, reflecting recent solid growth in Brazil, volatility in Colombia, and weakness in Mexico. Declines in headline inflation stalled in the second half of 2024, partly because of volatile food prices, while core inflation remains slightly above targets.

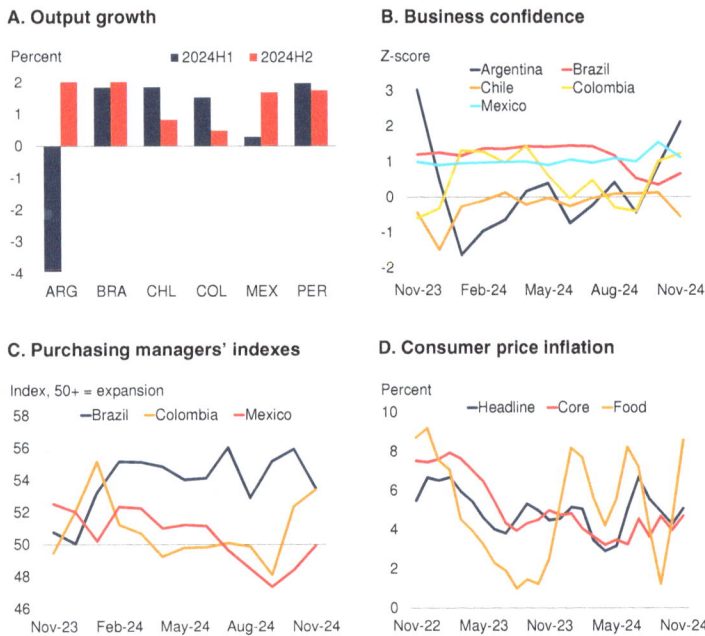

A. Output growth

B. Business confidence

C. Purchasing managers' indexes

D. Consumer price inflation

Sources: Haver Analytics; World Bank.
Note: ARG = Argentina; BRA = Brazil; CHL = Chile; COL = Colombia; LAC = Latin America and the Caribbean; MEX = Mexico; PER = Peru.
A. 2024H1 is seasonally adjusted GDP growth in the first half of 2024 compared with the second half of 2023. 2024H2 is seasonally adjusted GDP growth in the second half of 2024 compared with the first half of 2024. 2024H2 is estimated using the baseline projections in January 2025.
B. Figure shows the z-score for business confidence in Chile and consumer confidence in Brazil, Colombia, and Mexico. Last observation is November 2024.
C. A purchasing managers' index (PMI) of 50 or higher (lower) indicates expansion (contraction). Composite PMI for Brazil and manufacturing PMI for Colombia and Mexico. Last observation is November 2024.
D. Seasonally adjusted annual rate of consumer price inflation. Aggregate is three-month moving GDP-weighted average for Brazil, Chile, Colombia, Mexico, and Peru. Last observation is November 2024.

continued to reduce their rates significantly. Meanwhile, Mexico's central bank took a more cautious approach, lowering its benchmark rate but maintaining it at restrictive levels.

External factors, including weaker external demand and softening commodity prices, weighed on regional economic activity last year. While most countries ran trade deficits, Argentina recorded a significant trade surplus, mostly reflecting a sharp reduction in imports owing to the substantial currency depreciation. Although

some countries increased their exports, several economies faced challenges because of weaker demand from China. On a positive note, investor demand for regional debt remained resilient despite high debt levels and lingering uncertainties around fiscal policies.

Outlook

Regional growth is projected to rise to 2.5 percent in 2025 and 2.6 percent in 2026, primarily driven by Argentina's recovery following two years of economic contraction (table 2.3.1). Growth in the region's other major economies—Brazil and Mexico—is expected to slow this year, attributed to weak consumption and investment, with only a slight improvement anticipated in 2026. Inflation will likely remain above central bank targets in several countries, limiting the ability to cut policy rates and stimulate demand (figures 2.3.2.A and 2.3.2.B). Given limited fiscal space due to high debt levels, substantial deficits, and elevated global interest rates, fiscal policies are expected to be contractionary this year and remain broadly neutral in 2026 (figure 2.3.2.C). As central banks in the region cautiously normalize monetary policy, economic growth—apart from Argentina—is expected to approach potential. Changes in commodity prices and trade are unlikely to have a significant impact unless there are policy shifts in advanced economies that deviate from the expected baseline. Exports and imports are assumed to continue under a context of high uncertainty, with no substantial changes anticipated in migration flows.

Growth in Brazil is expected to moderate from 3.2 percent in 2024 to an average of 2.2 percent in 2025 and 2026. Private consumption and a robust labor market will remain the main drivers of growth. The moderation in activity partly reflects the effects of a still-restrictive monetary policy, with inflation projected to remain near the upper end of the target range in 2025. Fiscal policy is expected to have limited room to support economic activity as the government seeks to address pressing fiscal sustainability issues.

In Mexico, growth is forecast to slow slightly to an average of 1.5 percent in 2025-26, as continued fiscal consolidation efforts and tight monetary policy weigh on consumption and investment. Inflation, though edging down, is expected to remain close to the upper end of the central bank's target range in 2025. Trade disruptions are assumed to remain small within a context of high uncertainty, with limited effects on the outlook. This is expected to limit the central bank's ability to ease monetary policy, suggesting a continuing restrained approach to rate cuts.

Argentina's growth is projected to rebound 5 percent in 2025 and 4.7 percent in 2026, following two years of recession. Key activity drivers during the forecast horizon are expected to include agriculture, energy, and mining, supported by macroeconomic stability and newly enacted business-friendly legislation. The government is expected to maintain a tight fiscal policy to support sustained progress in reducing inflation and uphold the current policy framework's credibility.

Growth in Colombia is forecast to rise to an average of 3 percent in 2025-26. Following a subdued performance in 2024, private consumption and investment growth are expected to recover, underpinned by the continued easing of monetary policy as inflation moderates. However, restrictive fiscal policy will likely be a drag on activity. Rising policy uncertainty regarding reforms that challenge fiscal sustainability in the medium term could further delay the investment recovery.

Chile's growth is expected to slow to 2.2 percent in 2025 and remain at that pace in 2026. Inflation is projected to approach the central bank's target during the second half of 2025, providing additional room for further monetary easing to support domestic demand. External demand for green energy-related commodities, such as copper and lithium, is expected to bolster the country's exports, partly offsetting the reduction in demand caused by the slowdown in China's real estate sector.

Growth in Peru is projected to soften to 2.5 percent a year in 2025 and 2026, as consumption growth moderates following last year's one-time approval of pension fund withdrawals. Invest-

FIGURE 2.3.2 LAC: Outlook

Expected inflation remains close to the upper limit of central banks' target ranges. Consequently, central banks are maintaining elevated real policy interest rates, particularly in Brazil and Mexico, where inflation has been particularly persistent. Fiscal consolidation in LAC is projected to be more substantial this year than in 2026. Potential GDP growth in the region is forecast to be lower in 2022-30 than in 2000-21 but marginally higher in the Caribbean subregion.

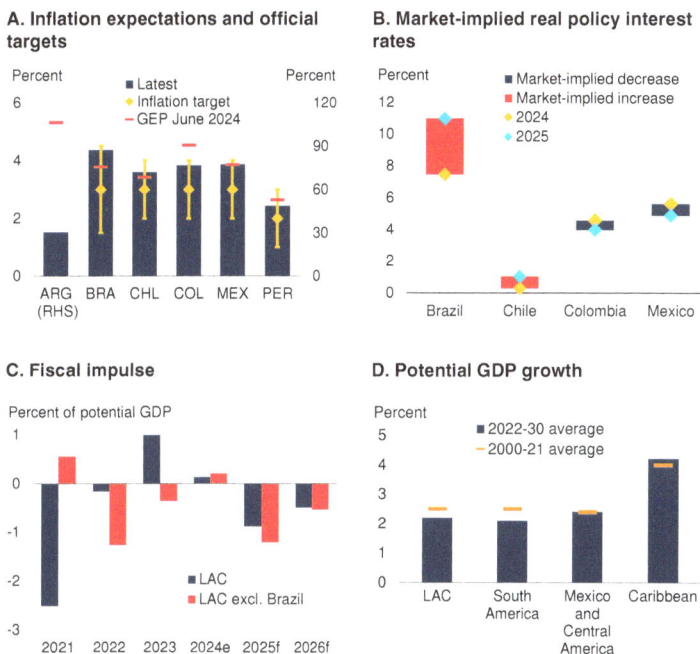

A. Inflation expectations and official targets

B. Market-implied real policy interest rates

C. Fiscal impulse

D. Potential GDP growth

Sources: Bloomberg; Consensus Economics; Haver Analytics; IMF *World Economic Outlook* (database); Kose and Ohnsorge (2023); World Bank.
Note: ARG = Argentina; BRA = Brazil; CHL = Chile; COL = Colombia; LAC = Latin America and the Caribbean; MEX = Mexico; PER = Peru.
A. Red lines show one-year-ahead inflation expectations reported in the June 2024 *Global Economic Prospects* report. Bars show the latest one-year-ahead inflation expectation based on Consensus Economics in December 2024. Inflation targets and target ranges are those set by the respective central banks.
B. Yellow diamonds denote the policy rate minus the 2024 inflation expectation from Consensus Economics. Blue diamonds denote the 30-day rolling average of one-year-ahead market implied policy rate, minus the 2025 inflation expectation from Consensus Economics. Bars show the expected change in real interest rates from 2024 to 2025. Last observation is December 18, 2024.
C. Fiscal impulse is the annual change in the structural primary balance for 18 LAC economies, using data from the October 2024 IMF *World Economic Outlook* (database). A positive value indicates fiscal expansion, while a negative value indicates contraction. Structural primary balance is the general government structural balance excluding net interest costs.
D. Period averages of annual GDP-weighted averages. GDP weights are calculated using average real U.S. dollar GDP (at average 2010-19 prices and market exchange rates) for the period 2000-21. Data for 2022-30 are forecasts. Estimates based on production function approach. South America includes Argentina, Bolivia, Brazil, Chile, Colombia, Ecuador, Peru, Paraguay, and Uruguay. Mexico and Central America include Costa Rica, Guatemala, Honduras, Mexico, and Nicaragua. Caribbean includes Dominican Republic and Jamaica.

ments in the mining sector and infrastructure are expected support growth in the coming years. Government consumption growth is expected to moderate relative to previous years, reducing the role of fiscal policy as a growth driver.

Growth in the Caribbean economies is projected to remain robust at 4.9 and 5.7 percent in 2025 and 2026, respectively, following an estimated strong pace of 7.7 percent in 2024. This performance partly reflects the continuing boom in Guyana, driven by the expansion of its new oil extraction sector following the discovery of oil a decade ago. Even excluding Guyana, the subregion's growth is expected to rise to an average of 3.8 percent annually in 2025-26. Exports to the United States are assumed to remain largely unaffected by trade tensions. However, prospects continue to diverge within the subregion. The Dominican Republic is forecast to grow strongly, by an average of 4.9 percent in 2025-26, supported by structural reforms to attract foreign direct investment. Jamaica's growth is expected to recover in 2025 from the impact of Hurricane Beryl, reaching 2.2 percent and stabilizing at 1.6 percent in 2026. Economic conditions in Haiti remain highly uncertain in the context of ongoing violence and political instability.

Growth in Central America is forecast to increase to 3.5 percent in 2025 and 2026, supported by increasing consumption. Growth in Costa Rica is expected to moderate to 3.5 percent in 2025 and 3.4 percent in 2026, while growth in Panama, underpinned by services exports, is projected to rebound to 3 percent this year and 3.5 percent in 2026. Inflation across the subregion varies, with El Salvador and Panama—both dollarized economies—and Costa Rica experiencing inflation rates comparable to those in the United States. Inflation in countries such as Guatemala, Honduras, and Nicaragua has decreased to more moderate levels than in previous years, aligning more closely with central bank targets due to restrictive monetary policies.

Estimated potential economic growth in LAC during 2011-21 was significantly lower than in the preceding decade. Projected potential growth in the 2020s suggests a further deceleration (figure 2.3.2.D). This trend reflects declines in the growth rates of both total factor productivity and the labor force (Kose and Ohnsorge 2023). This deceleration is also in part attributable to the enduring adverse effects of the pandemic—particularly on human capital formation—elevated violence, and a lack of competition (World Bank 2024k).

Risks

The growth forecast for the region faces several downward risks. Significant uncertainty surrounding trade and migration could have a negative impact on outcomes. Specifically, trade restrictions may result in decreasing exports. Additionally, a decline in migration flows to the United States could lead to reduced remittances. There are also other risks to consider. Large fiscal deficits are raising concerns about fiscal stability, and sustained core inflation may necessitate tighter monetary policies than previously anticipated. Furthermore, a more substantial decline in China's real estate sector, along with protectionist measures in advanced economies, could adversely affect exports from LAC. Lastly, climate change continues to threaten the region, particularly the Caribbean, including the potential shift in ocean currents toward La Niña, which could cause droughts in areas that rely heavily on agriculture, especially in the southern part of South America.

Trade restrictions have increased significantly and are now five times higher than the average levels observed between 2010 and 2019. Major economies, especially the United States, are increasingly discussing new trade-restrictive policies. The United States-Mexico-Canada Agreement includes a provision for revision in 2026, raising the possibility of additional protectionist measures. Moreover, universal tariffs could be imposed outside the framework of this treaty. If these changes are implemented, the region's exports are likely to decline, resulting in slower growth (figure 2.3.3.A). This downturn would be driven by both decreased demand and lower prices. The most vulnerable economies include Mexico and countries in Central America and the Caribbean. Additionally, stricter migration policies could further affect remittances to the region, especially affecting Central America and the Caribbean.

Although headline inflation has declined over the last year, core inflation has proven stickier than expected. The continuing persistence of core inflation above targets could compel central banks to further delay policy rate cuts (figure 2.3.3.B).

Higher-for-longer interest rates could result in growth falling below the baseline forecast.

Fiscal positions have become more precarious than in the pre-pandemic decade because of rising debt levels, higher interest rates, and weaker growth prospects. While fiscal deficits in most LAC economies have narrowed since the pandemic, they remain substantial. If markets perceive them as unsustainable, risk appetite for LAC government bonds could decline significantly, potentially leading to sharp currency depreciations amid elevated current account deficits. Such market reactions would require stronger fiscal consolidations than currently assumed (figure 2.3.3.C).

Developments in China, a key trading partner for the region, have significant implications for the region's growth. The real estate sector in China remains weak and subject to substantial downside risks. If its slump were to deepen and outweigh growth in other construction-related sectors, demand from China would fall, particularly for industrial commodities (figure 2.3.3.C). This would depress the prices of these commodities, especially metals, adding another downside risk to growth in some LAC economies, particularly Chile and Peru.

The effects of climate change could pose risks to sectors sensitive to extreme weather events, such as agriculture, fishing, and energy (Cai et al. 2015; Wang et al. 2019). Natural disasters, such as floods, could significantly strain countries in the region, particularly those with poor infrastructure. For example, a shift in ocean currents to La Niña could lead to droughts in southern South America, severely affecting agricultural production (figure 2.3.3.D).

FIGURE 2.3.3 LAC: Risks

LAC exports could decline if trade restrictions in the United States increase more than expected. High government debt and deficits pose risks to fiscal sustainability. Current accounts in the region have remained mostly in deficit, and significantly so in some countries, though smaller than in the 2010-19 period. Although LAC's vulnerability to climate change is relatively low, the region has been experiencing frequent extreme weather events, driving up energy and food costs.

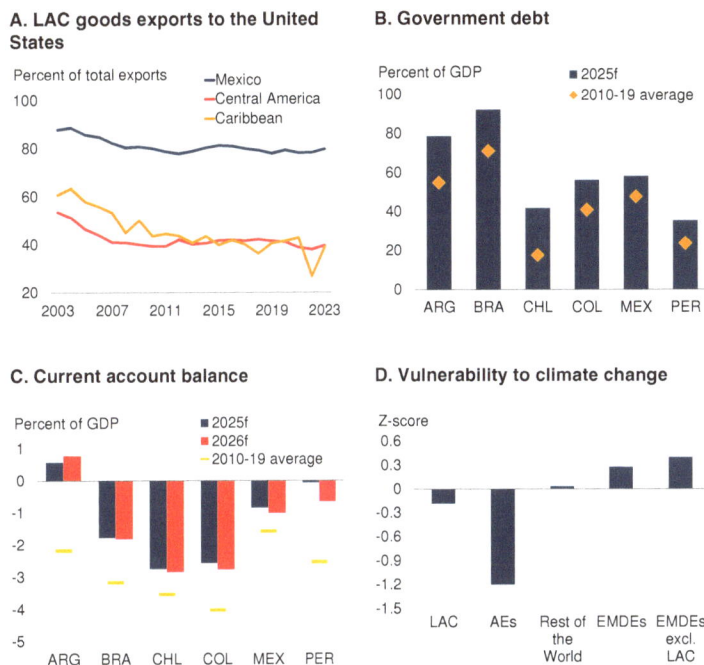

A. LAC goods exports to the United States

B. Government debt

C. Current account balance

D. Vulnerability to climate change

Sources: Haver Analytics; IMF *World Economic Outlook* (database); ND-GAIN (database); UN Comtrade (database); World Bank.
Note: f = forecast; AEs = advanced economies; ARG = Argentina; BRA = Brazil; CHL = Chile; COL = Colombia; EMDEs = emerging market and developing economies; LAC = Latin America and the Caribbean; MEX = Mexico; PER = Peru.
A. Goods exports to the United States as a share of total exports. Last observation is 2023.
B. General government gross debt as a percentage of GDP. Period averages of general government gross debt during 2010-19. 2025 is projection.
C. Period averages of current account balance during 2010-19; 2025 and 2026 are projections.
D. Vulnerability measures exposure, sensitivity, and capacity to adapt to the negative effects of climate change. The Notre Dame Global Adaptation Initiative measures overall vulnerability across six life-supporting sectors: food, water, health, ecosystem service, human habitat, and infrastructure. Z-score is calculated by normalizing the simple average of the respective group against the sample average of 187 countries. Higher values indicate higher vulnerability. Last observation is 2022.

TABLE 2.3.1 Latin America and the Caribbean forecast summary

(Real GDP growth at market prices in percent, unless indicated otherwise)

Percentage-point differences from
June 2024 projections

	2022	2023	2024e	2025f	2026f	2024e	2025f	2026f
EMDE LAC, GDP [1]	4.0	2.3	2.2	2.5	2.6	0.4	-0.2	0.0
GDP per capita (U.S. dollars)	3.3	1.5	1.5	1.8	1.9	0.5	-0.2	0.0
(Average including countries that report expenditure components in national accounts) [2]								
EMDE LAC, GDP [2]	3.9	2.2	2.1	2.5	2.5	0.4	-0.1	0.0
PPP GDP	4.0	2.1	2.0	2.5	2.5	0.3	-0.2	0.0
Private consumption	5.2	2.6	2.2	2.3	2.5	0.5	-0.1	0.2
Public consumption	2.3	1.9	0.0	1.1	1.2	0.3	-0.3	-0.2
Fixed investment	4.9	2.8	0.8	3.3	3.5	0.1	-0.8	-0.2
Exports, GNFS [3]	8.0	-0.5	2.9	3.0	3.4	-1.1	-0.7	-0.6
Imports, GNFS [3]	7.9	0.9	1.6	2.6	3.3	-0.9	-1.2	-0.7
Net exports, contribution to growth	-0.1	-0.3	0.3	0.0	0.0	0.0	0.1	0.1
Memo items: GDP								
South America [4]	3.7	1.6	2.1	2.7	2.7	0.8	0.0	0.2
Central America [5]	5.6	4.9	3.4	3.5	3.5	0.2	0.0	-0.1
Caribbean [6]	8.7	5.0	7.7	4.9	5.7	0.6	-0.8	-0.3
Caribbean excluding Guyana	5.5	2.3	3.5	3.7	3.9	-0.4	-0.3	0.0
Brazil	3.0	2.9	3.2	2.2	2.3	1.2	0.0	0.3
Mexico	3.7	3.3	1.7	1.5	1.6	-0.6	-0.6	-0.4
Argentina	5.3	-1.6	-2.8	5.0	4.7	0.7	0.0	0.2

Source: World Bank.

Note: e = estimate; f = forecast; PPP = purchasing power parity; EMDE = emerging market and developing economy. World Bank forecasts are frequently updated based on new information and changing (global) circumstances. Consequently, projections presented here may differ from those contained in other Bank documents, even if basic assessments of countries' prospects do not differ at any given moment in time. The World Bank is currently not publishing economic output, income, or growth data for República Bolivariana de Venezuela owing to a lack of reliable data of adequate quality. República Bolivariana de Venezuela is excluded from cross-country macroeconomic aggregates.

1. GDP and expenditure components are measured in average 2010-19 prices and market exchange rates.
2. Aggregate includes all countries in notes 4, 5, and 6, plus Mexico, but excludes Antigua and Barbuda, Barbados, Dominica, Grenada, Guyana, Haiti, St. Kitts and Nevis, St. Lucia, St. Vincent and the Grenadines, and Suriname.
3. Exports and imports of goods and nonfactor services (GNFS).
4. Includes Argentina, Bolivia, Brazil, Chile, Colombia, Ecuador, Paraguay, Peru, and Uruguay.
5. Includes Costa Rica, El Salvador, Guatemala, Honduras, Nicaragua, and Panama.
6. Includes Antigua and Barbuda, The Bahamas, Barbados, Belize, Dominica, the Dominican Republic, Grenada, Guyana, Haiti, Jamaica, St. Kitts and Nevis, St. Lucia, St. Vincent and the Grenadines, and Suriname.

TABLE 2.3.2 Latin America and the Caribbean country forecasts [1]

(Real GDP growth at market prices in percent, unless indicated otherwise)

Percentage-point differences from June 2024 projections

	2022	2023	2024e	2025f	2026f	2024e	2025f	2026f
Argentina	5.3	-1.6	-2.8	5.0	4.7	0.7	0.0	0.2
Bahamas, The	14.4	4.3	2.3	1.8	1.6	0.0	0.0	0.0
Barbados	13.5	4.4	3.9	2.8	2.3	0.2	0.0	0.0
Belize	8.7	4.7	4.3	1.2	0.5	0.9	-1.3	-2.0
Bolivia	3.6	3.1	1.4	1.5	1.5	0.0	0.0	0.0
Brazil	3.0	2.9	3.2	2.2	2.3	1.2	0.0	0.3
Chile	2.1	0.2	2.4	2.2	2.2	-0.2	0.0	0.0
Colombia	7.3	0.6	1.7	3.0	2.9	0.4	-0.2	-0.2
Costa Rica	4.6	5.1	4.0	3.5	3.4	0.1	-0.2	-0.3
Dominica	5.6	4.7	4.6	4.2	3.2	0.0	0.0	0.2
Dominican Republic	4.9	2.4	5.1	4.7	5.0	0.0	-0.3	0.0
Ecuador	6.2	2.4	-0.7	2.0	2.2	-1.0	0.4	0.0
El Salvador	2.8	3.5	2.9	2.7	2.5	-0.3	0.0	0.0
Grenada	7.3	4.7	4.2	3.8	3.4	-0.1	0.0	0.2
Guatemala	4.2	3.5	3.7	4.0	4.0	0.7	0.5	0.5
Guyana	63.3	33.8	43.0	12.3	15.7	8.7	-4.5	-2.5
Haiti [2]	-1.7	-1.9	-4.2	0.5	1.5	-2.4	-1.4	-0.5
Honduras	4.1	3.6	3.7	3.6	3.6	0.3	0.3	0.2
Jamaica	5.2	2.6	0.8	2.2	1.6	-1.2	0.6	0.0
Mexico	3.7	3.3	1.7	1.5	1.6	-0.6	-0.6	-0.4
Nicaragua	3.8	4.6	3.6	3.5	3.6	-0.1	0.0	0.1
Panama	10.8	7.3	2.6	3.0	3.5	0.1	-0.5	-0.5
Paraguay	0.2	4.7	4.0	3.6	3.6	0.2	0.0	0.0
Peru	2.8	-0.4	3.1	2.5	2.5	0.2	-0.1	0.1
St. Lucia	20.4	2.2	3.7	2.8	2.3	0.8	0.4	0.5
St. Vincent and the Grenadines	7.2	6.0	5.0	3.5	2.9	0.0	-0.4	-0.8
Suriname	2.4	2.5	2.9	3.0	3.1	-0.1	0.0	0.1
Uruguay	4.7	0.4	3.2	2.6	2.6	0.0	0.0	0.0

Source: World Bank.

Note: e = estimate; f = forecast. World Bank forecasts are frequently updated based on new information and changing (global) circumstances. Consequently, projections presented here may differ from those contained in other Bank documents, even if basic assessments of countries' prospects do not significantly differ at any given moment in time.

1. Data are based on GDP measured in average 2010-19 prices and market exchange rates.
2. GDP is based on fiscal year, which runs from October to September of next year.

MIDDLE EAST and NORTH AFRICA

Growth in the Middle East and North Africa (MNA) region is expected to pick up from an estimated 1.8 percent in 2024 to 3.4 percent in 2025 and 4.1 percent in 2026. The outlook for this year has deteriorated since June, primarily due to extended oil production cuts by major oil producers. The major downside risks to the outlook are the intensification of armed conflicts in the region, heightened policy uncertainty, and unexpected adverse global policy shifts. Delays in oil production hikes by major oil exporters could also slow regional growth. Other downside risks include persistent global inflation and a resulting tightening of global financial conditions, heightened domestic violence and social tensions, and more frequent extreme weather events. Upside risks to the outlook include the possibility of stronger growth in major economies and easier global financial conditions due to faster-than-expected disinflation.

Recent developments

Elevated geopolitical tensions and conflict have increased uncertainty in MNA, particularly in economies facing fragile and conflict-affected situations (FCS). The economy of West Bank and Gaza has been gravely affected, with a significant number of people in Gaza experiencing severe acute food insecurity and malnutrition. Neighboring countries have also suffered from repercussions of the conflict in the Middle East (figure 2.4.1.A). While a ceasefire agreed upon at the end of November 2024 has eased tensions in Lebanon, the conflict has resulted in serious economic damage, with output projected to contract by at least 5.7 percent in 2024 (World Bank 2024l). The transit of ships through the Suez Canal has declined as a result of attacks in the Red Sea by Houthi rebels based in the Republic of Yemen, causing disruptions to international trade and increased security concerns in neighboring countries. Uncertainty remains high in the Syrian Arab Republic following political upheaval in early December 2024.

Growth in MNA remained subdued at an estimated 1.8 percent in 2024, dampened by limited oil activity in oil exporters, mainly due to

the extension of voluntary oil production cuts initially agreed upon in November 2023 among member countries of the Organization of the Petroleum Exporting Countries and other affiliated oil producers (OPEC+). In December 2024, these countries agreed to maintain their cuts until the end of March 2025 and then gradually phase them out beginning in April. In addition, oil production adjustments announced in April 2023 were also extended until the end of 2026, following a one-year extension in June 2024 until the end of 2025. In countries belonging to the Gulf Cooperation Council (GCC), including Saudi Arabia, growth is estimated to have picked up to 1.6 percent in 2024, primarily because of strong non-oil activity supported by robust labor markets and a recovery in capital inflows (figure 2.4.1.B).

Among non-GCC oil exporters, growth in the Islamic Republic of Iran is estimated to moderate to 3 percent in fiscal year (FY) 2024/25 (late-March 2024 to late-March 2025) from 5 percent in FY2023/24, mainly owing to tighter fiscal and monetary policies amid heightened inflation. In Libya, activity is estimated to have declined 2.7 percent in 2024, largely as a result of earlier political turmoil. Growth in Algeria is estimated to have slowed to 3.1 percent in 2024, primarily because of constraints to oil activity stemming

Note: This section was prepared by Naotaka Sugawara.

FIGURE 2.4.1 MNA: Recent developments

Geopolitical tensions remain high in the region, with neighboring countries experiencing repercussions of the conflict in the Middle East. In oil exporters, non-oil activity in GCC countries has been bolstered by a recovery in capital inflows. The Arab Republic of Egypt experienced weak industrial activity prior to exchange rate liberalization, while agricultural production contracted in other oil importers. Headline inflation has declined since late 2023 in oil importers, but core inflation has been more persistent.

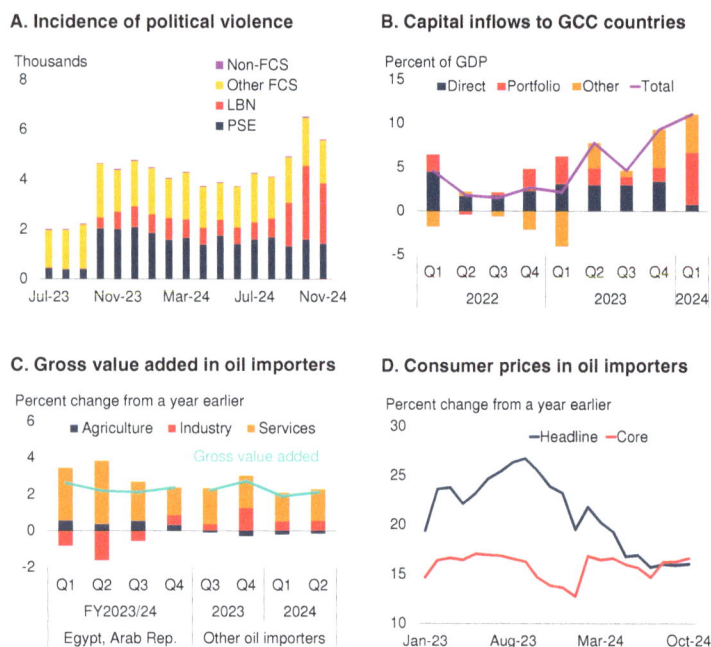

A. Incidence of political violence

B. Capital inflows to GCC countries

C. Gross value added in oil importers

D. Consumer prices in oil importers

Sources: ACLED (database); Haver Analytics; International Monetary Fund; World Bank.
Note: FCS = fragile and conflict-affected situations; GCC = Gulf Cooperation Council;
LBN = Lebanon; MNA = Middle East and North Africa; PSE = West Bank and Gaza.
A. Total number of political violent events, including battles, explosions and remote violence, and violence against civilians. Last observation is November 2024. Sample includes up to 14 MNA countries, including six FCS and eight non-FCS countries.
B. Capital inflows are measured as net incurrence of liabilities and divided by non-seasonally adjusted quarterly GDP. Sample includes five GCC countries.
C. Percent change in real gross value added from a year earlier, with sectoral contributions (in percentage points). The aggregate is computed as a weighted average, using gross value added at 2019 prices and market exchange rates as weights. Sample includes four non-FCS oil importers.
D. Percent change in headline and core consumer prices from a year earlier. The aggregate is calculated as a weighted average, using nominal GDP in U.S. dollars as weights. Last observation is October 2024. Sample includes five non-FCS oil importers.

from the OPEC+ oil production quota and a decline in natural gas production (World Bank 2024m).

In oil importers, elevated inflation has slowed the expansion of private sector demand and activity, and repercussions from the conflict in the region have also disrupted several economies. Growth in oil importers weakened further in 2024, to 2.2 percent, although this was still higher than in oil exporters. In the Arab Republic of Egypt, growth slowed to 2.4 percent in FY2023/24 (July 2023 to June 2024), reflecting a decline in shipping

through the Suez Canal, reduced natural gas production, contraction of the non-oil manufacturing sector mainly due to higher input costs and lingering supply bottlenecks, and earlier foreign exchange shortages (figure 2.4.1.C). However, the exchange rate liberalization in March 2024 improved investor confidence, strengthening private sector activity in the second half of 2024.

In Tunisia, persistent drought conditions and weak domestic demand contributed to a slower economic recovery in 2024 than previously projected, with growth estimated at 1.2 percent. Growth in Morocco decelerated to an estimated 2.9 percent in 2024, mainly owing to a slowdown in agricultural production due to drought conditions. In Djibouti, growth reached an estimated 5.9 percent in 2024—an upward revision of 0.8 percentage point relative to the June forecast, partly because of increased demand for transport services, primarily from Ethiopia. In West Bank and Gaza, the economy is estimated to have contracted by a further 25.6 percent in 2024—a downgrade of 19.1 percentage points from the June projection. The large-scale loss of life, widespread displacement of people, and destruction of fixed assets in Gaza, as well as restrictions on the mobility of workers in West Bank, have caused massive damage to society and the entire economy.

Among oil exporters, inflation has remained moderate in GCC countries—in almost all cases, reflecting exchange rates pegged to the U.S. dollar—with core inflation slightly above or below zero since July 2024. Inflation has declined from elevated levels in non-GCC oil exporters, particularly the Islamic Republic of Iran, in response to policy tightening, including stricter reserve requirements and an increase in official interest rates. In oil importers, headline inflation has remained elevated but has slowed gradually since late-2023, particularly in Egypt and Lebanon, supported by the stabilization of exchange rates (figure 2.4.1.D). In West Bank and Gaza, major shortages of essential products and supply chain disruptions, especially in Gaza, have substantially raised prices (World Bank 2024n). Core inflation in oil importers has declined more slowly than headline inflation. Easing financial conditions driven by interest rate cuts in the

United States since September 2024 have prompted looser monetary policy in GCC countries. In oil importers, policy rates have been relatively stable since early 2024, except in countries with pegged exchange rates such as Jordan.

Outlook

Growth in MNA is expected to pick up to 3.4 percent in 2025 and 4.1 percent in 2026, primarily reflecting gradual expansion of oil production (figure 2.4.2.A; table 2.4.1). The outlook for 2025 has been downgraded by 0.8 percentage point, mainly because OPEC+ members extended some of the voluntary oil production cuts—previously expected to be lifted at the end of 2024 in the June projections. However, the outlook is subject to particularly high uncertainty given the continuing conflict in the region.

Growth in GCC countries is forecast to increase to 3.3 percent in 2025 and 4.6 percent in 2026. Compared to the June forecasts, the projection for 2025 has been downgraded by 1.4 percentage points because of the extension of the voluntary production cuts by OPEC+. In Saudi Arabia, growth is projected to strengthen, driven by robust activity in the non-oil sector—especially in services—as well as higher oil production and exports (Chattha et al. 2024).

In other oil exporters, growth in the Islamic Republic of Iran is projected to moderate to 2.7 percent in FY2025/26 and 2.2 percent the following fiscal year, mainly reflecting softening external demand for oil, particularly from China, and slowing non-oil-related investment growth (table 2.4.2). Given elevated inflation, monetary policy is set to remain tight, weighing on near-term activity. Growth in Algeria and Iraq is expected to pick up in 2025, though it is envisaged to be weaker than in the June forecasts, primarily because of extended oil production adjustments. In Libya, growth is forecast to average 9 percent per year in 2025-26, assuming a full recovery in oil production.

In oil importers, growth is anticipated to pick up to 3.7 percent in 2025 and 4 percent in 2026,

FIGURE 2.4.2 MNA: Outlook

Growth in MNA is projected to rise to 3.4 percent in 2025 and 4.1 percent in 2026, with the improvement primarily driven by a gradual increase in oil production by oil exporters. Fiscal deficits in the region are expected to be broadly stable but with significant differences between oil exporters and importers. Inflation is projected to fall in 2025-26, while prospects for poverty reduction in oil importers are limited.

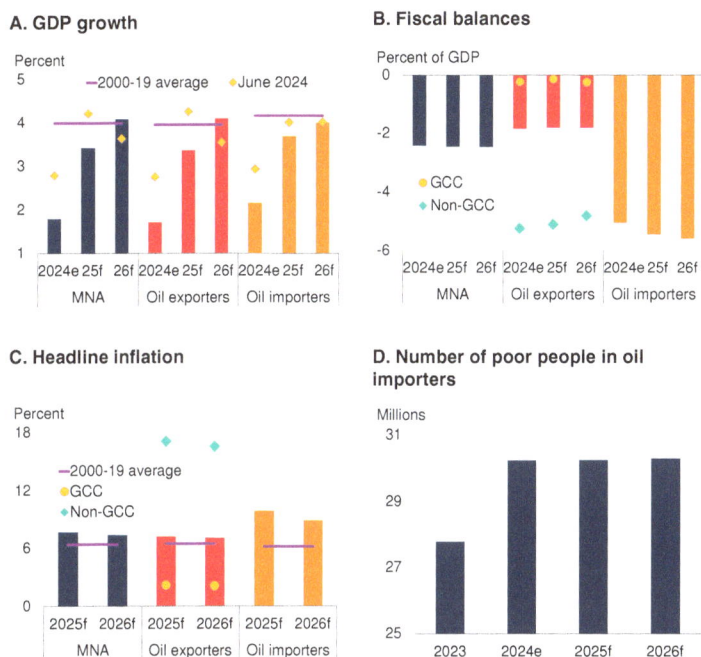

A. GDP growth

B. Fiscal balances

C. Headline inflation

D. Number of poor people in oil importers

Source: World Bank.
Note: e = estimate; f = forecast; GCC = Gulf Cooperation Council; MNA = Middle East and North Africa.
A. Aggregates are calculated as weighted averages using GDP at average 2010-19 prices and market exchange rates as weights. Diamonds for June 2024 refer to data presented in the June 2024 edition of the *Global Economic Prospects* report.
B.C. Aggregates are calculated as weighted averages using nominal GDP in U.S. dollars as weights.
D. The number of poor people is defined using the lower-middle-income poverty threshold of 3.65 international dollars per day in 2017 purchasing power parity. Sample includes five oil importers.

mainly driven by firming domestic demand, as inflationary pressures ease. In Egypt, growth is projected to strengthen to 3.5 percent in FY2024/25 and 4.2 percent in the following fiscal year, supported by private consumption growth amid gradually abating inflation, robust inflows of remittances, and improved sentiment. Investment in Egypt, particularly in infrastructure development, will be shored up by financing from the United Arab Emirates. Growth in Jordan is projected to edge up slightly, to 2.6 percent a year in 2025-26, with inflation set to remain contained (World Bank 2024o).

In Tunisia, growth is forecast to recover to 2.2 percent in 2025 and 2.3 percent in 2026, supported by improved external financing conditions and stronger external demand, particularly from Europe (World Bank 2024p). In Morocco, growth is projected to strengthen to 3.9 percent in 2025 before moderating to 3.4 percent in 2026, assuming an improvement in weather conditions raising agricultural production in 2025. Growth in Djibouti is expected to soften to about 5.1 percent a year in 2025-26, primarily as a result of the stabilization of port activity and related export earnings.

The growth outlook remains particularly uncertain for Lebanon, Syria, West Bank and Gaza, and the Republic of Yemen, given these countries' security and political challenges. In the Republic of Yemen, continued security concerns amid unsettled peace negotiations and high domestic tensions are expected to limit growth to 1.5 percent this year after two years of decline (World Bank 2024q).

Fiscal policies in the region are expected to have a neutral influence on growth in 2025, with region-wide fiscal deficits remaining broadly stable, though there are variations among countries (figure 2.4.2.B). Among oil exporters, expected declines in fiscal surpluses in GCC countries will be offset by smaller fiscal deficits in other countries. In GCC countries, despite projected declines in oil revenues, fiscal policies will likely support activity, particularly in Kuwait. Libya's fiscal position is set to improve as oil activity recovers. Meanwhile, the stance of fiscal policy in Iraq is forecast to ease, contributing to the recovery of activity but worsening the country's fiscal position. In 2026, a gradual increase in revenues resulting from the expansion of oil production is set to improve fiscal balances in oil exporters. In oil importers, fiscal deficits are expected to widen in 2025, increasing financing vulnerabilities. In Egypt, interest payments are projected to remain elevated. However, fiscal consolidations are set to proceed in several economies, including Jordan, Morocco, and Tunisia in 2025, and in several other economies, including Algeria, in 2026.

Monetary easing in GCC countries is anticipated to continue in tandem with projected monetary policy easing in the United States and favorable financial conditions, supporting activity over the forecast horizon. In oil importers, central banks are projected to start easing monetary policy in 2025 as inflationary pressures recede (figure 2.4.2.C). In much of the region, monetary policy easing will boost investment.

Per capita income growth in the region is forecast to rise to 2 percent in 2025 and 2.7 percent in 2026, well above the pre-pandemic decade average at 1.2 percent. In oil importers, the 2.5 percent average increase in per capita income growth in 2025-26 will reflect gradual progress toward narrowing the income gap with advanced economies. However, in these countries, poverty is projected to remain elevated, partly reflecting higher inflation, especially for food (figure 2.4.2.D). Heightened food price inflation will also exacerbate food insecurity, particularly in FCS economies.

Risks

Risks to the outlook for the region are tilted to the downside. An escalation of armed conflicts in the region and heightened policy uncertainty, particularly unexpected global policy shifts, are major downside risks. In oil exporters, lower global demand for oil and lower oil prices could further delay the end of the OPEC+ oil production cuts, reducing region-wide growth prospects. In oil importers, a further increase in protectionist measures by trading partners could reduce exports, while more persistent global inflation and tighter-than-expected monetary policy could adversely affect the cost and availability of foreign financing. Other downside risks to growth forecasts include surges in social unrest and more frequent extreme weather events and other natural disasters. On the upside, easier-than-expected global monetary policy amid faster-than-projected global disinflation could lead to an easing of financing conditions. Stronger-than-expected growth in the world's major economies is another upside risk, which would benefit activity in the region through higher global demand.

If the ongoing conflict in the Middle East expands to involve major oil producers more directly, significant disruptions in oil supply could be triggered. In addition, prolonged attacks on shipping in the Red Sea could dampen activity in

Egypt and other neighboring countries, including Djibouti and Saudi Arabia (World Bank 2024r). An escalation of these conflicts could lead to significant deteriorations in consumer and business sentiment, increased uncertainty, and tighter financial conditions, dampening investment and overall economic activity (Gatti et al. 2024).

Higher policy uncertainty, particularly related to global trade policy, could weigh on export activity. Unexpected policy shifts, notably intensified protectionist policies, in trading partners could reduce exports of agricultural and industrial goods, particularly from oil importers, weakening growth prospects (figure 2.4.3.A). High economic policy uncertainty, particularly in the United States, could also worsen investor sentiment and financial conditions, leading to an increase in borrowing costs and a decline in investment.

Heightened domestic violence and social unrest could weigh on productivity and investment, particularly in FCS economies, including Syria. Such unrest could also lead to increased food price inflation due to scarcity, exacerbating food insecurity and undermining economic development. Heightened social unrest could be amplified by lack of employment opportunities, which remains widespread, especially among the young (figure 2.4.3.B).

Weaker-than-projected global demand—for instance, because of weaker-than-expected growth in China and the United States—would put downward pressure on global oil prices, which would likely lead to reductions in oil production, negatively affecting overall growth in MNA. Countries in the region with strong economic relationships with China are more prone to fluctuations of growth in that country (Kazemi et al. 2024). In several oil importers, spillovers from growth shocks in major economies, including China, are estimated to be significant (chapter 3).

More persistent global inflation than assumed in the baseline could slow monetary policy easing across countries, weighing on consumption and investment while increasing debt-service burdens. A sudden adverse shift in global risk appetite and tightening global financial conditions could trigger

FIGURE 2.4.3 MNA: Risks

Increasing protectionist measures by major trading partners could reduce the region's exports and dampen growth prospects. Heightened violence and social unrest could be amplified by the lack of employment opportunities and weigh on productivity and economic activity. Oil importers face significant financing needs and are vulnerable to adverse changes in global financing conditions or shifts in risk appetite. The region is also prone to extreme weather events and other natural disasters.

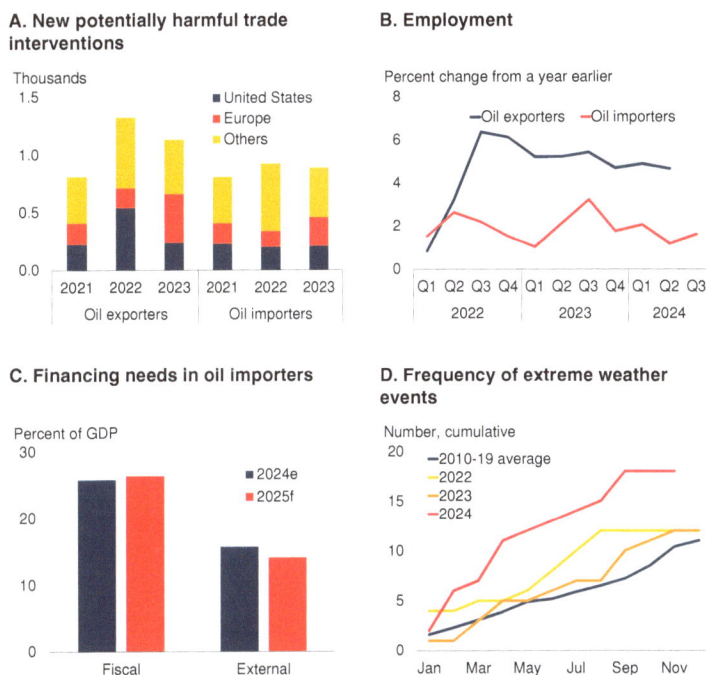

A. New potentially harmful trade interventions

B. Employment

C. Financing needs in oil importers

D. Frequency of extreme weather events

Sources: EM-DAT (database); Global Trade Alert (database); Haver Analytics; International Monetary Fund; Kose et al. (2022); World Bank.
Note: e = estimate; f = forecast; MNA = Middle East and North Africa.
A. The number of new trade interventions deemed likely or almost certainly discriminatory—defined as potentially harmful—against any country in respective groups on the horizontal axis, net of interventions removed within the year. Europe includes members of the European Union, the European Free Trade Association, European microstates, the United Kingdom, and their dependent territories. Sample includes 11 oil exporters and eight oil importers.
B. Percent change in total employment from a year earlier. Sample includes up to four oil exporters and four oil importers.
C. Fiscal financing needs are defined as a sum of short-term central government debt and fiscal deficits. External financing needs are defined as the sum of amortization of long-term external debt, stock of short-term external debt in the previous year, and current account deficits. Aggregates are calculated as weighted averages using nominal GDP in U.S. dollars as weights. Sample includes up to five oil importers.
D. Cumulative number of extreme weather events, including droughts, extreme temperatures, floods, storms, wildfire, and landslides. Last observation is November 2024. Sample includes 18 countries.

capital outflows, particularly from countries with elevated financial vulnerabilities. Given large external financing needs in several oil importers, reduced access to foreign borrowing could significantly weaken growth (figure 2.4.3.C). In oil importers with elevated government debt levels and large fiscal financing needs, further deterioration and delays in fiscal consolidation efforts could increase macroeconomic vulnerabilities, pushing up risk premiums and inflation expectations.

MNA is vulnerable to severe weather events induced by climate change, including extreme heat, droughts, and floods. The materialization of these adverse events could cause large-scale damage to infrastructure and reduce growth and productivity in the agricultural sector. Water scarcity is a serious concern, particularly in Morocco and Tunisia, and continued dry conditions could result in further reduced water supply (World Bank 2024s). More frequent and widespread natural disasters could cause food price spikes and exacerbate poverty and food insecurity, particularly given limited access to basic needs such as drinking water (figure 2.4.3.D). In countries with limited fiscal or institutional capacity to maintain and rebuild infrastructure, natural disasters, including earthquakes, could cause particularly large and long-lasting humanitarian and physical capital losses. In Djibouti, key industries, including transport and urban services, are exposed to climate change, with potential associated economic costs of 6 percent of GDP by mid-century (World Bank 2024t).

An upside risk to the baseline growth outlook for MNA is a faster-than-expected slowdown in global inflation and monetary policy easing. In oil exporters, especially countries with pegged exchange rates, a decline in policy rates in advanced economies may translate directly into monetary policy easing, which would support activity. In oil importers, easing financial conditions could increase consumption and investment and reduce debt-service burdens.

Another upside risk is positive growth surprises in major economies, including the United States and China, which could benefit the region's exports. In oil exporters, the likely boost to oil prices could lead to higher production. In oil importers, higher external demand for their industrial products and services, particularly those related to tourism, could lead to faster export growth.

TABLE 2.4.1 Middle East and North Africa forecast summary

(Real GDP growth at market prices in percent, unless indicated otherwise)

Percentage-point differences from
June 2024 projections

	2022	2023	2024e	2025f	2026f	2024e	2025f	2026f
EMDE MNA, GDP[1]	5.4	1.7	1.8	3.4	4.1	-1.0	-0.8	0.5
GDP per capita (U.S. dollars)	3.6	-0.2	0.2	2.0	2.7	-1.0	-0.7	0.4
(Average including countries that report expenditure components in national accounts)[2]								
EMDE MNA, GDP[2]	5.5	1.6	1.8	3.4	4.1	-1.0	-0.8	0.5
PPP GDP	5.3	2.0	2.0	3.4	4.0	-0.9	-0.8	0.4
Private consumption	4.9	4.3	4.1	3.7	3.7	0.9	0.5	0.5
Public consumption	4.8	3.3	2.2	3.1	2.7	-0.7	-0.7	-0.2
Fixed investment	8.1	3.2	4.1	4.5	5.0	-0.3	0.4	0.8
Exports, GNFS	12.5	1.1	0.3	5.1	5.2	-3.2	-1.6	0.0
Imports, GNFS	10.0	6.5	6.0	5.2	4.9	0.5	-0.1	-0.2
Net exports, contribution to growth	2.0	-1.7	-2.0	0.3	0.5	-1.6	-0.8	0.0
Memo items: GDP								
Oil exporters[3]	5.8	1.4	1.7	3.3	4.1	-1.1	-0.9	0.6
GCC countries[4]	7.1	0.4	1.6	3.3	4.6	-1.2	-1.4	1.1
Non-GCC oil exporters[5]	3.1	3.4	1.9	3.4	3.0	-0.8	0.0	-0.5
Oil importers[6]	4.0	2.7	2.2	3.7	4.0	-0.7	-0.3	0.0

Source: World Bank.

Note: e = estimate; f = forecast; EMDE = emerging market and developing economy; GCC = Gulf Cooperation Council; GNFS = goods and non-factor services; MNA = Middle East and North Africa; PPP = purchasing power parity. World Bank forecasts are frequently updated based on new information and changing (global) circumstances. Consequently, projections presented here may differ from those contained in other Bank documents, even if basic assessments of countries' prospects do not differ at any given moment in time.

1. GDP and expenditure components are measured in average 2010-19 prices and market exchange rates. Excludes Lebanon, the Syrian Arab Republic, and the Republic of Yemen as a result of the high degree of uncertainty.

2. Aggregate includes all economies in notes 3 and 6 except Jordan, for which data limitations prevent the forecasting of GDP components.

3. Algeria, Bahrain, the Islamic Republic of Iran, Iraq, Kuwait, Libya, Oman, Qatar, Saudi Arabia, and the United Arab Emirates.

4. Bahrain, Kuwait, Oman, Qatar, Saudi Arabia, and the United Arab Emirates.

5. Algeria, the Islamic Republic of Iran, Iraq, and Libya.

6. Djibouti, the Arab Republic of Egypt, Jordan, Morocco, Tunisia, and West Bank and Gaza.

TABLE 2.4.2 Middle East and North Africa economy forecasts[1]

(Real GDP growth at market prices in percent, unless indicated otherwise)

	2022	2023	2024e	2025f	2026f	Percentage-point differences from June 2024 projections 2024e	2025f	2026f
Calendar year basis								
Algeria	3.6	4.1	3.1	3.4	3.3	0.2	-0.3	0.1
Bahrain	6.0	3.0	3.5	3.3	3.3	0.0	0.0	-0.1
Djibouti	3.7	6.7	5.9	5.3	4.9	0.8	0.2	-0.3
Iraq[1]	7.6	-2.9	-0.8	3.5	3.0	-0.5	-0.3	-2.3
Jordan	2.6	2.7	2.4	2.6	2.6	-0.1	0.0	0.0
Kuwait	6.3	-3.6	-1.0	1.7	2.1	-3.8	-1.4	-0.6
Lebanon[2]	-0.6	-0.8	-5.7	..	..	-6.2	..	..
Libya	-8.3	10.2	-2.7	9.6	8.4	-7.5	4.3	2.6
Morocco	1.5	3.4	2.9	3.9	3.4	0.5	0.2	0.1
Oman	9.6	1.3	0.7	2.4	2.8	-0.8	-0.4	-0.4
Qatar	4.2	1.2	2.0	2.7	5.5	-0.1	-0.5	0.8
Saudi Arabia	7.5	-0.8	1.1	3.4	5.4	-1.4	-2.5	2.2
Syrian Arab Republic[2,3]	0.7	-1.2	-1.5	-1.0	..	0.0	..	..
Tunisia	2.7	0.0	1.2	2.2	2.3	-1.2	-0.2	0.1
United Arab Emirates	7.9	3.2	3.3	4.0	4.1	-0.6	-0.1	0.1
West Bank and Gaza	4.1	-5.4	-25.6	4.7	16.5	-19.1	-0.8	12.3
Yemen, Rep.[2]	1.5	-2.0	-1.0	1.5	..	0.0	0.0	..
Fiscal year basis[4]	**2022/23**	**2023/24**	**2024/25e**	**2025/26f**	**2026/27f**	**2024/25e**	**2025/26f**	**2026/27f**
Iran, Islamic Rep.	3.8	5.0	3.0	2.7	2.2	-0.2	0.0	-0.2
	2021/22	**2022/23**	**2023/24e**	**2024/25f**	**2025/26f**	**2023/24e**	**2024/25f**	**2025/26f**
Egypt, Arab Rep.	6.6	3.8	2.4	3.5	4.2	-0.4	-0.7	-0.4

Source: World Bank.

Note: e = estimate; f = forecast. World Bank forecasts are frequently updated based on new information and changing (global) circumstances. Consequently, projections presented here may differ from those contained in other Bank documents, even if basic assessments of economies' prospects do not significantly differ at any given moment in time.

1. Data are reported on a factor cost basis.
2. Forecasts for Lebanon (beyond 2024), the Syrian Arab Republic (beyond 2025), and the Republic of Yemen (beyond 2025) are excluded because of a high degree of uncertainty.
3. Forecast for 2025 was not included in June 2024 *Global Economic Prospects*, and therefore, the difference from June 2024 projection is not computed.
4. The fiscal year runs from March 21 to March 20 in the Islamic Republic of Iran, and from July 1 to June 30 in the Arab Republic of Egypt.

SOUTH ASIA

Growth in South Asia (SAR) is expected to remain high over the forecast period, averaging 6.2 percent in 2025-26, with the high level driven by resilient activity in India. Aggregate growth in the rest of the region is also projected to firm to 4.2 percent a year, on average, in 2025-26, with activity picking up in many countries. Risks to the outlook are tilted to the downside. Major downside risks include heightened policy uncertainty and adverse trade policy shifts in major trading partners, as well as higher commodity prices. Other downside risks include heightened domestic violence and social unrest, a slower pace of monetary easing and larger debt-service burdens, more frequent extreme weather events, and slower-than-projected growth in major global economies. An upside risk is stronger-than-expected growth in major economies, which would increase global demand and economic activity in the region.

Recent developments

Growth in SAR is estimated to have edged down to 6 percent in 2024 from 6.6 percent in 2023, as growth in India stabilizes from a high base. Excluding India, growth in SAR is estimated to have picked up to 3.9 percent last year from 3 percent in 2023, mainly reflecting recoveries in Pakistan and Sri Lanka, supported by improved macroeconomic policies aimed at addressing earlier economic difficulties.

In India, growth is expected to decelerate to 6.5 percent in fiscal year (FY) 2024/25 (April 2024 to March 2025) from 8.2 percent in FY2023/24, reflecting a slowdown in investment and weak manufacturing growth. However, services activity has been steady, while growth in the agricultural sector has recovered. Private consumption growth has remained resilient, primarily driven by improved rural incomes accompanied by a recovery of agricultural output. In contrast, higher inflation and slower credit growth have curbed consumption in urban areas (figure 2.5.1.A).

In Bangladesh, political turmoil in mid-2024 dampened economic activity and worsened

investor confidence. Growth in FY2023/24 (July 2023 to June 2024) is estimated to have slowed to 5 percent—a downward revision of 0.6 percentage point from previous projections. Supply constraints, including energy shortages and import restrictions, weakened industrial activity and led to increased price pressures (figure 2.5.1.B). High inflation reduced the purchasing power of households, slowing services growth.

Growth turned positive in Pakistan and Sri Lanka after recent periods of contraction. In Pakistan, growth is estimated to have picked up to 2.5 percent in FY2023/24 (July 2023 to June 2024). Agricultural output strengthened on account of improved weather conditions. Industrial production also increased, reflecting the earlier lifting of import controls and reduced political uncertainty following the general election in February. In Sri Lanka, GDP is estimated to have grown by 4.4 percent in 2024 after two years of significant contraction. Easing currency and inflationary pressures have contributed to faster macroeconomic stabilization and stronger industrial and services sector growth than previously envisaged.

Growth in Nepal is estimated to have picked up to 3.9 percent in FY2023/24 (mid-July 2023 to mid-July 2024), reflecting increased hydropower

Note: This section was prepared by Naotaka Sugawara.

FIGURE 2.5.1 SAR: Recent developments

Private consumption, particularly in rural areas, has remained resilient in India. While economic activity has eased in several countries, Pakistan and Sri Lanka have experienced a pickup in performance. Inflation in SAR has declined, staying below or within target ranges in most countries. Remittance inflows to the region have continued to grow strongly.

A. Vehicle and automotive sales in India

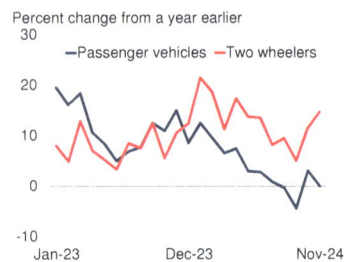

B. Gross value added, by sector

C. Headline consumer prices

D. Remittance receipts

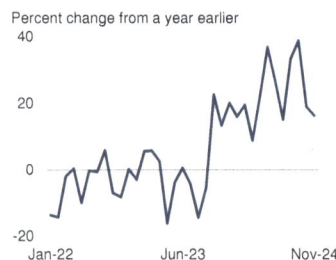

Sources: Haver Analytics; World Bank.

Note: BGD = Bangladesh; IND = India; LKA = Sri Lanka; MDV = Maldives; NPL = Nepal; PAK = Pakistan; SAR = South Asia.

A. Percent change in retail sales of passenger vehicles and two wheelers from a year earlier. Data are presented as three-month moving averages, covering data for the current and previous two months. Last observation is November 2024.

B. Percent change in real gross value added from a year earlier, with sectoral contributions (in percentage points).

C. Percent change in headline consumer price index from a year earlier. Aggregates are calculated as weighted averages, using nominal GDP in U.S. dollars as weights. Last observation is October 2024. Sample includes up to eight countries.

D. Percent change in remittance receipts, expressed in U.S. dollars, from a year earlier. Last observation is November 2024. Sample includes up to five countries (Bangladesh, Bhutan, Nepal, Pakistan, and Sri Lanka).

production and strong tourism-related services activity, including transport and hospitality. The strengthening of estimated growth to 5.3 percent in Bhutan in FY2023/24 (July 2023 to June 2024) was supported by solid services exports, particularly related to tourism, as well as by improved agricultural output. Tourism's strong performance also played a key role in boosting growth in Maldives last year to 4.7 percent, though it was partly offset by moderate spending per tourist, a slowdown in business activity related to a decline in capital expenditure and fisheries exports, and delays in completing an airport expansion.

Inflation in the region has gradually declined from elevated levels since mid-2022 (figure 2.5.1.C). In India, inflation has stayed within the central bank's target range since September 2023 except a breach in October 2024, driven by soaring food prices. Excluding India, regional inflation has been on a declining path, and headline inflation is within or below target ranges in most countries, including Nepal and Sri Lanka. In Pakistan, headline inflation fell to single digits in August 2024 for the first time since late 2021, mainly reflecting tight fiscal and monetary policies. As inflationary pressures waned, central banks in these countries started cutting policy rates in the second half of 2024. By contrast, inflation in Bangladesh has remained persistently high, and monetary policy has been tightened further.

Remittance inflows to the region have increased markedly since 2023, reflecting robust labor markets in worker destination countries—particularly the United States, member countries of the Gulf Cooperation Council, and India—and the stabilization of sender countries in the region (figure 2.5.1.D; chapter 2.4). The recovery of the tourism industry has also contributed to reductions in external imbalances in the region. Foreign exchange reserves increased last year in several countries, including Pakistan and Sri Lanka, reflecting reversals of exchange market pressures. However, in Bangladesh and Maldives, foreign reserves declined, reflecting currency pressures.

Outlook

Growth in SAR is expected to rise to 6.2 percent in 2025 and 2026, supported by the projected firm growth in India, though it will remain below the long-term average over 2000-19 (figure 2.5.2.A; table 2.5.1). Excluding India, growth in SAR is expected to strengthen to 4 percent this year and to 4.3 percent in 2026. The forecast for this year is slightly lower than in June, mainly because of a downgrade for Bangladesh amid policy uncertainty, despite upward revisions for several other countries driven by recent improvements in activity.

India is projected to maintain the fastest growth rate among the world's largest economies, at 6.7

percent in both FY2025/26 and FY2026/27 (table 2.5.2). The services sector is expected to enjoy sustained expansion, and manufacturing activity is anticipated to strengthen, supported by government initiatives to enhance logistics infrastructure and improve the business environment through tax reforms (World Bank 2024u). Private consumption growth is expected to be boosted by a strengthening labor market, expanding credit, and declining inflation. However, government consumption growth is likely to remain contained. Investment growth overall is expected to be steady, with rising private investment, supported by healthy corporate balance sheets and easing financing conditions.

In Bangladesh, growth is projected to decline to 4.1 percent in FY2024/25—1.6 percentage points lower than previous projections. Amid heightened political uncertainty, investment and industrial activity are expected to remain subdued in the near term (World Bank 2024v). Growth is projected to pick up to 5.4 percent in FY2025/26, assuming broad political stability, successful reforms in the financial sector, an improved business climate, and increased trade. Easing inflation is expected to boost private consumption.

In Pakistan, growth is projected to strengthen to 2.8 percent in FY2024/25 and 3.2 percent in FY2025/26—upgraded by 0.5 percentage point in both fiscal years since the June forecasts. Moderating inflation will support growth in industrial activity, while reduced uncertainty is expected to improve business and investor confidence, bolstering investment. Despite further stabilization of macroeconomic conditions, fiscal and monetary policies are expected to remain tight, keeping growth below potential over the forecast horizon (World Bank 2024w).

GDP in Sri Lanka is forecast to expand by 3.5 percent in 2025—an upward revision of 1 percentage point since June—largely reflecting stronger industrial activity than previously expected. Growth will moderate to 3.1 percent in 2026 but continue to be supported by recoveries in remittances and tourism, partly offset by tightening fiscal policy (World Bank 2024x). In Maldives, growth is projected to average 4.7 percent per year in 2025-26, primarily driven by

FIGURE 2.5.2 SAR: Outlook

Growth in SAR is projected to strengthen to 6.2 percent in 2025-26, with India remaining the engine of high regional growth. In SAR excluding India, growth is also forecast to firm over the forecast horizon. Fiscal policies in the region are expected to exert a modest drag on growth. However, moderating inflation is likely to support growth, particularly in private consumption, while poverty in the region is projected to decline.

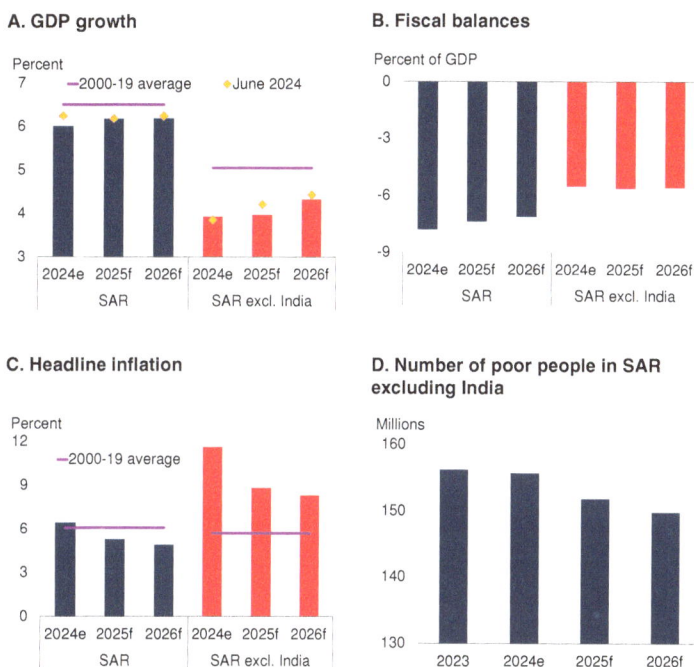

A. GDP growth

B. Fiscal balances

C. Headline inflation

D. Number of poor people in SAR excluding India

Source: World Bank.
Note: e = estimate; f = forecast; SAR = South Asia.
A. Aggregates are calculated as weighted averages, using GDP at average 2010-19 prices and market exchange rates as weights. Diamonds for June 2024 refer to data presented in the June 2024 edition of the *Global Economic Prospects* report.
B.C. Aggregates are calculated as weighted averages, using nominal GDP in U.S. dollars as weights.
D. The number of poor people is defined using the lower-middle-income poverty threshold of 3.65 international dollars per day in 2017 purchasing power parity. Sample includes four countries (Bangladesh, Bhutan, Pakistan, and Sri Lanka).

resilient tourism, while the planned fiscal adjustment is expected to dampen household income and government spending. Delays in constructing a new airport terminal have contributed to a downward revision to growth this year followed by an upgrade in 2026 (World Bank 2024y). The outlook assumes that the country will avoid a default on government debt by rescheduling debt repayments in an orderly manner.

In Nepal, growth is projected to strengthen to 5.1 percent in FY2024/25 and 5.5 percent in FY2025/26, mainly reflecting strengthening private investment alongside the expected easing of monetary policy and resilient hydropower exports to India. Growth in the services sector is also forecast to remain strong, especially in tourism and real estate (World Bank 2024z). In Bhutan, growth is projected to increase to 7.2 percent in FY2024/25—upgraded by 1.5 percentage points from the June projection—primarily because of a stronger-than-expected recovery in tourism and non-hydropower industrial activity. Activity will also be supported by the expected commissioning of a large hydropower plant and increased public investment driven by the country's new national economic plan focused on private sector growth and infrastructure investment. In FY2025/26, growth is forecast to moderate to 6.6 percent as the tourism rebound wanes, though robust electricity production and construction are expected to support growth.

Because of insufficient data, growth forecasts are not produced for Afghanistan. The economy is expected to experience modest expansion, partly supported by moderating inflation. However, unemployment is likely to remain elevated, food insecurity is forecast to be widespread, and per capita income is set to remain stagnant, leading to heightened poverty.

Fiscal policies in the majority of countries in the region are expected to be generally tight over the forecast horizon. In India, fiscal deficits are expected to continue shrinking, largely on account of growing tax revenues. Fiscal adjustment efforts are also projected to continue in other countries, including Maldives, Nepal, Pakistan, and Sri Lanka. In Bhutan, an increase in public investment in FY2024/25 is expected to widen the fiscal deficit, but fiscal consolidation is anticipated to start in the following fiscal year, with rising revenues from the commissioning of the new hydropower plant. However, region-wide fiscal deficits, particularly when India is excluded, are forecast to be stable, mainly reflecting the impact of fiscal adjustments offset by expected increases in interest payments in Pakistan and infrastructure investment in Bangladesh (figure 2.5.2.B). While government debt-to-GDP ratios in the region are expected to decline gradually, they will remain elevated. Debt-servicing costs are projected to remain high in several countries, partly reflecting persistently high borrowing costs.

Inflation in the region is expected to moderate further over the forecast period, especially as exchange rates stabilize in several countries (figure 2.5.2.C). It is projected to remain below or within inflation target ranges in most countries, including India, Nepal, and Sri Lanka. In contrast, inflation in Bangladesh is expected to remain above the target for FY2024/25, partly reflecting the adverse consequences of earlier political turmoil.

Per capita income growth in SAR is forecast to remain resilient at 5.2 percent a year, on average, in 2025-26. Even after India is excluded from the aggregate, the region is expected to see an increase in per capita income growth, from 2.5 percent in 2024 to 3 percent in 2026, with poverty set to decline further over the forecast period (figure 2.5.2.D). However, in Bangladesh, Pakistan, and Sri Lanka, per capita income growth is expected to be weaker in 2025-26 than in the decade preceding the pandemic, implying a slower pace of poverty reduction and, in some countries, a projected slowdown in income catch-up to economies with higher income levels.

Risks

Risks to the outlook remain tilted to the downside. Heightened policy uncertainty, including adverse trade policy shifts in major economies, is a key downside risk. Higher commodity prices could adversely affect growth prospects in the region, given that almost all countries in SAR are commodity importers. Other risks include surges in social unrest, tighter-than-expected monetary policy in response to more persistent inflation, climate-change-related natural disasters, and weaker-than-expected growth in major economies. Among upside risks, stronger-than-expected growth in major trading partners could improve global demand, benefiting activity in the region.

Heightened policy uncertainty, particularly concerning global trade policy, and adverse policy shifts in major trading partners that intensify protectionist measures could reduce export activity. Although recent trade-distorting measures against SAR countries have declined, further intensification of protectionist policies, especially in the United States and Europe, could reduce manufacturing and other industrial goods exports, dampening growth prospects (figure 2.5.3.A). In addition, high economic policy uncertainty outside the region, particularly in the United States, could also damage investor sentiment, raising borrowing costs and reducing investment and activity.

The escalation of armed conflicts, including the conflict in the Middle East, attacks on shipping in the Red Sea, and Russia's invasion of Ukraine, could cause significant disruptions in commodity markets. Prices of food, energy, and other commodities could increase as a result of higher production and trade costs. Since the poor and vulnerable are disproportionately affected by higher food and energy prices, such an increase could cause a surge in food insecurity, poverty, and inequality. Despite a recent moderation in hunger in several countries, including India, food insecurity has worsened since the decade preceding the pandemic in Afghanistan and Pakistan (figure 2.5.3.B).

Elevated social unrest could weigh on productivity and weaken investor confidence, reducing private investment, including foreign investment (World Bank 2024aa). In economies with high unemployment and limited job opportunities, particularly among the youth, adverse impacts of heightened social unrest could be amplified, undermining economic development. Youth unemployment remains elevated in the region, having risen since the pre-pandemic decade in many countries, including Bangladesh, Bhutan, Pakistan, and Sri Lanka, and is generally much higher than for other age groups (figure 2.5.3.C). High youth unemployment is partly associated with increased emigration, especially among skilled workers, because of limited employment opportunities, as seen in Bhutan. In addition, the incidence of political violence has increased in some countries in the region. Estimated economic damages from violent events are enormous in low-income countries, such as Afghanistan (chapter 4).

Government debt levels and debt-service burdens are elevated in the region. More persistent inflation could lead to slower monetary easing,

FIGURE 2.5.3 SAR: Risks

High trade policy uncertainty and increasing trade protection in major trading partners could hurt the region's exports. Food insecurity is widespread in several countries in the region, especially those facing major security threats or experiencing elevated food price inflation. Unemployment rates in SAR are high, particularly among youth, amplifying the risk of social unrest and exacerbating economic vulnerabilities. Countries with elevated government debt and financing needs are more susceptible to adverse changes in global financing conditions.

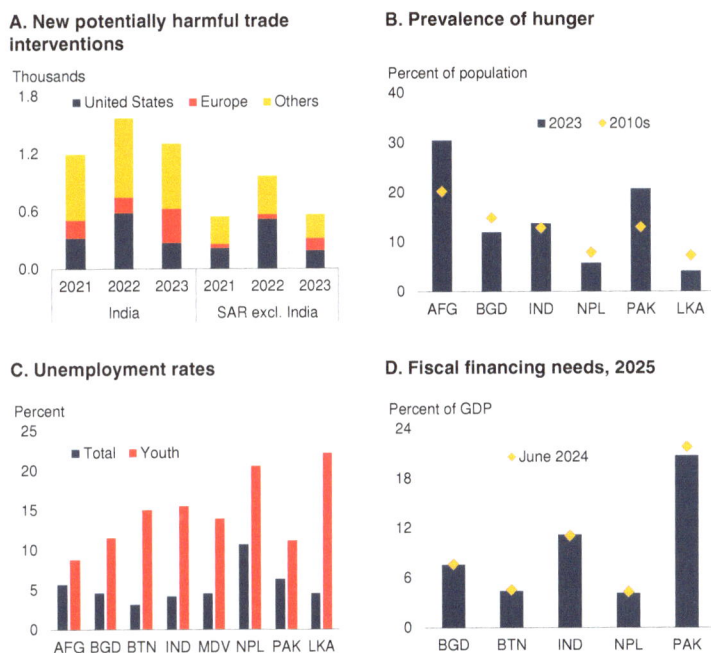

A. New potentially harmful trade interventions

B. Prevalence of hunger

C. Unemployment rates

D. Fiscal financing needs, 2025

Sources: Food and Agriculture Organization; Global Trade Alert (database); International Labour Organization; International Monetary Fund; Kose et al. (2022); World Bank.
Note: AFG = Afghanistan; BGD = Bangladesh; BTN = Bhutan; IND = India; LKA = Sri Lanka; MDV = Maldives; NPL = Nepal; PAK = Pakistan; SAR = South Asia.
A. The number of new trade interventions deemed likely or almost certainly discriminatory—defined as potentially harmful—implemented against India and any other countries in the region, net of interventions removed within the year. Europe includes members of the European Union, the European Free Trade Association, European microstates, the United Kingdom, and their dependent territories. Sample includes eight countries.
B. The share of the population that is undernourished. Data for 2010s refer to averages over 2010-19.
C. Total and youth (aged 15-24) unemployment rates, which are computed by the International Labour Organization with data from the national sources, for the most recent year: 2023 for Bhutan and India; 2022 for Bangladesh and Sri Lanka; 2021 for Afghanistan and Pakistan; 2019 for Maldives; and 2017 for Nepal.
D. Fiscal financing needs are defined as the sum of short-term central government debt and fiscal deficits. For countries where data are reported on a fiscal year basis, the year refers to fiscal year 2024/25. Diamonds for June 2024 refer to data presented in the June 2024 edition of the *Global Economic Prospects* report.

weighing on growth and increasing debt-servicing costs. In many countries, fiscal financing needs are expected to be marginally lower than projected in June 2024, mainly reflecting continued fiscal consolidation efforts (figure 2.5.3.D). However, a weakening of global risk appetite or tightening of global financial conditions could trigger capital outflows, particularly from economies with large fiscal and financial vulnerabilities. In addition, in several countries, including Maldives, Pakistan, and Sri Lanka, delays in implementing policy reforms, including under programs supported by the International Monetary Fund, could worsen investor confidence, causing capital outflows, increasing vulnerabilities, and dampening economic activity. Uncertainty about governments' resolve to maintain fiscal discipline could also damage confidence and increase fiscal and financial pressures, raising borrowing costs for the private sector and the government, with adverse consequences for private investment.

More frequent or more severe extreme weather events could reduce food production, drive up food price inflation, and raise living costs. The region is vulnerable to such events, including heatwaves, floods, and droughts. In addition to climate-change-induced events, other types of natural disasters, such as earthquakes, could cause significant humanitarian losses and damage to infrastructure, reducing output and productivity growth. In countries where the capacity to maintain and reconstruct infrastructure is limited, adverse impacts of natural disasters could be particularly large and long-lived. Maldives is

heavily exposed to the risk of rising sea levels and flooding, and the potential economic cost could be up to 11 percent of GDP by mid-century without sustained reconstruction and adaptation investments (World Bank 2024ab).

In SAR, spillovers from weaker-than-expected growth outside the region would be smaller than those in other regions owing to lower trade openness and limited infrastructure and connectivity (chapter 3). Nevertheless, slower-than-projected growth in major trading partners and the resulting weaker demand could dampen activity, particularly in countries with strong economic ties with Europe and the United States, including Bangladesh, Pakistan, and Sri Lanka. For example, countries in Europe account for about a half of total goods exports in Bangladesh.

An upside risk to the baseline forecast is stronger-than-expected activity in major economies, such as the United States and China. It could stimulate faster growth, particularly in countries with strong trade ties with these economies, such as India, Pakistan, and Sri Lanka. Stronger global demand would also benefit other economies in the region by boosting exports.

TABLE 2.5.1 South Asia forecast summary

(Real GDP growth at market prices in percent, unless indicated otherwise)

Percentage-point differences from June 2024 projections

	2022	2023	2024e	2025f	2026f	2024e	2025f	2026f
EMDE South Asia, GDP[1]	**5.8**	**6.6**	**6.0**	**6.2**	**6.2**	**-0.2**	**0.0**	**0.0**
GDP per capita (U.S. dollars)	4.8	5.6	5.0	5.1	5.2	-0.2	0.0	0.0
(Average including countries that report expenditure components in national accounts)[2]								
EMDE South Asia, GDP[2]	5.8	6.6	6.0	6.2	6.2	-0.2	0.0	0.0
PPP GDP	5.8	6.6	6.0	6.2	6.2	-0.2	0.0	0.0
Private consumption	6.7	4.2	4.8	5.2	5.4	0.5	-0.1	-0.4
Public consumption	5.6	2.8	3.3	5.1	5.6	-1.8	-0.7	-0.3
Fixed investment	7.4	6.9	7.5	7.3	7.4	-1.4	-0.7	0.0
Exports, GNFS	15.8	5.0	5.2	6.3	7.0	2.1	0.0	-0.4
Imports, GNFS	10.7	5.7	4.1	5.0	6.4	-0.5	-1.8	-1.3
Net exports, contribution to growth	0.2	-0.6	-0.1	-0.1	-0.3	0.5	0.5	0.3
Memo items: GDP								

	2022/23	2023/24	2024/25e	2025/26f	2026/27f	2024/25e	2025/26f	2026/27f
India[3]	7.0	8.2	6.5	6.7	6.7	-0.1	0.0	-0.1

	2022	2023	2024e	2025f	2026f	2024e	2025f	2026f
South Asia excluding India	3.3	3.0	3.9	4.0	4.3	0.0	-0.2	-0.1

Source: World Bank.

Note: e = estimate; f = forecast; EMDE = emerging market and developing economy; GNFS = goods and non-factor services; PPP = purchasing power parity. World Bank forecasts are frequently updated based on new information and changing (global) circumstances. Consequently, projections presented here may differ from those contained in other Bank documents, even if basic assessments of countries' prospects do not differ at any given moment in time.

1. GDP and expenditure components are measured in average 2010-19 prices and market exchange rates. Aggregates are presented in calendar year terms. Excludes Afghanistan because of the high degree of uncertainty.

2. Aggregate excludes Afghanistan and Maldives, for which data limitations prevent the forecasting of GDP components.

3. The fiscal year runs from April 1 through March 31.

TABLE 2.5.2 South Asia country forecasts

(Real GDP growth at market prices in percent, unless indicated otherwise)

Percentage-point differences from June 2024 projections

	2022	2023	2024e	2025f	2026f	2024e	2025f	2026f
Calendar year basis								
Afghanistan[1]	-6.2	2.7	..	..	..	..	..	..
Maldives	13.9	4.1	4.7	4.7	4.6	0.0	-0.5	0.5
Sri Lanka	-7.3	-2.3	4.4	3.5	3.1	2.2	1.0	0.1

	2022/23	2023/24	2024/25e	2025/26f	2026/27f	2024/25e	2025/26f	2026/27f
Fiscal year basis[2]								
India	7.0	8.2	6.5	6.7	6.7	-0.1	0.0	-0.1

	2021/22	2022/23	2023/24e	2024/25f	2025/26f	2023/24e	2024/25f	2025/26f
Bangladesh	7.1	5.8	5.0	4.1	5.4	-0.6	-1.6	-0.5
Bhutan	4.8	5.0	5.3	7.2	6.6	0.4	1.5	0.6
Nepal	5.6	2.0	3.9	5.1	5.5	0.6	0.5	0.2
Pakistan[3]	6.2	-0.2	2.5	2.8	3.2	0.7	0.5	0.5

Source: World Bank.

Note: e = estimate; f = forecast. World Bank forecasts are frequently updated based on new information and changing (global) circumstances. Consequently, projections presented here may differ from those contained in other Bank documents, even if basic assessments of countries' prospects do not significantly differ at any given moment in time.

1. Data beyond 2023 are excluded because of a high degree of uncertainty.

2. The fiscal year runs from April 1 through March 31 in India; from July 1 through June 30 in Bangladesh, Bhutan, and Pakistan; and from July 16 through July 15 in Nepal.

3. Data are reported on a factor cost basis.

SUB-SAHARAN AFRICA

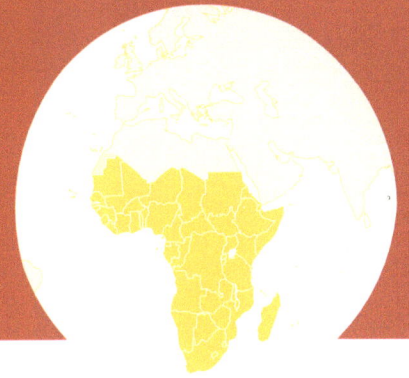

Growth in Sub-Saharan Africa (SSA) is projected to strengthen to an average of 4.2 percent in 2025-26, driven primarily by improvements in the outlook for industrial-commodity-exporting countries, including the region's largest economies. However, high government debt and elevated interest rates have narrowed fiscal space, prompting fiscal consolidation efforts in many countries, while financing needs remain high. Despite the projected pickup in growth, per capita income gains will remain inadequate to make significant progress in reducing extreme poverty in the region. Risks to the outlook remain tilted to the downside. These risks include weaker global growth due to heightened uncertainty and the potential for adverse changes in trade policies; a sharper-than-expected slowdown in China; increased regional or global instability, such as an escalation of conflicts in Sudan and in the Middle East, which could drive up energy and food price inflation in the region; increased risk of government distress amid a possibility of higher-for-longer global interest rates; and greater frequency and intensity of adverse weather events.

Recent developments

Growth in SSA picked up from 2.9 percent in 2023 to an estimated 3.2 percent in 2024. This was 0.3 percentage point lower than projected in June, reflecting the ongoing violent conflict in Sudan as well as various country-specific challenges that weighed on the region's economic recovery last year (figure 2.6.1.A). Growth in the region's two largest economies—Nigeria and South Africa—rose to an average of 2.2 percent in 2024, supported by improved electricity supply in South Africa and higher oil production in Nigeria. In the region's other countries, growth edged up to 4.0 percent.

In Nigeria, growth increased to an estimated 3.3 percent in 2024, mainly driven by services sector activity, particularly in financial and telecommunication services. Macroeconomic and fiscal reforms helped improve business confidence. In response to rising inflation and a weak naira, the central bank tightened monetary policy. Meanwhile, the fiscal deficit narrowed due to a surge in revenues driven by the elimination of the implicit foreign exchange subsidy, following the unification of

the exchange rate and improved revenue administration.

In South Africa, growth edged up in 2024, to an estimated 0.8 percent, supported by improved electricity supply and easing inflation. However, persistent structural constraints—especially transport bottlenecks, inefficient state-owned enterprises, and high crime rates—continued to impede economic activity.

Elsewhere in the region, growth in industrial-commodity-exporting countries, excluding Sudan, eased to 3.6 percent. Declines in energy and metal prices from their 2022 peaks made fiscal consolidation efforts necessary in several industrial-commodity-exporting economies, weighing on growth—especially among metal exporters (Central African Republic, Democratic Republic of Congo, Sierra Leone, Zambia). Contrary to the trend, growth in Angola recovered, driven by increased production of oil—the country's primary export and main source of tax revenue—and stronger services sector growth alongside the stabilization of the exchange rate. In Sudan, violent conflict caused GDP to contract for another year at a double-digit rate. As a result, the growth estimate for the region's metal exporters was revised down sharply.

Note: This section was prepared by Dominik Peschel.

FIGURE 2.6.1 SSA: Recent developments

Growth in SSA picked up in the first half of 2024 but remained subdued overall. Monetary policy interest rates in the region appear to have peaked last year as median inflation continued to abate, despite currency depreciations in several larger economies in 2024.

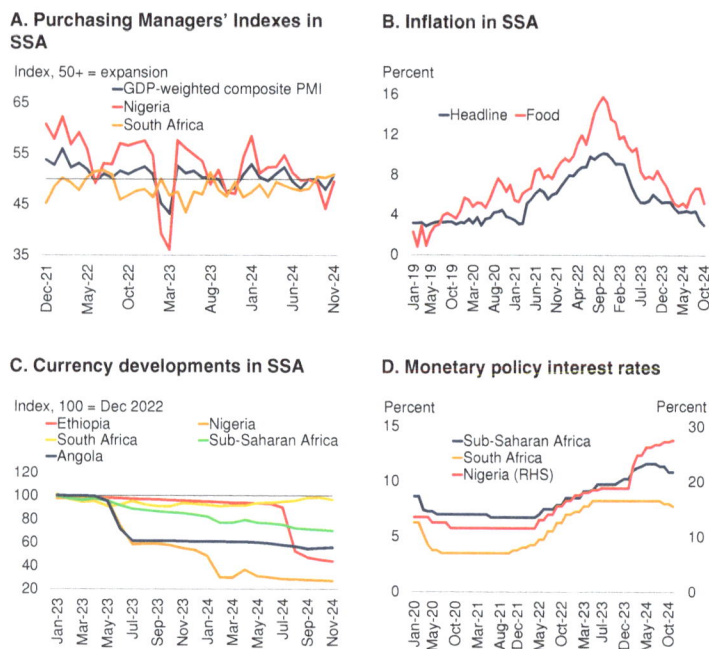

A. Purchasing Managers' Indexes in SSA

B. Inflation in SSA

C. Currency developments in SSA

D. Monetary policy interest rates

Sources: Bloomberg; Haver Analytics; International Monetary Fund; World Bank.
Note: EMDEs = emerging market and developing economies; GDP = gross domestic product; SSA = Sub-Saharan Africa.
A. GDP-weighted average. Sample comprises Ghana, Kenya, Mozambique, Nigeria, South Africa, Uganda, and Zambia. Last observation is November 2024.
B. Change in prices from 12 months earlier. Median for the sample of 20 SSA EMDEs. Last observation is October 2024.
C. U.S. dollars per local currency unit (monthly averages), indexed to 100 = December 2022. Values smaller than 100 indicate depreciation. Sub-Saharan Africa sample comprises 16 economies. Last observation is November 2024.
D. Median for the sample of 14 SSA EMDEs. Last observation is November 2024.

Growth in non-resource-rich countries edged down to 5.5 percent in 2024. This was mainly due to moderating growth in Ethiopia—SSA's largest agricultural commodity producer and its most populous low-income country—reflecting foreign exchange market reforms, including a substantial depreciation of the birr. After a brief uptick in 2023, growth in Kenya eased last year amid ongoing fiscal consolidation. In contrast, growth in Tanzania and Uganda accelerated in 2024, supported by higher private spending and, in the case of Uganda, stronger investment as well.

Consumer price inflation diverged across the region, with the majority of countries experiencing moderate and declining price increases, while food

price inflation remained relatively high (figure 2.6.1.B; World Bank 2024ac). However, sharp price rises persisted in some larger economies—partly reflecting significant currency depreciations (Angola, Ethiopia, Nigeria; figure 2.6.1.C). In countries where inflation has declined, many central banks eased monetary policy rates; however, policy rates were hiked in other cases (figure 2.6.1.D).

Food insecurity remained elevated across the region, partly because of adverse weather events, such as droughts in Southern Africa and floods elsewhere. Violent conflict exacerbated hunger vulnerability, particularly in East Africa. In particular, more than half of the populations of Sudan and South Sudan suffered high levels of acute food insecurity in 2024 (FSIN and GNAFC 2024).

Outlook

Growth in SSA is expected to firm to 4.1 percent in 2025 and 4.3 percent in 2026, as financial conditions ease alongside further declines in inflation (figure 2.6.2.A; table 2.6.1). Following weaker-than-expected regional growth last year, growth projections for 2025 have been revised upward by 0.2 percentage point, and for 2026 by 0.3 percentage point, with improvements seen across various subgroups (figure 2.6.2.B). At the country level, projected growth has been upgraded for nearly half of SSA economies in both 2025 and 2026.

The growth trajectory, however, is expected to be unevenly distributed among SSA economies. Growth rates in the region's largest two economies will continue to lag behind those of the rest of the region, despite projected growth pickups in both countries. Excluding the two largest economies, growth in the region is forecast to strengthen from 4 percent in 2024 to about 5.3 percent in 2025-26. Growth in non-resource-rich economies is projected to accelerate, partly driven by rising growth in Uganda. Meanwhile, growth in industrial-commodity-exporting economies, excluding Sudan, is forecast to recover amid a pickup in services sector growth as household consumption improves.

Against the backdrop of waning inflation, a gradual easing of policy interest rates should bolster private consumption and investment in many SSA economies during the forecast horizon. At the same time, limited fiscal space, resulting from high debt levels and increased borrowing costs, will continue to weigh on government spending across the region. Fiscal balances are expected to continue to improve, though at a moderating pace (World Bank 2024ac). Primary fiscal deficits are, on average, forecast to close over the forecast period, with declining deficits in non-resource-rich countries and increasing surpluses in commodity-exporting countries (figure 2.6.2.C).

Growth in Nigeria is forecast to strengthen to an average of 3.6 percent a year in 2025-26. Following monetary policy tightening in 2024, inflation is projected to gradually decline, boosting consumption and supporting growth in the services sector, which continues to be the main driver of growth. Oil production is expected to increase over the forecast period but remain below the OPEC quota. The baseline forecast implies that per capita income growth will remain weak over the forecast horizon.

Growth in South Africa is projected to rise to an average of 1.9 percent a year in 2025-26, about a half-percentage-point upgrade from the June forecast. Improving energy availability and further reforms in the transport sector are expected to support stronger growth. Household consumption is expected to rebound, supported by lower inflation and interest rates, while growth of private investment may gather momentum amid rising business confidence. Fiscal policy is anticipated to remain prudent, aiming to stabilize the public debt-to-GDP ratio by 2026. This requires the containment of pressures to raise expenditures, such as those related to the government wage bill, support for state-owned enterprises, and unfunded healthcare reforms.

Growth in SSA's resource-rich countries is projected to accelerate in 2025-26. Output in industrial-commodity exporters, excluding the region's two largest economies and Sudan, is forecast to expand by about 4.2 percent in 2025-26, up from 3.6 percent in 2024. This improvement is partly attributable to earlier fiscal

FIGURE 2.6.2 SSA: Outlook

Growth in SSA is forecast to pick up in 2025-26 as industrial-commodity-exporting economies recover, while non-resource-rich countries are expected to expand above their long-term trend. Revisions to the June forecasts are small but widespread. Primary fiscal balances are expected to improve amid continued fiscal consolidation efforts and higher growth. Improvements in income per capita will remain unevenly distributed with modest increases for most LICs.

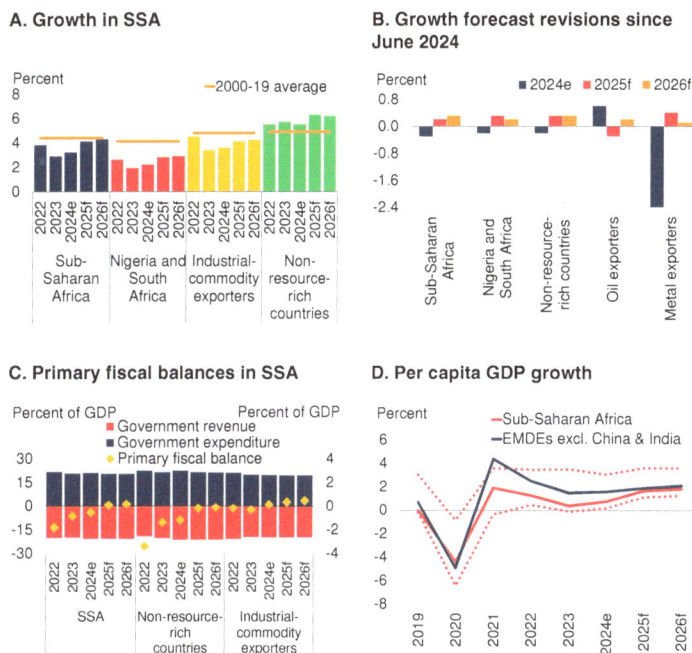

A. Growth in SSA

B. Growth forecast revisions since June 2024

C. Primary fiscal balances in SSA

D. Per capita GDP growth

Sources: International Monetary Fund; World Bank.
Note: e = estimates; f = forecasts; EMDEs = emerging market and developing economies; SSA = Sub-Saharan Africa. Non-resource-rich countries represent agricultural-commodity-exporting and commodity-importing countries.
A. Aggregate growth rates calculated using constant GDP weights at average 2010-19 prices and market exchange rates. Industrial-commodity exporters exclude Nigeria, South Africa, and Sudan.
B. Revisions relative to forecasts published in the June 2024 edition of the *Global Economic Prospects* report.
C. Simple averages of country groupings. Sample includes 47 SSA economies.
D. Dotted lines show the interquartile ranges for 47 SSA economies.

adjustments to lower commodity prices in many of these countries in 2023-24, coupled with expectations of less volatile prices in 2025-26. As inflation moderates further, growth in non-mining sectors, particularly services, is expected to improve, most prominently in Botswana, the Democratic Republic of Congo, Eritrea, and Niger. In Angola, growth is expected to ease in 2025-26 owing to structural constraints, despite an anticipated moderation in inflation.

Growth in non-resource-rich countries is projected to strengthen to an average of 6.3 percent in 2025-26, mainly driven by an oil-related infrastructure boom in Uganda ahead of the start of oil

FIGURE 2.6.3 SSA: Risks

Food insecurity remains a pressing issue, with more than 160 million people in SSA experiencing a food crisis or worse. Levels of violence in SSA remain high, weighing on economic activity. While public debt-to-GDP ratios should gradually decline, debt-service costs are expected to remain elevated, limiting fiscal space in many SSA economies to support the population and invest in growth-enhancing public projects. The share of population affected by adverse weather events, which destroy crops and adversely affect economic activity, has increased sharply in recent years.

A. Food insecurity in SSA

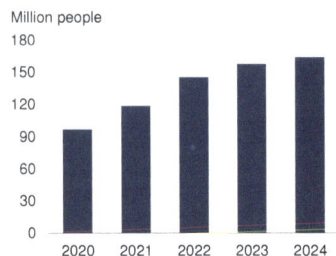

B. Violent events in SSA

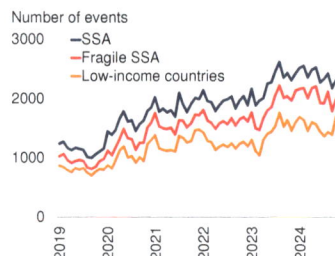

C. Public debt and interest payments in SSA

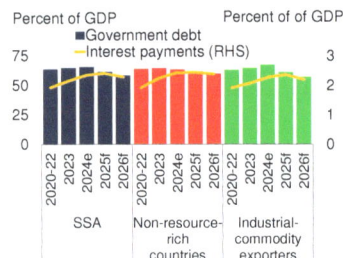

D. Share of population affected by adverse weather events

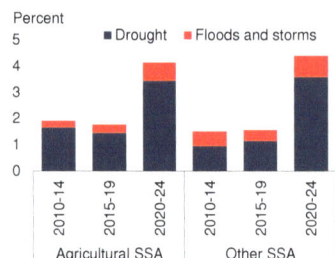

Sources: ACLED (database); EM-DAT (database); GRFC (database); International Monetary Fund; World Bank.
Note: e = estimates; f = forecasts. GDP = gross domestic product; RHS = right-hand scale; SSA = Sub-Saharan Africa.
A. Number of people facing food security crisis and worse. Sample includes at least 32 countries in Sub-Saharan Africa. Acute food insecurity numbers for 2023 and 2024 are estimates.
B. Violent events include battles, explosions, riots, and violence against civilians. Last observation is October 2024.
C. Simple averages of country groupings. Sample includes 45 SSA economies. Non-resource-rich countries represent agricultural-commodity-exporting and commodity-importing countries.
D. Bars indicate percent of population affected. Other SSA refers to non-agriculture-exporting countries. Last observation is December 5, 2024.

production. In Kenya, growth is expected to be boosted by private investment and supported by more accommodative monetary policy. In Tanzania, robust public investment, an improved business environment, and enhanced export competitiveness are anticipated to boost growth.

Per capita income in SSA is projected to expand by an average of 1.7 percent a year in 2025-26, which is below the average growth rate in emerging market and developing economies, even when China and India are excluded (figure 2.6.2.D). Moreover, per capita income growth in

SSA is expected to remain uneven, with incomes expected to decline in some countries. Per capita incomes are forecast to shrink over the forecast horizon in Angola, the Central African Republic, Equatorial Guinea, and Sudan. Even by 2026, GDP per capita in about 30 percent of the region's economies will not have recovered to their pre-pandemic levels. Thus, these economies will have lost several years in advancing per capita incomes and reducing poverty.

Risks

Risks to the outlook are tilted to the downside. Global growth could be weaker than projected on account of heightened uncertainty and the potential for adverse changes in trade policies. Further downside risks include a sharper-than-expected economic slowdown in China; escalating global geopolitical tensions, especially an intensification of the conflict in the Middle East; and worsening political instability and an escalation of violent conflicts in the region, especially in East Africa and the Sahel. Furthermore, more persistent inflation than expected could keep global interest rates elevated, compounding the challenges confronting highly indebted countries, while greater frequency and intensity of adverse weather events could exacerbate poverty in many countries across SSA.

Global growth could fall short of projections. Unexpected adverse changes in trade policies could result in further trade fragmentation, dampening economic activity, particularly in export-oriented EMDEs (chapter 1). New trade restrictions have already surged compared to pre-pandemic levels. An intensification of protectionist measures could lead to further trade barriers and retaliation between trading blocs, adversely affecting economic prospects.

Growth in China could weaken more than expected, with adverse effects on the demand for minerals and metals (chapter 1). Lower prices for these commodities, which are the main exports of several SSA countries—many of them low-income countries—would hit these countries especially hard. Furthermore, slower growth in China could reduce Chinese investment in SSA (Chen, Fornino, and Rawlings 2024).

An escalation of the conflict in the Middle East could exacerbate food insecurity in SSA, especially by disrupting supply chains, leading to less affordable food and an uptick in malnutrition rates in the region (figure 2.6.3.A). Similarly, intensified conflict in Sudan could drive up food prices—at least in parts of SSA—as a result of reduced supply and increased transportation costs. Even without an escalation of these conflicts, food insecurity in SSA is expected to exceed that in other regions of the world over the next decade (Cardell et al. 2024). A further destabilization of East Africa could result in a renewed pickup in violence that would lead to extended humanitarian crises in many of SSA's most economically vulnerable countries (chapter 4; figure 2.6.3.B). Besides the risk of food price inflation from intensifying conflicts, disruptions to global or local trade could also reignite inflation.

If regional or global policy interest rates decline more slowly than expected, there would be adverse effects on debt-service costs and debt dynamics in SSA (figure 2.6.3.C). Similarly, a decrease in global investors' risk appetite could increase debt-service costs. Coping with high debt-service costs is already a challenge, particularly for countries facing reduced donor support and depreciated local currencies. More than half of SSA countries under debt sustainability analysis for low-income countries were in or at high risk of government debt distress at the end of September 2024 (IMF 2024). Given the limited access to external financing at favorable interest rates for many economies in the region, higher-for-longer global interest rates could heighten the risk of government debt distress.

The SSA region remains highly vulnerable to extreme weather events linked partly to climate change (figure 2.6.3.D). An increase in the frequency or severity of droughts or floods would tend to exacerbate poverty in many countries across SSA. In the longer term, climate-change-induced increases in average temperatures could hurt crop yields across the region, reducing food supplies as well as exports.

TABLE 2.6.1 Sub-Saharan Africa forecast summary

(Real GDP growth at market prices in percent, unless indicated otherwise)

Percentage-point differences from June 2024 projections

	2022	2023	2024e	2025f	2026f	2024e	2025f	2026f
EMDE SSA, GDP [1]	3.8	2.9	3.2	4.1	4.3	-0.3	0.2	0.3
GDP per capita (U.S. dollars)	1.2	0.4	0.7	1.6	1.8	-0.4	0.2	0.2
(Average including countries that report expenditure components in national accounts) [2]								
EMDE SSA, GDP [2,3]	4.0	2.8	3.2	4.3	4.4	-0.4	0.3	0.3
PPP GDP	4.0	2.5	3.1	4.5	4.6	-0.6	0.4	0.3
Private consumption	3.6	2.7	2.9	3.8	4.0	-0.6	0.1	0.2
Public consumption	2.3	-0.2	2.3	2.3	2.0	0.3	0.5	0.4
Fixed investment	10.2	5.3	5.9	6.4	7.0	0.9	0.0	0.4
Exports, GNFS [4]	11.0	3.3	5.0	6.1	5.8	-0.3	1.2	0.6
Imports, GNFS [4]	15.3	3.7	4.4	5.6	5.5	-1.1	0.5	0.2
Net exports, contribution to growth	-1.8	-0.3	-0.1	-0.2	-0.2	0.2	0.1	0.1
Memo items: GDP								
Eastern and Southern Africa	3.8	2.5	2.6	4.1	4.2	-0.8	0.4	0.3
Western and Central Africa	3.8	3.3	4.0	4.2	4.3	0.2	0.1	0.1
SSA excluding Nigeria and South Africa	4.8	3.7	4.0	5.2	5.3	-0.5	0.2	0.2
Oil exporters [5]	3.2	2.5	3.4	3.4	3.7	0.3	0.0	0.1
CFA countries [6]	4.6	3.9	4.9	5.1	4.9	0.1	0.0	0.2
CEMAC	3.1	1.9	3.4	2.4	3.2	0.9	-0.4	0.2
WAEMU	5.4	5.0	5.7	6.6	5.8	-0.3	0.3	0.1
SSA2	2.6	1.9	2.2	2.8	2.9	-0.2	0.3	0.2
Nigeria	3.3	2.9	3.3	3.5	3.7	0.0	0.0	0.0
South Africa	1.9	0.7	0.8	1.8	1.9	-0.4	0.5	0.4

Source: World Bank.

Note: e = estimate; f = forecast; PPP = purchasing power parity; EMDE = emerging market and developing economy. World Bank forecasts are frequently updated based on new information and changing (global) circumstances. Consequently, projections presented here may differ from those contained in other World Bank documents, even if basic assessments of countries' prospects do not differ at any given moment in time.

1. GDP and expenditure components are measured in average 2010-19 prices and market exchange rates.

2. Subregion aggregate excludes the Central African Republic, Eritrea, Guinea, Nigeria, São Tomé and Príncipe, Somalia, and South Sudan, for which data limitations prevent the forecasting of GDP components.

3. Subregion growth rates may differ from the most recent edition of Africa's Pulse (https://www.worldbank.org/en/publication/africa-pulse) because of data revisions.

4. Exports and imports of goods and nonfactor services (GNFS).

5. Includes Angola, Cameroon, Chad, the Republic of Congo, Equatorial Guinea, Gabon, Ghana, Nigeria, and South Sudan.

6. The African Financial Community (CFA) franc zone consists of 14 countries in Sub-Saharan Africa, each affiliated with one of two monetary unions. The Central African Economic and Monetary Union (CEMAC) comprises Cameroon, the Central African Republic, Chad, the Republic of Congo, Equatorial Guinea, and Gabon; the West African Economic and Monetary Union (WAEMU) comprises Benin, Burkina Faso, Côte d'Ivoire, Guinea-Bissau, Mali, Niger, Senegal, and Togo.

TABLE 2.6.2 Sub-Saharan Africa country forecasts[1]

(Real GDP growth at market prices in percent, unless indicated otherwise)

Percentage-point differences from June 2024 projections

	2022	2023	2024e	2025f	2026f	2024e	2025f	2026f
Angola	3.0	1.0	3.2	2.9	2.9	0.3	0.3	0.5
Benin	6.3	6.4	6.3	6.4	6.3	0.3	0.4	0.3
Botswana	5.6	2.7	1.0	5.3	4.9	-2.5	1.0	0.9
Burkina Faso	1.5	3.0	3.7	3.9	4.1	0.0	0.1	-0.1
Burundi	1.8	2.7	2.2	3.5	4.2	-1.6	-0.9	-0.6
Central African Republic	0.5	0.7	0.7	1.1	2.0	-0.6	-0.6	0.1
Cabo Verde	17.4	5.1	5.2	4.9	4.8	0.5	0.2	0.2
Cameroon	3.6	3.3	3.7	4.0	4.2	-0.2	-0.2	-0.3
Chad	2.8	4.2	3.0	2.1	3.5	0.3	-1.2	0.6
Comoros	2.8	3.0	3.5	4.0	4.3	0.2	0.0	0.0
Congo, Dem. Rep.	8.9	8.4	4.9	5.0	4.6	-1.1	-0.9	-1.1
Congo, Rep.	1.5	1.9	2.1	3.5	3.3	-1.4	-0.2	0.1
Côte d'Ivoire	6.2	6.2	6.5	6.4	6.6	0.1	0.0	0.3
Equatorial Guinea	3.7	-5.7	4.7	-4.4	-0.8	9.0	-1.1	2.8
Eritrea	2.5	2.6	2.8	3.0	3.3	0.0	0.0	0.0
Eswatini	0.5	4.8	4.6	3.5	2.9	0.5	0.2	0.2
Ethiopia[2]	6.4	7.2	6.1	6.5	7.1	-0.9	-0.5	0.1
Gabon	3.1	2.4	3.1	2.4	3.0	0.1	0.1	0.2
Gambia, The	4.9	5.3	5.6	5.8	5.4	0.1	0.0	0.0
Ghana	3.8	2.9	4.0	4.2	4.9	1.1	-0.2	0.0
Guinea	4.0	6.7	5.3	6.0	6.4	0.4	-0.2	-0.1
Guinea-Bissau	4.2	5.2	5.0	5.0	5.0	0.3	0.2	0.1
Kenya	4.9	5.6	4.7	5.0	5.1	-0.3	-0.3	-0.2
Lesotho	1.3	0.9	2.5	2.3	2.0	0.3	-0.2	-0.3
Liberia	4.8	4.7	5.3	5.7	5.8	0.0	-0.5	-0.5
Madagascar	4.0	3.8	4.5	4.6	4.7	0.0	0.0	0.0
Malawi	0.9	1.6	1.8	4.2	3.3	-0.2	0.3	-0.8
Mali	3.5	3.5	3.7	4.0	4.5	0.6	0.5	0.0
Mauritania	6.8	6.5	6.5	7.8	7.5	2.7	3.3	1.2
Mauritius	8.9	7.0	5.6	4.4	3.8	0.6	0.3	-0.1
Mozambique	4.4	5.4	4.0	4.0	4.0	-1.0	-1.0	-0.4
Namibia	5.3	4.2	3.1	3.7	3.9	-0.3	0.1	0.1
Niger	11.5	2.0	5.7	8.5	4.6	-3.4	2.3	-0.5
Nigeria	3.3	2.9	3.3	3.5	3.7	0.0	0.0	0.0
Rwanda	8.2	8.2	7.6	7.8	7.5	0.0	0.0	0.0
São Tomé and Príncipe	0.2	0.4	1.1	3.3	3.6	-1.4	0.2	0.0
Senegal	3.8	4.6	6.1	9.7	6.0	-1.0	0.0	0.3
Seychelles	14.9	3.2	3.7	4.1	3.5	0.2	0.7	0.1
Sierra Leone	5.3	5.7	4.3	4.7	4.7	0.8	0.7	0.4
Somalia	2.7	4.2	4.4	4.5	4.5	0.7	0.6	0.5
South Africa	1.9	0.7	0.8	1.8	1.9	-0.4	0.5	0.4
Sudan	-1.0	-20.1	-15.1	1.3	2.9	-11.6	2.0	1.7
South Sudan[2]	-2.3	-1.3	-7.8	-11.4	6.1	-9.8	-15.2	2.1
Tanzania	4.6	5.1	5.4	5.8	6.2	0.0	0.0	0.0
Togo	5.8	6.4	5.3	5.4	5.8	0.2	0.0	0.2
Uganda[2]	4.7	5.3	6.0	6.2	10.8	0.0	0.0	4.2
Zambia	5.2	5.4	1.2	6.2	6.6	-1.5	0.1	0.7
Zimbabwe	6.1	5.3	2.0	6.2	4.8	-1.3	2.6	1.3

Source: World Bank.

Note: e = estimate; f = forecast. World Bank forecasts are frequently updated based on new information and changing (global) circumstances. Consequently, projections presented here may differ from those contained in other Bank documents, even if basic assessments of countries' prospects do not significantly differ at any given moment in time.

1. Data are based on GDP measured in average 2010-19 prices and market exchange rates.

2. Fiscal-year-based numbers.

References

ACLED (Armed Conflict Location & Event Data Project) database. Accessed on December 18, 2024. https://acleddata.com/data-export-tool/.

Arzoumanian, S. 2023. "Spillovers from Russia to Neighboring Countries: Transmission Channels and Policy Options." IMF Working Paper 23/185, International Monetary Fund, Washington, DC.

Cai, W., G. Wang, A. Santoso, M. J. McPhaden, L. Wu, F. Jin, A. Timmermann, et al. 2015. "Increased Frequency of Extreme La Niña Events under Greenhouse Warming." *Nature Climate Change* 5 (2): 132-37.

Cardell, L., Y. Zereyesus, K. Ajewole, J. Farris, M. Johnson, J. Lin, C. Valdes, and W. Zeng. 2024. *International Food Security Assessment, 2024-34.* Washington, DC: U.S. Department of Agriculture, Economic Research Service.

Chattha, M. K., H. Youssef, O. Ftomova, A. N. Maseeh, X. Wang, Ž. Bogetic, D. Naeher, C. Borja-Vega, and A. Ghosheh. 2024. "Gulf Economic Update: Navigating the Water Challenge in the GCC—Paths to Sustainable Solutions." December. World Bank, Washington, DC.

Chen, W., M. Fornino, and H. Rawlings. 2024. "Navigating the Evolving Landscape of China and Africa's Economic Engagements." IMF Working Paper 24/37, International Monetary Fund, Washington, DC.

EM-DAT (The International Disaster Database) database. Centre for Research on the Epidemiology of Disasters (CRED), UCLouvain, Brussels. Accessed on December 18, 2024. https://emdat.be.

European Court of Auditors. 2024. "Special Report 13/2024: Absorption of Funds from the Recovery and Resilience Facility – Progressing with Delays and Risks Remain Regarding the Completion of Measures and Therefore the Achievement of RRF Objectives." Report. September. European Court of Auditors.

Falagiarda, M. 2024. "Inflation in the Eastern Euro Area: Reasons and Risks." *The EC Blog* (blog). January 10, 2024. https://ecb.europa.eu/press/blog/date/2024/html/ecb.blog240110~4901f29da7.en.html.

FSIN (Food Security Information Network) and GNAFC (Global Network Against Food Crises). 2024. *Global Report on Food Crises 2024 Mid-Year Update.* Rome: Food Security Information Network and Global Network Against Food Crises.

GRFC (Global Report on Food Crisis) database. Accessed on December 20, 2024. https://fsinplatform.org/our-data.

Gatti, R., J. Torres, N. Elmallakh, G. Mele, D. Faures, M. E. Mousa, and I. Suvanov. 2024. *Growth in the Middle East and North Africa.* MENA Economic Update, October. Washington, DC: World Bank.

Global Trade Alert (database). Accessed on December 18, 2024. https://globaltradealert.org.

IEA (International Energy Agency). 2024. "Oil Market Report." December. International Energy Agency, Paris.

IMF (International Monetary Fund). 2024. "List of LIC DSAs for PRGT Eligible Countries (as of October 31, 2024)." International Monetary Fund, Washington, DC.

Kazemi, M., R. Zahedi, E. Osman, and E. W. Knippenberg. 2024. "Iran Economic Monitor: Sustaining Growth amid Rising Geopolitical Tensions." Spring. World Bank, Washington, DC.

Kose, M. A., S. Kurlat, F. Ohnsorge, and N. Sugawara. 2022. "A Cross-Country Database of Fiscal Space." *Journal of International Money and Finance* 128 (November): 102682.

Kose, M. A., and F. Ohnsorge, eds. 2023. *Falling Long-Term Growth Prospects: Trends, Expectations, and Policies.* Washington, DC: World Bank.

Wang, B., X. Luo, Y. Yang, W. Sun, M. A. Cane, W. Cai, S. Yeh, and J. Liu. 2019. "Historical Change of El Niño Properties Sheds Light on Future Changes of Extreme El Niño." *Proceedings of the National Academy of Sciences* 116 (45): 22512-17.

World Bank. 2024a. *Diminishing Growth amid Global Uncertainty: Ramping up Investment in the Pacific.* Pacific Economic Update. October. Washington, DC: World Bank.

World Bank. 2024b. *Jobs and Technology.* East Asia and Pacific Economic Update. October. Washington, DC: World Bank.

World Bank. 2024c. *Growing Beyond Property: Cyclical Lifts and Structural Challenges.* China Economic Update. June. Washington, DC: World Bank.

World Bank. 2024d. *Commodity Markets Outlook.* October. Washington, DC: World Bank.

World Bank. 2024e. *Livelihoods Under Threat.* Myanmar Economic Monitor. June. Washington, DC: World Bank.

World Bank. 2024f. *Global Economic Prospects.* June. Washington, DC: World Bank.

World Bank. 2024g. "Remittances Slowed in 2023, Expected to Grow Faster in 2024." Migration and Development Brief 40, World Bank, Washington, DC.

World Bank. 2024h. "Retaining the Growth Momentum." Western Balkans Regular Economic Report 26. October. World Bank, Washington, DC.

World Bank. 2024i. "Better Education for Stronger Growth." Europe and Central Asia Economic Update. October. World Bank, Washington, DC.

World Bank. 2024j. *Poverty, Prosperity, and Planet Report 2024: Pathways Out of the Polycrisis.* Washington, DC: World Bank.

World Bank. 2024k. *Competition: The Missing Ingredient for Growth?* Washington, DC: World Bank.

World Bank. 2024l. "Lebanon Interim Damage and Loss Assessment (DaLA)." November. World Bank, Washington, DC.

World Bank. 2024m. "Algeria Economic Update: A Holistic Framework for Sustained Export Growth." Fall. World Bank, Washington, DC.

World Bank. 2024n. "Impacts of the Conflict in the Middle East on the Palestinian Economy." December. World Bank, Washington, DC.

World Bank. 2024o. "Jordan Economic Monitor: Strength amidst Strain: Jordan's Economic Resilience." Summer. World Bank, Washington, DC.

World Bank. 2024p. "Tunisia Economic Monitor: Equity and Efficiency of Tunisia Tax System." Fall. World Bank, Washington, DC.

World Bank. 2024q. "Yemen Economic Monitor: Confronting Escalating Challenges." Fall. World Bank, Washington, DC.

World Bank. 2024r. "Djibouti Economic Monitor: Strengthening the Sustainability and Equity of Public Finances." Fall. World Bank, Washington, DC.

World Bank. 2024s. "Morocco Economic Monitor: Unlocking the Potential of the Private Sector to Spur Growth and Job Creation." Summer. World Bank, Washington, DC.

World Bank. 2024t. "Republic of Djibouti Country Climate and Development Report." November. World Bank, Washington, DC.

World Bank. 2024u. "India Development Update: India's Trade Opportunities in a Changing Global Context." September. World Bank, Washington, DC.

World Bank. 2024v. "Bangladesh Development Update." October. World Bank, Washington, DC.

World Bank. 2024w. "Pakistan Development Update: The Dynamics of Power Sector Distribution Reforms." October. World Bank, Washington, DC.

World Bank. 2024x. "Sri Lanka Development Update: Opening Up to the Future." October. World Bank, Washington, DC.

World Bank. 2024y. "Maldives Development Update: Seeking Stability in Turbulent Times." October. World Bank, Washington, DC.

World Bank. 2024z. "Nepal Development Update: International Migration and Well-being in Nepal." October. World Bank, Washington, DC.

World Bank. 2024aa. *South Asia Development Update: Women, Jobs, and Growth.* October. Washington, DC: World Bank.

World Bank. 2024ab. "Maldives Country Climate and Development Report." June. World Bank, Washington, DC.

World Bank 2024ac. *Africa's Pulse.* Volume 30. World Bank, Washington, DC.

CHAPTER 3

FROM TAILWINDS TO HEADWINDS

Emerging and Developing Economies in the Twenty-First Century

The first quarter of the twenty-first century has been transformative for emerging market and developing economies (EMDEs). These economies now account for about 45 percent of global GDP, up from about 25 percent in 2000, a trend driven by robust collective growth in the three largest EMDEs—China, India, and Brazil (the EM3). Collectively, EMDEs have contributed about 60 percent of annual global growth since 2000, on average, double the share during the 1990s. Their ascendance was powered by swift global trade and financial integration, especially during the first decade of the century. Interdependence among these economies has also increased markedly. Today, nearly half of goods exports from EMDEs go to other EMDEs, compared to one-quarter in 2000. As cross-border linkages have strengthened, business cycles among EMDEs and between EMDEs and advanced economies have become more synchronized, and a distinct EMDE business cycle has emerged. Cross-border business cycle spillovers from the EM3 to other EMDEs are sizable, at about half of the magnitude of spillovers from the largest advanced economies (the United States, the euro area, and Japan). Yet EMDEs confront a host of headwinds at the turn of the second quarter of the century. Progress implementing structural reforms in many of these economies has stalled. Globally, protectionist measures and geopolitical fragmentation have risen sharply. High debt burdens, demographic shifts, and the rising costs of climate change weigh on economic prospects. A successful policy approach to accelerate growth and development should focus on boosting investment and productivity, navigating a difficult external environment, and enhancing macroeconomic stability.

Introduction

The period around the turn of the twenty-first century was pivotal for development in many emerging market and developing economies (EMDEs).[1] A broad policy consensus on the benefits of integration into the global economy fueled rapid growth in cross-border trade and financial flows, while domestic structural reforms set the stage for growth.[2] The establishment of the World Trade Organization (WTO) in 1995 helped facilitate much greater market access for these economies, while a sharp reduction in tariffs embedded in trade agreements, as well as technological advances in communications and transportation, lowered the costs of international trade (World Bank 2002). Many EMDEs liberalized their domestic financial sectors and reduced restrictions on international financial

flows during this period. Many EMDEs also undertook reforms to strengthen monetary and fiscal policy frameworks and to improve the functioning of domestic markets.

During the 2000s, EMDEs registered annual growth of 5.9 percent, on average, as they benefited from expanded participation in global supply chains, increased capital inflows, and robust demand for commodities. This was their best growth performance since the 1970s, when growth averaged 6.1 percent. Many EMDEs weathered the 2009 global recession well because they were able to draw on sizable policy buffers accumulated during the pre-recession period of strong growth (Kose and Ohnsorge 2020).

With the winds of international integration and domestic reforms at their backs, the role of EMDEs in the global economy expanded markedly during the first quarter of the twenty-first century. In 2000, EMDEs accounted for about 25 percent of global GDP, in contrast with about 85 percent of the world's population. In 2024, EMDEs account for nearly 45 percent of global GDP and essentially the same share of the population (figure 3.1.A).[3] EMDEs contributed almost 60 percent of global output growth, on

---

Note: This chapter was prepared by a team led by Mirco Balatti, M. Ayhan Kose, and Dana Vorisek. The team included Kate McKinnon, Edoardo Palombo, Naotaka Sugawara, and Guillermo Verduzco-Bustos, with contributions from Amat Adarov, Tommy Chrimes, Alen Mulabdic, Hayley Pallan, Shijie Shi, and Kersten Stamm.

[1] This chapter covers all EMDEs, with a particular focus on middle-income EMDEs. Chapter 4 of this edition of the *Global Economic Prospects* presents a comprehensive assessment of the performance of low-income countries in the twenty-first century and their prospects and policy priorities.

[2] For discussions on the impact of international financial integration, structural reforms, and policy to enhance macroeconomic stability in EMDEs, see Chari, Blair, and Reyes (2021); Kose et al. (2009); Obstfeld (2009); and Rodrik and Subramanian (2009).

[3] GDP is measured at average 2010-19 prices and market exchange rates. EMDEs account for larger shares of global output and growth when GDP at purchasing power parity (PPP) is used. In 2024, in PPP terms, EMDEs accounted for about 60 percent of global GDP, compared to 40 percent in 2000.

FIGURE 3.1 EMDEs' contribution to global output and growth

EMDEs have accounted for a growing share of global output over the past 25 years Their contribution to global growth increased from about one-quarter in the 1990s to about three-fifths in the 2000s, 2010s, and 2020s.

A. Shares of global GDP

B. Shares of global GDP growth

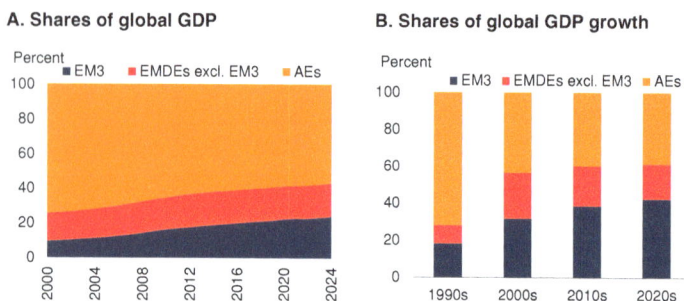

Source: World Bank.
Note: AEs = advanced economies; EM3 = China, India, and Brazil; EMDEs = emerging market and developing economies. Gross domestic product (GDP) is measured in average 2010-19 prices and market exchange rates. Sample includes 154 EMDEs and 38 advanced economies. EMDEs and advanced economies are defined in table 1.2.
A. Data for all economies in 2024 are estimates.
B. Bars show the average contributions to annual growth. Data for the 2020s includes 2020-24.

average, during 2000-24, compared to 30 percent in the 1990s (figure 3.1.B). They have accounted for steadily growing shares of trade flows, investment flows, and commodity demand and supply since 2000. Since 2010, each of the three largest EMDEs (EM3)—China, India, and Brazil—have been among the 10 largest economies in the world.

Today, however, EMDEs face daunting headwinds—both global and domestic. Compared to its pace in the early part of the twenty-first century, cross-border integration has slowed, with trade growth falling and the ratio of foreign direct investment (FDI) inflows to EMDEs declining. Integration through global value chains (GVCs) peaked in the late 2000s (Caldara et al. 2020; Constantinescu et al. 2020; Freund et al. 2024). In more recent years, trade and investment policy fragmentation and a rise in protectionism among major economies have complicated policy making.

Following a decade of remarkable expansion at the dawn of the century, EMDEs have since encountered subdued growth and a significant drop in long-term growth projections. As of 2025, EMDEs face the lowest five-year-ahead potential growth rate since 2000. Fiscal space in many EMDEs narrowed, in part because of the increase in government spending to mitigate the damage

associated with the overlapping crises of the past five years (World Bank 2021a, 2024a). Progress implementing structural reforms has stalled, with little improvement in the quality of institutional environments in the majority of these economies since the 2000s. Climate-related disasters have become more frequent and costly, adversely affecting economic activity and straining limited fiscal resources in some cases. In many EMDEs in two regions, East Asia and Pacific (EAP) and Europe and Central Asia (ECA), population aging is already limiting long-term growth prospects.

Against this backdrop, this chapter first analyzes EMDEs' progress during the first quarter of the twenty-first century. In particular, it reviews EMDEs' integration into the global economy and studies business cycle linkages among EMDEs and between EMDEs and the rest of the global economy. This analysis is critical given the seismic changes in EMDEs' integration into the global economy and business cycles linkages during this period. The chapter then systematically examines the main challenges confronting these economies. Finally, it utilizes the lessons from their progress and challenges to offer a menu of policies that EMDEs can use to overcome the headwinds they face. Specifically, the chapter addresses the following questions:

- How has EMDEs' integration into the global economy evolved during the first quarter of the twenty-first century?

- How have business cycle linkages between EMDEs and the rest of the global economy changed during this period?

- What are the main economic challenges facing EMDEs?

- What are the key policy interventions EMDEs need to undertake to boost productivity and investment, navigate a difficult external environment, and improve macroeconomic stability?

The chapter makes the following contributions to the literature:

- *Evolution of EMDEs' integration into the global economy.* The chapter traces how EMDEs' footprint in the global economy has changed over the past 25 years and documents how these economies have become much more integrated into the global economy through multiple channels, including trade, commodity markets, and finance. It also reviews how the global economic landscape has shifted during this period.

- *Business cycle synchronization.* The chapter studies how business cycle synchronization among EMDEs and between EMDEs and advanced economies has changed during the first quarter of the twenty-first century. Linkages are estimated by employing a model that decomposes the sources of business cycle fluctuations into global, group-specific, and idiosyncratic (economy-level) forces.

- *Spillovers from EMDEs.* The chapter estimates spillovers from growth shocks in the three largest EMDEs, the EM3 (China, India, and Brazil), and compares these to the magnitude of spillovers from the three largest advanced economies, the AE3 (the United States, the euro area, and Japan). Similar analysis compares the magnitude of spillovers from China, the largest EMDE, to those from the United States, the largest advanced economy. This analysis uses a large and diverse country sample covering the first quarter of the century, including the deep global recession of 2020 and its aftermath.

- *Challenges and policy priorities.* In light of the insights from their experience with respect to international integration and business cycle linkages, the chapter presents a systematic assessment of the main challenges confronting EMDEs. It then reviews policies that can best help these economies navigate the challenges they face as they enter the second quarter of this century. Specifically, it provides guidance on how EMDEs can pursue a broad agenda to improve their growth prospects through structural reforms; navigate the difficult external environment through changes in trade and investment policy; and enhance macroeconomic stability through improvements in fiscal, monetary, and financial sector policy.

The chapter presents the following key findings.

The role of EMDEs in the global economy has grown substantially during the first quarter of the twenty-first century. They accounted for almost 45 percent of global GDP in 2024, up from about 25 percent in 2000, and have contributed most of global growth in since 2000. EMDEs' growing share of the global economy has been powered by the EM3: they produced about 25 percent of global GDP in 2024, compared to 10 percent in 2000. EMDEs accounted for about 35 percent of global trade in 2023, versus about 20 percent in 2000. Together, the EM3 were responsible for two-fifths of EMDE trade in 2023. Increasingly, EMDEs are trading with each other. As of 2023, more than 45 percent of goods exports from EMDEs go to other EMDEs, compared to about 25 percent in 2000. EMDEs received 21 percent of global capital inflows during 2019-23, compared to just 6 percent during 2000-04. They have outstripped advanced economies' demand for primary energy since 2004 and for metals since 2007. China alone accounts for 60 percent of global metals demand, versus 13 percent in 2000.

Business cycle synchronization among EMDEs has risen during the past quarter century. Multiple measures suggest that the synchronization of business cycles among EMDEs increased sharply from the 1990s to the 2000s, and further strengthened in the subsequent decade and a half. The degree of synchronization between EMDEs and advanced economies has also increased since the 1990s. During the 2010s, an EMDE-specific factor, which captures common business cycle movements in these economies, accounted for about one-quarter of business cycle variation in EMDEs, more than twice as much as in the 2000s, suggesting that a more distinct EMDE-wide business cycle has emerged. By contrast, in advanced economies, the contribution of the advanced-economy-specific factor was mostly stable during the first two decades of this century.

Growth spillovers from the EM3 to other EMDEs have increased, but spillovers from the AE3 remain considerably larger. In the period 2000-23, a one-time increase in GDP growth in the EM3 of 1 percentage point is associated with a

GDP expansion in other EMDEs of 0.3 percent on impact and a cumulative increase of nearly 2 percent after three years. In contrast, a one-time 1-percentage-point increase in growth in the AE3 yields a 0.8 percent GDP expansion in other EMDEs on impact and a cumulative increase of 4 percent after three years. Global GDP expands by nearly 1 percent, cumulatively, after three years following a one-time 1-percentage- point increase in growth in the EM3, compared to a 3 percent cumulative expansion following a 1-percentage-point growth acceleration in the AE3. Growth spillovers from the EM3 to other EMDEs have become larger over time, with the cumulative effect on output after three years of a 1-percentage-point increase in EM3 annual growth rising from near zero in 1971-2001 to 1.5 percent in 1993-2023.

EMDEs confront a host of global and domestic challenges as they enter the second quarter of the twenty-first century. Growth in EMDEs has declined along with an overall slowdown in the global economy. Growth in these economies averaged 3.5 percent per year during 2020-24, compared to 5.1 percent during 2010-19 and 5.9 percent during 2000-09. Trends in productivity, investment, and labor supply, among the fundamental drivers of growth, suggest that EMDEs' potential growth will slow to about 4 percent in the 2020s, on average, compared to more than 5 percent in the 2010s and nearly 6 percent in the 2000s. The slowdown in growth has coincided with a record increase in government debt and a greater cost of debt service since the early 2010s, reinforced by the overlapping shocks that have buffeted the global economy since 2020. Government debt in EMDEs has surged since the early 2010s, reaching 70 percent in 2024, the highest level since 1970. Despite a rise in government expenditures in EMDEs as a share of GDP since the 2000s, on average, there has been no accompanying rise in government revenues.

The pace of EMDEs' integration into the global economy has slowed since the 2000s, and various other headwinds have also started to weigh on growth prospects. Global trade growth weakened in the 2010s compared to the 2000s, while the expansion of GVCs has leveled off. The slowdown in trade has been experienced by the majority of EMDEs. The decline in the pace of integration is attributable partly to increasing trade restrictions and geopolitical fragmentation, particularly in recent years (Fernández-Villaverde, Mineyama, and Song 2024). In 2023, the number of global trade restrictions reached the highest level on record since 2009. FDI inflows to EMDEs have averaged 1.8 percent of GDP in the 2020s, down from 3.1 percent in the 2000s. Many EMDEs have been negatively affected, either directly or indirectly, by trade tensions between major economies (Amiti, Redding, and Weinstein 2019; IMF 2019a). In addition, rapid sectoral transitions, climate change, and demographic shifts weigh on growth prospects in many EMDEs. The impact of multiple challenges facing EMDEs is amplified due to their interconnected nature. For instance, the stagnation in structural and institutional reforms has played a role in the growth slowdown. Similarly, the increase in trade and investment restrictions has hindered cross-border integration, further exacerbating the impact of other challenges.

Given these challenges, EMDEs need to prioritize boosting investment and productivity, navigating a difficult external environment, and improving macroeconomic stability. While policies should be tailored to each country's circumstances, three equally important themes dominate the policy agendas needed across these economies.

- EMDEs need to improve sustainable growth prospects by reinvigorating key policy reforms. These reforms can accelerate investment and productivity growth by improving the institutional and business environment, human capital development, and digital transformation.

- In the increasingly difficult international economic environment shaped by slowing integration and trade tensions between major economies, EMDEs need to adopt a comprehensive set of policies to mitigate the adverse effects of fragmentation and protectionist measures while seeking ways to take advantage of untapped opportunities for cross-border cooperation.

- EMDEs need to enhance macroeconomic stability by implementing well-designed, credible policy frameworks and putting in place sufficient buffers against shocks. With the bulwarks established by these policies, EMDEs will be less vulnerable to external shocks and are more likely to be able to use countercyclical policy when needed.

The list of necessary policy interventions may appear extensive, but the significant synergies among these policies can help address multiple challenges. Structural policies to reverse the growth slowdown, such as human capital development and business environment improvements, help EMDEs better withstand external shocks. Enhanced macroeconomic stability paves the way for effective structural reforms. Policy makers in EMDEs have a rich set of policy tools to address their economic challenges and will often need to use a combination of approaches.

EMDEs' integration into the global economy

EMDEs have become far more deeply connected economically, both among themselves and with advanced economies, since 2000. In aggregate, EMDEs are key export markets, major contributors to global commodity supply and demand, and, increasingly, significant sources of FDI and remittances for other EMDEs. EMDEs' integration into GVCs has also grown substantially. In some cases, geographic proximity has promoted trade and financial linkages among EMDEs, although considerable diversity remains in the nature and extent of regional integration (box 3.1).

The EM3 have played a major role in expanding the global footprint and influence of EMDEs: China, as the largest EMDE and a key driver of global growth in the past quarter century; India, as the fastest-growing large economy in recent years; and Brazil, as the leading exporter of agricultural products. Together, the EM3 have consistently accounted for a sizable share of global activity and growth over the past two decades. The EM3, which accounted for about 55 percent of the GDP

of EMDEs in 2024, will remain key to global economic prospects in the years ahead, particularly given the expected continuing rise of India's share in the world economy. The AE3—the United States, the euro area, and Japan—provides a benchmark for advanced economies, accounting for about 75 percent of their GDP in 2024. Through trade, financial, commodity market, and confidence channels, economic conditions in the EM3 affect the rest of the world, just as conditions in the AE3 often do (box 3.2).

Trade linkages

Global trade flows have expanded significantly during the first quarter of the twenty-first century, supporting output and income growth, technology spillovers, and poverty reduction in EMDEs.[4] In nominal U.S. dollar terms, global exports and imports of goods and services increased nearly four-fold between 2000 and 2023. EMDEs' share of global trade rose from 22 percent in 2000 to 37 percent in 2023, while the EM3's share rose from 5 percent to 15 percent during the same period (figures 3.2.A and 3.2.B). China alone accounted for 11 percent of global trade 2023, up from 3 percent in 2000, just before its accession to the WTO in 2001. The AE3's share of global trade declined, in relative terms, falling from 78 percent in 2000 to 62 percent in 2023.

As EMDEs' share of global trade has risen, their trade partnerships have evolved. Increasingly, EMDEs are trading with other EMDEs. Between 2000 and 2023, the share of goods exports from EMDEs to other EMDEs rose from 27 percent to 46 percent (figure 3.2.C). The growth of EMDEs' goods exports to other EMDEs has been faster than the growth of their goods exports to advanced economies in the 2000s, 2010s, and thus far in the 2020s (figure 3.2.D).

Global trade growth has been underpinned by, and has in turn reinforced the expansion of, international production networks. The 2000s were a second consecutive decade of rapid growth in GVCs as technological advances eased the outsourcing of goods and services and continued

---

[4] See, for example, World Bank and WTO (2015); World Bank (2020a); and WTO (2024).

FIGURE 3.2 EMDEs in global trade

An increasing share of global trade is attributable to EMDEs, especially the EM3. Increasingly, EMDEs are trading with other EMDEs. Although services represent a smaller share of global trade than goods, services trade growth has outpaced goods trade growth since the early 2010s, and EMDEs account for an increasing share of services trade.

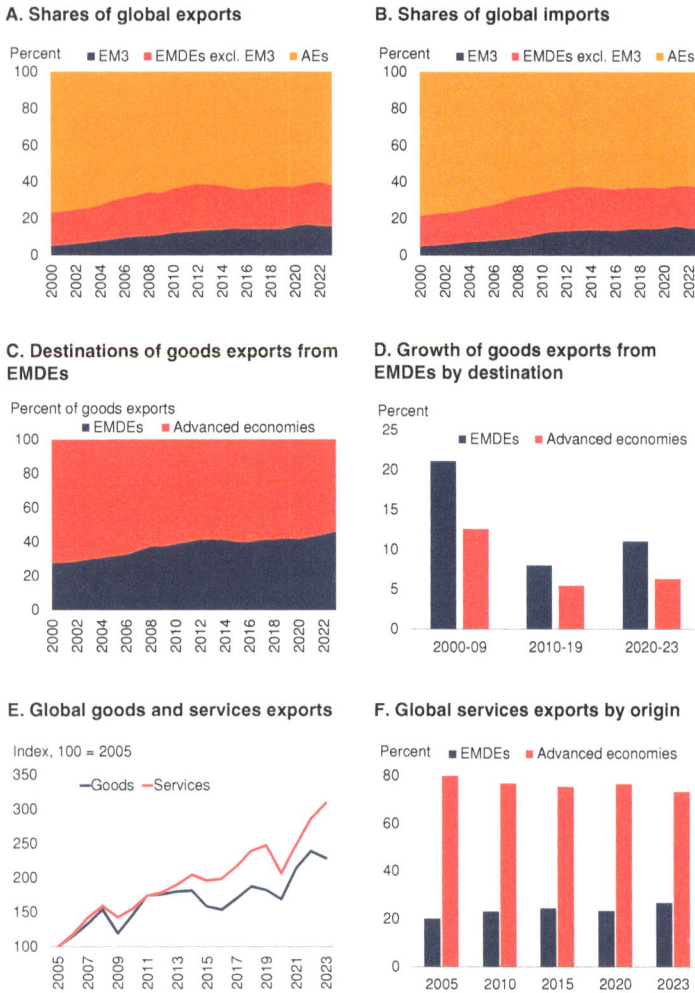

A. Shares of global exports

B. Shares of global imports

C. Destinations of goods exports from EMDEs

D. Growth of goods exports from EMDEs by destination

E. Global goods and services exports

F. Global services exports by origin

Sources: IMF Direction of Trade Statistics (database); UNCTAD; World Bank; World Development Indicators (database).
Note: AEs = advanced economies; EM3 = China, India, and Brazil; EMDEs = emerging market and developing economies; EMDEs excl. EM3 = emerging market and developing economies excluding China, India, and Brazil. Sample includes 154 EMDEs and 38 advanced economies.
A.-F. Exports and imports are measured in nominal U.S. dollars.
A.B. Data include goods and services trade. Last observation is 2023.
C.D. Last observation is 2023.
D. Bars show simple averages of year-over-year growth during each decade. Last observation for the 2020s is 2022.
E.F. Data begin in 2005 in the original source.

to reduce transport costs (World Bank 2020a). In real terms, global trade expanded at a brisk pace in the early part of the twenty-first century, at about 5 percent per year, on average, in 2000-09. Much of EMDEs' increased participation in GVCs during this period was attributable to increased backward participation (the proportion of foreign

value-added embedded in an economy's exports), although the intensity of forward participation (the proportion of domestic value-added embedded in foreign countries' exports) has also increased, most notably among the EM3.

The services trade landscape has also changed dramatically. The value of global services trade— business and communication services, financial services, transport services, tourism, and the like— remains far smaller than the value of goods trade, accounting for 24 percent of global trade (exports plus imports) in 2023. Yet services trade growth has outpaced goods trade growth since the early 2010s. Between 2005 and 2023, services trade, in nominal U.S. dollar terms, expanded more than threefold (figure 3.2.E). EMDEs accounted for more than one-quarter of global services exports in 2023, a share that has slowly but steadily risen since 2005, with the exception of a temporary dip during the pandemic (figure 3.2.F).

Commodity market linkages

Rapid growth of EMDEs has underpinned surging demand for commodities, especially energy and metals, in the past quarter century, and it fueled a price boom during the first decade (Baffes et al. 2018). The share of demand for key commodities from EMDEs surpassed that of advanced economies in the mid-2000s and has continued to increase, albeit at a slowing pace (figures 3.3.A and 3.3.B). EMDEs' share of global energy demand rose from 46 percent in 2000 to 67 percent in 2023, while their share of metals demand rose from 32 percent to 77 percent.

Rapid industrialization and urbanization in China account for a sizable share of the increase in EMDEs' demand for commodities in recent decades. China alone accounted for 17 percent of global oil demand, 28 percent of primary energy demand, and 60 percent of metals demand in 2023 (figure 3.3.C). India's demand for primary energy and metals has also grown substantially, despite the comparatively services-oriented nature of its economy, albeit from a much lower base. The EM3 also play an outsized role in the global supply of key commodities. China's production of refined metals (namely, aluminum, copper, and zinc) and coal has increased sharply since 2000 (figure 3.3.D). Brazil is now the world's largest exporter of agricultural commodities.

Three-fifths of EMDEs are commodity exporters; together, these economies account for a major share of global commodity exports.[5] EMDE commodity exporters tend to be specialized according to their natural resource base, with associated substantial regional concentrations of commodity production (figure 3.3.E). For instance, the Middle East and North Africa (MNA) accounts for about a quarter of global oil exports, while ECA contributes a further 12 percent. Latin America and the Caribbean (LAC) exports large shares of global exports in metals (14 percent) and food (14 percent). The production of some tropical commodities, including cocoa (West Africa) and natural rubber (East Asia), is also highly concentrated regionally. EAP—and within the region, predominantly China—absorbs a large share of global imports of several commodity subcategories (figure 3.3.F).

Financial linkages

EMDEs account for a growing share of global capital flows as both recipients and sources (figures 3.4.A and 3.4.B). On average, EMDEs received 21 percent of global capital inflows during 2019-23, compared to only 6 percent during 2000-04. The integration of EMDEs into the global financial system varies according to the type of flows, however. The share of global FDI going to these economies continues to be much higher than the shares of portfolio investment and bank lending.

Between 2000-04 and 2019-23, EMDEs' average share of global FDI inflows nearly tripled, from 18 percent to 51 percent, although the value of inflows dropped sharply during the pandemic. During both of these periods, nearly half of the inflows to EMDEs were channeled to the EM3. EMDEs' combined share of global FDI outflows remains far lower than their share of global inflows, though it increased nine-fold between 2000-04 and 2019-23, from 3 percent to 27 percent. Advanced economies remain the predominant source of FDI inflows to EMDEs,

---

[5] Table 1.2 describes the parameters used for classifying countries as commodity exporters.

FIGURE 3.3 EMDEs in global commodity markets

Since the mid-2000s, EMDEs' consumption of energy and metals has exceeded that of advanced economies, reflecting rapid growth in China and some other major EMDEs. At the regional level, concentrated shares of commodity exports reflect the geographical distribution of natural resources.

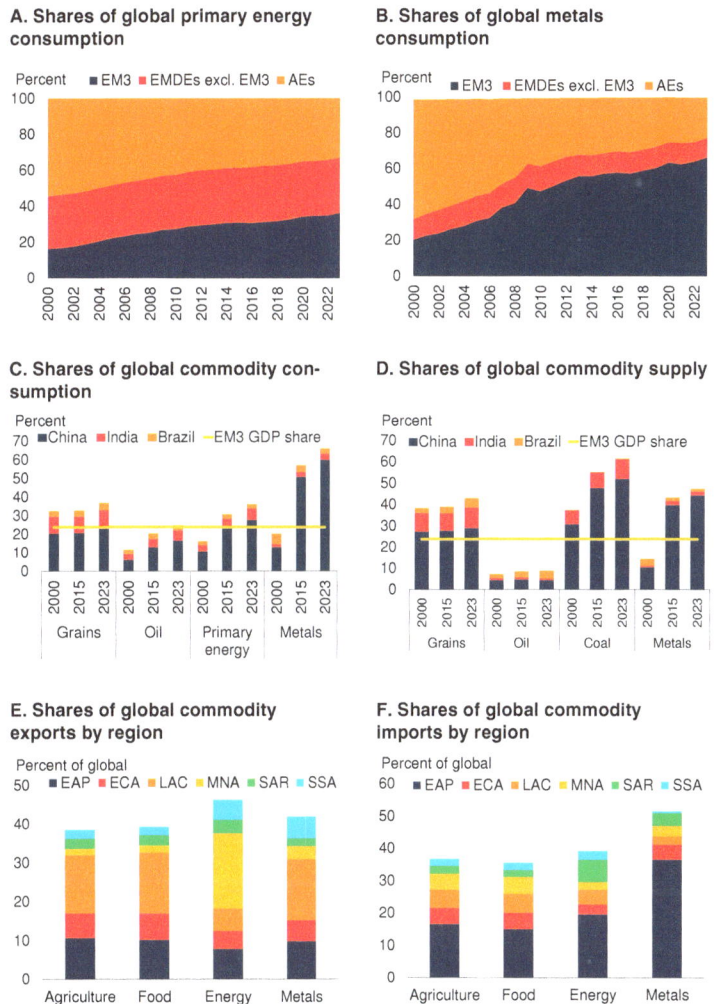

A. Shares of global primary energy consumption

B. Shares of global metals consumption

C. Shares of global commodity consumption

D. Shares of global commodity supply

E. Shares of global commodity exports by region

F. Shares of global commodity imports by region

Sources: Refinitiv (database); UN Comtrade (database); U.S. Department of Agriculture; The Energy Institute; World Bank.
Note: Geographic regions include only EMDEs. AEs = advanced economies; EM3 = China, India, and Brazil; EAP = East Asia and Pacific; ECA = Europe and Central Asia; EMDEs = emerging market and developing economies; LAC = Latin America and the Caribbean; MNA = Middle East and North Africa; SAR = South Asia; SSA = Sub-Saharan Africa. Sample includes 154 EMDEs and 38 advanced economies.
A. Primary energy includes oil, coal, and natural gas. Last observation is 2023.
B. Metals include aluminum, nickel, copper, lead, zinc and tin. Last observation is 2023.
C.D. Primary energy includes oil, coal, and natural gas. GDP share is for 2024.
E.F. Data for 2023. Sample includes 17 economies in EAP, 19 in ECA, 29 in LAC, 12 in MNA, 5 in SAR, and 34 in SSA.

although China has become a major source, accounting for 12 percent of global outflows in 2019-23. Even as the value of FDI flows has increased, inflows to EMDEs as a share of their GDP have fallen since the global financial crisis (figures 3.4.C). In some regions—in particular,

FIGURE 3.4 EMDEs in global financial markets

EMDEs account for a growing share of global inflows and outflows of FDI and remittances. Between 2000-04 and 2019-23, EMDEs' average share of global FDI inflows nearly tripled. Advanced economies continue to be the source of most inflows of FDI and remittances to EMDEs.

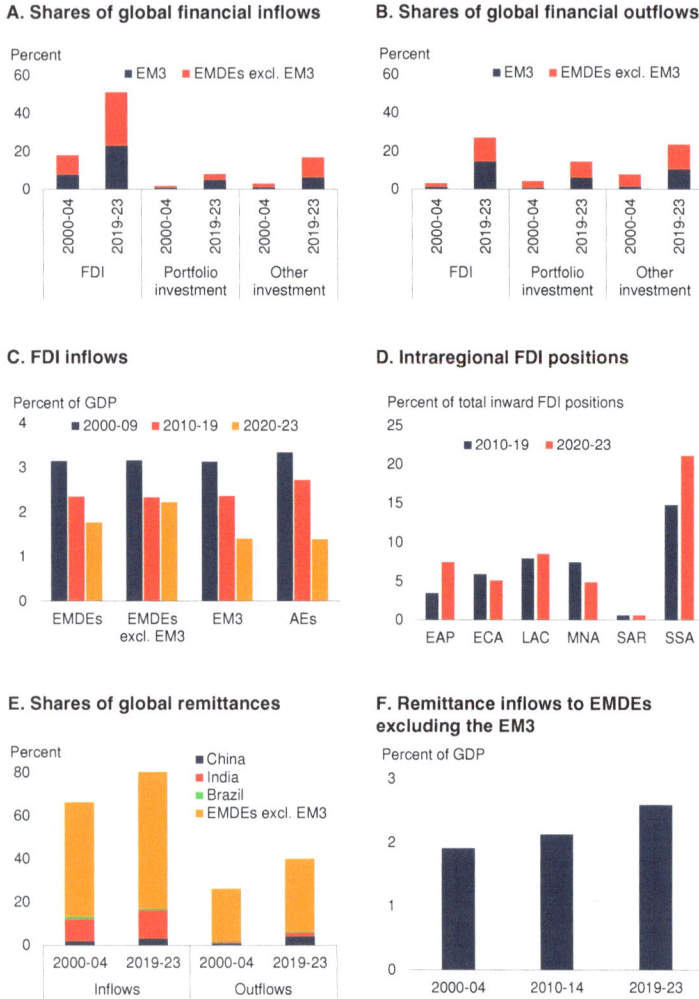

A. Shares of global financial inflows

B. Shares of global financial outflows

C. FDI inflows

D. Intraregional FDI positions

E. Shares of global remittances

F. Remittance inflows to EMDEs excluding the EM3

Sources: IMF Balance of Payments and International Investment Position (database); IMF Coordinated Direct Investment Survey (database); World Development Indicators (database); World Bank.

Note: Geographical regions include EMDEs only. AEs = advanced economies; EAP = East Asia and Pacific; ECA = Europe and Central Asia; EM3 = China, India, and Brazil; EMDEs = emerging market and developing economies; LAC = Latin America and the Caribbean; MNA = Middle East and North Africa; SAR = South Asia; SSA = Sub-Saharan Africa.

A.B. FDI, portfolio investment, and other investment data are net inflows and outflows from balance of payments data. Other investment is a proxy for bank lending flows.

C. FDI data are net inflows. Bars show decade averages of annual GDP-weighted group averages.

D. Bars show inward FDI positions by economies in the same regions as a share of total inward positions in respective regions.

E. Remittances inflows and outflows refer to remittances received and remittances paid, respectively.

F. Data are aggregated using GDP weights.

EAP and Sub-Saharan Africa (SSA)—FDI positions are increasingly from economies in the same region (figure 3.4.D).

The proportion of global portfolio debt and equity inflows that went to EMDEs more than quadrupled between 2000-04 and 2019-23, though it remains modest at 8 percent, partly reflecting restrictive capital account restrictions and relatively shallow financial markets in host EMDEs (Combes et al. 2019). Similarly, banking networks remain a limited channel of integration among EMDEs, although there has been an increase in involvement by EMDE banks in cross-border lending at both the regional and global levels (Cerutti, Casanova, and Pradhan 2018). Most notably, international banking networks headquartered in China have expanded rapidly, accounting for 6 percent of global cross-border lending per year, on average, in 2019-23.

For decades, EMDEs have received most of global remittance inflows. EMDEs' proportion of inflows has continued to rise, reaching 80 percent in 2019-23, compared to about 65 percent in 2000-04 (figure 3.4.E). EMDEs have also accounted for a rising share of global remittance outflows—40 percent in 2019-23, up from about 25 percent in 2000-04. These shifts in the destination and origin of remittances reflect the growing migration of people to and from EMDEs, triggered by push and pull factors such as income gaps, armed conflict, and climate change (World Bank 2023a). Remittance inflows as a proportion of GDP in EMDEs excluding the EM3 have also steadily increased since the early 2000s (figure 3.4.F).

Official development assistance (ODA) is an important source of external financing for many EMDEs, particularly those where per capita income is lowest. Yet ODA as a proportion of gross national income in low-income countries has generally declined since 2000 (chapter 4). While most ODA to EMDEs continues to originate in advanced economies, major EMDEs play a growing role in the provision of aid (Benn and Luijkx 2017). China is now the largest single bilateral creditor to other EMDEs (World Bank 2021b). A large share of ODA from China and Brazil is directed to SSA, while India is an important source of ODA within the South Asia (SAR) region.

BOX 3.1 Regional aspects of integration

Emerging market and developing economies (EMDEs) have become increasingly integrated into the global economy during the first quarter of the twenty-first century. However, there remains considerable heterogeneity in the nature and extent of trade and financial linkages across and within regions.

Trade. Trade openness has increased toward advanced-economy levels in most EMDE regions since 2000, despite these economies continuing to employ relatively more restrictive trade policies than advanced economies (Estefania-Flores et al. 2024; figure B3.1.1.A). Likewise, EMDE participation in global value chains (GVCs) has expanded, although many economies rely heavily on primary commodity exports.

Economies in EAP are generally characterized by a high degree of trade openness, with exports and imports together equivalent to more than 100 percent of GDP in many economies. China is an exception: despite being a globally important export market and a major source of imports, trade as a share of GDP has averaged less than 40 percent since 2015, contributing to the relatively low GDP-weighted regional average trade openness in EAP. ECA is highly open to trade, with exports and imports together ranging from nearly 70 to 80 percent of GDP in the 2020s, the highest across regions. Countries that joined the European Union (EU) in the 2000s—including Bulgaria, Hungary, and Poland—exhibit particularly high trade openness and GVC integration through backward participation. High trade openness in MNA is driven by sizable fuel exports, while SSA is home to many commodity exporters specializing in natural resource products, such as raw, unprocessed minerals and crude oil.

Overall, trade openness in LAC is lower than in ECA, MNA, and SSA. However, the region is a globally significant supplier of agricultural products such as soybeans, sugar, poultry, and corn, and is also rich in critical minerals necessary for the green transition. Some LAC economies are substantially engaged in manufacturing exports (for example, Mexico, Costa Rica, and El Salvador) or services exports (for example, Panama). The extent of trade openness in SAR remains low relative to other regions, owing to restrictive trade policies, including high tariffs, and limited infrastructure and connectivity (World Bank 2024b). Rapid growth in services exports in India has contributed to increased trade integration in SAR since 2000, however.

Finance. Financial openness in EMDEs generally lags that of advanced economies. However, the scale and composition of capital inflows are quite different across the six EMDE regions (figure B3.1.1.B). De jure financial openness is highest, on average, in LAC and MNA.[a] FDI inflows as a share of GDP in LAC, at an average 3 percent per year in 2019-23, are the highest among EMDE regions, while the ratio of portfolio inflows to GDP has increased since 2000 from a low base. MNA has become increasingly open to capital inflows since 2000, boosted by inflows to the Gulf Cooperation Council countries. The ratio of portfolio inflows to GDP in MNA, more than 1 percent per year in 2019-23, is substantially higher than in other regions but still markedly lower than 4 percent of GDP in advanced economies. In ECA, the average annual ratio of FDI inflows to GDP was almost 3 percent in 2019-23, despite outflows from the Russian Federation since 2022, although portfolio inflows are comparatively modest.

In EAP, FDI inflows as a share of GDP have fallen since the late 2000s and averaged just 1.5 percent per year in 2019-23, less than in most other regions. Portfolio inflows a share of GDP similarly trail. SSA has recorded a decrease in FDI inflows as a share of GDP since 2000, while the region's ratio of portfolio inflows to GDP has stagnated. SAR remains the least financially open region on a de jure basis, although it has seen an increase in FDI inflows as a share of GDP since 2000, largely attributable to India.

Remittances represent a significant source of external financing for many EMDEs; they are of a larger or similar in magnitude as FDI inflows in ECA, MNA, SAR, and SSA (figure B3.1.1.C). SAR, a significant source of global migrants, received remittance inflows equivalent to 4 percent of GDP in 2022, the highest among all regions. SSA is the region most reliant on official development assistance (ODA), although inflows relative to GDP have declined since 2000.

Note: This box was prepared by Kate McKinnon.

a. De jure capital openness as measured by the Chinn-Ito index.

BOX 3.1 Regional aspects of integration (*continued*)

FIGURE B3.1.1 Trade and financial openness

Most EMDE regions have become increasingly integrated through trade since 2000. Although capital inflows as a share of GDP have stagnated or receded in some regions, remittance inflows have risen and are now larger than foreign direct investment (FDI) inflows in MNA, SAR, and SSA.

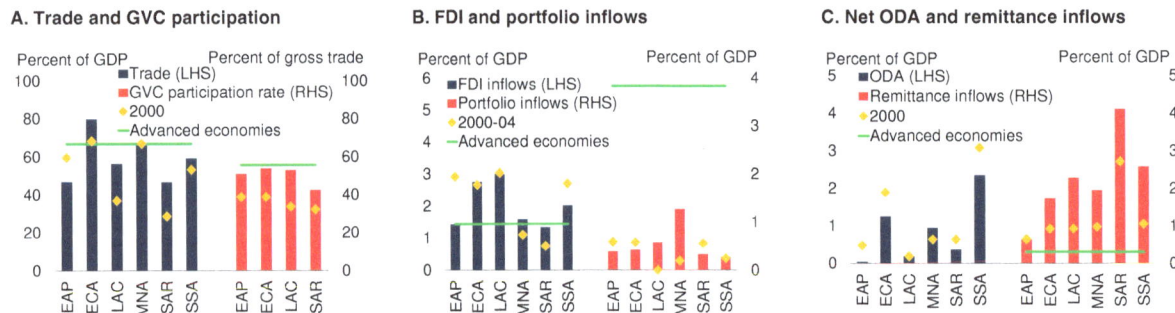

A. Trade and GVC participation

B. FDI and portfolio inflows

C. Net ODA and remittance inflows

Sources: Asian Development Bank; IMF Balance of Payments and International Investment Position (database); OECD TiVA; WBG-KNOMAD; World Bank; World Development Indicators (database).

Note: Regions include only EMDEs. EAP = East Asia and Pacific; ECA = Europe and Central Asia; EMDEs = emerging market and developing economies; FDI = foreign direct investment; GDP = gross domestic product; GVC = global value chains; LAC = Latin America and the Caribbean; LHS = left-hand scale; MNA = Middle East and North Africa; RHS = left-hand scale; SAR = South Asia; SSA = Sub-Saharan Africa.

A. Trade refers to the sum of imports and exports, expressed as a share of GDP (i.e., the trade openness ratio). Regional values are GDP-weighted averages. Bars show data for 2022. GVC participation rate includes backward and forward participation, where backward participation measures the proportion of foreign value added embedded in a domestic economy's exports and forward participation measures the proportion of domestic value added embedded in foreign exports. GVC data are unavailable for MNA and SSA. Regional values are simple averages. Bars show data for 2022.

B. FDI and portfolio investment are net inflows. Regional values are GDP-weighted averages. Bars show averages for 2019-23.

C. Regional values are GDP-weighted averages. Bars show data for 2022.

Global linkages. The trade and financial linkages of EMDEs tend to be predominantly with the large, advanced economies, particularly the United States and the euro area. However, China is a major trading partner for several regions.

The United States and the euro area are important economic partners for EAP, together accounting for a relatively large share of the region's exports, inward FDI, and remittance inflows (figure B.3.1.2.A). EAP also retains strong trade and financial linkages with advanced economies in geographic proximity, including Japan and Singapore, although their role as export markets has waned somewhat as trade linkages with China have expanded.

ECA has deep economic linkages with the euro area, its largest trading partner, a key source of remittances, and the source of more than 70 percent of the region's inward FDI stock as of 2023 (figure B.3.1.2.B). China's role as an export destination and source of FDI is comparatively limited, although its importance as an export market has increased for several economies in the region.

The United States remains the most important external economic partner for LAC , accounting for a large share of exports, inward FDI, remittance inflows, and tourism. Mexico has particularly strong trade ties, supported by the North American Free Trade Agreement, and, more recently, the United States-Mexico-Canada Agreement. About 80 percent of Mexico's exports are directed to the United States. LAC also has strong financial ties to the euro area, which accounted for one-quarter of the region's inward FDI stock in 2023. China has become an increasingly important export destination and source of FDI for LAC, particularly for economies in South America.

MNA retains strong financial ties with the United States and the euro area, which together account for approximately one-third of the region's remittance inflows in 2021 and almost 60 percent of the inward FDI stock as of 2023. While the United States is still an important export market for some economies in the region, its reliance on oil imports has decreased since the mid-to-late 2000s, owing to increased domestic production associated partly with the "shale revolution." Oil exports from MNA to the euro area have picked up since Russia's invasion of Ukraine in 2022.

BOX 3.1 Regional aspects of integration (*continued*)

FIGURE B3.1.2 Within-region integration

Within-region exports account for a relatively high share of total exports in ECA and SSA. SSA exhibits a high degree of intraregional financial integration through FDI and remittances, while more than half of remittances to ECA and MNA are from within the region. SAR exhibits minimal intraregional trade and financial integration.

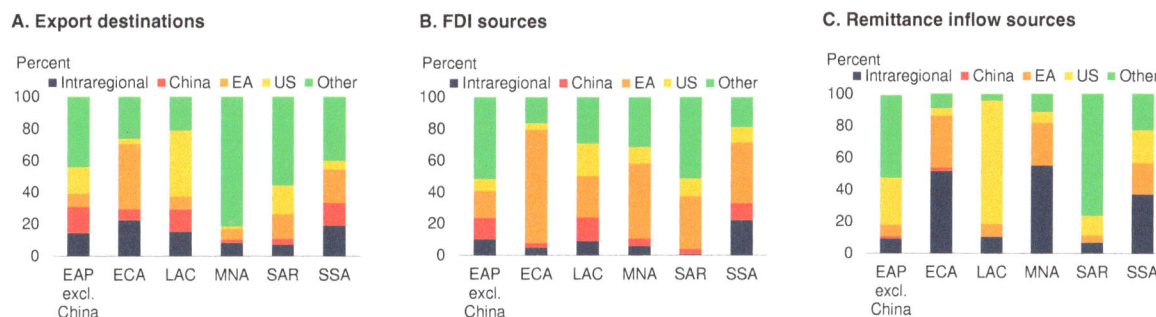

A. Export destinations

B. FDI sources

C. Remittance inflow sources

Sources: IMF Coordinated Direct Investment Survey (database); World Integrated Trade Solution (database); WBG-KNOMAD; World Bank.
Note: CHN = China; EA = euro area; EAP = East Asia and Pacific; ECA = Europe and Central Asia; FDI = foreign direct investment; LAC = Latin America and the Caribbean; MNA = Middle East and North Africa; SAR = South Asia; SSA = Sub-Saharan Africa; US = United States. "Intraregional" means emerging market and developing economies within the same region.
A. Bars show exports for each region in percent of each region's total, categorized by destination. Data are for 2022 for EAP, LAC, MNA, SAR, and SSA and 2021 for ECA.
B. Bars show FDI positions for each region in percent of each region's total, categorized by origin. Data are for 2023.
C. Bars show remittances for each region in percent of each region's total, categorized by origin. Data are for 2021.

SAR's financial and trade linkages are also predominantly with large, advanced economies, with the United States and euro area together accounting for about one-third of export demand and about 45 percent of the inward FDI stock. In addition, many of SAR's large number of emigrants work in MNA, particularly in Gulf Cooperation Council countries, which accordingly form a large source of remittance inflows. For SSA, advanced economies—including the euro area, United States, and United Kingdom—remain important export markets and sources of remittances, FDI, and ODA. However, SSA's exports have increasingly been directed to EMDEs. China is now the region's largest bilateral trading partner.

Intraregional linkages. Given EMDEs' deep economic ties with advanced economies and large extraregional EMDEs, intraregional connectivity remains comparatively modest. However, there are robust within-region trade and financial linkages in some cases, underpinned by major regional EMDEs that serve as fulcrums for integration.

China has helped forge deeper integration across EAP through its prominent footprint in regional trade and finance. It absorbed 16 percent of goods exports from other economies in the region in 2022 and was the

source of 14 percent of the inward FDI of other EAP economies in 2023. ECA economies are also highly integrated through trade and finance channels, with more than 20 percent of their exports and imports traded within ECA in 2022 and more than half of remittance inflows originating in the region in 2021. Though its role has diminished recently, the Russian Federation has traditionally had deep economic linkages with several other ECA countries, while the extent of Türkiye's intraregional linkages are more modest, with its top trade and financial partners outside the region.

Within LAC, close economic linkages are largely confined to a narrower set of economies. Mexico does not play a large role in driving integration within Central America. In contrast, Brazil is an important trading partner and source of FDI for several South American economies, particularly Argentina, Paraguay, and Uruguay.

SSA is characterized by strong trade and financial linkages among some economies. As a major export market and source of imports, as well as an important source of FDI and remittances for several economies, South Africa plays a key role in driving this integration, especially within the Southern African Customs Union (Botswana, Eswatini, Lesotho, Namibia, and South

BOX 3.1 Regional aspects of integration (*continued*)

Africa). Despite having the largest economy and population in SSA, Nigeria has a modest intraregional role as an export destination and does not yet have a substantial role as a source of FDI or remittances, although its banks have a regional presence.

Although trade within MNA is somewhat constrained by limited economic diversity, financial linkages are generated through migration, with more than half of remittance inflows originating within the region in 2021, typically flowing from oil-exporting to oil-importing economies. Economic linkages are relatively weak within SAR, consistent with the region's low trade and financial openness, although India is a source of significant remittances for some SAR economies.

Synchronization of business cycles in EMDEs with those in the rest of the world

Deepening integration between EMDEs and the rest of the world over the past few decades has enabled these countries to benefit from shared growth dynamics. Yet integration has exposed EMDEs to shared vulnerabilities, magnifying the impact of external shocks. The literature provides robust evidence that increased trade intensity fosters greater international synchronization of business cycles, although the strength of this relationship varies depending on the estimation methods employed and the particular trade relationships considered.[6] Financial linkages are likewise found to be a crucial driver of business cycle synchronization. Economies that are more integrated through FDI or financial market openness tend to experience more synchronized economic fluctuations.[7] Financially interconnected economies are also more susceptible to common shocks transmitted via capital flows, credit markets, and financial institutions, which also contribute to business cycle alignment.

Evolution of synchronization

The increasing integration of EMDEs into the global economy has contributed to greater synchronization of business cycles among EMDEs and between EMDEs and advanced economies. Three measures explore how the degree of synchronization has evolved in recent decades. First, a concordance index captures the proportion of time that two countries are in the same phase of the business cycle.[8] Second, the correlation of growth rates between economies goes beyond a comparison of expansion-contraction periods by measuring the degree of synchronization in terms of how closely economies' growth performances are related. A third measure, the average pairwise concordance index of a country with all other countries, allows all economies to be ranked in terms of their business cycle synchronization with all other economies. Each of these measures suggests that business cycles among EMDEs have become more synchronized since the 1990s. Higher synchronization could be the result of more frequent common shocks, more correlated shocks, or more potent cross-border spillovers.

The concordance index shows that the synchronization of business cycles among EMDEs increased sharply, on average, from the 1990s to the 2000s, and somewhat further in the 2010s and early 2020s (figure 3.5.A). A similar upward trend is observed in the business cycle synchronization between EMDEs and advanced economies. In the

---

[6] See, for example, Baxter and Kouparitsas (2005); Frankel and Rose (1997, 1998); Gong and Kim (2018); Imbs (2004); and Inklaar, Jong-A-Pin, and de Haan (2008).

[7] See, for example, Davis (2008); Imbs (2004, 2006); Kose, Prasad, and Terrones (2003); and Otto, Voss, and Willard (2001).

[8] The concordance index is calculated by, first, identifying the two phases of business cycles—expansions and contractions—in each economy. A value of one is assigned when two economies share the same phase in a given period, and zero otherwise. The index measures the percent of periods when the two countries are in the same business cycle phase. Two countries are perfectly procyclical (countercyclical) if the concordance index is equal to 100 (zero). The phases of business cycles are identified using the statistical algorithm of Harding and Pagan (2002), with each phase lasting at least two quarters and the entire cycle lasting at least five quarters.

1990s, the synchronization of business cycles between EMDEs and advanced economies tended to be higher than the synchronization among EMDEs, likely because of larger exports to advanced economies. However, as cross-border trade and financial linkages within the group have strengthened, their business cycles have become more synchronized over time. In the 2020s, the average degree of synchronization among EMDEs has become closer to that between EMDEs and advanced economies.

Since extreme growth outcomes, especially during periods of global recessions and recoveries, could distort correlation results, the effects of these events are removed by computing a partial correlation.[9] The results suggest that GDP growth has been more correlated among EMDEs in the 2020s than in the previous decades, and that the correlation increased slightly from the 2000s to the 2010s (figure 3.5.B). The correlation of growth between EMDEs and advanced economies has tended to be higher than that among EMDEs during all decades except the 2010s, when growth in EMDEs was more weakly correlated with growth in AE3, reflecting the moderation of China's growth during this period (figure 3.5.C).

In the 1990s, EMDEs accounted for about half of the number of economies with the highest synchronization of economic activity with the rest of the world (figure 3.5.D). However, since 2000, the number of EMDEs among the most synchronized economies has been significantly higher. This also highlights the increased comovement of activity in EMDEs with the global economy, reflecting a notable shift in the dynamics of cross-country economic and financial linkages.

Drivers of synchronization

The sources of changes in the synchronization of business cycles are explored using a dynamic factor model (DFM). The model decomposes

---

[9] The partial correlation measures the relationship between two variables after the effects of control variables are adjusted. It is calculated as the correlation of residuals of the two variables after being regressed on controls. The results reported in figures 3.5.B and 3.5.C control for the effects of global recessions in 1991, 2009, 2020 and the immediate rebounds from these recessions (Guénette, Kose, and Sugawara 2022).

FIGURE 3.5 Synchronization of business cycles

Synchronization of business cycles across EMDEs and between EMDEs and advanced economies has strengthened since the 1990s.

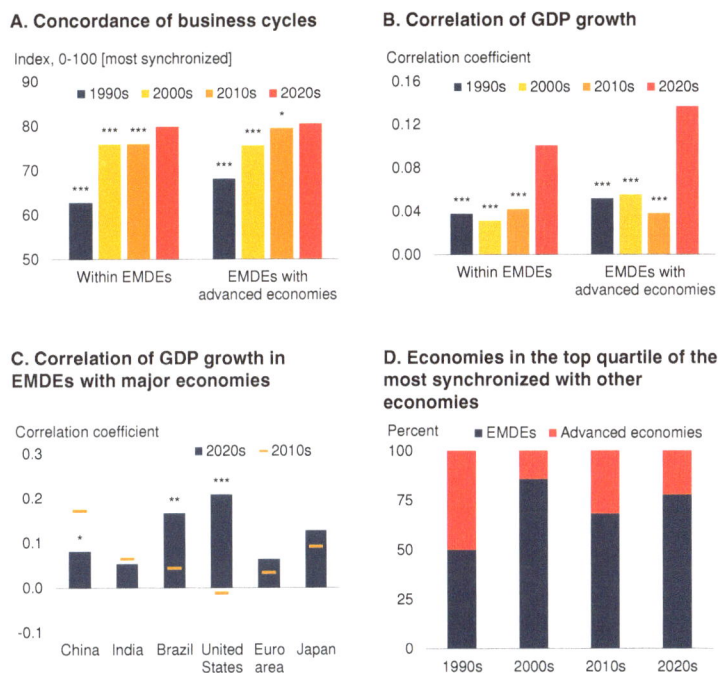

A. Concordance of business cycles

B. Correlation of GDP growth

C. Correlation of GDP growth in EMDEs with major economies

D. Economies in the top quartile of the most synchronized with other economies

Source: World Bank.
Note: EMDEs = emerging market and developing economies; GDP = gross domestic product. Sample includes 72 EMDEs and 19 advanced economies (treating euro area economies as a single economy).
A. Unweighted average of all the two-country concordance indices, based on quarterly real GDP, between two EMDEs or between an EMDE and an advanced economy over each decade. Data for the 2020s include 2020Q1-2023Q4. * and *** denote that the concordance index for the 1990s, 2000s, and 2010s is statistically significantly different from that for the 2020s at the 10 percent and 1 percent levels, respectively.
B. Unweighted average of all the correlation coefficients of quarter-over-quarter annualized real GDP growth between two EMDEs or between an EMDE and an advanced economy over each decade. A bar for the 2020s reflects data for 2020Q1-23Q4. The coefficients are obtained by partial correlation, after the effects of global recessions in 1991 (1990Q4-1991Q1), 2009 (2008Q3-2009Q1), and 2020 (2020Q1-Q2) and the following quarters (1991Q2, 2009Q2, and 2020Q3) as immediate rebounds from respective recessions are removed. *** denotes that correlation coefficients for the 1990s, 2000s, and 2010s are statistically significantly different from that for the 2020s at the 1 percent level.
C. Unweighted average of all the correlation coefficients of quarter-over-quarter annualized real GDP growth between an EMDE and each of six major economies, as denoted on the horizontal axis, over each decade. Data for the 2020s cover 2020Q1-23Q4. The coefficients are obtained by partial correlation, as explained in the note for panel B. *, **, and *** denote that the correlation coefficient for the 2010s is statistically significantly different from that for the 2020s at the 10 percent, 5 percent, and 1 percent levels, respectively.
D. The shares of EMDEs and advanced economies in the top quartile of countries, based on the degree of synchronization in each decade. Synchronization in each country is measured by the average concordance index, based on quarterly real GDP, of an economy with all other economies.

fluctuations in growth into three components: a global factor, a group factor, and an idiosyncratic factor (technical details are provided in annex 3.1). The global factor captures growth fluctuations common across all economies, representing synchronized cyclical movements; this factor can be interpreted as the global business cycle. The group factor captures growth fluctuations specific to a particular group of economies (in this case, EMDEs or advanced

BOX 3.2 Transmission channels of spillovers

Trade and financial linkages are major channels through which growth spillovers are transmitted across countries, with exposure depending on the nature of bilateral partnerships and economic openness. For EMDEs, commodity prices are an important conduit for shocks emanating from shifts in the external environment. The confidence channel can generate or magnify growth spillovers beyond those transmitted through real and financial channels.

Trade channel. In the long-run, trade integration promotes shared growth by facilitating the transfer of technology and knowledge embedded in imports and exports, allowing exporters to exploit economies of scale, and fostering domestic competition and innovation (Ohnsorge and Quaglietti 2024).[a] Goods and services trade can also serve as a major channel through which fluctuations in growth are transmitted from one country to another (Montinari and Stracca 2016). Exporting countries are directly exposed to shifts in import demand linked to economic activity in destination markets, while production and consumption in importing countries is affected by output shocks in suppliers (Rigobon 2019).[b]

Susceptibility to spillovers through the trade channel beyond direct trading partners is driven by participation in global value chains (GVCs), which propagate economic shocks through international production networks while promoting the diffusion of productivity gains (Carvalho and Tahbaz-Salehi 2019). The degree of a country's integration into GVCs, as well as general trade openness, are found to be key drivers of the magnitude of growth spillovers (Altomonte, Colantone, and Bonacorsi 2018; Yilmazkuday 2024).

Spillovers through services trade are also important—in particular, many EMDEs rely on inbound tourism as an engine for economic growth, yet revenues are sensitive to economic conditions in tourists' home countries and global shocks, as highlighted by the COVID-19 pandemic (Milesi-Ferretti 2023; Rasool, Maqbool, and Tarique 2021).

Commodity price channel. Three-fifths of EMDEs are commodity exporters, rendering them vulnerable to commodity price fluctuations resulting from shifts in global demand and supply, which are often driven by large economies such as China and the United States (Chatterjee and Saraf 2024; Kose et al. 2020). Although an increase in global demand for commodities raises prices and can bolster output and employment in commodity-exporting economies, negative commodity price shocks may hinder growth in these economies through adverse effects on the terms of trade, export income, and public revenues (Dabla-Norris, Espinoza, and Jahan 2015; Naraidoo and Paez-Farrell 2023; Roch 2019). The impact of commodity price changes on the GDP of a commodity exporter depends on the responsiveness of supply to price movements and the size of the commodity sector in the domestic economy (Housa, Mohimont, and Otrok 2023).[c] For commodity-importing economies, a shock that raises global commodity prices puts upward pressure on domestic inflation and can impair growth (Igan et al. 2022; Gelos and Ustyugova 2017).

Financial channel. External financing is crucial for growth and economic stability in many EMDEs. Foreign direct investment (FDI), for example, can help plug gaps in domestic investment, generate employment, and boost productivity (Benetrix, Pallan, and Panizza 2023). Portfolio investment has the potential to support economic growth and development by improving international risk sharing and enhancing liquidity and efficiency of domestic capital markets (Kose, Prasad, and Terrones 2009; Vita and Kyaw 2009).[d] While capital inflows are connected to specific characteristics of host countries—"pull" factors—they are also vulnerable to fluctuations tied to cyclicality in investors' home countries, forging a conduit for business cycle spillovers (Jansen and Stokman 2004).

Note: This box was prepared by Kate McKinnon.

a. The benefits may be accentuated as capital accumulation and concentration of trade in labor-intensive or technologically sophisticated goods increases, and as the share of advanced economies or rapidly growing economies in the composition of trading partners rises (Didier and Pinat 2017).

b. Although deeper trade linkages may amplify spillovers, the effect on business cycle synchronization may be attenuated to the extent that trade catalyzes cross-country specialization in industries that are key drivers of domestic business cycles (Kose, Prasad, and Terrones 2003).

c. The effects of fluctuations in particular commodity prices tend to be largest in the economies that specialize in their production: for instance, output in Chile is strongly affected by movements in copper prices, while output in Indonesia is affected by movements in the prices of oil and tin (Hegerty 2016).

d. Related research emphasizes that the link between increased capital inflows and economic growth is often contingent on characteristics of host countries, particularly the level of institutional and financial market development (Baharumshah, Slesman, and Devadason 2015).

BOX 3.2 Transmission channels (*continued*)

Portfolio flows, in particular, are also prone to instability linked to external "push" factors related to global financial conditions and portfolio allocation decisions, which can transmit real economic shocks across borders (Calvo 2014; Cerutti, Claessens, and Puy 2019; Koepke 2019).

The global banking network can also act as an important transmission mechanism for economic growth shocks across countries. For instance, sharp contractions in cross-border lending from foreign banks and their affiliates can exacerbate negative spillovers to EMDEs during periods of widespread economic tumult, as evidenced during the global financial crisis (Cetorelli and Goldberg 2010; Hale, Kapan, and Minoiu 2016). While EMDE banks are, in general, still not deeply integrated into the international banking system, the rise in cross-border banking linkages between EMDEs, and increasing regionalization of banking networks represents a nascent channel for spillovers (Cerutti, Casanova, and Pradhan 2018; Cerutti and Zhou 2018).

The financial channel also includes remittances, an important source of total external financing for many low- and lower-middle-income countries (Beaton, Cerovic, and Galdamez 2017; Poghosyan 2023). Changes in labor market conditions in workers' host countries may curtail or augment remittance inflows, depending on the type of shock. Official development assistance also remains an important source of funding for many low- and lower-middle-income EMDEs,

although the effective scale of support has fallen since the turn of the twenty-first century, likely dampening transmission of cross-border shocks via this channel. While official multilateral lending may be comparatively stable, bilateral lending is prone to swings linked to conditions in the origin country (Avellán et al. 2024; Galindo and Panizza 2018).

Confidence channel. Business cycles are linked to consumer and investor sentiment at both the domestic and global levels (Nowzohour and Stracca 2020). For instance, heightened global uncertainty can dampen global economic activity through the confidence channel, likely attributable in part to the postponement of consumption and investment by individuals and firms (Ha and So 2023). Economic, financial market, and policy developments in major economies can transmit to sentiment and activity elsewhere, amplifying cross-border growth spillovers beyond those transmitted through the trade and financial channels (Fei 2011; Kose et al. 2020; Levchenko and Pandalai-Nayar 2020). Elevated financial market uncertainty in the United States, for example, can reverberate widely through increased risk aversion in international bond, equity, and currency markets, while heightened U.S. policy uncertainty can have a negative effect on global consumption and investment growth (Ehrmann, Fratzscher, and Rigobon 2011; Miranda-Agrippino and Rey 2022). Given its considerable role in the global economy, a negative shock to GDP growth in China could also precipitate a deterioration in global risk sentiment (Ahmed et al. 2022).

economies); this factor can be interpreted as representing the group-specific business cycle. Finally, the idiosyncratic factor captures growth fluctuations not explained by the global or group factors—that is, country-specific factors.

To identify the group factor, the economy-level data is divided into two groups: EMDEs and advanced economies. An additional exercise decomposes growth fluctuations within the EM3 and the AE3. To examine how the roles of the three factors in explaining business cycle fluctuations in EMDEs have evolved, data for the full sample period, 2000Q1 to 2023Q4, is divided into three subperiods: two ten-year windows

roughly aligned with the decade of rapid globalization prior to the global financial crisis (2000-09) and the decade following that crisis (2010-19), and a four-year period overlapping the COVID-19 pandemic (2020-23).[10]

The results suggest that, for EMDEs, the role of the group factor in explaining the variance of business cycles increased substantially in the

---

[10] An alternative version of the baseline DFM is estimated after grouping economies into geographic regions, without taking into account whether they are EMDEs or advanced economies. The results, summarized in annex 3.1, show that the global factor remains the dominant contributor to fluctuations in economic growth.

FIGURE 3.6 Decomposition of business cycle variance

An EMDE-specific factor contributed more to the variation of business cycles in EMDEs in the 2010s than in the 2000s, suggesting that business cycles in EMDEs have become more synchronized. In contrast, for advanced economies, the share of business cycle variation explained by the advanced-economy-specific factor was mostly stable between the 2000s and 2010s, although it increased in the AE3.

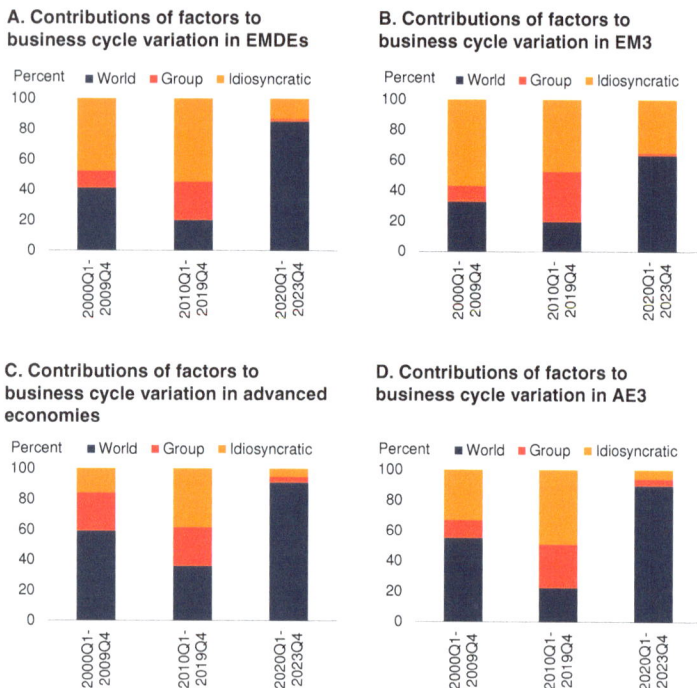

A. Contributions of factors to business cycle variation in EMDEs

B. Contributions of factors to business cycle variation in EM3

C. Contributions of factors to business cycle variation in advanced economies

D. Contributions of factors to business cycle variation in AE3

Source: World Bank.
Note: AE3 = United States, euro area, and Japan. EMDEs = emerging market and developing economies; EM3 = China, India, and Brazil. Sample includes 15 EMDEs and 15 advanced economies. Annex 3.1 contains additional methodological information.

2010s, accounting for 25 percent of the variance in that decade, more than double the 11 percent in the 2000s (figure 3.6.A). For the EM3, the importance of the group factor increased even more between the two decades, accounting for 33 percent of the business cycle variation in the 2010s, about three times as much as in the 2000s (figure 3.6.B). These findings indicate that a more pronounced EMDE business cycle has emerged in the 2010s, likely reflecting stronger cross-border trade and financial linkages among EMDEs.

For advanced economies, by contrast, the relative size of the group-specific factor was roughly unchanged, at about 25 percent during the 2000s and 2010s, although it increased for the AE3 (figures 3.6.C and 3.6.D). In the early 2020s, the world factor contributed the most, by far, to the variance of growth in EMDEs and advanced

economies (although somewhat less markedly among the EM3), largely reflecting the global nature of shocks during this subperiod.

Business cycle spillovers from major economies

The increase in the relative size of major EMDEs—in particular, China—may have changed the nature and extent of cross-border business cycle spillovers during the twenty-first century. The expanding footprint of major EMDEs in the global economy, combined with the evidence that business cycle synchronization among these economies has strengthened, points to the possibility of larger cyclical spillovers from economic growth in major EMDEs to other economies.

Analysis of spillovers from EMDEs remains scant compared to the large literature on spillovers from advanced economies. Notable contributions provide evidence of growth spillovers from emerging market economies to LICs and underscore the global significance of spillovers from large EMDEs (Dabla-Norris, Espinoza, and Huidrom et al. 2020; IMF 2024a; Jahan 2015). There is also evidence of rising spillovers from EMDEs since the 1990s, although spillovers from advanced economies remain larger in comparison (Arezki and Liu 2020). Trade, particularly through GVCs and commodity markets, is a key transmission channel for spillovers from large EMDEs and advanced economies. In contrast, financial linkages predominantly transmit spillovers from advanced economies, with limited evidence of such effects from EMDEs (Feldkircher and Huber 2016; Furceri, Jalles, and Zdzienicka 2017; Kose et al. 2020).[11]

---

[11] Research on the contribution of the financial channel to business cycle spillovers from EMDEs remains sparse, yet findings suggest its limited importance in global transmission. Insights from existing studies focus on spillovers associated with unexpected changes in monetary policy, equity prices, sovereign spreads, exchange rates, and capital flows. Monetary policy in China generates only short-lived effects, largely transmitted through trade linkages with regional economies (Cho and Kim 2021; Johansson 2012; Lei, Mei, and Zhang 2024). Similarly, EMDEs equity markets, though regionally integrated, exhibit limited spillovers to global markets (Hedström et al. 2020). Evidence of financial spillovers from sovereign spreads and exchange rates tends to be modest and geographically contained (Dell'Erba, Baldacci, and Poghosyan 2013; Kelejian, Tavlas, and Hondroyiannis 2006).

The magnitude of spillovers depends on both the size of the initial growth shock and the strength of the transmission channels that underpin cross-border linkages. A structural vector autoregression (SVAR) model, with a standardized shock calibration to ensure comparability, is used to estimate spillovers from major economies to other economies. To help with the interpretation of the results, box 3.2 provides a detailed discussion of transmission channels—including trade, commodities, financial markets, and confidence effects—and the associated mechanisms driving spillovers. The SVAR analysis covers 40 economies, divided into three groups—the EM3, the AE3, and other EMDEs—using data for 2000Q1 to 2023Q4 (technical details are provided in annex 3.2 and Balatti et al. 2024). The variables in the analysis include AE3 GDP growth, the U.S. interest rate, EMBI spreads, EM3 GDP growth, oil price growth, and GDP growth of other EMDEs. Dummy variables are also included to control for the impact of the COVID-19 pandemic. Spillovers are inferred by tracing cumulative GDP growth responses to a one-off exogenous increase in GDP growth of 1 percentage point.

Estimated responses to shocks are identified with a combination of sign and zero restrictions, grounded in economic theory. In general, an increase in GDP growth in major economies is assumed to boost GDP growth in these economies further than the shock itself and to increase oil prices, reflecting higher commodity demand. The response of other EMDEs to an increase in growth in the EM3 or AE3 is left unrestricted, allowing for direct estimation of spillovers from the data.

Spillovers from the EM3 and AE3

A growth increase in the EM3 is found to have sizable spillover effects on other EMDEs and the global economy. Specifically, a one-time 1-percentage-point increase in output growth in the EM3 is associated with a cumulative 1.9 percent expansion of output in other EMDEs and a cumulative 0.9 percent expansion in global output after three years (figures 3.7.A and 3.7.B). These findings underscore the interconnectedness of emerging markets with the rest of the global economy and align with findings in the previous literature (Huidrom et al. 2020; World Bank

2016). Spillovers to the AE3 from an increase in growth in the EM3 are not statistically significant. This can be attributed partly to factors such as offsets from rising oil prices that result from the initial growth shock and macroeconomic policies employed by the AE3.

An increase in growth in the AE3 is associated with larger spillovers than an equivalent growth increase in the EM3, both on impact and after each of the subsequent three years. A 1-percentage-point increase in growth in the AE3 is associated with a cumulative 4 percent output expansion in other EMDEs after three years, about twice the effect of an equivalent growth increase in the EM3, and a cumulative 3.1 percent expansion of global output after three years, roughly three times the effect of a growth increase in the EM3.

Growth fluctuations in the AE3 also account for a larger share of growth fluctuations elsewhere than those originating in the EM3. The AE3 account for about 35 percent of the variance in growth rates of other EMDEs at the three-year horizon, compared to a 10 percent contribution from the EM3 (figure 3.7.C). Similarly, the AE3 account for approximately 40 percent of the variance in global growth, whereas the EM3 contribute about 10 percent (figure 3.7.D). These results underscore the continued dominant role of advanced economies in driving global economic cycles, although EMDEs exert significant influence (World Bank 2016).

The relatively large spillovers from the AE3 can be attributed to their relatively large economic size and their dominant role in global trade and finance. With a greater share of global GDP and financial flows, the AE3 have the capacity to transmit shocks more strongly and rapidly through financial channels, influencing economic conditions worldwide. Although the EM3 still account for a smaller portion of the global GDP, their growing influence is evident in the substantial spillovers an increase in their output growth generates for other EMDEs and the global economy.

Spillovers from China and the United States

To investigate the extent of spillovers from China, the largest EMDE, and the United States, the largest advanced economy, the benchmark SVAR

FIGURE 3.7 Spillovers from the EM3 and AE3

Growth shocks in the EM3 have sizable spillovers on output in other EMDEs and globally. A 1-percentage-point increase in EM3 output growth is associated with a cumulative increase n output of 1.9 percent in other EMDEs and 0.9 percent growth in the global economy after three years. However, growth spillovers from the EM3 are considerably smaller than spillovers from the AE3. Growth shocks in the EM3 also explain less of the growth variance in other EMDEs and the global economy than do shocks in the AE3.

A. Cumulative output responses in other EMDEs from a 1-percentage-point growth increase in the EM3 and AE3

B. Cumulative output responses in the global economy from a 1-percentage-point growth increase in the EM3 and AE3

C. Other EMDEs' growth variance explained by growth variations in the EM3 and AE3

D. Global growth variance explained by growth variations in the EM3 and AE3

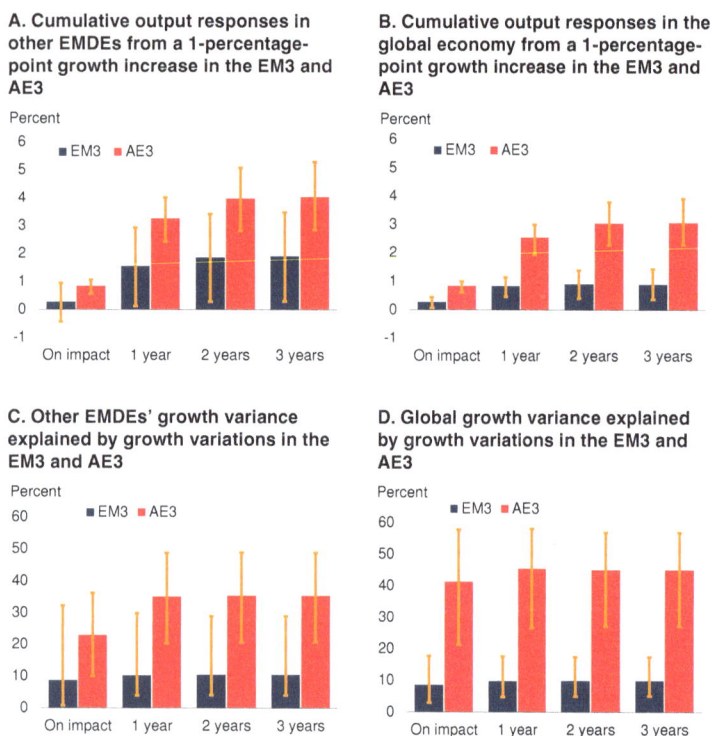

Source: World Bank.
Note: AE3 = United States, euro area, and Japan; EM3 = China, India, and Brazil; other EMDEs = emerging market and developing economies, excluding the EM3. Solid bars represent medians from the posterior distribution; error bars show 16-84 percent confidence bands. Results are based on quarterly data covering the period 2000Q1-2023Q4. Annex 3.2 contains further methodological information.
A. Bars show the cumulative impulse responses of output in other EMDEs to a 1 percentage point increase in output growth in the EM3 and the AE3.
B. Bars show the cumulative impulse responses of output in the global economy to a 1 percentage point increase in output growth in the EM3 and the AE3. Impulse responses are calculated as the GDP-weighted average of EM3, other EMDEs, and AE3 responses.
C. Bars show the (forecast error) variance of other EMDEs explained by growth variations in the EM3 versus the AE3.
D. Bars show the (forecast error) variance of the global economy explained by growth variations in the EM3 versus the AE3. The variance share of the global economy is calculated as the GDP-weighted average of the variance shares of the EM3, other EMDEs, and the AE3.

model is revised by replacing the EM3 with China and replacing the AE3 with the United States. The country-specific results mirror the benchmark results. In short, although an increase in growth in China has considerable effects on output elsewhere after two years, particularly in other EMDEs, the impact of an increase in growth in the United States is larger, a finding that is consistent with previous work on spillovers from the two

economies (Inoue, Kaya, and Ohshige 2015; Kose et al. 2020; Osborn and Vehbi 2015).

Specifically, a 1-percentage-point increase in China's GDP growth rate is associated with a 1.8 percent cumulative output expansion in other EMDEs and a 0.8 percent cumulative output expansion in the global economy after three years (figures 3.8.A and 3.8.B). This findings of sizable spillovers from China confirms findings from previous studies (Copestake et al. 2023; Furceri, Jalles, and Zdzienicka 2017; Kose et al. 2020). However, a 1-percentage-point increase in growth in the United States is associated with larger spillovers: a cumulative 2.9 percent output expansion in other EMDEs and a cumulative 2 percent expansion in the global economy after three years. Nevertheless, the magnitude of spillovers from China relative to those from the United States is closer than the magnitude of spillovers from the EM3 relative to those from the AE3. At the three-year horizon, spillovers from the United States to the global economy are approximately twice as large as those from China, while spillovers from the AE3 to the global economy are about three times as large as those from the EM3.

As in the results described above for the EM3 and AE3, the share of growth variance in other EMDEs and the global economy attributable to growth shocks in China is small relative to the share attributable to growth shocks in the United States. Between 2000Q1 and 2023Q4, growth shocks in China explained about 10 percent of the growth variance in other EMDEs and the global economy over a three-year horizon, while shocks in the United States explained approximately 25 percent of growth variation in other EMDEs and 30 percent of the global growth variation (figures 3.8.C and 3.8.D).

Spillovers over time and across country groups

The analysis of spillovers above indicates that changes in growth in the EM3 lead to sizable output growth spillovers elsewhere, but also that spillovers from changes in growth in the AE3 remain much larger than those from the EM3 in the first quarter of the twenty-first century. It is possible, though, given the EM3's increasing integration into, and contribution to, the global economy, that spillovers from these economies have increased over time.

To obtain a longer-term perspective, and in view of the limited availability of long, high-frequency time-series data for many EMDEs, the benchmark model is extended using annual data, with modifications in some variables to accommodate data availability.[12] Specifically, the model is estimated using annual data for two overlapping 30-year time spans—1971-2001 and 1993-2023. A comparison of estimates for these periods indeed shows a rise in the responsiveness of other EMDEs and commodity prices to an increase in growth in the EM3, substantiating the growing influence of major EMDEs on the global economy (figure 3.9.A). The increased responsiveness of output in other EMDEs signals a notable shift in interdependencies and an amplification of spillovers since the turn of the century. However, spillovers from an increase in growth in the AE3 remain substantially larger than spillovers from the EM3.

Consistent with the findings in the previous sections on integration and synchronization and in the literature, the analysis corroborates the important roles of trade and commodity prices in transmitting cross-border shocks. As EMDEs have opened further to trade, EM3 growth shocks have had larger global spillovers. The integration of major EMDEs into GVCs, particularly during the 1990s and 2000s, has likely amplified these spillovers. Commodity prices are also important transmission channels. Rising commodity prices, driven by growing demand, can spill across borders and boost economic activity in commodity-exporting countries (Kose et al. 2020). Conversely, for commodity importers, this channel could moderate adverse spillovers from

FIGURE 3.8 Spillovers from China and the United States

A 1-percentage-point increase in growth China leads to substantial output spillovers in other EMDEs and the global economy. Yet the cumulative magnitude of spillovers to the global economy is about half of that of spillovers from the United States. Growth shocks in China also explain a smaller share of the growth variance in other EMDEs and the global economy than do shocks in the United States.

A. Cumulative output responses in other EMDEs from a 1-percentage-point growth increase in China and the United States

B. Cumulative output responses in the global economy from a 1-percentage-point growth increase in China and the United States

C. Other EMDEs' growth variance explained by growth variations in China and the United States

D. Global growth variance explained by growth variations in China and the United States

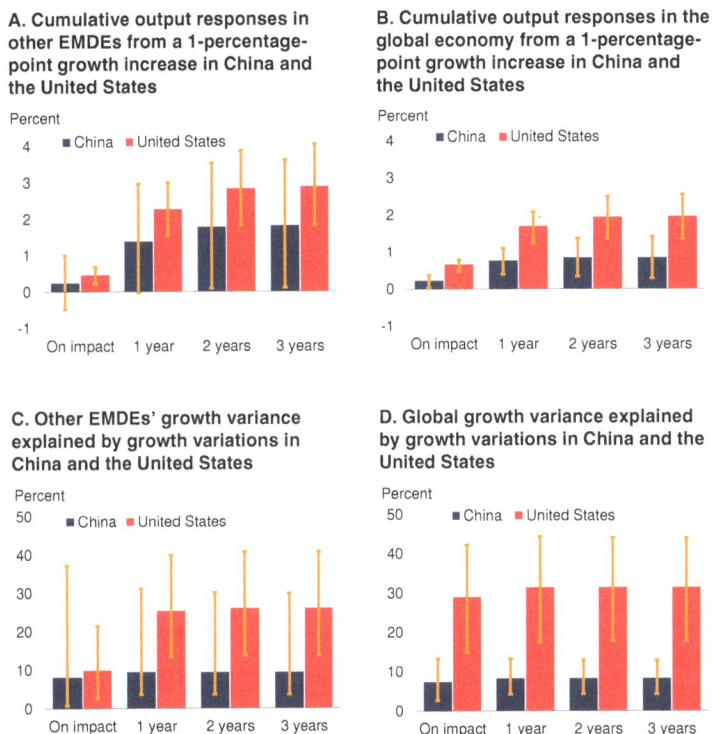

Source: World Bank.
Note: AE3 = United States, euro area, and Japan; EM3 = China, India, and Brazil; other EMDEs= emerging market and developing economies, excluding the EM3. Solid bars represent medians from the posterior distribution; error bars show 16-84 percent confidence bands. Results are based on quarterly data covering the period 2000Q1-2023Q4. Annex 3.2 contains further methodological information.
A. Bars show the cumulative impulse responses of output in other EMDEs to a 1 percentage point increase in output growth in China and the United States.
B. Bars show the cumulative impulse responses of output in the global economy to a 1 percentage point increase in output growth in China and the United States. Impulse responses are calculated as the GDP-weighted average of EM3, other EMDEs, and AE3 responses.
C. Bars show the (forecast error) variance of other EMDEs explained by growth variations in China versus the United States.
D. Bars show the (forecast error) variance of the global economy explained by growth variations in China versus the United States. The variance share of the global economy is calculated as the GDP-weighted average of the variance shares of the EM3, other EMDEs, and the AE3.

slumps in EM3 growth. In particular, stronger-than-expected growth in the EM3 tends to raise oil prices, amplifying positive spillovers to oil-exporting economies while muting positive spillovers to oil-importing economies (figure 3.9.B). While the financial channel is also important, the relatively limited financial integration of the EM3 constrains the extent of global spillovers.

---

[12] In addition to the SVAR exercise using annual data described here, the baseline SVAR model is re-estimated using quarterly data for 2009-23. The results show that, although the impact on oil prices has increased somewhat, there is no noticeable rise in business cycle spillovers to other EMDEs, advanced economies, or the global economy in the post-global financial crisis period. Several factors may explain the lack of significant increases in spillovers with quarterly data over a shorter period. These factors are summarized in annex 3.2.

FIGURE 3.9 Spillovers over time and across country groups

Spillovers from the EM3 to other EMDEs have increased over time. Commodity prices play an important role in transmitting cross-border shocks.

A. Cumulative output responses in other EMDEs after three years from a 1-percentage-point growth increase in the EM3 and AE3

B. Cumulative output responses in other EMDE commodity exporters and importers after three years from a 1-percentage-point growth increase in the EM3

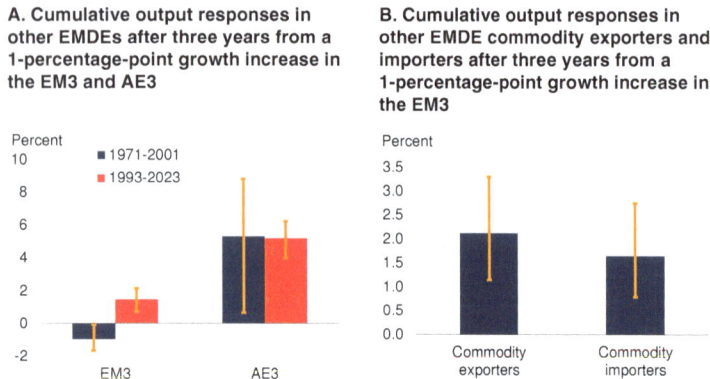

Source: World Bank.

Note: AE3 = United States, euro area, and Japan; EM3 = China, India, and Brazil; other EMDEs = emerging market and developing economies, excluding the EM3. Solid bars represent medians from the posterior distributions; error bars show 16-84 percent confidence bands.

A. Chart shows the cumulative impulse responses of output at a 3-year horizon to a 1 percentage point increase in EM3 and AE3 growth. Annex 3.2 contains further methodological information.

B. Chart shows the cumulative impulse responses of output at a 3-year horizon to a 1 percentage point increase in EM3 growth.

Taken together, these findings indicate that although spillovers from EM3 to the global economy are substantial and have become more potent since the turn of the century, they remain smaller than spillovers from the AE3.

Challenges confronting EMDEs

For many EMDEs, the period around the turn of the twenty-first century was transformative. As they became more integrated with advanced economies, they did not just embrace the global policy consensus on the benefits of globalization, but they also undertook measures to improve monetary and fiscal policy frameworks and liberalize their domestic financial sectors. The combination of global integration, domestic policy reforms, and robust commodity demand led to historically strong economic growth and better development outcomes. During the 2000s, EMDEs registered their best collective growth performance and fastest income convergence toward advanced economies since the 1970s. Thanks to strong growth and improvements in policy frameworks during this period, a large

number of EMDEs also accumulated significant policy buffers, better enabling them to weather the 2009 global recession (Kose and Prasad 2020).

Although they form a larger part of the global economy than they did at the start of the twenty-first century, EMDEs face many challenges as they enter the second quarter of the century. Output growth—actual as well as potential—has been weakening, the pace of structural reforms has stagnated, and fiscal space has narrowed. A surge in cross-border trade and investment restrictions and geopolitical tensions has dramatically altered the global economic landscape over the past decade. Rapid sectoral shifts and adverse effects of climate change have also become more pronounced, weighing on growth prospects. In addition, demographic conditions have been progressively less supportive of growth in several regions. Many EMDEs, particularly China, have, through their success, moved closer to the global technology frontier, so that their growth potential has waned. These developments have taken place against a backdrop of multiple global shocks, including the COVID-19 pandemic, Russia's invasion of Ukraine, renewed conflict in the Middle East, large commodity price swings, and a surge in global inflation accompanied by a sharp increase in global interest rates.

The impact of these challenges is magnified by significant linkages between them. For example, the lack of progress on structural and institutional reforms has contributed to the growth slowdown, as has the loss of momentum in cross-border integration resulting from the proliferation of trade and investment restrictions. Limited fiscal space has constrained the availability of financing for infrastructure investment, and climate-related adaptation and mitigation efforts. Multiple global shocks have contributed to the rapid accumulation of debt in many EMDEs, further eroding fiscal space.

Weakening growth prospects

Reflecting a combination of cyclical and structural factors, there has been a sustained slowdown in EMDEs' growth since the global financial crisis. On average, output in EMDEs grew by only 3.5 percent per year during 2020-24, compared to

5.1 percent during 2010-19 and 5.9 percent during 2000-09 (figure 3.10.A). The slowdown in growth has been widespread across EMDEs. Three-quarters of EMDEs had lower average growth during 2020-24 than in 2010-19, and nearly three-fifths already had lower average growth in the 2010s than in 2000-09. Average annual growth in the EM3 slowed to 4.5 percent during 2020-24, from 6.7 percent during the 2010s and 8.1 percent during the 2000s.[13] The slowdown in growth has also extended to advanced economies.

As growth in EMDEs has slowed, the pace of convergence to the per capita income levels of advanced economies has also weakened: the difference in per capita growth between EMDEs and advanced economies, which averaged more than 3 percentage points during the 2000s, has narrowed significantly. During 2020-24, annual per capita growth in EMDEs averaged only 1.2 percentage points above that in advanced economies (figure 3.10.B). Excluding China and India, per capita growth in EMDEs has switched from catching up with that in advanced economies to falling further behind. Nearly half of EMDEs had slower per capita growth than advanced economies in 2020-24 (figure 3.10.C). The sluggish pace of per capita growth in EMDEs will not be sufficient to allow many of these economies to make meaningful progress toward key global development goals. The pace of poverty reduction was already slower in the years after the global financial crisis than in the decade preceding the crisis, and poverty rates in some EMDEs rose following the COVID-19 pandemic (figure 3.10.D). By 2030, about 7 percent of the global population is expected to remain in extreme poverty (World Bank 2024c). An estimated 600 million people will be facing hunger (UN 2024).

The decline in growth in EMDEs reflects a slowdown in potential growth, or the maximum growth rate that can be sustained in the long term

---

[13] Although China explains much of the growth slowdown in the EM3 because of its size, growth has weakened in all three economies since the 2000s. In China, growth slowed from 10.3 percent in the 2000s to 4.8 percent in 2020-24. Growth in India decelerated from 6.3 percent in the 2000s to 5.1 percent in 2020-24, while Brazil also experienced a slowdown from 3.4 percent to 2.1 percent during the same period.

FIGURE 3.10 Growth, convergence, and poverty

As growth in EMDEs has slowed, the pace of convergence to the income levels of advanced economies has also weakened. During 2020-24, annual per capita growth in EMDEs averaged only 1.2 percentage points above that in advanced economies. The sluggish pace of per capita growth in EMDEs will not be sufficient to allow many of these economies to make meaningful progress toward key global development goals, including further progress on poverty reduction.

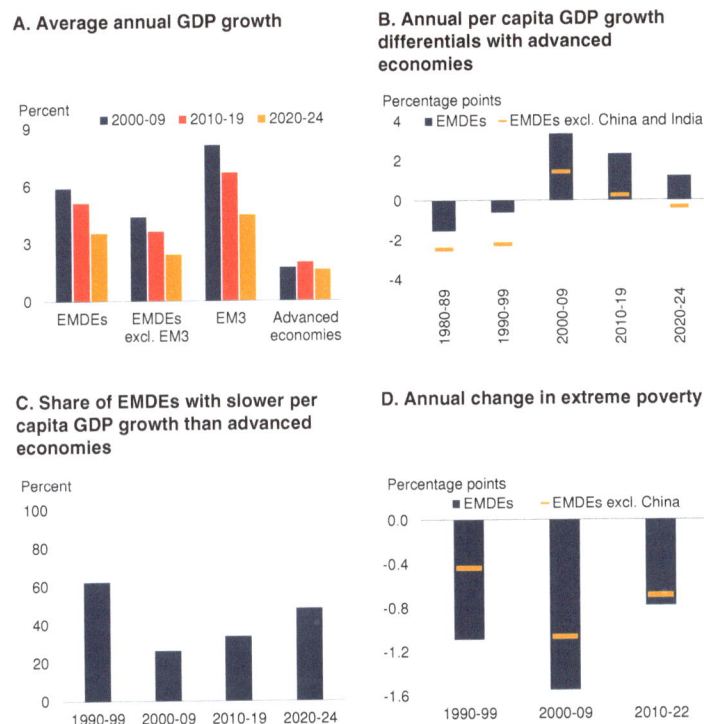

A. Average annual GDP growth

B. Annual per capita GDP growth differentials with advanced economies

C. Share of EMDEs with slower per capita GDP growth than advanced economies

D. Annual change in extreme poverty

Sources: UN World Population Prospects; World Bank; World Bank Poverty and Inequality Platform.
Note: EM3 = China, India, and Brazil; EMDEs = emerging market and developing economies.
A. Bars show simple average for each decade of annual GDP-weighted average growth in each group of economies. Data for the 2020s include 2020-24. Growth rates for 2024 are estimated.
B.C. Per capita GDP is calculated as the total GDP for each group of economies divided by the total population in each group. GDP aggregates are calculated using real U.S. dollar GDP weights at average 2010-19 prices and market exchange rates. Per capita growth rates for 2024 are estimated.
D. Bars show average annual change in extreme poverty rates.

---

at full employment and full capacity without igniting inflation. All fundamental drivers of growth have weakened since the global financial crisis. Potential growth in EMDEs is projected to slide to 4.1 percent per year, on average, in 2020-29, lower than the average of 5.3 percent per year in 2010-19, which in turn was already lower than 5.9 percent in the 2000s (figure 3.11.A). Potential growth in the EM3 is on track to slow more sharply, from 6.3 percent in 2010-19 to 4.7 percent in 2020-29. As of 2025, EMDEs face the lowest five-year-ahead potential growth rate since the start of the century. Like the slowdown in actual growth, the slowdown in potential growth

FIGURE 3.11 Potential output growth and long-term growth expectations

EMDEs' potential output growth and long-term growth forecasts have slowed significantly since the 2000s. The slowdown has been even more pronounced in the EM3, mainly reflecting the slowdown in China. Even with the post-pandemic recovery, growth of actual and potential GDP is set to remain below the averages achieved in the early 2000s.

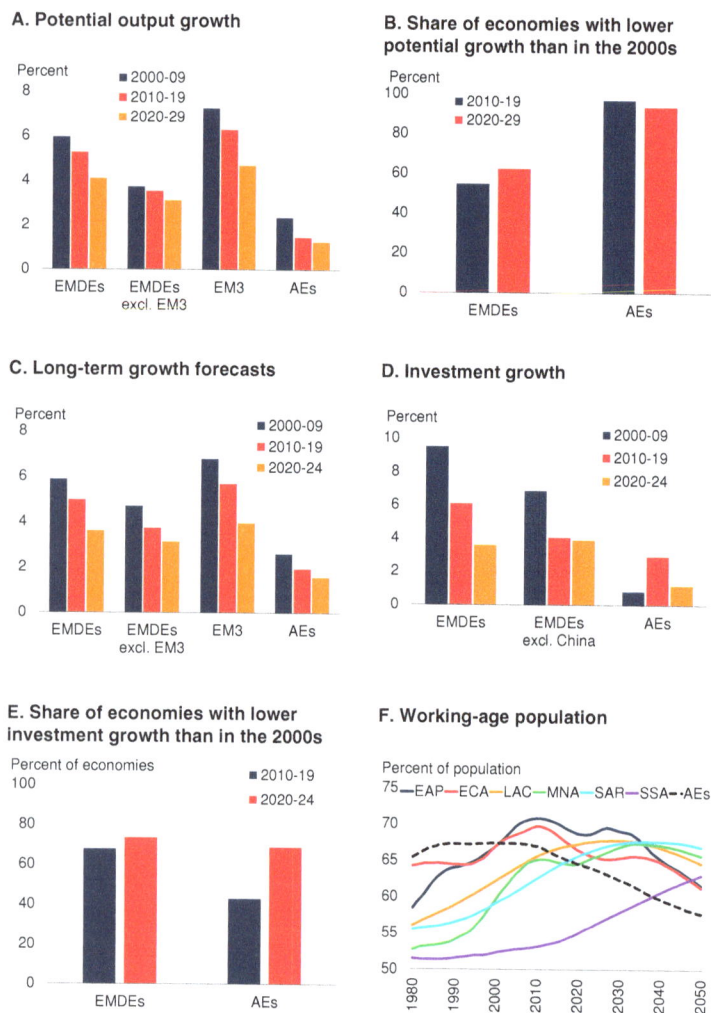

A. Potential output growth

B. Share of economies with lower potential growth than in the 2000s

C. Long-term growth forecasts

D. Investment growth

E. Share of economies with lower investment growth than in the 2000s

F. Working-age population

Sources: Consensus Economics; Haver Analytics; Penn World Tables; Kilic Celik, Kose, and Ohnsorge (2024); United Nations World Population Prospects; World Bank; World Development Indicators database.

Note: AEs = advanced economies; EAP = East Asia and Pacific; ECA = Europe and Central Asia; EM3 = China, India, and Brazil; EMDEs = emerging market and developing economies; EMDEs excl. EM3 = emerging market and developing economies excluding China, India, and Brazil; LAC = Latin America and the Caribbean; LICs = low-income countries; MNA = Middle East and North Africa; SAR = South Asia; SSA = Sub-Saharan Africa.

A.B. Potential growth is the maximum GDP growth rate that can be sustained in the long term at full employment and full capacity without igniting inflation. It is measured using a production function approach as in Kilic Celik, Kose, and Ohnsorge (2024). Sample includes 53 EMDEs and 30 advanced economies.

A. Bars show simple averages across years of GDP-weighted averages for each year.

B. Bars show the fraction of countries with weaker average potential output growth during the 2010s and 2020s compared to the 2000s.

C. Bars show simple averages across years of GDP-weighted averages of Consensus Economics growth forecasts for 6-10 years ahead. Sample includes 52 EMDEs and 34 advanced economies.

D.E. "Investment" refers to gross fixed-capital formation. Investment growth is calculated using countries' real annual investment in constant U.S. dollars as weights. Investment growth for 2024 is estimated. Sample includes 71 EMDEs and 35 advanced economies.

F. Lines show population-weighted averages. Working-age is defined as people ages 15-64.

has been global. In advanced economies, potential growth is projected to average about 1.3 percent per year in 2020-29, about half of the rate during the 2000s. Sixty percent of EMDEs are on track to have slower potential growth during the 2020s than during the 2000s (figure 3.11.B).

Consistent with the slowing of potential growth, long-term growth expectations of EMDEs have also softened considerably. In 2000, EMDEs were projected by private-sector forecasters to grow by 6 percent in 2010. In 2010, the long-term growth forecast for these economies peaked at 6.2 percent. Since 2010, it has steadily declined, falling to 3.4 percent in 2024 (figure 3.11.C). For advanced economies, long-term growth forecasts have been declining since the early 2000s. Weak prospects for advanced economies, still critical trade and investment partners of EMDEs, will make it additionally challenging for EMDEs to improve their growth outlooks.

Three fundamental factors explain the slowdown in potential growth in EMDEs. First, investment growth in EMDEs was substantially slower in the 2010s than in the 2000s, and the slowing continued in the early 2020s (figure 3.11.D). In both the 2010s and the 2020s, about 70 percent of EMDEs has lower investment growth, on average, than in the 2000s (figure 3.11.E). The post-global financial crisis slowdown in investment growth initially reflected, in part, the withdrawal of crisis-related policy stimulus. The plunge in commodity prices in 2014-16 also hit investment, particularly in commodity-exporting EMDEs, while in China, the rebalancing of growth away from investment contributed to the global investment slowdown. Flagging investment growth may also have reflected discouraging investment climates and bouts of elevated policy uncertainty (Stamm and Vorisek 2024).

Second, labor productivity growth softened in EMDEs during the 2010s, in part because of weakening investment growth, but also due to several other factors (Dieppe 2021). Productivity gains during previous decades from sectoral reallocation of resources, particularly of the labor force out of the agricultural sector, have faded. Populations begin to age in some EMDEs. And innovation slowed, partly owing to narrowing gaps between technology in use and the global technological frontier.

Third, the demographic profiles of some EMDEs have become less favorable for economic growth. In EAP and ECA, the working-age (aged 15-64) share of the population has been declining since the early 2010s following the trend in advanced economies starting in the mid-2000s (figure 3.11.F). In LAC, the working-age share of the population will begin a slow, steady decline from the early 2030s. In MNA and SAR, the decline is expected to begin somewhat later. In contrast, in SSA, the working-age share of the population is projected to continue to expand for decades, presenting an opportunity to accelerate growth if workers can be employed more productively.

Difficult external environment

Despite EMDEs' significant progress in integrating into the global economy over the past 25 years, the global economic cooperation that characterized the years around the turn of the century has wound down since the global financial crisis and, more recently, has gone into reverse. The frequency of new trade and investment agreements has been substantially lower in the early 2020s than in the two preceding decades (figures 3.12.A and 3.12.B). In 2023, the number of global trade restrictions reached the highest level on record since 2009. Trade and investment restrictions, along with trade distortions stemming from behind-the-border industrial policies, have proliferated (figures 3.12.C and 3.12.D). Advanced economies are responsible for about 70 percent of the trade-distorting policy measures introduced in 2022-24, while EMDEs have borne most of the effects. The momentum of trade and financial globalization has stalled, and geopolitical fragmentation has risen, reaching a peak in 2020 and remaining elevated (figures 3.12.E and 3.12.F). These developments present challenges for EMDEs (Aiyar and Ohnsorge 2024; Fernández-Villaverde, Mineyama, and Song 2024).

As protectionist measures have risen, global economic integration has slowed, reflecting a raft of cyclical and structural challenges (Constantinescu, Mattoo, and Ruta 2020). During 2000-19, global trade in real terms

FIGURE 3.12 Trade and investment fragmentation

Trade and investment restrictions have increased sharply in recent years, while the number of new trade and investment agreements has declined. Geopolitical fragmentation has been trending upwards since around 2008, peaking in 2020, and remains high.

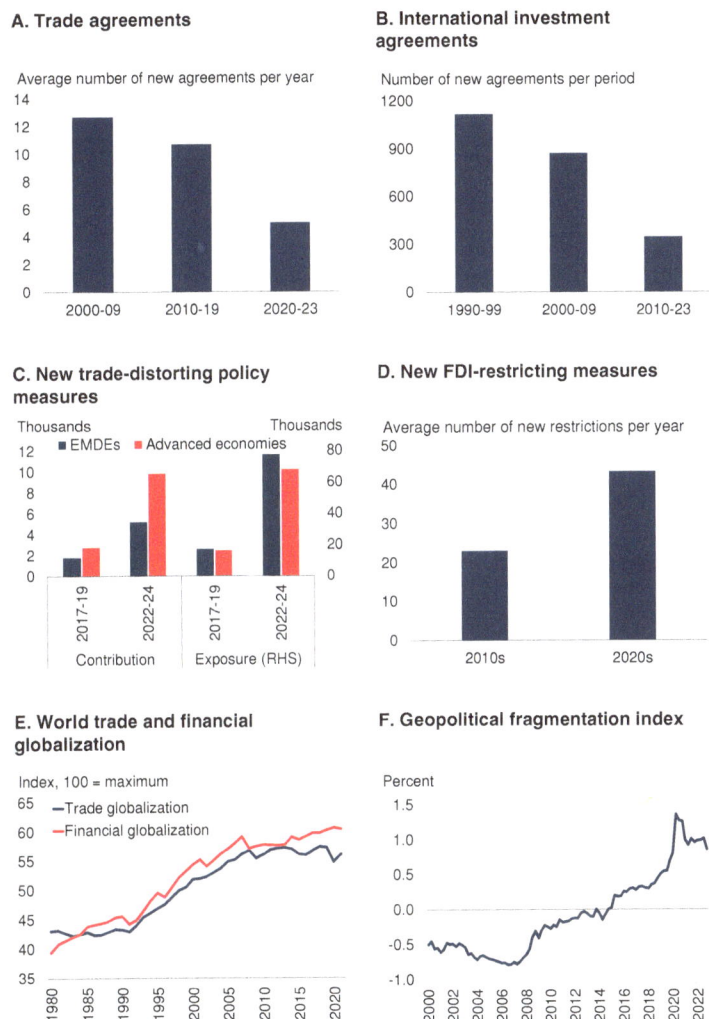

A. Trade agreements

B. International investment agreements

C. New trade-distorting policy measures

D. New FDI-restricting measures

E. World trade and financial globalization

F. Geopolitical fragmentation index

Sources: Fernández-Villaverde, Mineyama, and Song (2024); Global Trade Alert (database); UNCTAD International Investment Agreements Navigator (database); KOF Economic Research Institute; World Bank; World Trade Organization.
Note: EMDEs = emerging market and developing economies; FDI = foreign direct investment; RHS = right-hand scale.
A. Bars show simple averages of annual data. Sample excludes agreements signed by the United Kingdom.
B. Data include new international investment agreements that are in force.
C. Panel shows implemented interventions by countries that discriminate against foreign interests. Contribution represents the number of measures implemented by each country group. Exposure represents the number of measures affecting each country group. Each measure can be implemented by and target multiple countries. Adjusted data (for reporting lags) as of December 19, 2024.
D. Bars for the 2020s include data available through November 2024.
E. The trade globalization index is calculated using trade in goods and services, trade partner diversity, trade regulations, trade taxes and tariffs, and trade agreements. The financial globalization index is calculated using FDI; portfolio investment; international debt, reserves, and income payments; investment restrictions; capital account openness; and international investment agreements. The indexes use time-varying weights of the individual variables, determined using principal components analysis on 10-year rolling windows of annual data.
F. The geopolitical fragmentation index extracts a common factor across various indicators relating to trade and financial flows, restrictions, and global uncertainty (Fernández-Villaverde, Mineyama, and Song 2024). Line shows the percent responses to a one-standard-deviation fragmentation shock. A higher value implies greater fragmentation.

FIGURE 3.13 Global trade integration

Trade as a share of GDP leveled off in advanced economies and EMDEs excluding the EM3 in the early 2010s, after rising rapidly in the decade before the global financial crisis, and has not risen back to its peaks since then. In the EM3, trade as a share of GDP has declined significantly. Trade growth in the early 21st century was underpinned by robust growth in global value chains (GVCs) in the 2000s, which has since leveled off.

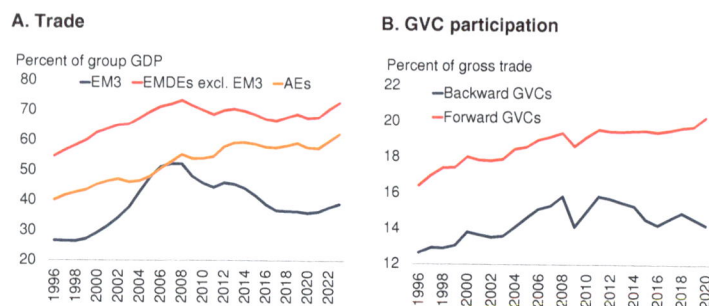

A. Trade

B. GVC participation

Sources: OECD TiVA; World Bank; World Development Indicators (database).
Note: AEs = advanced economies; EM3 = China, India, and Brazil; EMDEs = emerging market and developing economies; EMDEs excl. EM3 = emerging market and developing economies excluding China, India, and Brazil.
A. Lines show three-year moving averages of annual GDP-weighted averages in each group of economies. Trade is measured as the sum of exports and imports and includes goods and services trade. Last observation is 2023.
B. Lines show GDP-weighted averages of 39 EMDEs and 34 advanced economies. Backward GVC participation measures the proportion of foreign value-added embedded in a domestic economy's exports; forward GVC participation measures the proportion of domestic value added embedded in foreign exports.

expanded at an average rate of about 5 percent per year. That pace slowed to about 2.5 percent per year during 2020-24. Moreover, after peaking in 2008, the ratio of trade to GDP in EMDEs has since trended downward (figure 3.13.A). The decline has been particularly marked in the EM3. The trade slowdown has been concentrated in goods trade, while the pace of services trade has remained robust (Ohnsorge and Quaglietti 2024). The rapid expansion of GVCs, instrumental in promoting trade growth in the 2000s, has leveled off since the early 2010s, in line with slowing global growth and rising protectionist measures, but also reflecting a degree of natural maturation as potential gains from further specialization became more limited (figures 3.13.B). Supply chain vulnerabilities exposed during the COVID-19 pandemic further slowed GVC growth (Javorcik 2020).

FDI to EMDEs, as a share of their GDP, has also dropped, from an average of 3.1 percent of GDP in the 2000s to 1.8 percent in the 2020s, partly because of elevated policy uncertainty (Adarov and Pallan forthcoming). The decline has been widespread: FDI as a share of GDP has been lower

in more than three-fifths of EMDEs in the 2020s relative to the 2000s. Although EMDEs are receiving a larger share of global FDI inflows—about one-half in the early 2020s, compared to one-fifth in the 2000s—that larger share is based on a lower volume of global flows. After reaching more than $3 trillion in 2007, global net FDI inflows fell to an annual average of about $1.5 trillion in the early 2020s.

Restrictions on cross-border investment flows have also been proliferating alongside barriers to trade. For example, inward FDI screening mechanisms have become more widespread, with the number of countries adopting such measures more than doubling in the past decade, in part reflecting elevated geopolitical tensions and concerns relating to national security (UNCTAD 2024a). Additionally, there has been a rising incidence of outward FDI screening by large economies, which may hinder FDI flows to EMDEs (Myles 2024; UNCTAD 2024b).

Protectionist trade measures and investment restrictions tend to result in distortions that inhibit economic growth, increase prices paid by domestic consumers, disrupt value chains, and impede cross-border productivity spillovers.[14] Rising use of protectionist measures also increases policy uncertainty, disrupting firms' decisions and trade flows while creating a less stable, more costly environment for global trade. These measures often lead to retaliatory actions, creating a cycle of escalating trade barriers that harm cross-border commerce well beyond the countries targeted by the original measures. This uncertainty discourages investment and innovation and forces firms to reconfigure supply chains, often at significant cost (Grossman, Helpman, and Redding 2024). While industrial policies can support sectoral development and address market failures, poorly designed or long-lasting interventions risk distorting markets, suppressing competition and innovation, adversely affecting price formation, and reducing the availability of goods and services (EBRD 2024; Millot and Rawdanowicz 2024).

---

[14] See, for example, Amiti, Redding, and Weinstein (2019); Cavallo et al. (2021); and World Bank (2023b).

Narrowing fiscal space

Many EMDEs have limited fiscal space, reducing their ability to use countercyclical policy to stabilize activity in the face of adverse (domestic or external) shocks. Public spending to respond to the COVID-19 pandemic drove up debt levels in the 2020s, but debt had already increased substantially in the decade before the pandemic, from a GDP-weighted average of 37 percent in 2010 to 55 percent in 2019—the largest and most widespread of four global debt waves since 1970 (Kose et al. 2021; figure 3.14.A). By 2024, government debt-to-GDP ratio in EMDEs stood at 70 percent, the highest since 1970. The widening of fiscal deficits and the speed at which both government and private debt rose far exceeded changes in previous waves of debt.

This surge in debt in the 2010s coincided with a significant policy shift that has been increasingly more supportive of expansionary fiscal measures (Cao, Dabla-Norris, and Di Gregorio 2024). These developments have resulted in a steady worsening of government debt in EMDEs (figure 3.14.B). Against a background of weak growth and elevated interest rates, debt-servicing costs have risen sharply in many cases, making the need for fiscal consolidation more pressing (figure 3.14.C). Longstanding challenges related to rampant informality, domestic revenue mobilization, and public spending efficiency hinder EMDEs' ability to improve the fiscal outlook in the near term (Ohnsorge and Yu 2022; figure 3.14.D).

Underdeveloped financial markets

Financial sector depth and access, as well as efficiency, tend to be far lower in EMDEs than in advanced economies (World Bank 2019). Many EMDEs have bank-dominated financial systems with underdeveloped capital markets and inadequate regulatory capacity. Small- and medium-sized enterprises face particular challenges accessing finance. Measured by domestic credit to the private sector by banks, financial sector depth averaged 42 percent of GDP in EMDEs in 2023, compared to 96 percent in advanced economies. The bank lending -to-deposit spread, a measure of financial system

FIGURE 3.14 Debt and fiscal conditions

Elevated public debt and persistent fiscal deficits in EMDEs limit their policy space. Amid weak growth, higher interest rates and debt-service costs, and long-standing structural challenges, the urgency of fiscal consolidation and reforms to restore and maintain debt sustainability has intensified.

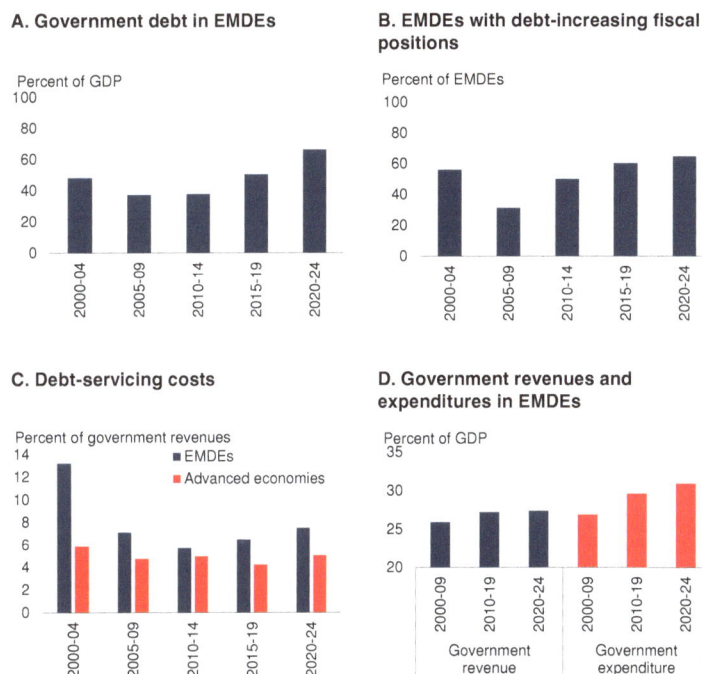

A. Government debt in EMDEs

B. EMDEs with debt-increasing fiscal positions

C. Debt-servicing costs

D. Government revenues and expenditures in EMDEs

Sources: International Monetary Fund; Kose et al. (2021, 2022); World Bank.
Note: EMDEs = emerging market and developing economies; GDP = gross domestic product.
A. Period averages, with data for 2024 referring to estimates. The aggregate is computed with current GDP in U.S. dollars as a weight, based on data for up to 153 EMDEs.
B. Bars show the share of EMDEs with a primary balance sustainability gap of less than zero. The primary balance sustainability gap is calculated as the difference between the primary balance and the debt-stabilizing primary balance. Sample includes 82 EMDEs.
C. Debt servicing costs are represented by net interest payments in percent of government revenues. Net interest payments are, computed as the difference between primary and overall fiscal balances. The aggregates are computed with government revenues in U.S. dollars as weights. Sample includes 150 EMDEs and 38 advanced economies.
D. Bars show unweighted averages.

efficiency, averaged about 8 percentage points in EMDEs during 2019-23, compared to about 3 percentage points in advanced economies.

Although some EMDEs have made progress in deepening their financial sectors since the global financial crisis, including through the development of local currency bond markets, many continue to face challenges in addressing information asymmetries and strengthening regulatory frameworks (Hashimoto et al. 2021; Wooldridge 2020). These features of EMDEs' financial systems make it challenging for policymakers to protect their financial systems from disruptions, whether such disruptions emerge as internal pressures or cross-border spillovers. In 2024, 52 percent of low- and lower-middle income EMDEs were assessed to be at a high risk of financial instability, versus only 8 percent of high and upper-middle-income EMDEs (World Bank 2024d). Shallow financial markets also hamper monetary policy transmission and reduce the feasibility of exchange rate flexibility, making EMDEs more vulnerable to external shocks. In the medium to long term, financial sector limitations and fragilities constrain EMDEs' ability to promote inclusive growth.

Failure to reform amid elevated policy uncertainty

Since the early 2000s, progress with structural and institutional reforms in many EMDEs has stalled (IMF 2019b; figures 3.15.A and 3.15.B). Lack of progress in implementing institutional reforms is one factor contributing to the sustained decline in FDI inflows as a share of GDP in these economies since the early 2010s (Adarov and Pallan forthcoming). In contrast, in EMDEs where there has been sustained institutional improvement, there has been higher productivity and investment growth (Kilic Celik, Kose, and Ohnsorge 2024; World Bank 2024e).

Lower-middle-income countries and LICs may have more limited capacity to implement the comprehensive structural reforms necessary to foster trade and FDI, rendering them especially vulnerable to risks associated with increasing global economic fragmentation (chapter 4). An adverse or unclear regulatory environment would likely be a key concern for investors considering the viability of FDI projects in EMDEs (MIGA 2024). Some EMDEs may also be experiencing a weakening of institutions associated with the rise of populist movements, an increasing phenomenon since the early 2000s (Funke, Schularick, and Trebesch 2023).

Policy uncertainty has increased since the global financial crisis. Multiple measures of global economic and trade policy uncertainty have risen markedly since the 2000s (figures 3.15.C and 3.15.D). Contributing factors have included security challenges and armed conflicts, geopolitical tensions between major economies,

acute domestic political challenges in some EMDEs, and changing approaches to cross-border trade and investment flows. Uncertainty plays a critical role in firms' decision-making processes (Alfaro, Bloom, and Lin 2024). Trade policy uncertainty—including relating to tariffs, transport costs, customs and border processes, and other nontariff restrictions—is associated with weaker investment and output growth.

Adaptation to sectoral and technological change

EMDEs face major structural changes in the global economy, including sectoral shifts and technological advances, and they need to position themselves to benefit from these changes. For example, between 2000 and 2023, the services sector accounted for two-thirds of global GDP growth and three-fourths of global employment growth. The transition to services-based economies in EMDEs is occurring without the large productivity gains that accompanied the transition from agriculture to manufacturing in some of these economies decades ago, in part because a large share of services sector jobs are in low-skilled, nontradable services. At the same time, digitalization has improved prospects for economies of scale and innovation in the services sector by reducing the need for physical proximity and physical capital (Nayyar and Davies 2024). Policies to support the availability and adoption of digital technologies may thus be an effective way to advance productivity-enhancing services sector growth.

Climate change and natural disasters

Climate change is a major challenge for EMDEs. It has already caused significant damage to lives and livelihoods, disproportionately affecting the poor. The frequency and severity of extreme weather events such as droughts, floods and storms affecting EMDEs has risen sharply (figure 3.16.A). Damages and losses from such disasters, already large—especially in the smallest EMDEs—are expected to continue rising as the effects of climate change become more intense (figure 3.16.B). In an adverse scenario, climate change could push more than 130 million people into extreme poverty by 2030, most of them in low- and lower-middle-income EMDEs (figure 3.16.C; Hallegatte and Rozenberg 2017; Jafino et al. 2020). A 1°C upward temperature shock could potentially lead to a peak medium-term decline in global GDP as large as 12 percent (Bilal and Kanzig 2024; Nath, Ramey, and Klenow 2024). A major investment push is needed to accelerate mitigation and adaptation efforts related to climate change in EMDEs, yet significant financing constraints make achieving the scale of investment needed very difficult (figure 3.16.D).

Policy priorities in EMDEs

Given the challenges they face, EMDEs need to prioritize policy actions to boost investment and productivity, navigate the difficult external environment, and enhance macroeconomic stability and resilience. With appropriate policy interventions, some challenges can be converted into opportunities. For example, EMDEs have massive investment needs to address infrastructure gaps, speed up climate transition, boost economic growth, and meet broader development goals. However, if they employ prudent policies to accelerate investment, these could translate not only into higher near-term growth but also into stronger potential and long-term growth that would help them achieve broader development and climate-related goals. Policies to enhance the human capital of younger generations provide another example: if effective, they will allow some EMDEs to reap demographic dividends, and help enhance potential growth prospects. While there is no one-size-fits-all recipe to overcome the challenges facing EMDEs, three fundamental and equally important policy objectives lead to a common set of thematic priorities.

- *Boost investment and productivity.* EMDEs need to reinvigorate structural reforms. Especially for the least developed EMDEs, such reforms should aim to boost the growth of both physical capital, including by improving the investment and institutional environment, and foster human capital development (see chapter 4). For more developed EMDEs, additional policy initiatives are needed to spur innovation and promote the diffusion of efficiency-enhancing

FIGURE 3.15 Institutional environment and policy uncertainty

Progress with institutional reforms in EMDEs has stalled since the 2000s, weakening the investment climate and discouraging FDI inflows. Heightened policy uncertainty—driven by geopolitical tensions, armed conflicts, and changing approaches to trade policy shifts—constrains investment and growth prospects in EMDEs.

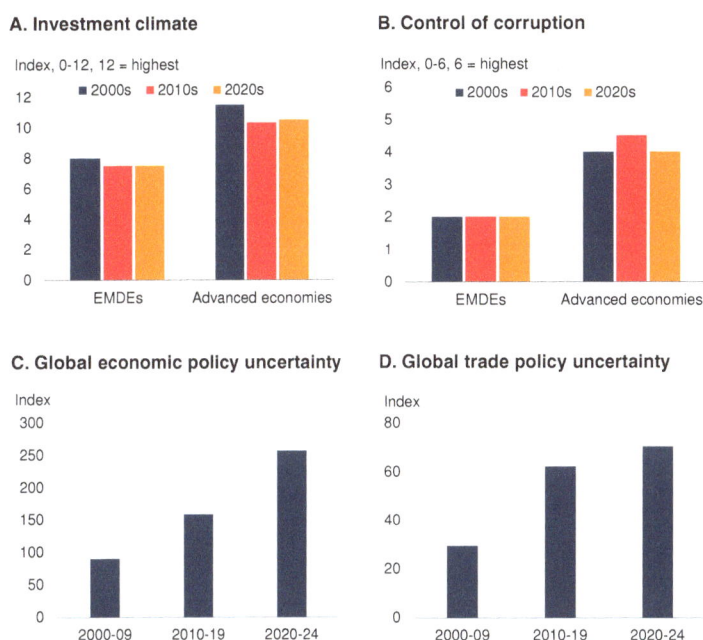

A. Investment climate
Index, 0-12, 12 = highest

B. Control of corruption
Index, 0-6, 6 = highest

C. Global economic policy uncertainty
Index

D. Global trade policy uncertainty
Index

Sources: Caldara et al. (2020); Federal Reserve Economic Data (database); PRS Group; World Bank.
Note: EMDEs = emerging market and developing economies; FDI = foreign direct investment.
A.B. Bars show group medians. Data for the 2020s cover 2020-23. Sample includes 36 advanced economies and 102 EMDEs.
C. Index is a GDP-weighted average of 15 advanced economies and 5 EMDEs using current price adjusted GDP. Last observation is September 2024.
D. The global trade policy uncertainty index quantifies changes in trade policy uncertainty by measuring the frequency of related terms in major newspapers; higher values indicate increased uncertainty. Last observation is November 2024.

technologies that can accelerate growth and create the conditions necessary to benefit more from integration (World Bank 2024f).

- *Navigate the difficult external environment.* In an increasingly difficult global economic environment marked by rising trade restrictions and geopolitical tensions, EMDEs need to implement a comprehensive set of policies to mitigate the adverse effects of trade tensions between major economies and to fully reap the benefits of cross-border linkages.

- *Enhance macroeconomic stability.* To maintain macroeconomic stability in the face of external shocks, EMDEs will need to ensure that sufficient buffers are in place, supported by

FIGURE 3.16 Natural disasters and climate change

The frequency and severity of extreme weather events have risen sharply. Climate change and climate-related disasters have caused significant damage to lives and livelihoods in some EMDEs and could push a large number of people into poverty in the future. Large-scale investment is needed for mitigation of, and adaptation to, the effects of climate change, but this is obstructed by EMDEs' major financing constraints.

A. Extreme weather events in EMDEs

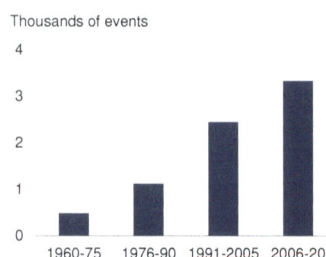

B. Damages and losses from natural disasters

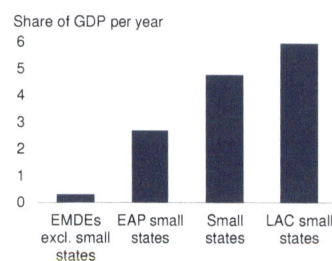

C. Impact of climate change on extreme poverty by 2030

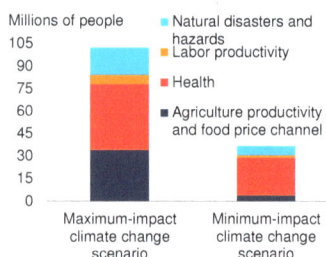

D. Additional investment needs for a resilient and low-carbon pathway, 2022-30

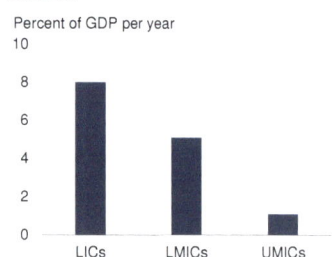

Sources: EM-DAT (database); Jafino et al. (2020); World Bank (2022a); World Bank.
Note: EAP = East Asia and Pacific; EMDEs = emerging market and developing economies; LAC = Latin America and the Caribbean; LICs = low-income countries; LMICs = lower-middle-income countries; UMICs = upper-middle-income countries.
A. Extreme weather events include droughts, floods, and storms. Sample includes 123 economies for droughts, 144 for floods, and 125 for storms.
B. Small states are EMDEs with a population of less than 1.5 million. Aggregates are calculated using nominal GDP weights.
C. Bars show the number of additional people in extreme poverty in 2030 owing to climate change. Based on Jafino et al. (2020), baseline scenarios are created without accounting for climate change impacts but with factoring in possible changes to demography, education, labor force participation, economic structure, productivity, and redistribution. Then, climate change is introduced in these baselines. The maximum and minimum levels of climate impacts represent the uncertainty on the physical impacts of climate and local adaptation policies.
D. Bars show the annual investment needs to build resilience to climate change and put countries on track to reduce emissions by 70 percent by 2050. Depending on availability, estimates include investment needs related to transport, energy, water, urban adaptations, industry, and landscape. In some Country Climate and Development Reports, especially those for low-income and lower-middle-income countries, estimated investments include development needs, especially those linked to closing the infrastructure gaps—such as solar mini grids to provide energy access—and cannot be considered entirely "additional" to pre-existing financing needs.

well-designed and credible policy frameworks. With these bulwarks, EMDEs will be better able to use countercyclical policy when needed.

Although these common policy objectives cover a wide range of actions, the actions can involve

significant synergies. Structural policies to reverse the growth slowdown, such as human capital development and business environment improvements, will also help put EMDEs in a better position to withstand external shocks. Enhanced macroeconomic stability often sets the stage for effective structural reforms. Policy makers in EMDEs have a rich toolkit at their disposal to overcome the challenges confronting their economies, and in most cases they will need to deploy a combination of policy instruments.

Improving growth prospects by boosting investment and productivity

Growth is the single most important driver to improve living standards, reduce poverty, and make progress in broader goals of development. The appropriate sequencing and focus of policy interventions to improve sustainable and inclusive growth outcomes differ depending on specific country circumstances. However, policies generally need to focus on three key areas. First, EMDEs need to accelerate investment, particularly in infrastructure. Second, improving the business climate is key not only to boosting private investment growth but also to spurring innovation and the diffusion of technology (World Bank 2024f). Third, many EMDEs need to take further action to enhance human capital, setting the stage to boost labor productivity.

Investment acceleration

Investment is a critical engine of economic growth in EMDEs. Indeed, capital accumulation has been responsible for more than half of the potential output growth in these economies since 2000.[15] Reversing the prolonged, broad-based slowdown in investment growth in EMDEs since the 2009 global recession is thus critical for improving their growth prospects. Accelerating investment growth is also essential for addressing the large investment gaps in many EMDEs and for making progress

---

[15] The standard growth accounting framework to decomposes output growth into estimated contributions of the growth in factor inputs and the growth of total factor productivity. See, for example, Kilic Celik, Kose, and Ohnsorge (2024).

toward broader development goals, including climate change-related objectives. Substantially higher investment is required to build and maintain infrastructure, adapt to climate change, facilitate the energy transition away from fossil fuels, accelerate poverty reduction, and advance shared prosperity.[16]

Many EMDEs have experienced investment accelerations, defined as periods of sustained increases in investment growth to relatively rapid rates, although the frequency of these episodes has decreased sharply since the 2000s (Stamm and Yu 2024). During the early 2000s, nearly half of EMDEs experienced an investment acceleration, while only about a quarter had an investment acceleration in the 2010s (figure 3.17.A). Investment accelerations tend to be accompanied by not only higher output growth, but also faster productivity growth (figure 3.17.B).

Policy reform is paramount for EMDEs to spark a new round of investment acceleration episodes. Well-designed fiscal, financial sector, and trade policy reforms all increase the likelihood of an investment acceleration (figure 3.17.C). A regulatory environment that promotes business dynamism and enables efficient capital and labor reallocation will help accelerate domestic private investment and make EMDEs more attractive as trade and investment partners, setting the stage for their economies to benefit from increased international integration. Past episodes of investment acceleration also suggest that while individual policy reforms increased the likelihood of starting a new episode, comprehensive packages of reforms resolving structural bottlenecks and enhancing macroeconomic stability tended to be more effective in triggering investment accelerations. This indicates that significant and wide-ranging policy reform efforts—drawing on experience gained in many countries—could promote an acceleration of investment that could help reverse the projected decline in potential growth expected in EMDEs during the coming years (figure 3.17.D). Effective scaling-up of

FIGURE 3.17 Investment accelerations in EMDEs

Investment accelerations in EMDEs—a key means of boosting potential growth in these economies—have become less common since the 2009 global recession, reducing output growth and hindering progress toward development and climate goals. Comprehensive policy reforms that ease cross-border trade and financial flows, remove structural bottlenecks, and enhance macroeconomic stability can trigger new investment accelerations and reverse projected declines in potential growth.

A. Share of EMDEs with investment accelerations

B. Annual growth of investment, output, and productivity before and during investment accelerations in EMDEs

C. Change in probability of investment acceleration

D. Impact of investment surges and policy reforms on potential growth in EMDEs

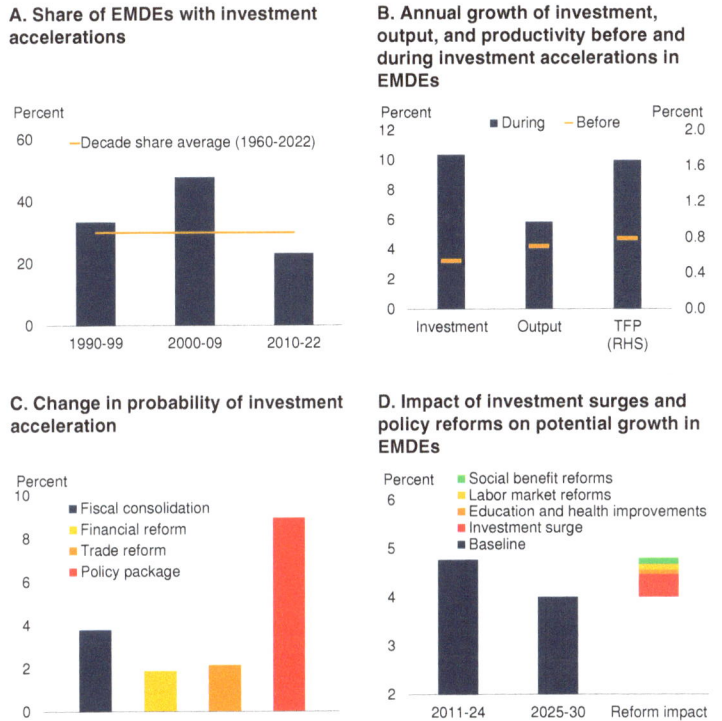

Source: Stamm and Yu (2024); World Bank.
Note: EMDEs = emerging market and developing economies; TFP = total factor productivity.
"Investment accelerations" are sustained periods when investment growth typically accelerates to more than 10 percent per year—more than three times the growth rate in other (nonacceleration) years over the past seven decades.
A. Bars show the decade average share of EMDEs that started an investment acceleration during the corresponding periods. The line shows the average percent of countries that started an investment acceleration over the past six decades.
B. "Before" indicates the six years before an investment acceleration. "During" indicates the full duration of an investment acceleration. The markers indicate median growth before acceleration years in the sample.
C. Bars show the increase in the probability of an investment acceleration following a one-standard deviation improvement in economic policy. Right bar shows the combined impact of increasing all three policy variables by one standard deviation.
D. GDP-weighted arithmetic averages. Scenarios assume annual growth rates of underlying variables during 2025-30, in each country. The investment surge is defined as the best 10-year average annual investment growth for each country. Education improvements assume that secondary and tertiary enrollment and completion rates rise over 2022-30 as much as their largest historical 10-year gain in 2000-21. Labor market changes assume female labor force participation grows annually at each country's fastest historical 10-year pace in 1990-2020. Health improvements assume life expectancy increases over 2022-30 at each country's highest recorded 10-year rate in 2000-21. Social benefits assume reforms raise older workers' participation rates over two decades by gradually lifting rates for each 5-year age and gender group from 55-59 years onward to match those of the next-younger age group.

investment would be key to this, and is also vital for broader sustainable development objectives.

Accelerating investment in infrastructure is especially critical for many EMDEs: high-quality

---

[16] For details on the links between investment and climate and infrastructure needs, see G20 Independent Experts Group (2023), Rozenberg and Fay (2019), Stamm and Vorisek (2024), Stamm and Yu (2024), and UNEP (2023).

infrastructure can bring numerous economic benefits but is lacking in many cases. Robust transportation, electricity, and digital networks can enhance access to jobs, labor productivity, and economic diversification. High-quality transport infrastructure, paired with low transport costs, is key for improving EMDEs' international trade competitiveness and for attracting investment—and, increasingly, for complying with climate-related regulations of trading partners (Chen and Lin 2020; Dappe, Lebrand, and Stokenberga 2024; Maliszewska et al. forthcoming). Moreover, resilient infrastructure can act as a shock absorber during and after weather- and climate-related disasters (Hallegatte, Rentschler, and Rozenberg 2019).

Many EMDEs have made significant progress since 2000 on building and upgrading infrastructure, yet progress has been uneven across countries, and large gaps persist. In SSA, for example, where 600 million people lack access to electricity, expanding reliable coverage is vital for boosting productivity and enhancing the region's capacity to integrate into the global economy. To accelerate infrastructure investment, given fiscal constraints, policy makers in EMDEs will need to draw on private as well as government financing and ensure efficient project implementation (World Bank 2024a).

Business environment reforms

By lowering barriers to entry, reducing bureaucratic hurdles, and stimulating competition, regulatory reforms can drive innovation and, in the medium to long term, foster more diverse economies that are less vulnerable to sector-specific shocks. Some middle-income EMDEs have succeeded in becoming among the top economies in the world in terms of private sector regulatory environment and operational efficiency (World Bank 2024g). Other EMDEs can draw lessons from their experience. Implementation of structural reforms is more likely to be successful when it is well communicated and designed with input from a variety of stakeholders (IMF 2024b).

Strengthening competition policy is crucial to ensuring a fair and dynamic marketplace. By preventing monopolistic practices and acting to ensure a level playing field, and by effectively regulating markets that remain uncompetitive, competition policy can stimulate innovation and drive economic efficiency (World Bank 2020a, 2024f). A competitive environment benefits consumers through better products and services at lower prices, and fosters the growth of new and existing businesses.

Innovation policy can contribute to overall dynamism, promoting productivity growth and making economies more adaptable and resilient to change. Many EMDEs also need to prioritize enhancing the capacity of the domestic economy to benefit from innovation. In this regard, it is important for policy to meet the needs of both incumbent firms and new entrants. The former can move an economy closer to the global technological frontier, while the latter can expand an economy's technological frontier (World Bank 2024c). Fostering collaboration and knowledge transmission through partnerships between academic institutions, the private sector, and international networks can accelerate the diffusion of new technologies developed elsewhere (OECD 2024). By advancing R&D, technological innovation, and knowledge sharing, EMDEs can build more resilient and innovative economies, not only with stronger productivity growth but also better equipped to navigate global challenges and seize emerging opportunities (Amaglobeli et al. 2023).

Human capital development and labor market policy

Policies to support the development of human capital are crucial not only to the growth of labor productivity but also to the achievement of inclusive and equitable economic growth. A multifaceted approach is needed. Investing in education, skills, training, and re-training is essential to boost labor productivity growth and to enable workers to adapt to structural change. Changing economic dynamics and new opportunities, including in the services sector, and boosting labor productivity and living standards. Also vital are access to early education, nutrition, and health care, which are still lacking in EMDEs, especially for those with the lowest incomes.

Progress in these areas can significantly enhance the long-run growth of employment and incomes (Fox and Gandhi 2021). Improving the quality of education is also critical for raising the productivity of workers (Hanushek 2013).

Appropriate labor market policies differ across regions, partly due to differing demographic conditions. In SSA, policy makers will need to focus particularly on reforms designed to serve the needs of growing working-age populations, by creating the conditions for young entrants to the labor force to become productively employed (Filmer and Fox 2014). Even in economies with aging and declining working-age populations, youth unemployment can still be a significant concern for policy makers (World Bank 2022b). Some EMDEs, particularly those in MNA and SAR, could boost growth significantly by reducing barriers to female labor force participation (Cuberes and Teignier 2016; Pennings 2022; World Bank 2024b).

For middle-income EMDEs, where human capital is typically better developed than in LICs, growth can be raised through more efficient allocation of labor—for instance, by enhancing education-related selection processes and improving inefficient job matching in the labor market (Donovan, Lu, and Schoellman 2023). Effective coordination between educational institutions and employer needs can help ensure that individual training and development are relevant and applicable (Cunningham and Villaseñor 2016).

Navigating a difficult external environment

In an external trade environment marked by increasing protectionist measures, disrupted value chains, and high uncertainty about the trade policy of major economies, EMDEs need to navigate their own policy making carefully, adopting a comprehensive approach to mitigate the adverse consequences of rising trade and investment restrictions and to take advantage of opportunities for cross-border cooperation. This approach can include multiple elements: (1) seeking strategic trade and investment partnerships with rapidly expanding economies and markets, including other EMDEs, thus furthering the growth of intra-EMDE trade that has become

a feature of these economies' development path since 2000; (2) tackling high trade costs and low trade efficiency; (3) pursuing avenues to diversify trade and making wise use of industrial policy; (4) putting in place policies to protect vulnerable segments of the society from adverse effects of trade-related policy changes; and (5) reinvigorating engagement in global trade governance, with support from multilateral institutions, because global challenges require global cooperation and solutions.

Strategic trade and investment agreements

EMDEs need to work with willing partners to reduce barriers to trade and investment flows. Against the backdrop of ebbing global cooperation, they could consider pursuing stronger regional trade linkages. Regional trade agreements are not a perfect substitute for global initiatives to boost trade, but they can offer a means to diversify export destinations, reduce dependence on major economies, and provide an effective means for resolving trade disputes.

Two recent agreements that provide good examples of regional cooperation to ease cross-border trade and investment flows are the African Continental Free Trade Area (AfCFTA) and the Regional Comprehensive Economic Partnership (RCEP) in East Asia. If fully and effectively implemented, measures to facilitate trade and FDI under the AfCFTA stand to boost exports from Africa by more than 30 percent and intraregional exports by more than 100 percent by 2035 (Echandi, Maliszewska, and Steenbergen 2022). Incomes in Africa could be raised by 7 percent under the AfCFTA in the same period (World Bank 2020b). The RCEP, effective from January 2022 among 15 economies in EAP, aims to phase out tariffs on goods and reduce nontariff barriers to increase regional trade and value chain integration among members. Trade cost reductions, coupled with liberal rules of origin, could increase trade among members by 12 percent and boost real incomes by up to 2.5 percent by 2035, lifting 27 million people into middle-class status (Estrades et al. 2022).

EMDEs can also benefit from trade agreements between regions. The recent EU-Mercosur Free

FIGURE 3.18 Trade policy

Deep trade agreements that tackle behind-the-border barriers as well as explicit trade restrictions could yield broader benefits—boosting output in and beyond member countries. Reforms that reduce persistently high trade costs could also deliver sizable macroeconomic gains and efficiency improvements for EMDEs.

A. Effect of deepening existing trade agreements on output

B. Cost of goods traded internationally in excess of goods traded domestically

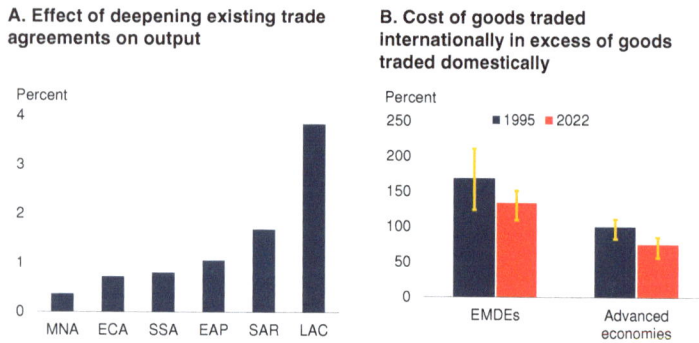

Sources: ESCAP-World Bank Trade Cost Database; Fontagné et al. (2023); World Integrated Trade Solution (database); World Bank.

Note: EAP = East Asia and Pacific; ECA = Europe and Central Asia; EMDEs = emerging market and developing economies; LAC = Latin America and the Caribbean; MNA = Middle East and North Africa; SAR = South Asia; SSA = Sub-Saharan Africa.

A. Bars show estimates of percent change in GDP by region resulting from deepening existing trade agreements to their highest level of ambition. Data for 2018.

B. Bars show averages of the percentage by which the costs of a good traded internationally exceed the costs of the same good traded domestically and are expressed as ad valorem tariff equivalents. Costs are aggregated into individual-country measures using 2021 bilateral country export shares. Bars show unweighted averages of individual-country measures; whiskers show interquartile ranges. Sample in 1995 includes 62 EMDEs and 34 advanced economies; sample in 2022 includes 86 EMDEs and 28 advanced economies.

Trade Agreement, although still subject to ratification, signals support for rules-based international trade despite the global rise in protectionist policy. The agreement, expected to remove more than 90 percent of tariffs on goods between the two blocs, would significantly increase trade between them in agricultural products, critical minerals, and manufactured goods, and would also facilitate services trade.

Achieving the full potential of trade and investment agreements requires diligence in implementing the specific commitments made as part of those agreements. In the longer term, with EMDEs' shares of global trade and investment flows expected to continue growing, they are likely to rely increasingly on each other to expand their export markets, regardless of the changes in global trade policies and protectionist trends.

Elevated uncertainty in the global trade environment increases the importance of depth in trade agreements, such that they reduce behind-the-border barriers associated with subsidies and industrial policies as well as tariffs and other direct

trade-restricting measures such as tariffs. Deep trade agreements tend to generate more trade and FDI than shallow agreements, and the broader policy areas they address provide their members with more opportunities to reap the benefits of economic integration (Mattoo, Mulabdic, and Ruta 2022; Mattoo, Rocha, and Ruta 2020). These types of agreements can also prevent the trade and investment distortions associated with industrial policies, and can have positive spillover effects on excluded countries (Barattieri, Mattoo, and Taglioni 2024; Lee, Mulabdic, and Ruta 2023). It follows that deepening existing trade agreements can produce sizable macroeconomic benefits: it is estimated that deepening all existing preferential trade agreements to their highest level of ambition could increase GDP by an estimated 0.8 percent in SSA and by 1.7 percent in SAR (Fontagné et al. 2023; figure 3.18.A).

Trade costs and efficiency

In addition to pursuing cross-border agreements, EMDEs can adjust domestic policy to reduce trade costs and enhance trade efficiency. Despite falling over time, goods trade costs are substantially higher in EMDEs than in advanced economies (figure 3.18.B; Ohnsorge and Quaglietti 2024). The difference is especially pronounced for agricultural trade costs. For goods trade, substantial cost reductions could be achieved by lowering transportation costs, including through infrastructure upgrades. Efficiency-raising improvements in ports, roads, and airport facilities can all reduce costs (Chen and Mattoo 2008; Moïsé and Le Bris 2013). There is also significant scope to reduce services trade costs, which are nearly double goods trade costs (WTO 2019). EMDEs would also benefit from initiatives to improve trade efficiency, such as streamlining customs procedures, easing regulatory compliance, improving logistics, and reducing nontariff barriers. Recent evidence suggests that some upper-middle-income EMDEs have achieved higher efficiency than advanced economies in moving goods across borders (World Bank 2023c).

Trade diversification

EMDEs should ensure that their policies meet the needs of a changing trade and investment landscape—in particular, rapid growth in trade and investment in services fueled by technological advances (Baldwin, Freeman, and Theodora-kopoulos 2023). EMDEs' share of global services trade is already rising. To further benefit from services trade, they need to ensure that workers have the education and skills needed for services-based jobs and that they are equipped to participate in services trade delivered digitally (World Bank 2024h; World Bank and WTO 2023). Digital technologies can increase services sector productivity and generate more opportunities than traditional (nondigital) services for firms to participate in GVCs, in addition to helping reduce services trade costs (World Bank 2024i; WTO 2019). Services trade can also contribute to inclusive growth by expanding opportunities for small enterprises and for female and young workers.

Industrial policy

The use of industrial policy to support certain economic sectors—interventions such as subsidies and preferential regulatory treatment, often intended to promote exports—has become increasingly widespread since the late 2000s, particularly among advanced economies (Juhász et al. 2022; World Bank 2024b). Designed and implemented well, these policies can facilitate knowledge and technology spillovers, input-output linkages, and job creation, as well as address sector-specific coordination failures and reduce costs and uncertainty for private investors (Harrison and Rodríguez-Clare 2010). They can help EMDEs attract FDI and, later, integrate domestic businesses into GVCs (Adarov and Stehrer 2021). In addition to strategic competitiveness, industrial policy has been employed to address challenges related to climate change, supply chain resilience, and national security (Evenett et al. 2024; Juhász, Lane, and Rodrik 2024). Industrial policies that are relatively more successful tend to focus on technology adoption, competition, avoidance of trade-restrictive measures, and transparency and accountability (World Bank 2024b).

However, there are also downsides to industrial policy (Pop and Connon 2020). The fiscal costs of industrial policy can be high. The intended effects can be hindered by institutional weaknesses such as corruption, regulatory challenges, and public sector inefficiency. It is also often argued that industrial policies are anticompetitive, and that they distort private investment in the long term. Successful industrial policy requires that the protected sectors eventually operate without public support and that discounted future benefits outweigh the cost of protection.

EMDEs should carefully assess the costs and benefits when implementing industrial policies, including alignment with WTO commitments. Support for industries should be time-bound, targeted, transparent, and based on specific, measurable objectives, with outcomes closely monitored. EMDEs should aim to minimize cross-border spillovers from industrial policy. While industrial policies can help steer foreign investment toward priority certain priority sectors and regions, policies to strengthen institutions, human capital development, R&D, macroeconomic stability, and financial development remain important for long-term development in these economies.

Protection of the vulnerable

Policy makers in EMDEs, as in advanced economies, may need to take action to contain and offset the adverse effects on their economies, and particularly on the most vulnerable, of trade tensions between major economies, as well as tensions resulting from rapid technological change and shifting supply and demand conditions. If protectionist policies and heightened trade uncertainty lead to significant job and earnings losses, carefully designed temporary income support, retraining programs, and targeted tax policy changes may be needed (Goldberg and Reed 2023). Well-designed active labor market policies can help reduce the duration of unemployment episodes and maintain relatively low unemployment rates (Andersen and Svarer 2012; Card, Kluve and Weber 2018). Targeted technical assistance programs can also be provided to firms negatively affected by trade disruptions.

Multilateral institutions

Global challenges require global cooperation and solutions. Although EMDEs may pursue new or improved trade agreements with regional or other strategic partners, these efforts should be complemented by renewed engagement in global trade governance. Multilateral institutions play important roles in preserving a rules-based international trade system, promoting dialogue to reduce uncertainty about trade and investment policies, and analyzing the global consequences of protectionist policies (World Bank 2020a). They provide fora for coordinating efforts to reduce trade barriers, and advice on policy strategies to avoid distortive and damaging protectionist and industrial policies, and to establish level playing fields for cross-border trade and investment flows. These institutions also provide needed technical and financial assistance to enable structural reforms in EMDEs.

To prevent further trade fragmentation and reinvigorate trade growth, it is essential to restore a fully functioning, rules-based, multilateral trade system, complete with an efficient and effective dispute settlement system at the World Trade Organization (WTO) accessible to all its members. EMDEs should actively engage in multilateral negotiations and reforms to ensure the system meets their needs (WTO 2024). Additionally, the international community needs to find ways to mitigate the adverse effects of geopolitical tensions on trade, foster a level playing field for international commerce, reduce trade policy uncertainty, and enhance transparency, especially regarding distortions caused by industrial policy measures (IMF et al. 2022).

With regard to such global challenges as climate change and pandemics, the multilateral institutions need to be well positioned and adequately resourced to help countries better identify and mitigate adverse cross-border spillovers (Aiyar et al. 2023; World Bank 2021c). This includes developing and promoting internationally agreed-upon standards for the measurement and reporting of carbon emissions. Multilateral institutions can also help establish and strengthen mechanisms to facilitate the availability of vital goods, including food and medical equipment, that are acutely needed during crises. The urgency of facilitating the free movement of vital goods was evident during the COVID-19

pandemic, and such facilitation will be increasingly important as climate change-related disasters become more frequent and intense.

Enhancing macroeconomic stability

With the global growth outlook sluggish and the risk of external shocks high, it is imperative that EMDEs strengthen their fiscal, monetary, and financial sector policy frameworks. Fiscal space and financial cushions provide a crucial line of defense to mitigate the adverse impact of sharp movements in currencies and global interest rates. Policy reforms aimed at strengthening macroeconomic stability are likewise key for maintaining investor confidence and managing systemic risks.

In the past quarter century, many EMDEs have employed countercyclical policies to stabilize activity in the face of macroeconomic fluctuations. Buffers accumulated and policy improvements implemented in the period preceding the global financial crisis allowed many EMDEs to use countercyclical policies to mitigate its impact (Koh and Yu 2019). EMDEs also used a large array of support measures during the COVID-19 pandemic, although a narrowing of fiscal space in the 2010s meant that the policy response in these economies had to be notably smaller than that in advanced economies (World Bank 2021a).

Fiscal policy

Building and maintaining fiscal buffers remains a cornerstone of sound fiscal policy in EMDEs, in part because many of these economies have limited capacity to respond to shocks with monetary policy alone. Capacity to provide temporary fiscal support in response to adverse shocks—by increasing public spending or reducing taxes—is contingent on having adequate fiscal space. Yet fiscal space in EMDEs, already narrower than in advanced economies, has been eroded further in recent years, particularly by the policy actions required to meet needs arising from the COVID-19 pandemic and other crises, and by the increase in financing costs stemming from the rise in global interest rates and the large and growing stocks of government debt.

For many EMDEs, greater revenue mobilization is essential for restoring fiscal space. Broadening the tax base, undertaking measures to reduce informal transactions, curbing exemptions, and upgrading tax administration capacity can improve compliance and increase revenues (Dom et al. 2022; Ohnsorge and Yu 2022; World Bank 2023d). On the expenditure side, EMDEs need to improve spending efficiency. Different public expenditure items affect growth and equity in different ways, requiring that expenditure restraint be selective. Targeting social benefits and subsidies more effectively would reduce distortions and generate budgetary savings while preserving support for vulnerable groups. Growth-enhancing public investment, including infrastructure upgrades, should generally be prioritized, although projects should be rigorously evaluated in terms of their economic returns and alignment with development priorities (Adarov 2024). Investment in human capital through effective education and health expenditures should also be prioritized. Increasing the efficiency of government administration and avoiding investments that carry little economic return may offer ways of reducing unproductive government spending.

In part because of limited fiscal buffers, fiscal policy in EMDEs has tended to be more procyclical than in advanced economies, especially in the three-fifths of EMDEs that are commodity exporters. Procyclical fiscal policy accentuates macroeconomic fluctuations, thereby adversely affecting growth in EMDEs. Credible rules-based fiscal frameworks can reduce fiscal volatility and procyclicality, build investor confidence, and improve resilience to shocks. In this regard, EMDEs are much better positioned than they were in 2000, when only 23 EMDEs used fiscal rules. By 2021, 70 EMDEs used at least one type of fiscal rule, most often balanced budget rules and debt rules, while 61 employed more than one type of rule (figure 3.19.A). Such rules are credible, however, only when countries consistently adhere to the specified numerical limits. Implementing best practices in debt management can help ensure that fiscal policy remains disciplined and responsive to economic cycles rather than influenced by short-term political pressures (World Bank 2024e). Stabilization funds can also be effective in managing public revenue volatility, especially in resource-rich EMDEs, by

saving windfall revenues during boom periods for use during downturns (Gill et al. 2014; World Bank 2024e).

Monetary and financial sector policy

The primary objectives of central banks in EMDEs, as in advanced economies, should be the maintenance of reasonable price stability in the medium term together with financial sector stability. To achieve these objectives, EMDEs need to have countercyclical monetary policy instruments available, as well as adequate international reserves that can be used to mitigate currency and capital flow volatility when needed, and instruments to regulate financial institutions and markets. Because of their susceptibility to terms-of-trade shocks, commodity-reliant economies may need to be particularly diligent in accumulating reserve buffers, bearing in mind that reserve accumulation may cause excessive monetary expansion unless it is sterilized.

Monetary policy frameworks in many EMDEs have become better defined and more disciplined in recent decades. Inflation-targeting frameworks have become more common: as of 2022, they were in use in 35 EMDEs, compared to 22 in 2010 and only six in 2000 (figure 3.19.B). Increased use of inflation targeting may have contributed to lower macroeconomic volatility during the 2010s relative to the 2000s (figure 3.19.C). However, it did not prevent a marked increase in volatility in 2020-23, which may be attributed in large part to the pandemic, Russia's invasion of Ukraine, supply chain disruptions, and sharp movements in oil and food prices.

Improved monetary policy frameworks helped many EMDE central banks to better manage the surge in inflation that started in 2021 (World Bank 2024a). For some EMDEs, these improvements include greater central bank independence, which allows central banks to make decisions in line with established mandates, mainly to contain inflation, rather than being swayed by short-term political considerations. Central banks operating independently, without political interference, are more likely to maintain credibility and to be effective at managing actual and expected inflation expectations and responding to macroeconomic

FIGURE 3.19 Fiscal and monetary policy frameworks

The volatility of output and inflation in EMDEs decreased somewhat between 2000 and 2019 but spiked up following the global pandemic. Fiscal and monetary frameworks in EMDEs have improved since the early 2000s as a growing number of countries adopt fiscal rules and central banks use inflation-targeting frameworks. Inflation and inflation volatility are better controlled in EMDEs where central banks have a high degree of independence.

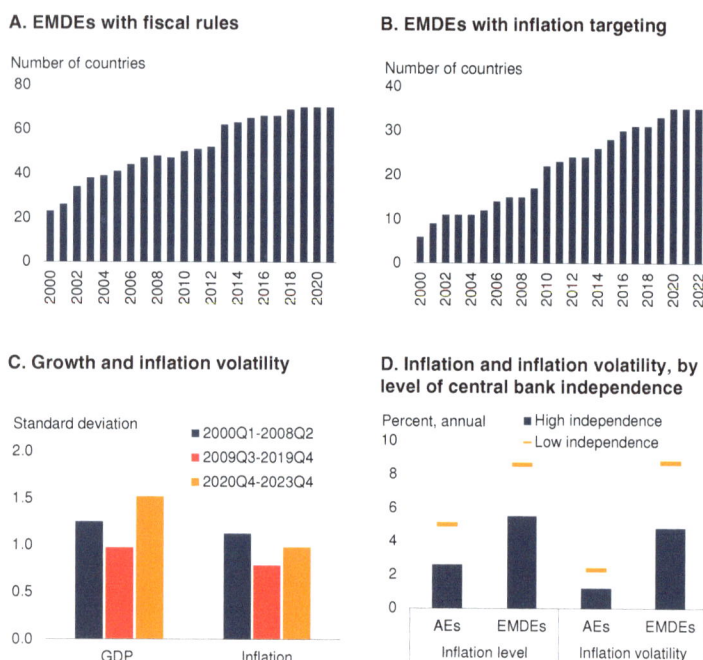

A. EMDEs with fiscal rules

Number of countries

B. EMDEs with inflation targeting

Number of countries

C. Growth and inflation volatility

Standard deviation

■ 2000Q1-2008Q2
■ 2009Q3-2019Q4
■ 2020Q4-2023Q4

D. Inflation and inflation volatility, by level of central bank independence

Percent, annual   ■ High independence   − Low independence

Sources: Dincer and Eichengreen (2014); Ha, Kose, and Ohnsorge (2023); Haver Analytics; IMF AREAER database; World Bank.
Note: AEs = advanced economies; EMDEs = emerging market and developing economies.
A. An economy is considered to implement a fiscal rule if it has one or more fiscal rules on expenditure, revenue, budget balance or debt.
C. Bars show median volatility of quarterly real GDP and CPI growth during indicated subsamples. Sample includes the same 37 EMDEs as shown in annex 3.2.
D. Bars show median inflation rates and inflation volatility in country-year pairs with a central bank independence and transparency index in the top quartile of the sample. Markers show medians for country-year pairs in the bottom quartile.

shocks (figure 3.19.D; Garriga and Rodriguez 2020; Kose et al. 2019).

The increasing role of global factors in explaining inflation and international financial flows, stemming partly from increasing trade and financial integration, can amplify the cross-border spillovers of interest rate movements and be a source of financial market volatility. Central banks and other regulatory institutions need to employ flexible and well-targeted policy interventions to reduce financial market volatility, and to mitigate foreign currency risk and asset price misalignment. If capital flows are a source of external imbalances,

employing capital flow management measures to correct the underlying imbalances and stabilize currency markets can be appropriate, although they should not impede necessary adjustments to fundamentals. Coordinated actions across countries—including information sharing and regulatory alignment—can help reduce financial market volatility by enhancing the design and effectiveness of monetary and financial sector policies (Eichengreen 2016; Clarida 2023).

Amid heightened uncertainty, EMDEs need to strengthen their macroprudential policy frameworks to ensure that financial institutions have adequate capital buffers to cope with shocks. The risk of financial instability can be minimized through improved monitoring and management of credit flows. Since financial markets in most EMDEs are dominated by the banking sector, enhancing financial sector regulation and supervision can contain the risk of banks with weak balance sheets generating contagion affecting the entire financial system (Ferreira, Jenkinson, and Wilson 2019; Jones and Knaack 2019). However, such frameworks should match each country's institutional capacity and stage of financial sector development, and should be expanded in a way that allows effective enforcement (Anginer, Demirgüç-Kunt, and Mare 2018).

The development of the financial sector is an integral part of economic growth and plays an important role in absorbing shocks, but the depth, access, and efficiency of the financial sector are limited in many EMDEs (World Bank 2019). Financial development could be promoted by establishing a strong business and regulatory environment, but the pace of development needs to be carefully monitored to mitigate financial stability risks, particularly given that the effect of financial vulnerabilities could be amplified in an environment of high uncertainty (IMF 2024). The stability-oriented foundation would help create conditions for sustainable financial deepening and market development over time. To promote the development of domestic capital markets, particularly related to local currency bond and equity transactions, financial infrastructure and legal frameworks, including reliable trading and settlement systems, clear disclosure requirements, and strong creditor rights protections, need to be put in place (Hashimoto et al. 2021).

Conclusion

The period around the turn of the twenty-first century was transformative for many EMDEs. Their ascendance in the global economy was propelled by tailwinds associated with a broad-based embrace of the advantages of trade and financial integration. They liberalized their domestic financial markets; undertook structural reforms; and made improvements in fiscal, monetary, and financial sector policy frameworks that have bolstered macroeconomic stability. As they experienced a surge in cross-border trade and financial flows, EMDEs became increasingly important players in global supply chains and commodity markets. Highlighting their growing prominence in the global economy, EMDEs have accounted for the majority of global growth since the beginning of the century.

EMDEs' rapid integration into the global economy has coincided with substantial changes in their international business cycle linkages. Business cycle synchronization both among EMDEs and between EMDEs and advanced economies has increased markedly since the 1990s, reflecting stronger interdependence through trade, financial, and commodity price channels. An EMDE-specific business cycle has also emerged over time, reflecting deepening integration among these economies. Spillovers from the largest EMDEs, the EM3, to other EMDEs are sizable but they remain more limited than those from the largest advanced economies, the AE3.

Despite these developments, EMDEs face daunting headwinds that threaten to reverse their earlier gains. Global trade and financial integration has slowed since the late 2000s. Although the share of global FDI inflows directed to EMDEs has risen, FDI inflows as a proportion of their GDP are now substantially lower than in the 2000s. Rising protectionist measures and geopolitical fragmentation have made navigating

the external environment more challenging. EMDEs have made little progress in reforming their institutions since the 2000s. Climate-related disasters have become more frequent and costly. Moreover, fiscal constraints have intensified, exacerbated by external shocks such as the COVID-19 pandemic, armed conflicts, and rising geopolitical tensions.

Potential growth in EMDEs is expected to slow to about 4 percent in the 2020s—down from more than 5 percent in the 2010s. Long-term growth projections for these economies have repeatedly been revised downward. Investment growth has been weakening over time. They also have experienced a slowdown in productivity growth as some of them have moved closer to the global technology frontier and begun to exhaust the scope for reallocation of labor from low-productivity agriculture. Population aging and slower growth of working-age populations have been adverse for GDP growth in some EMDEs.

To overcome these challenges and sustain progress, many EMDEs need to prioritize policy actions in three fundamental and equally important areas. EMDEs adopted policy in each of these three areas in the early 2000s, when they also achieved robust growth rates and made progress on development goals. First, EMDEs need to reinvigorate structural reforms to accelerate investment and productivity growth. This includes improving institutional quality, fostering human capital development, and advancing digital transformation. Policies also need to mitigate the adverse effects of protectionist policies and geopolitical fragmentation while taking advantage of opportunities for untapped cross-border cooperation. Strengthening multilateralism and fostering international diversification in trade and financial networks are essential to addressing shared challenges such as climate change and ensuring that EMDEs continue to play a pivotal role in the global economy. Finally, EMDEs need credible macroeconomic frameworks with appropriate policy buffers.

ANNEX 3.1 Dynamic factor model methodology

Dynamic factor model (benchmark version)

Dynamic factor models are commonly utilized for identifying common elements in national business cycles (Crucini, Kose, and Otrok 2011; Kose, Otrok, and Prasad 2012; Hirata, Kose, and Otrok 2013). This chapter estimates a dynamic factor model to capture commonalities in fluctuations of real GDP growth. The benchmark model uses a sample of 30 economies and quarterly data for 2000Q1-2023Q4 (table A3.1.1). Real quarterly GDP (seasonally adjusted and in local currency) is obtained from Haver Analytics and converted to continuously compounded growth rates by taking the quarter-over-quarter change in the natural logarithm of the series.

Dynamic factor models are designed to extract a small number of unobservable common elements from the comovement between macroeconomic time series across economies. In this application, the variance of quarterly GDP growth is decomposed into three factors:

- A global factor common to all economies;

- A group factor common to a subset of economies. In the benchmark model, the sample is split into two groups, advanced economies and EMDEs;

- Idiosyncratic factors specific to each individual GDP growth series.

A major advantage of the model is that it allows for a parsimonious representation of the data in terms of unobservable common elements, obviating the need to explicitly identify all relevant observable independent variables.

The model has thirty equations, in which GDP growth for each economy is specified as a function of the global, group, and idiosyncratic factors. For example, under the benchmark approach to grouping economies, Mexico is categorized as an EMDE, such that the equation for economic growth for this economy is:

$$Y_t^{\text{MEX}} = \beta_{\text{GLOBAL}}^{\text{MEX}} f_t^{\text{GLOBAL}} + \beta_{\text{EMDE}}^{\text{MEX}} f_t^{\text{EMDE}} + \varepsilon_t^{\text{MEX}},$$

where Y denotes growth in output. The global and group factors are represented by f_t^{EMDE} and f_t^{global}, respectively. The coefficients capture the sensitivities of the GDP growth in each economy to these factors. The error term $\varepsilon_t^{\text{MEX}}$ is assumed to be uncorrelated at all lead and lags. The error term and the factor loadings follow autoregressive processes:

$$f_t^m = \phi^m(L) f_{t-1}^m + \mu_t^m,$$

$$\varepsilon_t = \psi(L)\varepsilon_{t-1} + \chi_t$$

where $m = \{\text{GLOBAL, GROUP}\}$, $\phi^m(L)$ and $\psi(L)$ are lag polynomial operators, and the terms μ_t^m and χ_t are normally distributed and mutually orthogonal across all equations and variables in the system.

The model is estimated using the Bayesian approach outlined in Kose, Otrok, and Whiteman (2003) and using priors described in detail in Jackson et al. (2016). Dummy series are included as external variables in the system for each of the quarters of 2020 and 2021 to avoid any bias produced by the unconventional variance that observations exhibit during this period.

To measure the importance of each factor, the total variance of output growth is decomposed according to the contributions of each factor. This is achieved by applying the variance operator to each equation in the system. For the case of GDP growth in Mexico:

$$\text{Var}(Y^{\text{MEX}}) = (\beta_{\text{GLOBAL}}^{\text{MEX}})^2 \text{Var}(f_t^{\text{GLOBAL}})$$
$$+ (\beta_{\text{EMDE}}^{\text{MEX}})^2 \text{Var}(f_t^{\text{EMDE}}) + \text{Var}(\varepsilon^{\text{MEX}}),$$

Since the factors are assumed to be orthogonal to each other, the variance in output attributable to the global factor can be represented as:

$$\frac{(\beta_{\text{GLOBAL}}^{\text{MEX}})^2 \text{Var}(f_t^{\text{GLOBAL}})}{\text{Var}(Y^{\text{MEX}})}$$

The variance share attributable to the group factor is computed using an analogous approach. The idiosyncratic factor explains the residual variance unaccounted for by the global and group factors. In reporting results, the variance attributable to the respective factors is averaged across economies in each group (the change in the contribution of the factors is robust to using medians instead of means).

The analysis is extended to examine the dynamic nature of the variance contributions by adopting more granular time frames. To do this, the coefficient matrix of the system of equations is estimated using the entire sample, making use of the maximum number of available data to avoid estimation issues. Then, the variance decomposition exercises are performed employing the coefficients estimated before and the variance of the factor and data within 10-year windows. For example, the variance explained by the global factor for Mexico between 2000 and 2009 is:

$$\frac{(\beta_{\text{GLOBAL}}^{\text{MEX}})^2 \text{Var}(f_{2000-09}^{\text{GLOBAL}})}{\text{Var}(Y_{2000-09}^{\text{MEX}})}$$

This approach mitigates estimation biases that could arise from relying on shorter sub-periods to estimate the model, at the time in which it allows to capture dynamic properties of the data, such as autocorrelations and cross-autocorrelations across variables over time.

TABLE A3.1.1 Sample, benchmark DFM

Group	Economies
Advanced economies (15)	Australia; Austria; Belgium; Canada; France; Germany; Italy; Japan; Korea, Rep.; Netherlands; New Zealand; Spain; Sweden; the United Kingdom; and the United States
EMDEs (15)	Brazil, Chile, China, Colombia, Hungary, India, Malaysia, Mexico, Peru, Philippines, Poland, the Russian Federation, South Africa, Thailand, and Türkiye

Note: DFM = dynamic factor model; EMDEs = emerging market and developing economies.

Dynamic factor model (alternative version)

In an alternative exercise, the sample is extended to 58 economies, using quarterly data for the same period as in the benchmark model (2000Q1-2023Q4), and grouped into six geographic regions (table A3.1.2). Given geographic proximity, North American countries (Canada and the United States) are combined with the LAC region. The results are robust to treating these countries as a separate region. For SAR, the model is estimated with four additional countries (Maldives, Nepal, Pakistan, and Sri Lanka), using data for a shorter time period, 2005Q4 to 2023Q4, given data availability for these countries.

The purpose of the alternative DFM is to provide insights into how the contributions of specific group factors change when considering geographic proximity. For example, under the geographic approach to grouping economies, Mexico is categorized in the Latin America and the Caribbean, United States, and Canada region:

$$Y_t^{\text{MEX}} = \beta_{\text{GLOBAL}}^{\text{MEX}} f_t^{\text{GLOBAL}} + \beta_{\text{LAC}}^{\text{MEX}} f_t^{\text{LAC}} + \varepsilon_t^{\text{MEX}}$$

TABLE A3.1.2 Sample, alternative DFM

Region	Economies
East Asia and Pacific (10)	Australia; China; Hong Kong SAR, China; Indonesia; Japan; New Zealand; the Philippines; Singapore; Republic of Korea; and Thailand
Europe and Central Asia (22)	Austria, Belgium, Bosnia and Herzegovina, Bulgaria, Denmark, Finland, France, Germany, Iceland, Ireland, Italy, Kazakhstan, Luxembourg, the Netherlands, North Macedonia, Norway, the Russian Federation, Serbia, Spain, Sweden, Türkiye, and the United Kingdom
Latin America and the Caribbean, United States, and Canada (16)	Argentina, Belize, Bolivia, Brazil, Canada, Chile, Colombia, Costa Rica, the Dominican Republic, Ecuador, El Salvador, Mexico, Paraguay, Peru, the United States, and Uruguay
Middle East and North Africa (5)	Israel, Jordan, Morocco, Tunisia, and West Bank and Gaza
South Asia (5)	India, Maldives, Nepal, Pakistan, and Sri Lanka
Sub-Saharan Africa (4)	Botswana, Cameroon, Namibia, and South Africa

Note: DFM = dynamic factor model; EMDEs = emerging market and developing economies.

The variance decomposition exercise is estimated using the same strategy described for the benchmark DFM. Figure A3.1.1 shows the results of this exercise. When countries are grouped by geographic regions, global factors remain the dominant contributors to fluctuations in economic growth, explaining 54 percent of the variance across countries. Here, the group (that is, regional) factor accounts for a smaller share of the variance than in the benchmark model, explaining, on average, 9 percent of the variability in growth across the six regions. The results are heterogeneous across regions, however.[17]

---

[17] Dynamic factor models are designed to capture underlying trends and patterns in multivariate time series data. Even when the factors extracted explain a relatively small part of the variance of growth, they still represent meaningful underlying economic processes. These factors highlight systematic relationships and latent structures that are crucial for understanding the dynamics of the data.

FIGURE A3.1.1 Variance decomposition, by geographic region

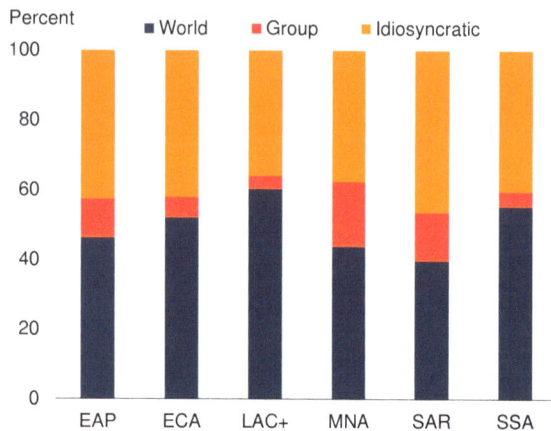

Source: World Bank.

Note: The figure shows the variance decomposition when grouping countries by geographical region. EAP = East Asia and Pacific; ECA = Europe and Central Asia; LAC+ = Latin America and the Caribbean, United States, and Canada; MNA = Middle East and North Africa; SAR = South Asia; and SSA = Sub-Saharan Africa.

ANNEX 3.2 SVAR methodology

Benchmark SVAR model

Growth spillovers are investigated using a structural vector autoregression (SVAR) model. The data set includes 40 economies—EM3 countries, AE3 countries, and 34 other EMDEs—at a quarterly frequency covering the period 2000Q1-2023Q4 (table A3.2.1). The starting date is selected based on data availability. The starting date of 2000 is also chosen so that the sample does not mix data from before and after the launch of the euro at the beginning of 1999, avoids the immediate aftermath of the Asian financial crisis of 1997 and the Russian financial crisis of 1998, and captures data at the time of China's WTO accession in 2001.

The benchmark SVAR model is used to investigate the growth spillovers from EM3 countries, where several global developments are controlled for. The model includes the endogenous variables of AE3 growth, the U.S. interest rate, EMBI spreads, EM3 growth, oil price growth, and other EMDEs growth. The U.S. interest rate (measured as the yield on 10-year U.S. Treasuries) and EMBI spreads are used as proxies for financial conditions in AE3 and EM3, respectively. The EMBI (Emerging Market Bond Index) is a commonly used benchmark for tracking yields on sovereign debt in EMDEs. Oil price growth (with oil prices measured as a simple average of Brent, Dubai, and West Texas Intermediate crude oil prices) captures developments in production costs and demand conditions. Four dummies are included as exogenous variables, one for each quarter of 2020, to control for the economic effects of the COVID-19 pandemic.

Country-specific growth rates are calculated as log-differences based on the quarterly real GDP data obtained from Haver Analytics. The market yield on 10-year U.S. Treasuries is sourced from the Federal Reserve Economic Data. The EMBI spread is obtained from J.P. Morgan. Nominal oil prices are obtained from the World Bank's Pink Sheet (crude oil, average) and deflated using seasonally adjusted U.S. CPI series from the Federal Reserve Economic Data.

TABLE A3.2.1 Sample, benchmark SVAR model

Group	Economies
AE3	United States, euro area, and Japan
EM3	China, India, and Brazil
Other EMDEs (34 economies)	Argentina, Belize, Bolivia, Bosnia and Herzegovina, Botswana, Bulgaria, Cameroon, Chile, Colombia, Costa Rica, Ecuador, El Salvador, Honduras, Hungary, Indonesia, Jordan, Kazakhstan, Mexico, Morocco, Namibia, North Macedonia, Paraguay, Peru, the Philippines, Poland, Romania, the Russian Federation, Serbia, South Africa, Thailand, Tunisia, Türkiye, Uruguay, and West Bank and Gaza

Note: EMDEs = emerging market and developing economies; SVAR = structural vector autoregression.

The formal investigation is based on the following model with a lag length of four quarters (standard for SVAR models using quarterly data):

$$A_0 z_t = a + \sum_{k=1}^{4} A_k z_{t-k} + u_t,$$

where u_t is a vector of serially and mutually uncorrelated structural innovations. The model is expressed in reduced form for estimation purposes:

$$z_t = b + \sum_{k=1}^{4} B_k z_{t-k} + e_t,$$

where $b = A_0^{-1} a$ and $B_k = A_0^{-1} A_k$ for all k and $e_t = A_0^{-1} u_t$. The identification of the shocks is achieved by imposing the following sign and zero restrictions on the matrix A_0^{-1} (table A3.3.2). The restrictions are deliberately minimal, as the secondary shocks are not the main subject of the analysis and the aim is to avoid imposing overly restrictive assumptions.

The motivation for the restrictions imposed on each shock is as follows:

- A positive growth shock in major emerging markets (EM shock) increases GDP growth in EM3, decreases the EMBI spread, and increases oil price growth amid higher demand. It is assumed that the two advanced economy variables (AE3 GDP growth and the U.S. interest rate) do not respond contemporaneously to EM shocks.

- A positive growth shock in major advanced economies (AE shock) is associated with an increase in AE3 GDP growth, EM3 GDP growth, and oil price growth. U.S. interest rates also rise as a result, as standard during the business cycle. Importantly, the response of other EMDEs growth to EM and AE shocks is left unrestricted.

- A positive growth shock in other EMDEs (other EMDEs shock) increases GDP growth in other EMDEs but is not associated with a contemporaneous impact on GDP growth in both AE3 and EM3, nor is it associated with a change in the U.S. interest rate.

- A rate shock is akin to a monetary policy shock, as it slows GDP growth in AE3 while the U.S. interest rate rises.

- An EMBI shock is assumed to be a rise in the EMBI spread decrease of EM3 GDP growth. AE3 growth is assumed to have no contemporaneous reactions.

- An oil shock resembles a supply shock in that it is associated with higher oil price growth and lower economic activity in all regions analyzed (AE3, EM3, and other EMDEs).

In the results presented in the main text of the chapter, shocks are normalized to a 1-percentage-point increase in GDP growth for the respective aggregate. For instance, an EM3 shock corresponds to a 1-percentage-point increase in EM3 growth upon impact, with persistence determined by the model. The bar charts depicting responses in other EMDEs and the global economy display the cumulative effect over time, expressed as percent increase in GDP. The "global" results are based on the GDP-weighted average of the impact in the AE3, the EM3, and other EMDEs.

The estimation uses a Bayesian approach with Minnesota priors. This corresponds to generating posterior draws for the structural model parameters by transforming each reduced-form posterior draw. For each draw of the covariance matrix from its posterior distribution, the corresponding posterior draw for A_0^{-1} is constructed by discarding non admissible solutions of the structural shocks that do not satisfy the sign restrictions until 1,000 admissible draws are obtained. While the median of each distribution is considered as the Bayesian estimator, the 16th and 84th percentiles of distributions are used to construct 68 percent confidence intervals (the standard measure in the related literature).

Several tests are conducted to ensure the robustness of the baseline SVAR findings. First, oil prices are replaced with a broad index of energy and non-energy prices from the World Bank's Pink Sheet. The results indicate that a positive growth shock in EM3 countries leads to expansions in other EMDEs and the global economy of a similar magnitude as in the baseline results. Second, the consistency of the estimates is tested by replacing China's GDP with the China Activity Tracker from the San Francisco Fed. Although this adjustment necessitates a slightly shorter sample period, starting from 2001Q1, the results are closely aligned with the baseline results, with growth shocks in China yielding comparable effects on other EMDEs and the global economy. Third, the sensitivity of the baseline model to alternative groupings of economies is tested by replacing the AE3 and EM3 aggregates with G7 and EM7 aggregates, where EM7 is Brazil, China, India, Indonesia, Mexico, Russia, and Türkiye. Again, the results are comparable to the baseline results.

TABLE A3.2.2 Sign and zero restrictions imposed to identify shocks in the SVAR models

	EM shock	AE shock	Other EMDEs shock	Rate shock	EMBI shock	Oil shock
AE3	0	+	0	-	0	-
U.S. rates	0	+	0	+	*	*
EMBI	-	*	*	*	+	*
EM3	+	+	0	*	-	-
Oil	+	+	*	*	*	+
Other EMDEs	*	*	+	*	-	-

Note: Asterisks indicate that no restrictions were imposed on these variables. AE3 = United States, euro area, and Japan; EM3 = China, India, and Brazil; other EMBI = Emerging Markets Bond Index; EMDEs = emerging market and developing economies; other EMDEs = emerging market and developing economies excluding the EM3; SVAR = structural vector autoregression.

Multiple subsample estimations provide sensitivity analysis of the results. Excluding the post-2020 period from the estimation sample indicates that the findings are not driven by the COVID-19 period. Additionally, the baseline model is re-estimated using data for 2009-23. The results show that although the impact on oil prices has increased somewhat, there is no noticeable rise in business cycle spillovers to other EMDEs, advanced economies, or the global economy in the post-global financial crisis period. Similar findings emerge from re-estimating the model using 10-year rolling windows over the full sample, which indicate broadly stable spillovers from EM3 growth shocks since 2000.

Several factors may explain the lack of significant increases in spillovers over time. First, the shorter sub-periods may limit the ability to detect longer-term changes in spillover dynamics. Second, while EM3 economies have deepened their trade and financial linkages globally, the changes may not be large enough to drive a noticeable rise in spillovers, particularly given the more gradual pace of integration since the early 2010s. Third, the relatively low variability of aggregate growth in the EM3, especially driven by the reduced GDP volatility of China in the 2010s compared to the previous decade, could dampen the effects of business cycle spillovers. Finally, the estimated models do not explicitly account for potential regime changes or nonlinearities, which may limit the capacity to capture variations in spillovers over time. For instance, although China's growth delivered substantial regional spillovers to developing economies in the 2000s, these effects appear to have diminished in recent years (World Bank 2024j).

Country-specific SVAR model

Country-specific SVAR models are used to estimate growth spillovers from China (the largest of the EM3 economies) and the United States (the largest advanced economy). In technical terms, this investigation is achieved by replacing the EM3 aggregate in the benchmark model with China and replacing the AE3 aggregate in the benchmark model with the United States. The exogenous COVID-19 dummies are also included to ensure consistency with the baseline specification. In the model estimating spillovers from China, the endogenous variables in the benchmark model are modified to include AE3 GDP growth, the U.S. interest rate, EMBI, China's GDP growth, oil price growth, and other EMDEs GDP growth. In the model estimating spillovers from the United States, the endogenous variables in the benchmark model are modified to include U.S. GDP growth, U.S. interest rate, EMBI, EM3 GDP growth, oil price growth, and other EMDEs GDP growth.

References

Adarov, A. 2024. "Harnessing the Benefits of Public Investment." In *Global Economic Prospects,* 103-45. June. Washington, DC: World Bank.

Adarov, A., and H. Pallan. Forthcoming. "Foreign Direct Investment: Trends, Implications, and Policies." World Bank, Washington, DC.

Adarov, A., and R. Stehrer. 2021. "Implications of Foreign Direct Investment, Capital Formation and Its Structure for Global Value Chains." *The World Economy* 44 (11): 3246-99.

Ahmed, S., R. Correa, D. A. Dias, N. Gornemann, J. Hoek, A. Jain, E. Liu, and A. Wong. 2022. "Global Spillovers of a Chinese Growth Slowdown." *Journal of Risk and Financial Management* 15 (12): 596.

Aiyar, S., J. Chen, C. H. Ebeke, R. Garcia-Saltos, T. Gudmundsson, A. Ilyina, A. Kangur, et al. 2023. "Geoeconomic Fragmentation and the Future of Multilateralism." IMF Staff Discussion Note 2023/001, International Monetary Fund, Washington, DC.

Aiyar, S., and F. Ohnsorge. 2024. "Geoeconomic Fragmentation and 'Connector' Countries." CEPR Discussion Paper 19352, Centre for Economic Policy Research, Paris and London.

Alfaro, L., N. Bloom, and X. Lin. 2024. "The Finance Uncertainty Multiplier." *Journal of Political Economy* 132 (2): 577-614.

Altomonte, C., I. Colantone, and L. Bonacorsi. 2018. "Trade and Growth in the Age of Global Value Chains." BAFFI CAREFIN Centre Research Paper 97.

Amaglobeli, D., R. A. de Mooij, A. Mengistu, M. Moszoro, M. Nose, S. Nunhuck, S. Pattanayak, et al. 2023. "Transforming Public Finance Through GovTech." IMF Staff Discussion Note 23/004, International Monetary Fund, Washington, DC.

Amiti, M., S. J. Redding, and D. E. Weinstein. 2019. "The Impact of the 2018 Tariffs on Prices and Welfare." *Journal of Economic Perspectives* 33 (4): 187-210.

Andersen, T. M., and M. Svarer. 2012. "Active Labour Market Policies in a Recession." *IZA J Labor Policy* 1 (7).

Anginer, D., A. Demirgüç-Kunt, and D. S. Mare. 2018. "Bank Capital, Institutional Environment and Systemic Stability." *Journal of Financial Stability* 37: 97-106.

Arezki, R. and Y. Liu. 2020. "On the (Changing) Asymmetry of Global Spillovers: Emerging Markets vs. Advanced Economies." *Journal of International Money and Finance* 107 (October): 102219.

Avellán, L., A. J. Galindo, G. Lotti, and J. P. Rodríguez. 2024. "Bridging the Gap: Mobilization of multilateral Development Banks in Infrastructure." *World Development* 176 (April): 106498.

Baffes, J., A. Kabundi, and P. Nagle. 2021. "The Role of Income and Substitution in Commodity Demand." *Oxford Economic Papers* 74 (2): 498-522.

Baffes, J., A. Kabundi, P. Nagle, and F. Ohnsorge. 2018. "The Role of Major Emerging Markets in Global Commodity Demand." Policy Research Working Paper 8495, World Bank, Washington, DC.

Baharumshah, A.Z., L. Slesman, and E.S. Devadason. 2017. "Types of Foreign Capital Inflows and Economic Growth: New Evidence on Role of Financial Markets." *Journal of International Development* 29 (6): 768-89.

Balatti, M., M. A. Kose, F. L. Ohnsorge, and H. Yilmazkuday. 2024. "Business Cycle Spillovers from Emerging Market Economies." Mimeo.

Baldwin, R., R. Freeman, and A. Theodorakopoulos. 2023. "Deconstructing Deglobalization: The Future of Trade is in Intermediate Services." *Asian Economic Policy Review* 19 (1): 17-38.

Barattieri, A., A. Mattoo, and D. Taglioni. 2024. "Trade Effects of Industrial Policy: Are Preferential Agreements a Shield?" Policy Research Working Paper 10806, World Bank, Washington, DC.

Baxter, M., and M. Kouparitsas. 2005. "Determinants of Business Cycle Co-movement: A Robust Analysis," *Journal of Monetary Economics* 52 (1): 113-57.

Beaton, K., S. Cerovic, M. Galdamez, M. Hadzi-Vaskov,F. Loyola, Z. Koczan, B. Lissovolik, J. K. Martijn, Y. Ustyugova, and J. Wong. 2017. "Migration and Remittances in Latin America and the Caribbean: Engines of Growth and Macroeconomic Stabilizers?" IMF Working Paper 17/144, International Monetary Fund, Washington, DC.

Bénétrix, A., H. Pallan, and U. Panizza. 2023. "The Elusive Link between FDI and Economic Growth." Policy Research Working Paper 10422, World Bank, Washington, DC.

Benn, J., and W. Luijkx. 2017. "Emerging Providers' International Co-operation for Development." OECD

Development Co-operation Working Paper 33, Organisation for Economic Co-operation and Development, Paris.

Bilal, A., and D. R. Känzig. 2024. "The Macroeconomic Impact of Climate Change: Global vs. Local Temperature." NBER Working Paper 32450, National Bureau of Economic Research, Cambridge, MA.

Caldara, D., M. Iacoviello, P. Molligo, A. Prestipino, and A. Raffo. 2020. "The Economic Effects of Trade Policy Uncertainty" *Journal of Monetary Economics* 109 (January): 38-59.

Calvo, G. A. 2014. "Sudden Stop and Sudden Flood of Foreign Direct Investment: Inverse Bank Run, Output, and Welfare Distribution." *The Scandinavian Journal of Economics* 116 (1): 5-19.

Cao, Y., E. Dabla-Norris, and E. Di Gregorio. 2024. "Fiscal Discourse and Fiscal Policy." IMF Working Paper 24/194, International Monetary Fund, Washington, DC.

Card, C., J. Kluve, and A. Weber. 2018. *Journal of the European Economic Association* 16 (3): 894-931.

Carvalho, V. M., and A. Tahbaz-Salehi. "Production Networks: A Primer." *Annual Review of Economics* 11: 635-63.

Cavallo, A., G. Gopinath, B. Neiman, and J. Tang. 2021. "Tariff Pass-Through at the Border and at the Store: Evidence from US Trade Policy." *American Economic Review: Insights* 3 (1): 19-34.

Cerutti, E., C. Casanova, and S.-K. Pradhan. 2018. "The Growing Footprint of EME Banks in the International Banking System." *BIS Quarterly Review* (December): 27-37.

Cerutti, E., S. Claessens, and D. Puy. 2019. "Push Factors and Capital Flows to Emerging Markets: Why Knowing Your Lender Matters More Than Fundamentals." *Journal of International Economics* 119: 133-49.

Cerutti, E., and H. Zhou. 2018. "Cross-border Banking and the Circumvention of Macroprudential and Capital Control Measures." IMF Working Paper 18/217, International Monetary Fund, Washington, DC.

Cetorelli, N., and L. S. Goldberg. 2010. "Global Banks and International Shock Transmission: Evidence from the Crisis." NBER Working Paper 15974, National Bureau of Economic Research, Cambridge, MA.

Chari, A., P. B. Henry, and H. Reyes. 2021. "The Baker Hypothesis: Stabilization, Structural Reforms, and Economic Growth." *Journal of Economic Perspectives* 35 (3): 83-101.

Chatterjee, A., and R. Saraf. 2024. "Impact of China on Commodity Exporters." *Review of International Economics* 32 (3): 1462-91.

Chen, M. X., and C. Lin. 2020. "Geographic Connectivity and Cross-Border Investment: The Belts, Roads and Skies." *Journal of Development Economics* 146 (September): 102469.

Chen, M. X., and A. Mattoo. 2008. "Regionalism in Standards: Good or Bad for Trade?" *Canadian Journal of Economics* 41 (3): 383-863.

Chinn, M. D., and H. Ito. 2008. "A New Measure of Financial Openness." *Journal of Comparative Policy Analysis* 10 (3): 309-22.

Cho, Y., and S. Kim. 2021. "International Transmission of Chinese Monetary Policy Shocks to Asian Countries." Working Paper 18, Bank of Korea, Seoul.

Clarida, R. H. 2023. "Perspectives on Global Monetary Policy Coordination, Cooperation and Correlation." *Journal of International Money and Finance* 130 (February): 102749.

Combes, J. L., T. Kinda, R. Ouedraogo, and P. Plane. 2019. "Financial Flows and Economic Growth in Developing Countries." *Economic Modelling* 83 (December): 195-209.

Constantinescu, C., A. Mattoo, and M. Ruta. 2020. "The Global Trade Slowdown: Cyclical or Structural?" *The World Bank Economic Review* 34 (1): 121-42.

Copestake, A., M. Firat, D. Furceri, and C. Redl. 2023. "China Spillovers: Aggregate and Firm-Level Evidence." IMF Working Paper 23/206, International Monetary Fund, Washington, DC.

Crucini, M. J., M. A. Kose, and C. Otrok. 2011. "What Are the Driving Forces of International Business Cycles?" *Review of Economic Dynamics* 14 (1): 156-75.

Cuberes, D., and M. Teignier. 2016. "Aggregate Effects of Gender Gaps in the Labor Market: A Quantitative Estimate." *Journal of Human Capital* 10 (1): 1-32.

Cunningham, W., and P. Villaseñor. 2016. "Employer Voices, Employer Demands, and Implications for Public Skills Development Policy Connecting the Labor and Education Sectors." Policy Research Working Paper 7582, World Bank, Washington, DC.

Dabla-Norris, E., R. Espinoza, and S. Jahan. 2015. "Spillovers to Low-Income Countries: Importance of Systemic Emerging Markets." *Applied Economics* 47 (53): 5707-25.

Dabla-Norris, E., and S. Narapong. 2013. "Revisiting the Link between Finance and Macroeconomic Volatility." IMF Working Paper 13/029, International Monetary Fund, Washington, DC.

Dappe, M., M. Lebrand, and A. Stokenberga. 2024. *Shrinking Economic Distance: Understanding How Markets and Places Can Lower Transport Costs in Developing Countries*. Washington, DC: World Bank.

Davis, J. S. 2014. "Financial Integration and International Business Cycle Co-movement." *Journal of Monetary Economics* 64 (May): 99111.

De Vita, G., and K. S. Kyaw. 2009. "Growth Effects of FDI And Portfolio Investment Flows to Developing Countries: A Disaggregated Analysis by Income Levels." *Applied Economics Letters* 16 (3): 277-83.

Dell'Erba, S., E. Baldacci, and T. Poghosyan. 2013. "Spatial Spillovers in Emerging Market Spreads." *Empirical Economics* 45: 735-56.

Dieppe, A., ed. 2021. *Global Productivity: Trends, Drivers, and Policies*. Washington, DC: World Bank.

Dincer, N. N., and B. Eichengreen. 2014. "Central Bank Transparency and Independence: Updates and New Measures." *International Journal of Central Banking* 10 (1): 189-259.

Didier, T., and M. Pinat. 2017. "The Nature of Trade and Growth Linkages." Policy Research Working Paper 8168, World Bank, Washington, DC.

Dom, R., A. Custers, S. Davenport. and W. Prichard. 2022. *Innovations in Tax Compliance: Building Trust, Navigating Politics, and Tailoring Reform*. Washington, DC: World Bank.

Donovan, K., W. J. Lu, and T. Schoellman. 2023. "Labor Market Dynamics and Development." *The Quarterly Journal of Economics* 138 (4): 2287-325.

EBRD (European Bank for Reconstruction and Development). 2024. *Transition Report 2024-25: Navigating Industrial Policy*. London: European Bank for Reconstruction and Development.

Echandi, R., M. Maliszewska, and V. Steenbergen. 2022. *Making the Most of the African Continental Free Trade Area*. Washington, DC: World Bank.

Ehrmann, M., M. Fratzscher, and R. Rigobon. 2011. "Stocks, Bonds, Money Markets and Exchange Rates: Measuring International Financial Transmission." *Journal of Applied Econometrics* 26 (6): 948-74.

Eichengreen, B. 2016. "International Policy Coordination and Emerging-Market Economies" In *Monetary Policy in India: A Modern Macroeconomic Perspective*, edited by C. Ghate and K. M. Kletzer. Springer, New Delhi.

Estefania-Flores, J., D. Furceri, S. A. Hannan, J. D. Ostry, and A. K. Rose. 2022. "A Measurement of Aggregate Trade Restrictions and Their Economic Effects." IMF Working Paper 22/001, International Monetary Fund, Washington, DC.

Estrades, C., M. Maliszewska, I. Osorio-Rodarte, and M. Seara e Pereira. 2022. "Estimating the Economic and Distributional Impacts of the Regional Comprehensive Economic Partnership." Policy Research Working Paper 9939, World Bank, Washington, DC.

Evenett, S., A. Jakubik, F. Martín, and M. Ruta. 2024. "The Return of Industrial Policy in Data." *The World Economy* 47: 2762-88.

Fei, S. 2011. "The Confidence Channel for the Transmission of Shocks." Banque de France Working Paper 314, Banque de France, Paris.

Feldkircher, M., and F. Huber. 2016. "The International Transmission of US Shocks—Evidence from Bayesian Global Vector Autoregressions." *European Economic Review* 81 (January): 167-88.

Fernández-Villaverde, J., T. Mineyama, and D. Song. 2024. "Are We Fragmented Yet? Measuring Geopolitical Fragmentation and Its Causal Effect." NBER Working Paper 32638, National Bureau of Economic Research, Cambridge, MA.

Ferreira, C., N. Jenkinson, and C. Wilson. 2019. "From Basel I to Basel III: Sequencing Implementation in Developing Economies." IMF Working Paper 19/127, International Monetary Fund, Washington, DC.

Filmer, D., and L. Fox. 2014. *Youth Employment in Sub-Saharan Africa*. Washington, DC: World Bank.

Fontagné, L., N. Rocha, M. Ruta, and G. Santoni. 2023. "The Economic Impact of Deepening Trade Agreements." *World Bank Economic Review* 37 (3): 366-88.

Fox, L., and D. Gandhi. 2021. "Youth Employment in Sub-Saharan Africa: Progress and Prospects." Brookings

Africa Growth Initiative Working Paper 28, Brookings Institution, Washington DC.

Frankel, J. A., and A. K. Rose. 1997. "Economic Structure and the Decision to Adopt a Common Currency." Seminar Paper 611, The Institute for International Economic Studies, Stockholm University, Stockholm.

Frankel, J. A., and A. K. Rose. 1998. "The Endogeneity of the Optimum Currency Area Criteria." Royal Economic Society, Vol. 108 (499): 1009-25.

Freund, C., A. Mattoo, A. Mulabdic, and M. Ruta. 2024. "Is US Trade Policy Reshaping Global Supply Chains?" *Journal of International Economics* 152 (November): 104011.

Funke, M., M. Schularick, and C. Trebesch. 2023. "Populist Leaders and the Economy." *American Economic Review* 113 (12): 3249-88.

Furceri, D., J. T. Jalles, and A. Zdzienicka. 2017. "China Spillovers: New Evidence from Time-Varying Estimates." *Open Economies Review* 28 (3): 413-29.

G20 (Group of Twenty) Independent Experts Group. 2023. "Strengthening Multilateral Development Banks: The Triple Agenda." Report of the Independent Expert Group.

Galindo, A. J., and U. Panizza. 2018. "The Cyclicality of International Public Sector Borrowing in Developing Countries: Does the Lender Matter?" *World Development* 112 (December): 119-35.

Garriga, A. C., and C. M. Rodriguez. 2020. "More Effective Than We Thought: Central Bank Independence and Inflation in Developing Countries." *Economic Modelling* 85 (February): 87-105.

Gelos, G., and Y. Ustyugova. 2017. "Inflation Responses to Commodity Price Shocks–How and Why Do Countries Differ?" *Journal of International Money and Finance* 72: 28-47.

Gill, I. S., I. Izvorski, W. van Eeghen, and D. De Rosa. 2014. *Diversified Development: Making the Most of Natural Resources in Eurasia*. Washington, DC: World Bank.

Global Trade Alert (database). Accessed on December 18, 2024. https://globaltradealert.org.

Goldberg, P. K., and T. Reed. 2023. "Presidential Address: Demand-Side Constraints in Development: The Role of Market Size, Trade, and (In)equality." *Econometrica* 91 (6): 1915-50.

Gong, C., and S. Kim. 2018. "Regional Business Cycle Synchronization in Emerging and Developing Countries: Regional or Global Integration? Trade or Financial Integration?" *Journal of International Money and Finance* 84 (June): 42-57.

Grossman, G. M., E. Helpman, and S. J. Redding. 2024. "When Tariffs Disrupt Global Supply Chains." *American Economic Review* 114 (4): 988-1029.

Guénette, J. D., M. A. Kose, and N. Sugawara. 2022. "Is a Global Recession Imminent?" Equitable Growth, Finance, and Institutions Policy Note 4, World Bank, Washington, DC.

Ha, J., M. A. Kose, and F. Ohnsorge. 2023. "One-Stop Source: A Global Database of Inflation." *Journal of International Money and Finance* 137: 102896.

Ha, J., and I So. 2021. "Global Confidence, Uncertainty, and Business Cycles. Uncertainty, and Business Cycles." SSRN Scholarly Paper 3748156, Social Science Research Network, Rochester, NY.

Hale, G., T. Kapan, and C. Minoiu. 2016. "Crisis Transmission in the Global Banking Network." IMF Working Paper 16/91, International Monetary Fund, Washington, DC.

Hallegatte, S., J. Rentschler, and J. Rozenberg. 2019. *Lifelines: The Resilient Infrastructure Opportunity*. Washington, DC: World Bank.

Hallegatte, S., and J. Rozenberg. 2017. "Climate Change through a Poverty Lens." *Nature Climate Change* 7: 250-56.

Hanushek, E. A. 2013. "Economic Growth in Developing Countries: The Role of Human Capital." *Economics of Education Review* 37 (December): 204-12.

Harding, D., and A. Pagan. 2002. "Dissecting the Cycle: A Methodological Investigation." *Journal of Monetary Economics* 49 (2): 365-81.

Harrison, A., and A. Rodríguez-Clare. 2010. "Trade, Foreign Investment, and Industrial Policy for Developing Countries." In *Handbook of Development Economics, Volume 5*, edited by D. Rodrik and M. Rosenzweig, 4039-214. Oxford, U. K., and Amsterdam: North-Holland.

Hashimoto, H., Y. Mooi, G. Pedras, A. Roy, K. Chung, T. Galeza, M. G. Papaioannou, et al. 2021.

"Developing Government Local Currency Bond Markets." Guidance Note 2021/01, International Monetary Fund and World Bank, Washington, DC.

Hedström, A., N. Zelander, J. Juntilla, and G. S. Uddin. 2020. "Emerging Market Contagion under Geopolitical Uncertainty." *Emerging Markets Finance and Trade* 56: 1377-401.

Hegerty, S. W. 2016. "Commodity-price Volatility and Macroeconomic Spillovers: Evidence from Nine Emerging Markets." *The North American Journal of Economics and Finance* 35 (January): 23-37.

Hirata, H., M. A. Kose, and C. Otrok. 2013. "Regionalization Versus Globalization." IMF Working Paper 13/19, International Monetary Fund, Washington, DC.

Housa, R. J. Mohimont, and C. Otrok. 2023. "Commodity Exports, Financial Frictions, and International Spillovers." *European Economic Review* 158: 104465.

Huidrom, R., M. A. Kose, H. Matsuoka, and F. Ohnsorge. 2020. "How Important Are Spillovers from Major Emerging Markets?" *International Finance* 23 (1): 47-63.

Igan, D., E. Kohlscheen, G. Nodari, and D. Rees, 2022. "Commodity Market Disruptions, Growth and Inflation." BIS Bulletins 54, Bank for International Settlements, Basel.

Imbs, J., and I. Mejean. 2017. "Trade Elasticities." *Review of International Economics* 25 (2): 383-402.

Imbs, J., 2004. "Trade, Specialization and Synchronization." *Review of Economics and Statistics* 86 (3): 723-34.

Imbs, J., 2006. "The Real Effects of Financial Integration." *Journal of International Economics* 68 (March): 296-324.

IMF (International Monetary Fund). 2019a. "Drivers of Bilateral Trade and Spillovers from Tariffs." In *World Economic Outlook.* April 2019. Washington, DC: International Monetary Fund.

IMF (International Monetary Fund). 2019b. "Reigniting Growth in Emerging Market and Low-Income Economies: What Role for Structural Reforms." In *World Economic Outlook: Global Manufacturing Downturn, Rising Trade Barriers.* October. Washington, DC: International Monetary Fund.

IMF (International Monetary Fund). 2024a. "Trading Places: Real Spillovers from G20 Emerging Markets." In *World Economic Outlook.* April. Washington, DC: International Monetary Fund.

IMF (International Monetary Fund). 2024b. "Understanding the Social Acceptability of Structural Reforms." In *World Economic Outlook, October 2024.* Washington, DC: International Monetary Fund.

IMF (International Monetary Fund), OECD (Organisation for Economic Co-operation and Development), World Bank, and WTO (World Trade Organization). 2022. "Subsidies, Trade, and International Cooperation." Staff report, International Monetary Fund, Washington, DC.

Inklaar, R., R. Jong-A-Pin, and J. de Haan. 2008. "Trade and Business Cycle Synchronization in OECD Countries—A Re-examination." *European Economic Review* 52 (May): 646-66.

Inoue, T., D. Kaya, and H. Ohshige. 2015. "The Impact of China's Slowdown on the Asia Pacific Region: An Application of the GVAR Model." Policy Research Working Paper 7442, World Bank, Washington, DC.

Jackson, L. E., M. A. Kose, C. Otrok, and M. T. Owyang. 2016. "Specification and Estimation of Bayesian Dynamic Factor Models: A Monte Carlo Analysis with an Application to Global House Price Comovement." In *Dynamic Factor Models*, 361-400. Emerald Group Publishing, Bingley, U.K.

Jafino, B. A., B. Walsh, J. Rozenberg, and S. Hallegatte. 2020. "Revised Estimates of the Impact of Climate Change on Extreme Poverty by 2030." Policy Research Working Paper 9417, World Bank, Washington, DC.

Jansen, W. J., and A. C. J. Stokman. 2004. "Foreign Direct Investment and International Business Cycle Comovement." ECB Working Paper No. 401, European Central Bank, Frankfurt.

Javorcik, B. 2020. "Global Supply Chains Will Not Be the Same in the Post-COVID-19 World." In *COVID-19 and Trade Policy: Why turning Inward Won't Work*, edited by R. E. Baldwin and S. J. Evenett, 111-16. Paris and London: Centre for Economic Policy Research.

Johansson, A. C. 2012. "China's Growing Influence in Southeast Asia–Monetary Policy and Equity Markets." *The World Economy* 35 (7): 816-37.

Jones, E., and P. Knaack. 2019. "Global Financial Regulation: Shortcomings and Reform Options." *Global Policy* 10 (2): 193-206.

Juhász, R., N. Lane, E. Oehlsen, and V. C. Pérez. 2022. "The Who, What, When, and How of Industrial Policy: A Text-Based Approach." SSRN Scholarly

Paper 4198209, Social Science Research Network, Rochester, NY.

Juhász, R., N. Lane, and D. Rodrik. 2024. "The New Economics of Industrial Policy." *Annual Review of Economics* 16: 213-24.

Kelejian, H. H., G. S. Tavlas, and G. Hondroyiannis. 2006. "A Spatial Modelling Approach to Contagion among Emerging Economies." *Open Economies Review* 17 (4): 423-41.

Kilic Celik, S., A. Kose, and F. Ohnsorge. 2024. "Prospects for Potential Growth: Risks, Rewards, and Policies." In *Falling Long-term Growth Prospects: Trends, Expectations, and Policies*, edited by M. A. Kose and F. Ohnsorge, 57-124. Washington, DC: World Bank.

Koepke, R. 2019. "What Drives Capital Flows to Emerging Markets? A Survey of the Empirical Literature." *Journal of Economic Surveys* 33 (2): 516-40.

Koh, W. C., and S. Yu. 2019. "Macroeconomic and Financial Sector Policies." In *A Decade After the Global Recession: Lessons and Challenges for Emerging and Developing Economies,* edited by M. A. Kose and F. Ohnsorge, 209-53. Washington, DC: World Bank.

Kose, M. A., S. Kurlat, F. Ohnsorge, and N. Sugawara. 2022. "A Cross-Country Database of Fiscal Space." *Journal of International Money and Finance* 128 (November): 102682.

Kose, M. A., C. Lakatos, F. Ohnsorge, and M. Stocker. 2020. "The Global Role of the United States and China." *Seoul Journal of Economics* 33 (3): 283-305.

Kose, M. A., H. Matsuoka, U, Panizza, and D. Vorisek. 2019. "Inflation Expectations: Review and Evidence." CEPR Discussion Paper 13601, Centre for Economic and Policy Research, London.

Kose, M. A., P. Nagle, F. Ohnsorge, and N. Sugawara. 2021. *Global Waves of Debt: Causes and Consequences.* Washington, DC: World Bank.

Kose, M. A., and F. Ohnsorge, eds. 2020. *A Decade after the Global Recession: Lessons and Challenges for Emerging and Developing Economies*, Washington, DC: World Bank.

Kose, M. A., and F. Ohnsorge, eds. 2024. *Falling Long-term Growth Prospects: Trends, Expectations, and Policies.* Washington, DC: World Bank.

Kose, M. A., C. Otrok, and E. Prasad. 2012. "Global Business Cycles: Convergence or Decoupling?" *International Economic Review* 53 (2): 511-38.

Kose, M. A., C. Otrok, and C. H. Whiteman. 2003. "International Business Cycles: World, Region, and Country-Specific Factors." *American Economic Review* 93 (4): 1216-39.

Kose, M. A., and E. S. Prasad. 2010. *Emerging Markets: Resilience and Growth amid Global Turmoil.* Washington, DC: Brookings Institution.

Kose, M. A., E. Prasad, K. Rogoff, and S.-J. Wei. 2009. "Financial Globalization: A Reappraisal." *IMF Staff Papers* 56 (1): 8-62.

Kose, M. A., E. S. Prasad, and M. E. Terrones. 2003. "Financial Integration and Macroeconomic Volatility." IMF Working Paper 03/50, International Monetary Fund, Washington, DC.

Kose, M. A., E. S. Prasad, and M. E. Terrones. 2009. "Does Financial Globalization Promote Risk Sharing?" *Journal of Development Economics* 89 (2): 258-70.

Lee, W., A. Mulabdic, and M. Ruta. 2023. "Third-Country Effects of Regional Trade Agreements: A Firm-Level Analysis." *Journal of International Economics* 140 (January): 103688.

Lei, W., D. Mei, and M. Zhang. 2024. "Global Spillovers of China's Monetary Policy." *China & World Economy* 32 (3): 1-30.

Levchenko, A. A., and N. Pandalai-Nayar. 2020. "TFP, News, and "Sentiments": The International Transmission of Business Cycles." *Journal of the European Economic Association* 18 (1): 302-41.

Maliszewska, M., P. Brenton, V. Chemutai, M. Chepeliev, and I. Sikora. Forthcoming. "Climate Policies and Their Impact on Developing Countries' Trade." EFI Insights Series, World Bank, Washington, DC.

Mattoo, A., A. Mulabdic, and M. Ruta. 2022. "Trade Creation and Trade Diversion in Deep Agreements." *Canadian Journal of Economics* 55 (3): 1598-637.

Mattoo, A., N. Rocha, and M. Ruta. 2020. *Handbook of Deep Trade Agreements.* Washington, DC: World Bank.

MIGA (Multilateral Investment Guarantee Agency). 2024. "Shifting Shores: FDI Relocations and Political Risk." Multilateral Investment Guarantee Agency, World Bank, Washington, DC.

Milesi Ferretti, G. M. 2021. "The Travel Shock." Hutchins Center on Fiscal and Monetary Policy

Working Paper 74, Brookings Institution, Washington, DC.

Millot, V., and Ł. Rawdanowicz, 2024. "The Return of Industrial Policies: Policy Considerations in the Current Context." *Economic Policy Papers* 34, Organisation for Economic Co-operation and Development, Paris.

Miranda-Agrippino, S., and H. Rey. 2022. "The Global Financial Cycle." In *Handbook of International Economics, Volume 6*, edited by G. Gopinath, E. Helpman, and K. Rogoff, 1-43. Amsterdam: Elsevier.

Moïsé, E., and F. Le Bris. 2013. "Trade Costs—What Have We Learned?: A Synthesis Report." OECD Trade Policy Paper 150, Organisation for Economic Co-operation and Development, Paris.

Montinari, L., and L. Stracca. 2016. "Trade, Finance or Policies: What Drives the Cross-Border Spill-over of Business Cycles?" *Journal of Macroeconomics* 49 (September): 131-48.

Myles. D. 2024. "US Outbound Screening Countdown Enters Final Stretch." *FDI Intelligence*. August 8.

OECD (Organisation for Economic Cooperation and Development). 2024. *OECD Economic Outlook, Volume 2024 Issue 1*. Paris: Organisation for Economic Co-operation and Development.

Naraidoo, R., and J. Paez-Farrell. 2023. "Commodity Price Shocks, Labour Market Dynamics and Monetary Policy in Small Open Economies." *Journal of Economic Dynamics and Control* 151: 104654.

Nath, I. B., V. A. Ramey, and P. J. Klenow. 2024. "How Much will Global Warming Cool Global Growth?" NBER Working Paper 32761, National Bureau of Economic Research, Cambridge, MA.

Nayyar, G., and E. Davies. 2024. "Services-Led Growth: Better Prospects after the Pandemic?" In *Falling Long-term Growth Prospects: Trends, Expectations, and Policies*, edited by M. A. Kose and F. Ohnsorge, 493-528. Washington, DC: World Bank.

Obstfeld, M. 2009. "International Finance and Growth in Developing Countries: What Have We Learned?" *IMF Staff Papers* 56 (1): 63-111.

Ohnsorge, F., and L. Quaglietti. 2024. "Trade as an Engine of Growth: Sputtering but Fixable." *Falling Long-term Growth Prospects: Trends, Expectations, and Policies*, edited M. A. Kose and F. Ohnsorge, 443-91. Washington, DC: World Bank.

Ohnsorge, F., and S. Yu, eds. 2022. *The Long Shadow of Informality: Challenges and Policies*. Washington, DC: World Bank.

Osborn, D. R., and T. Vehbi. 2015. "Growth in China and the US: Effects on a Small Commodity Exporter Economy." *Economic Modelling* 45 (February): 268-77.

Otto, G., G. Voss, and L. Willard. 2001. "Understanding OECD Output Correlations." Research Discussion Paper 2001-05, Reserve Bank of Australia, Sydney.

Pennings, S. M. 2022. "A Gender Employment Gap Index (GEGI): A Simple Measure of the Economic Gains from Closing Gender Employment Gaps, with an Application to the Pacific Islands." Policy Research Working Paper 9942, World Bank, Washington, DC.

Poghosyan, T. 2023. "Remittances in Russia and Caucasus and Central Asia: The Gravity Model." *Review of Development Economics* 27 (2): 1224-41.

Pop, G., and D. Connon. 2020. "Industrial Policy Effects and the Case for Competition." Equitable Growth, Finance and Institutions Insight. World Bank, Washington, DC.

Prasad, E. S. 2010. "Financial Sector Regulation and Reforms in Emerging Markets: An Overview." NBER Working Paper 16428, National Bureau of Economic Research, Cambridge, MA.

Rasool, H., S. Maqbool, and M. Tarique. 2021. "The Relationship Between Tourism and Economic Growth Among BRICS Countries: A Panel Cointegration Analysis." *Future Business Journal* 7 (1): 1-11.

Rigobon, R. 2019. "Contagion, Spillover, and Interdependence." *Economía* 19 (2): 69-100.

Roch, F. 2019. "The Adjustment to Commodity Price Shocks." *Journal of Applied Economics* 22 (1): 437-467.

Rodrik, D., and A. Subramanian. 2009. "Why Did Financial Globalization Disappoint?" *IMF Staff Papers* 56 (1): 112-38.

Rozenberg, J., and M. Fay. 2019. *Beyond the Gap: How Countries Can Afford the Infrastructure They Need while Protecting the Planet*. Washington, DC: World Bank.

Stamm, K., and D. Vorisek. 2024. "The Global Investment Slowdown: Challenges and Policies." In *Falling Long-term Growth Prospects: Trends, Expectations, and Policies*, edited by M. A. Kose and F. Ohnsorge, 227-98. Washington, DC: World Bank.

Stamm, K., and S. Yu. 2024. "The Magic of Investment Accelerations." In *Global Economic Prospects,* 97-147. January. Washington, DC: World Bank.

UNCTAD (United Nations Conference on Trade and Development). 2024a. "Investment Policy Trends." In *2024 Trade and Development Report: Rethinking Development in the Age of Discontent.* New York: UNCTAD.

UNCTAD (United Nations Conference on Trade and Development). 2024b. "Outward FDI Policies: Promotion and Facilitation—Regulation and Screening." Investment Policy Monitor 27, UNCTAD, New York.

UNEP (United Nations Environment Programme). 2023. *Adaptation Gap Report 2023.* New York: United Nations Environment Programme.

United Nations. "Goal 2: Zero Hunger." UN Sustainable Development Goals. https://un.org/sustainable development/hunger/.

Wooldridge, P. 2020. "Implications of Financial Market Development for Financial Stability in Emerging Market Economies." Note submitted to the G20 International Financial Architecture Working Group, Bank for International Settlements, Basel.

World Bank. 2002. *Globalization, Growth, and Poverty: Building an Inclusive Global Economy.* Washington, DC: World Bank; New York: Oxford University Press.

World Bank. 2016. *Global Economic Prospects: Spillovers amid Weak Growth.* Washington, DC: World Bank.

World Bank. 2019. *Global Financial Development Report 2019/2020: Bank Regulation and Supervision a Decade after the Global Financial Crisis.* Washington, DC: World Bank.

World Bank. 2020a. *World Development Report 2020: Trading for Development in the Age of Global Value Chains.* Washington, DC: World Bank.

World Bank. 2020b. *The African Continental Free Trade Area: Economic and Distributional Effects.* Washington, DC: World Bank.

World Bank. 2021a. *Global Economic Prospects,* January. Washington, DC: World Bank.

World Bank. 2021b. "A Changing Landscape: Trends in Official Financial Flows and the Aid Architecture." World Bank, Washington, DC.

World Bank. 2021c. "Prevention, Preparedness, and Response: The WBG's Role in Future Crises." Development Committee Meeting Paper, World Bank, Washington, DC.

World Bank. 2022a. "Climate and Development: An Agenda for Action. Emerging Insights from World Bank Group 2021-22 Country Climate and Development Reports." World Bank, Washington, DC.

World Bank. 2022b. "Navigating Uncertainty: China's Economy in 2023." China Economic Update. World Bank, Washington, DC.

World Bank. 2023a. *World Development Report 2023: Migrants, Refugees, and Societies.* Washington, DC: World Bank.

World Bank. 2023b. *Unfair Advantage: Distortive Subsidies and Their Effects on Global Trade.* Washington, DC: World Bank.

World Bank. 2023c. "Connecting to Compete 2023: Trade Logistics in an Uncertain Global Economy." World Bank, Washington, DC.

World Bank. 2023d. *World Bank Support for Domestic Revenue Mobilization: An Independent Evaluation.* Independent Evaluation Group. Washington, DC: World Bank.

World Bank. 2024a. *Global Economic Prospects.* June. Washington, DC: World Bank.

World Bank. 2024b. *Women, Jobs, and Growth.* South Asia Economic Update. Washington, DC: World Bank.

World Bank. 2024c. *Poverty, Prosperity, and the Planet Report: Pathways Out of Prosperity.* Washington, DC: World Bank.

World Bank. 2024d. *Finance and Prosperity 2024.* Washington, DC: World Bank.

World Bank. 2024e. *Global Economic Prospects.* January. Washington, DC: World Bank.

World Bank. 2024f. *World Development Report 2024: The Middle-Income Trap.* Washington, DC: World Bank.

World Bank. 2024g. *Business Ready 2024.* Washington, DC: World Bank.

World Bank 2024h. "Viet Nam 2045: Trading Up in a Changing World—Pathways to a High-Income Future." World Bank, Washington, DC.

World Bank. 2024i. *Services Unbound: Digital Technologies and Policy Reform in East Asia and Pacific*. Washington, DC: World Bank.

World Bank. 2024j. *Jobs and Technology*. East Asia and Pacific Economic Update. October. Washington, DC: World Bank.

World Bank and WTO (World Trade Organization). 2015. "The Role of Trade in Ending Poverty." World Trade Organization, Geneva.

World Bank and WTO (World Trade Organization). 2023. "Trade in Services for Development: Fostering Sustainable Growth and Economic Diversification." World Trade Organization, Geneva.

WTO (World Trade Organization). 2012. *A Practical Guide to Trade Policy Analysis*. Geneva: World Trade Organization.

WTO (World Trade Organization). 2019. *World Trade Report 2019: The Future of Services Trade*. Geneva: World Trade Organization.

WTO (World Trade Organization). 2024. *World Trade Report 2024: Trade and Inclusiveness. How to Make Trade Work for All*. September. Geneva: World Trade Organization.

Yilmazkuday, H. 2024. "International Spillover Effects of Geopolitical Risks on Economic Growth." SSRN Scholarly Paper 4801817, Social Science Research Network, Rochester, NY.

CHAPTER 4

FALLING GRADUATION PROSPECTS

Low-Income Countries in the Twenty-First Century

Rapid growth underpinned by domestic reforms and a benign global environment allowed many low-income countries (LICs) to attain middle-income status in the first decade of the twenty-first century. Since then, the rate at which LICs are graduating to middle-income status has slowed markedly. The prospects for today's LICs appear much more challenging. In recent years, per capita growth has been anemic amid heightened levels of conflict and fragility and adverse global developments. Across a wide array of development metrics, today's LICs are behind where LICs that since turned middle-income stood in 2000. They are also more susceptible to domestic shocks, including those related to climate change. Many LICs that graduated in the past underwent growth accelerations—extended periods of robust economic expansion, during which output became far more trade- and investment-intensive. These accelerations were generally preceded by reforms that tended to increase market orientation and channeled resources into rapid investment growth. To kick-start stronger growth, today's LICs can harness large resource endowments to, among other things, supply the green transition, and find advantage in youthful and growing populations, untapped tourism potential, and regional trade integration. However, harnessing these factors and improving productivity hinges on engineering increased investment in human and physical capital, closing gender gaps, addressing fiscal risks, and improving governance. For LICs in fragile and conflict-affected situations, attaining greater peace and stability is paramount. LICs will also need international support to mobilize additional resources and foster institutions that can drive durable reforms. Throughout, policy makers should be guided by deep knowledge of country circumstances—there is no one-size-fits-all recipe for growth and graduation to middle income status in LICs.

Introduction

At the turn of the twenty-first century, nearly 1.8 billion people lived in extreme poverty world-wide—more than 60 percent of them in 63 nations classified as low-income countries (LICs).[1] Since then, the number of extreme poor globally has declined by more than 60 percent, while 39 countries that were low income have achieved middle-income country status (figure 4.1.A). Among these previous LICs are some of the largest emerging market and developing economies (EMDEs), including Bangladesh, India, and Indonesia. Countries that graduated to middle-income since 2000—referred to in this chapter as LICs turned into middle-income countries (LTMs)—were often among the richer LICs in 2000, but they have also grown at solid pace, with substantial improvements in many wider development metrics.[2]

Yet, 24 countries that were low income at the turn of the century remain so today.[3] In addition, South Sudan and the Syrian Arab Republic have regressed from middle-income status during protracted conflicts, bringing the total of number of LICs to 26. These countries have annual GNI per capita of less than $1,145 or a little more than $3 per day.[4] In all, they currently account for less than 1 percent of global output, but about 9 percent of the global population (figure 4.1.B and 4.1.C). Twenty-two of them are in Sub-Saharan Africa (SSA) and seventeen of them are classified as being in fragile and conflict-affected situations (FCS; figure 4.1.D).

Over the last decade, the rate at which LICs have been graduating to middle-income status has slowed, set back by anemic growth, high levels of conflict and violence, and escalating effects from climate change. In the face of overlapping global shocks, poverty in LICs has increased since 2019—LICs now account for more than 40 percent of extreme poverty worldwide and about

---

Note: This chapter was prepared by Philip Kenworthy, Joseph Mawejje, and Max Rudibert Steinbach.

[1] LICs in 2000 reflect the country classification of the 2001/02 World Bank fiscal year and are defined as countries with GNI per capita of $755 or less in 2000 (World Bank Atlas method). The LIC threshold for the 2024/25 fiscal year is set at GNI per capita of $1,145 or less in 2023. New thresholds are determined at the start of each World Bank fiscal year.

[2] In addition to 39 LTMs that graduated after being LICs in 2000, there are three middle-income countries that have been low-income at some point since 2000 that are included in this group (Equatorial Guinea, Papua New Guinea, and Timor Leste). See tables 1 and 2 for a list of LICs and LTMs.

[3] The Democratic People's Republic of Korea is included in the total of 26 LICs, but excluded from all subsequent analysis, because of lack of data.

[4] The GNI is based on Atlas method which uses a convergence factor to U.S. dollars taking account of a moving average of the market-exchange rate, adjusted for differences between domestic and international inflation. For full details, see: https://www.datahelpdesk.worldbank.org/knowledgebase/articles/378832-what-is-the-world-bank-atlas-method.

FIGURE 4.1 Developments in LICs and LTMs

The rate at which low-income countries are graduating to middle-income status has slowed markedly since 2010. Current LICs account for about 9 percent of the global population and less than 1 percent of global output, but they are home to more than 40 percent of people experiencing extreme poverty. Geographically, LICs are heavily concentrated in Sub-Saharan Africa. Acute food insecurity in LICs has recently increased and is mainly in countries affected by fragility and conflict.

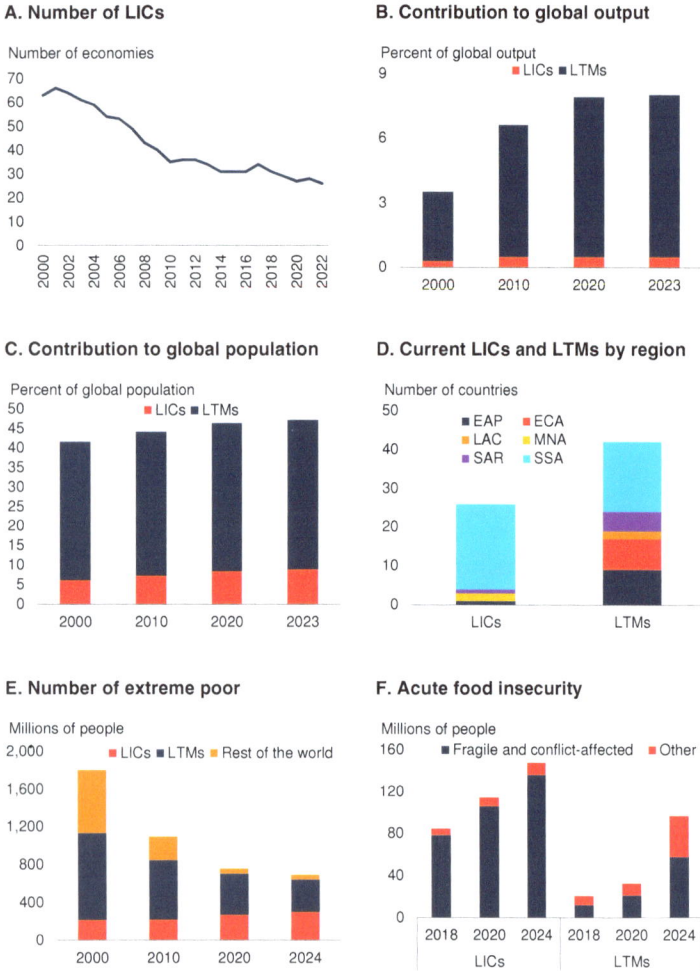

A. Number of LICs

B. Contribution to global output

C. Contribution to global population

D. Current LICs and LTMs by region

E. Number of extreme poor

F. Acute food insecurity

Sources: Global Report on Food Crises (database); WDI (database); World Bank.
Note: EAP = East Asia and the Pacific; ECA = Europe and Central Asia; LAC = Latin America and the Caribbean; MNA = Middle East and North Africa; SAR = South Asia; SSA = Sub-Saharan Africa. LICs = low-income countries; LTMs = LICs turned into middle-income countries.
A.D. LICs count includes the Democratic People's Republic of Korea.
B. Share of LICs and LTMs output in world output.
C. Share of LICs and LTMs population in world population.
E. The number of poor in today's LICs, LTMs, and the rest of the world.
F. Bars show the number of people in food crisis as classified by the Integrated Food Security Phase Classification Phase 3, that is, in acute food insecurity crisis or worse.

four-in-ten of their population are estimated to have experienced extreme poverty last year (figure 4.1.E; World Bank 2024a). Food insecurity, which is concentrated in fragile and conflict-affected situations, has intensified (figure 4.1.F).

Reflecting these forces, in LICs, only about 4 percent of Sustainable Development Goals adopted by the United Nations in 2015 are on track (Sachs, Lafortune, and Fuller 2024).

Reversing these trends and delivering global development priorities will require sustainably increasing growth rates in LICs so that many more become middle-income. Against this backdrop, this chapter presents a comprehensive review of the progress made by LICs and LTMs in the first quarter of this century. It seeks to illuminate factors that helped drive graduation to middle-income status (hereafter, "graduation") in the past and analyze growth and graduation prospects for LICs today. It addresses the following questions:

- What are the salient macroeconomic features of today's LICs?

- How has growth evolved in LICs since the turn of the century?

- What challenges and opportunities stand between today's LICs and graduation?

- What are the policy priorities to improve graduation prospects?

Contributions. This chapter makes several contributions to the literature.

- *Main features and performance of LICs.* The chapter analyzes how the structural features of LICs today differ from countries that were considered low-income in the past. In addition, it documents a dismal growth performance in many LICs over the past 15 years and highlights how, despite the global rebound from the 2020 global recession, the poorest countries have fallen further behind LTMs across a wide variety of key develop-ment indicators. It also assesses implications for the future pace of graduation to middle-income status. Previous studies have examined the macroeconomic developments of different groups of EMDEs, including the larger group of lower-middle-income and low-income countries (Chrimes et al. 2024; IMF 2024a). Some others examined transitions at higher income levels, with a focus on the middle-income group (World Bank 2024b). This study focuses exclusively on LICs because of their particular characteristics: they have substantial development gaps relative to other EMDEs; are geographically concentrated; and face greater vulnerability to a range of shocks including those related to conflict, climate change, and commodity price swings.

- *Growth accelerations.* The chapter assesses the recent history of growth accelerations in LICs—periods defined by robust and sustained economic growth, with concomitant large improvements in varied economic and development metrics. It highlights how these sustained growth surges have been central to many LTM graduations, and how the COVID-19 pandemic snuffed out all but one of the ongoing low-income accelerations in 2020. Selected case studies shed light on the drivers behind the comparatively narrow set of growth accelerations that took root in countries at income levels similar to today's LICs.

- *Opportunities and challenges.* The chapter discusses growth opportunities and challenges that could accelerate or derail graduation. For example, in the context of the clean energy transition, it considers how key macroeconomic variables evolve around energy and mineral discoveries. In addition, the chapter systematically surveys how LICs could take advantage of endowments—such as natural resources (including tourism potential), youthful populations, and scope for greater economic integration—to kick-start growth and transformation. The chapter then analyzes various risks which, if they crystallized, could further worsen economic performance in LICs, including those related to conflict, climate change, fiscal vulnerabilities, geographical challenges, declining domestic productivity, and a less favorable external environment.

- *Policy priorities.* The chapter provides a rich appraisal of national and global policy priorities to help LICs tackle the challenges

confronting them, capitalize on their comparative advantages, and accelerate growth and graduation. The chapter does not attempt to rank policy recommendations, recognizing that country circumstances differ and may dictate different priorities. Instead, the chapter categorizes policies into those that are broadly cross-cutting, and those that are most relevant to subsets of LICs.

Main findings. The chapter presents the following main findings:

Adverse initial conditions. LICs today are poorer than LTMs were in 2000. Commensurately, physical and human capital scarcity is more pronounced in the former group. Low-productivity agriculture comprises a larger share of output in LICs today than it did in LTMs in the past. LICs today also tend to be less open to trade and are more geographically concentrated. They are also more reliant on official development assistance (ODA) than LTMs were in 2000.

Fifteen lost years in LICs. Annual per capita GDP growth in LICs averaged 2.2 percent in the first decade of this century. However, over the last 15 years, incomes have barely increased, with per capita growth averaging less than 0.1 percent annually.[5] Amid increased conflict in some LICs, debt-related challenges in others, and a general deterioration in institutional quality, structural transformation has lost momentum and progress in reducing extreme poverty has stalled. On average, LICs have become poorer relative to LTMs and other EMDEs. Based on 2010-19 average growth rates, only six LICs—less than a quarter of eligible countries—would be on course to graduate by 2050, as compared with 42 graduations between 2000 and today, nearly two-thirds of eligible countries.

Correlates of growth accelerations. Most macroeconomic and development improvements occur during growth accelerations. Since 1990, the typical growth acceleration starting from low-

---

[5] Summary statistics for output in LICs may differ between chapter 1 and this chapter because of the omission in the former of some LICs for which forecasts are not available.

income levels has lasted almost 16 years, with per capita growth rising to nearly 7 percent annually. This compares with close to no per capita growth, on average, in non-acceleration years. Growth accelerations have coincided with improvements in a wide range of economic and development indicators—including investment, education, poverty reduction, and governance—compared with slower or no improvement, on average, outside accelerations.

Triggers of growth accelerations. A diverse range of productivity- and stability-enhancing policies have helped to ignite growth accelerations. Case studies of growth accelerations and graduations from low income levels indicate there is no one-size-fits-all strategy to kick-start growth, but there are apparent commonalities. First, peace and a baseline level of political stability are essential. Second, rapid investment growth tends to yield large dividends in low-income contexts. Third, accelerations were often preceded by reforms that increased the market orientation of the economy.[6] Fourth, although institutions do not need to be fully developed to initially enter an acceleration, policies that promote macroeconomic stability and improve conditions for private enterprise, backed by comparatively capable governance, help sustain accelerated growth.

Challenges to graduation. Daunting obstacles stand between today's LICs and graduation. First, there are many pressing institutional challenges. Two-thirds of LICs are in fragile and conflict-affected situations, with some experiencing intense conflicts. Wider institutional and social fragilities further impede graduation prospects. And, following an acutely challenging decade, appetite for necessary reforms may be waning—especially where macroeconomic adjustments have resulted in social frustration or where growth has been perceived as poor quality, jobless, and not inclusive. Second, domestic macro-financial vulnerabilities are mounting. Fiscal space has

narrowed since the mid-2010s, with half of LICs in or at high risk of debt distress in 2024. Even in some LICs where growth has been comparatively faster, the recent drivers of growth may be reaching their limits. Finally, LICs confront a barrage of external hindrances to growth. Declining global potential growth and advancing trade fragmentation pose headwinds to export-led development. Geopolitical tensions complicate the outlook and threaten further shocks. Meanwhile, clustered in Sub-Saharan Africa, LICs are geographically concentrated, highly exposed to climate shocks, and lack resources for adaptation.

Growth opportunities in LICs. There is latent potential in LICs that, if properly harnessed, could raise growth rates and accelerate graduation. First, as the rest of the world confronts demographic aging, the majority of LIC populations will become prime working age, facilitating increased domestic savings. Second, some LICs with ample natural resources could reap dividends supplying climate transition industries. Many LICs have great potential for agricultural productivity growth and agro-industrialization. Others have substantial potential as tourism destinations. Most LICs also have promising conditions for generating cheap solar energy. Third, even with sluggish global trade growth, trade integration in SSA could facilitate economies of scale and better access to global value chains. However, capturing the potential gains from these opportunities will require them to address a broad range of related constraints.

Policy priorities. LICs will have to generate sustained and stronger investment growth to meet development and climate objectives and durably raise incomes. Such efforts are far more likely to work in concert with improved institutions and reforms that foster macroeconomic stability. Sustaining an investment push in many LICs will likely also require the creation of fiscal space, both to finance projects directly and to lower the cost of finance across the economy. Meanwhile, for LICs in fragile and conflict-affected situations, fostering peace and greater stability is a first order prerequisite for growth and transformation. Commodity dependent LICs—especially energy and metals exporters—will need to strengthen the

---

[6] Growth accelerations were often preceded by policy reforms to boost competitiveness. Such reforms included: eliminating price controls, reforming exchange rate policies, liberalizing financial sectors and capital accounts, reducing trade barriers, easing tax and regulatory burdens, and reforming state-owned enterprises, among others.

management of natural resource extraction and revenues to deliver broad economic benefits. The global community has a critical role to play. Over the medium term, LICs will have much-improved chances of raising living standards if the global trading system is open, rather than sympathetic to beggar-thy-neighbor policies. Along with open trade, increased flows of concessional finance and technical assistance will be needed, given the large climate-related and other investment gaps. For many LICs, receipt of timely debt relief is an urgent priority.

Macroeconomic features of LICs and LTMs

Today, there are sizeable income and development gaps between LICs and LTMs that reflect both differing initial conditions in 2000 and contrasting development trajectories over the last quarter century. Today's LICs remain substantially poorer and more capital scarce than LTMs were at the turn of the century, with weaker institutions, higher shares of informal employment, and a greater proportion of output concentrated in low productivity agriculture. LICs also remain less open than were LTMs, limiting gains from trade, with more precarious fiscal positions. Despite these more challenging circumstances, LICs receive about the same level of development assistance per person as LTMs did in 2000, and less than LTMs do today. These characteristics indicate that, in aggregate, LICs face a steeper climb to graduate to middle-income than LTMs did in the past.

Lower per capita GDP. As a group, LTMs have long been wealthier than today's LICs. Indeed, current LICs remain substantially poorer than LTMs were at the turn of the century. In 2000, the population-weighted per capita GDP of LICs was less than 60 percent of the LTM level. Since then, the income gap has widened dramatically: in 2023, the population weighted per capita GDP in LICs was about 30 percent of the LTM level (figure 4.2.A). Many LTMs graduated partly because they started the century with higher incomes (figure 4.2.B). Nonetheless, several LTMs were poor by LIC standards in 2000. For example, Cambodia, the Kyrgyz Republic, the Lao People's

FIGURE 4.2 Macroeconomic features of LICs and LTMs

LICs today are far poorer than LTMs were in 2000, and the income gap between the two groups has widened over time. LICs also are younger but are gradually converging toward the population structure of LTMs in 2000. Capital stock per capita in LICs is estimated to be about one fifth of the level in LTMs, while proxies for physical and human capital are much weaker.

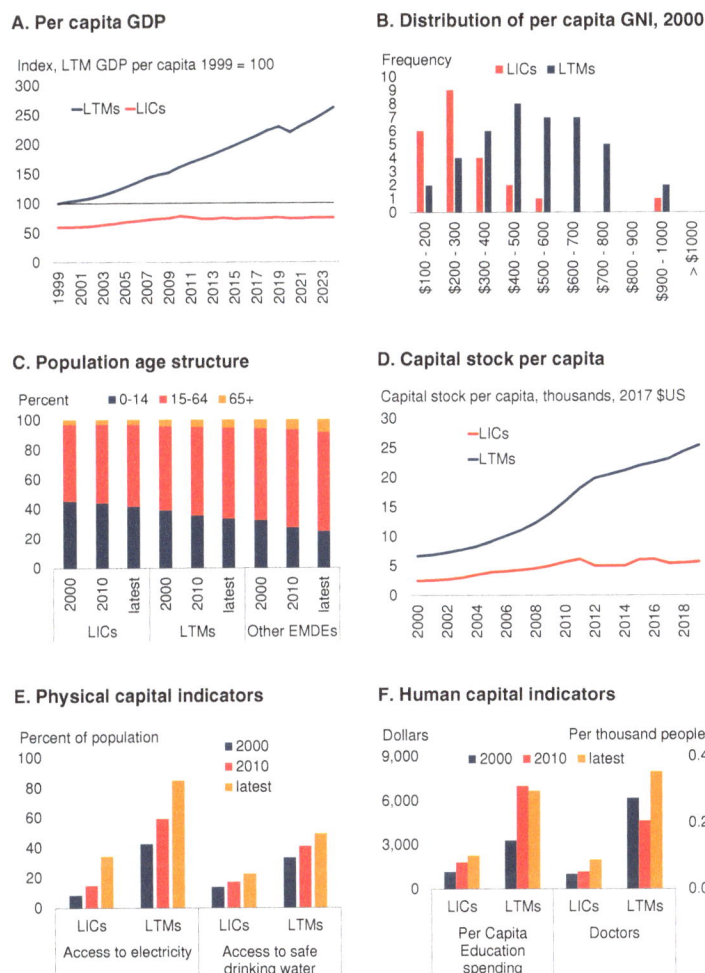

A. Per capita GDP

B. Distribution of per capita GNI, 2000

C. Population age structure

D. Capital stock per capita

E. Physical capital indicators

F. Human capital indicators

Sources: Penn-World Tables (database); WDI (database); World Bank.
Note: EMDEs = emerging market and developing economies; LICs = low-income countries; LTMs = LICs turned into middle-income countries.
A. Lines represent population-weighted GDP per capita. Country groups are consistent over time.
B. Horizontal axis numbers represent upper end of $100 bins for GNI per capita in 2000 (current U.S. dollars, Atlas method).
C. Simple averages of country groups. "Latest" shows data for 2022.
D. Lines represent population-weighted averages. Estimated with PPP exchange rates in real 2017 U.S. dollars.
E.F. Medians of country groups. "2000", "2010", and "latest" are calculated as the five-year average per country from 1998-2002, 2008-12, and 2018-22, respectively, to maximize available observations.

Democratic Republic, Nepal, and Tajikistan were all at about or below median for LIC living standards in 2000. As such, the incomes levels of LICs today reflect weaker growth rates than in LTMs, as well as worse starting points.

Younger populations. Demographics largely determine the potential size of the country's workforce, which is a key driver of trend growth rates in EMDEs. LIC populations are considerably younger than those in LTMs, which in turn tend to be younger than in other EMDEs. In the average LIC, about 40 percent of the population is under age 15 compared to a third in LTMs (figure 4.2.C). The proportion of children in LICs remains slightly higher today than it was in LTMs in 2000, while the proportion of working-age adults and those 65 or older is marginally lower. Over the coming decade today's LICs are likely to converge to broadly the population age structure that characterized LTMs in 2000.

Limited physical capital. The stock of physical capital per worker is critical to per capita incomes, because greater capital depth enables increased productivity. Physical capital is more severely limited in LICs than in LTMs. Prior to the COVID-19 pandemic, capital stock per capita in LICs was estimated to be about one-fifth of its level in LTMs and still materially lower than the level in LTMs in 2000 (figure 4.2.D). Proxies for the availability of infrastructure services underscore acute capital scarcity. About a third of the population in the average LIC has access to electricity compared to just over 40 percent in LTMs in 2000 and more than 80 percent in recent years. Similarly, just over 20 percent of the population in the average LIC has access to safe drinking water, less than half the proportion in LTMs today and about two-thirds of the proportion in 2000 (figure 4.2.E).

Lower levels of human capital development. Human capital—embodied in education, technical know-how, and healthcare provision—is a further key determinant of productivity levels and is relatively scarce in LICs. The secondary school enrollment rate in the median LIC is currently 39 percent—well below the 56 percent attained by the median LTM in the year of graduation to middle-income status, and per capita education spending in today's LICs is only about 70 percent of the LTM level in 2000. Comparatively low per capita outlays on education reflect low incomes rather than government priorities—education spending in LICs relative to

GDP is higher than in LTMs. The number of doctors per person has roughly doubled since 2000 in the average LIC but remains less than a third of the comparable number in LTMs in 2000 (figure 4.2.F).

Sectoral composition of output. The breakdown of GDP into agricultural, industrial and services output offers a broad marker of the sophistication of an economy's production process—a lower share of agricultural output in GDP tends to correlate with higher per capita incomes. Services has been the largest sector in both LICs and LTMs over the past quarter century, although by a larger margin in LTMs (figure 4.3.A). The proportion of agricultural output in GDP has declined across the board, but agriculture remained the second-largest sector in LICs throughout the period. This contrasts with LTMs, where industry formed the second largest sector, with a gradually growing share of output. In LICs, the industrial output share increased between 2000 and 2010, but subsequently receded again. The average agriculture share in LICs has consistently been more than 10 percentage points higher than in LTMs and averages 28 percent today compared with 19 percent in the average LTM when it became middle-income.

Informality. Consistent with lower incomes and smaller non-agricultural sectors, informality is substantially more prevalent in LICs than in LTMs. At about 82 percent in the median LIC in 2022, the proportion of informal employment is estimated to be 18 percentage points higher than in the median LTMs, with the informality gap having grown over time (ILO 2024).[7] Informality also remains 8 percentage points greater in the typical LICs today than it was in LTMs in 2000. Greater informality is sometimes a correlate of lesser development rather than a cause—lower wages among informal workers may reflect pre-existing skills rather than informality per se (Ohnsorge and Yu 2022). However, informality can also be exacerbated by poor governance and regulatory frameworks, which can disincentivize formalizing business activity, and by a lack of

---

[7] Estimated values for self-employment are used as a proxy for informal employment.

financial development that constraint entrepreneurs' access to capital. Elevated informality also tends to worsen fiscal policy challenges and curb resources for development by constraining the taxable base of activity.

Weaker fiscal positions. Fiscal capacity—especially tax revenue as a share of output—constrains government sector development efforts, while elevated debt burdens increase the risk of financial crises. LICs generally have lower government spending and revenue ratios than LTMs. Although the size of the general government sector in LICs has increased in the last quarter-century, it remains materially smaller than in LTMs in 2000. General government expenditures in LICs are currently lower by about 2 percentage points of GDP than in LTMs in 2000 while revenues are lower by 4 percentage points. LICs have modestly closed the revenue gap with LTMs since 2000, while the differential in government spending is little changed (figure 4.3.B). Today's LICs are running larger government deficits, on average, than LTMs have at any point since 2000. They also tend to have larger debt-to-GDP ratios with weaker buffers, and a greater share of LICs are in or at high risk of debt distress (Mawejje 2024a).

Lower levels of trade openness. Trade can embody the transfer of technology, as well as facilitate more efficient resource allocation. Accordingly, greater trade openness is generally associated with higher per capita incomes (Cerdeiro and Komaromi 2017). Trade-to-GDP ratios have been consistently lower in LICs than LTMs—about 50 percent in LICs compared with over 70 percent in LTMs (figure 4.3.C). Even so, the trade openness gap between LICs and LTMs has narrowed from an average of 26 percentage points of GDP in 2000 to about 18 percentage points in recent years. This pattern reflects a sharper increase in trade openness in LICs due to higher average import ratios. Trade openness in LTMs is not significantly different from other EMDEs.

Greater commodity reliance. Most LICs and LTMs are commodity exporters. This preponderance is more marked among LICs, only three of which do not have export baskets dominated by

FIGURE 4.3 Macroeconomic features of LICs and LTMs (*continued*)

Agriculture's share of total output is larger in LICs than in LTMs and has declined less, on average, since 2000. Government expenditure is constrained by revenue weakness in LICs. Trade openness has increased somewhat in the average LICs since 2000, although it remains well below levels typical in LTMs. Most LICs are commodity exporters, primarily of agricultural products and metals, whereas more LTMs export energy.

A. GDP share by sector

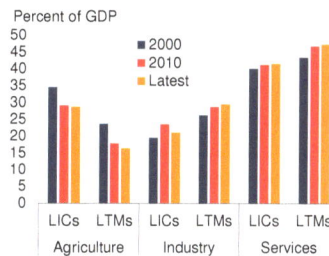

B. General government expenditure and revenues

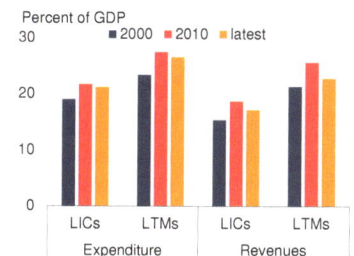

C. Trade openness

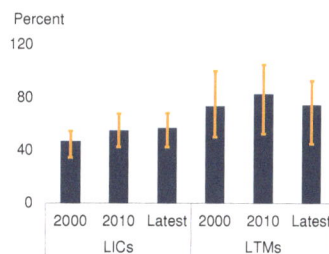

D. Share of commodity exporters

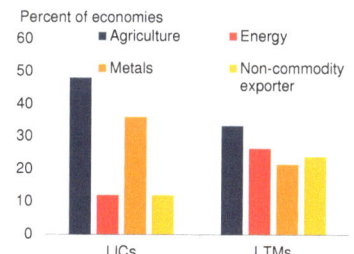

Source: International Monetary Fund; WDI (database); World Bank.
Note: EMDEs = emerging market and developing economies; LICs = low-income countries; LTMs = LICs turned into middle-income countries.
A. Simple averages of country groups. "2000", "2010", and "latest" are calculated as the five-year average per country from 1998-2002, 2008-12, and 2019-23, respectively, to maximize available observations.
B. Simple averages of country groups. "2000", "2010", and "latest" are calculated as averages per country from 1998-2002, 2008-12, and 2022-23, respectively.
C. Bars indicate simple averages of country groups. Whiskers indicate interquartile range. "2000", "2010", and "latest" are calculated as the five-year average per country from 1998-2002, 2008-12, and 2019-23, respectively. Trade openness is defined as the ratio of the sum of exports and imports to GDP.
D. Taxonomy of commodity exporters follows the definition in chapter 1 of *the Global Economic Prospects, January 2025.*

primary products, compared with about a quarter of LTMs. The profile of commodity exports differs between the two groups, however. Agricultural products dominate exports in more than half of LIC commodity exporters, with most of the remainder exporting metals (figure 4.3.D). Only three LICs have substantial export shares of energy products, with the majority of LICs reliant on energy imports. By contrast, more than one-third of LTM commodity exporters are energy exporters.

FIGURE 4.4 Macroeconomic features of LICs and LTMs (*continued*)

Governance measures indicate a substantial shortfall in the quality of institutions in LICs, and the gaps between LICs and LTMs in this regard have widened over time. Financial institutions remain underdeveloped in the average LIC but have surpassed the comparable measure for LTMs in 2000. LICs have recently received less real ODA per person than LTMs and about the same amount as LTMs were receiving in 2000.

A. Governance indicators

B. Governance indicators (*continued*)

C. Development of financial institutions

D. ODA received

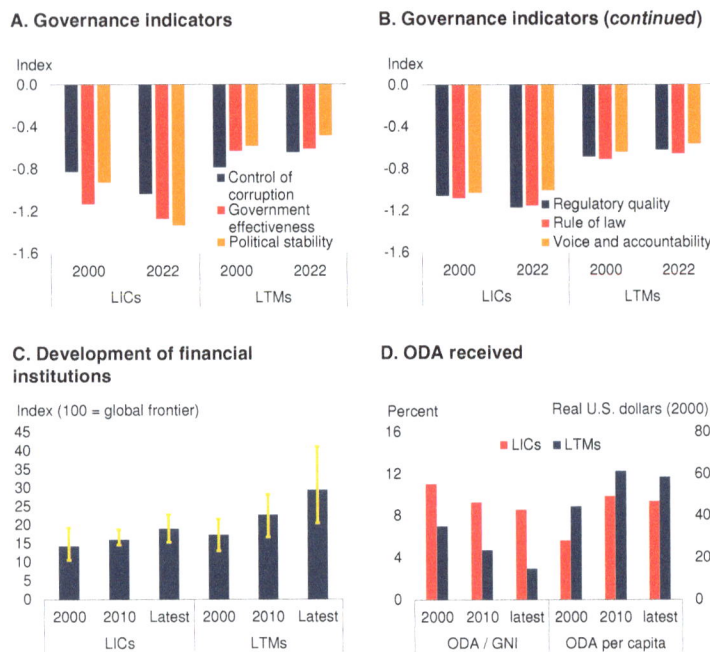

Sources: International Monetary Fund; WDI (database); WGI (database); World Bank.
Note: EMDEs = emerging market and developing economies; LICs = low-income countries; LTMs = LICs turned into middle-income countries; ODA = official development assistance.
A.B. Simple averages of Worldwide Governance Indicators by country group and year. Indices are in units of a standard normal distribution, with mean = zero, a standard deviation of one, and running from approximately –2.5 to 2.5, with higher values corresponding to better governance.
C. Bars show simple average of financial institutions development index. Whiskers indicate interquartile range. Index is normalized such that 1 = the intertemporal frontier and 0 = the intertemporal lowest reading. Latest = 2021.
D. Median ODA-to-gross national income ratios. ODA per capita calculated as ODA per head in current U.S. dollars, deflated by the U.S. consumer price index. "2000" and "2010" are calculated as the five-year average per country from 1998-2002, 2008-12. Latest = 2022.

Weaker governance and institutional quality. Institutional quality has been posited as a major factor in creating conditions that cause low incomes, such as capital scarcity. Improve institutional quality is commonly found to enhance the effectiveness of other possible growth drivers, such as public investment (Acemoglu and Robinson 2013; World Bank 2024c). Measures of governance and institutions indicate that institutional frameworks are significantly weaker in LICs than LTMs. According to the World Bank's Worldwide Governance Indicators, LICs

are substantially further from the frontier than LTMs in the areas of control of corruption, government effectiveness, political stability, regulatory quality, the rule of law, and the accountability of governments (figures 4.4.A and 4.4.B). Importantly, the institutional gap between LTMs and LICs has widened as measures generally have deteriorated for LICs and improved for LTMs. For example, while control of corruption was comparable among LICs and LTMs in 2000, by 2022 the average LIC lagged the average LTM by 11 percentile ranks. Other governance indicators underscore a widening gap. Political stability in the average LIC is 16 percentile ranks lower than in the average LTM, a 10-percentile rank divergence since 2000.

Weaker financial development. LICs have shallow and narrow financial sectors characterized by limited credit creation and extensive capital account controls. Compared with other EMDEs, LTMs also have relatively underdeveloped financial sectors, but to a lesser degree, and with greater variation among economies. The early development of financial institutions—such as increasing coverage of, and competition between, such foundational sectors as commercial banking and basic insurance—has been associated with stronger growth in low-income settings (Arcand, Berkes and Panizza 2012; Sahay et al. 2015). Measures of the depth and sophistication of financial institutions suggest that LICs today are roughly at parity with LTMs in 2000, after which point LTMs underwent material financial deepening (figure 4.4.C).

Official development assistance. The typical LIC has long received more official development assistance (ODA) as a proportion of GNI than the typical LTM (figure 4.4.D). This difference has widened somewhat over time even as ODA-to-GNI ratios have generally declined. In 2000, the ODA-to-GNI ratio was about 4 percentage points greater in LICs than in LTMs whereas in recent years it was close to 6 percentage points greater. However, this discrepancy reverses when considering real ODA per capita, with LICs currently receiving less on this measure than LTMs, as was also the case in 2000 and 2010. Indeed, LICs are now receiving essentially the same quantum of real development assistance per person as flowed to LTMs at the turn of the century, despite their more challenging conditions.

Growth and structural transformation

Rapidly advancing globalization in the 2000s, as well as the integration of China into the global economy and the resultant surge in commodity demand, offered opportunities for LICs to raise productivity and living standards through trade and financial integration (Kose and Ohnsorge 2020). Since the late 2000s, the external environment has proved more turbulent, with bouts of financial stress, large commodity price swings, and the COVID-19 pandemic buffeting the global economy. In addition, greater geopolitical tensions and increasing trade fragmentation have emerged as new and broad headwinds in a global economy already strained by declining potential growth.

These trends and shocks have weighed on per capita growth and development in LICs and LTMs. In addition, many LICs have experienced adverse domestic developments such as civil and cross-border conflicts. In aggregate, the record shows slowing progress in LTMs, after a period of rapid catch-up in the 2000s. In LICs, the pace of economic progress has been anemic since 2000, worsening after 2010 and further stalling following the COVID-19 pandemic. At the same time, structural transformation has lost momentum.

Declining per capita growth. Dividing the 25 years since 2000 into three periods (2000-09, 2010-19, and 2020-24), an overall trend of decelerating per capita growth in both LTMs and LICs is evident (figure 4.5.A). Most LTMs made solid progress over the 2000s with the median country registering per capita growth of 3.8 percent. Notably high growth rates were achieved by transition economies in Europe and Central Asia that recovered from the deep recessions associated with the end of the Soviet Union, as well as some economies in East Asia and the

FIGURE 4.5 Growth and structural transformation since 2000

Per capita growth has declined in LTMs over the last quarter century. In LICs, per capita GDP has nearly flatlined for 15 years, in part reflecting conflict-driven economic collapses in several countries. The global shocks of the early 2020s set back LIC prospects of graduating to middle-income status, with extreme poverty rates in LICs no longer declining. Per capita GDP as a proportion of advanced economy levels has doubled in LTMs since 2000, but LICs have made no progress in this regard. Progress on poverty reduction has stalled in LICs.

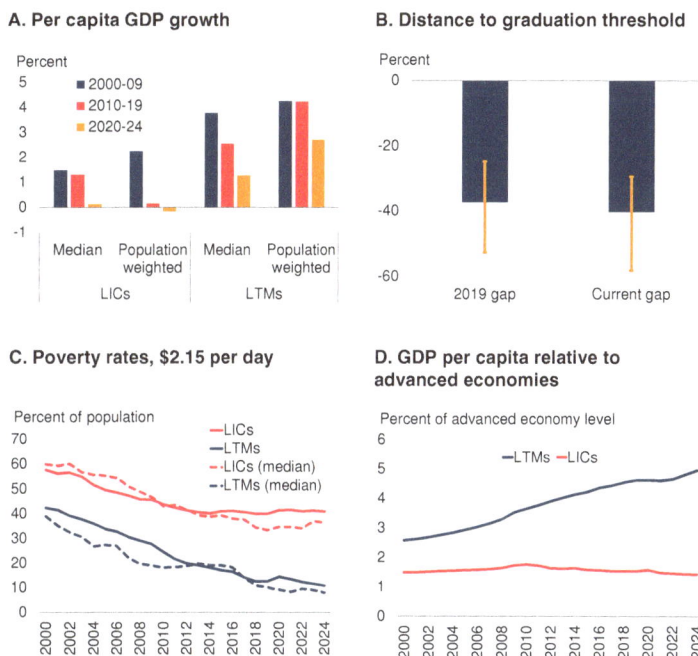

A. Per capita GDP growth

B. Distance to graduation threshold

C. Poverty rates, $2.15 per day

D. GDP per capita relative to advanced economies

Sources: Mahler, Yonzan, and Lakner (2022); World Bank Poverty and Inequality Platform (database); WDI (database); World Bank.

Note: LICs = low-income countries; LTMs = LICs turned into middle-income countries.

A. GDP aggregates are calculated using real U.S. dollar GDP weights at average 2010-19 prices and market exchange rates. GDP per capita population weighted aggregates are calculated as aggregated GDP divided by aggregate population. Median growth rates represent the median annual average growth rate for each country group in each period.

B. Bars represent distance in percentage points of GNI per capita (Atlas method) from the respective graduation thresholds; whiskers represent the 25th and 75th percentiles. Pre-COVID gap represents the median distance from the graduation threshold of $1035 in FY2021 based on 2019 data; the current gap represents the median distance from the FY2025 threshold of $1145 based on 2023 data.

C. Solid lines represent population-weighted poverty rates in country groups. Dotted lines indicate the median poverty rate in each group each year.

D. Population-weighted GDP per capita as a percent of population-weighted GDP per capita in advanced economies.

Pacific (Cambodia, Viet Nam) where integration into global supply chains accelerated (Steinbach 2019).

In contrast, per capita growth was muted in LICs and the group largely missed out on the potential dividends of rapid global growth. Per capita growth in the median LIC was just 1.5 percent in 2000-09, although progress was markedly faster in some economies (Ethiopia, Mozambique,

Rwanda, Uganda). Even in a period characterized by favorable global conditions and rapidly rising commodity prices, there was virtually no increase in incomes in the bottom quartile of LICs.

In the 2010s, median per capita growth slowed appreciably in LTMs, to an average of 2.6 percent, mirroring a broader deceleration in EMDE growth. Some of this deterioration reflected the protracted decline in commodity prices that started in about 2014 and weighed on LTM commodity exporters (Angola, Azerbaijan, Equatorial Guinea, Nigeria). In addition, weakening external demand growth and cross-border financial flows from advanced economies following the global financial crisis and euro area debt crisis created a less supportive global environment.

Per capita growth in the median LIC slowed slightly in 2010-19, edging down to 1.3 percent annually. However, sharp slowdowns or outright contractions in some large LICs resulted in population-weighted per capita income growth slowing to a crawl, increasing by just 0.2 percent annually. Conflicted-related growth collapses in Sudan, Syria, and the Republic of Yemen played an outsized role in pinning back progress. Ethiopia and Rwanda stood out as LICs that still made substantial strides in raising average incomes. Aided by domestic growth strategies (see box 4.1), they posted per capita growth rates of 6.5 percent and 4.6 percent, respectively.

The global shocks of the early 2020s were markedly more adverse for LICs than those of the preceding two decades. The median LIC is estimated to have registered annual average per capita growth of just 0.1 percent in 2020-24, with population-weighted per capita GDP contracting slightly. Headwinds in the wake of the COVID-19 pandemic included large import price shocks, sluggish global trade growth, and sharply higher interest rates in advanced economies. In all, the median LIC is now close to 5 percentage points further from the graduation threshold than it was in 2019 (figure 4.5.B). Per capita growth also slowed markedly in LTMs in 2020-24, but higher initial incomes and greater fiscal resources endowed greater resilience than in LICs. The median LTM grew 1.3 percent annually in per capita terms. Growth was materially faster in LTMs when weighted by population, primarily reflecting relatively strong growth in India.

Slower extreme poverty reduction. More than 40 percent of the population in LICs is estimated to remain in extreme poverty (that is, living on less than $2.15 per day in 2017 PPP), about four times the proportion of the LTM population in extreme poverty (figure 4.5.C). About two-thirds of people in LICs live on less than $3.65 per day, compared with closer to one-third in LTMs. At the start of the century, the two groups were more closely comparable, but while the extreme poverty rate in LTMs has fallen by more than 31 percentage points since 2000, it has declined by just 17 percentage points in LICs.

Much weaker progress on poverty reduction in LICs than in LTMs is a relatively recent phenomenon. In the 2000s, LICs and LTMs reduced poverty at a broadly similar pace. Progress on poverty reduction in LICs slowed sharply thereafter, in part as a result of conflicts in the Middle East, Sudan, and South Sudan in the first half of the 2010s. Extreme poverty levels in LICs increased in 2020 and have since stagnated. The confluence of these earlier deep shocks in a handful of LICs—from which there has generally been limited recovery—and broader recent weakness has resulted in a slight rise in extreme poverty over the last decade. In contrast, the typical LTM appears on pace to essentially eliminate extreme poverty in the 2030s.

A reversal of per capita GDP catch-up. All else being equal, capital accumulation and growth should be faster in capital-scarce economies, where the marginal product of capital is greater. Indeed, if other structural factors that influence growth rates—such as access to technology, education, and the quality of institutions—are controlled for, then lower-income economies generally exhibit a tendency toward faster income gains than higher-income economies (Dieppe 2021). However, large and persistent shortfalls in other structural growth drivers mean that, in practice, poorer countries have often not made much progress towards the income levels of richer countries, even over extended periods of time (Barro 2012).

The per capita GDP trajectory in LICs since 2000 illustrates just such a failure of income convergence. Per capita GDP in LICs in aggregate has made no progress toward the advanced economy frontier since 2000, with considerable gains in a handful of LICs offset by much weaker performance elsewhere (figure 4.5.D). LICs made some progress between 2000 and 2010, with per capita incomes increasing from 1.5 to 1.8 percent of advanced economy levels. Since then, however, LICs have backslid, regressing to 1.4 percent of advanced economy levels in 2023-24. In contrast, per capita GDP in LTMs has made solid, albeit slowing, gains on advanced economies, with per capita GDP as a proportion of the advanced economy level near-doubling in the first quarter of the twenty-first century, from 2.6 percent to 4.9 percent.

Structural transformation. Rapid structural transformation has been crucial to long-term growth successes in EMDEs (Hallward-Driemeier and Nayyar 2017). Structural transformation primarily entails the transfer of agricultural labor into industrial and services sectors with higher productivity. This process can be facilitated both by advances in agricultural productivity that free up surplus labor, and by the active development of tradable sectors that offer higher wages, incentivizing labor reallocation (Herrendorf, Rogerson, and Valentinyi 2014; McMillan and Headey 2014). This process, especially when combined with industrialization and integration into global value chains, has historically proved powerful for accelerating labor productivity and broader development, for example in economies in East Asia and the Pacific and Europe and Central Asia. Overall, structural transformation has made notable strides in many LTMs since 2000, albeit to differing degrees. In contrast, structural transformation in LICs appears to be stalling.

LICs have substantially larger shares of employment in agriculture than do LTMs (figure 4.6.A). Since 2000, the agricultural share of employment has also declined more quickly in LTMs, falling by about 15 percentage points, compared to 12 percentage points in LICs. Expanding services sectors have absorbed the bulk of freed-up labor,

FIGURE 4.6 Growth and structural transformation since 2000 (*continued*)

Agricultural employment accounts for a much greater share of total employment in LICs than in LTMs, and the share has declined less in LICs since 2000. Industrial employment's share of total employment has increased significantly faster in LTMs than in LICs. Although services employment shares have risen in both groups, weakening services productivity trends have been the largest contributor to productivity slowdowns since 2010. After the 2000s, productivity is estimated to have declined outright in all employment sectors in LICs, with this decrease offset only slightly by continuing labor reallocation out of agriculture. At 2010-19 average growth rates, less than a quarter of LICs appear on course to graduate to middle-income status by 2050.

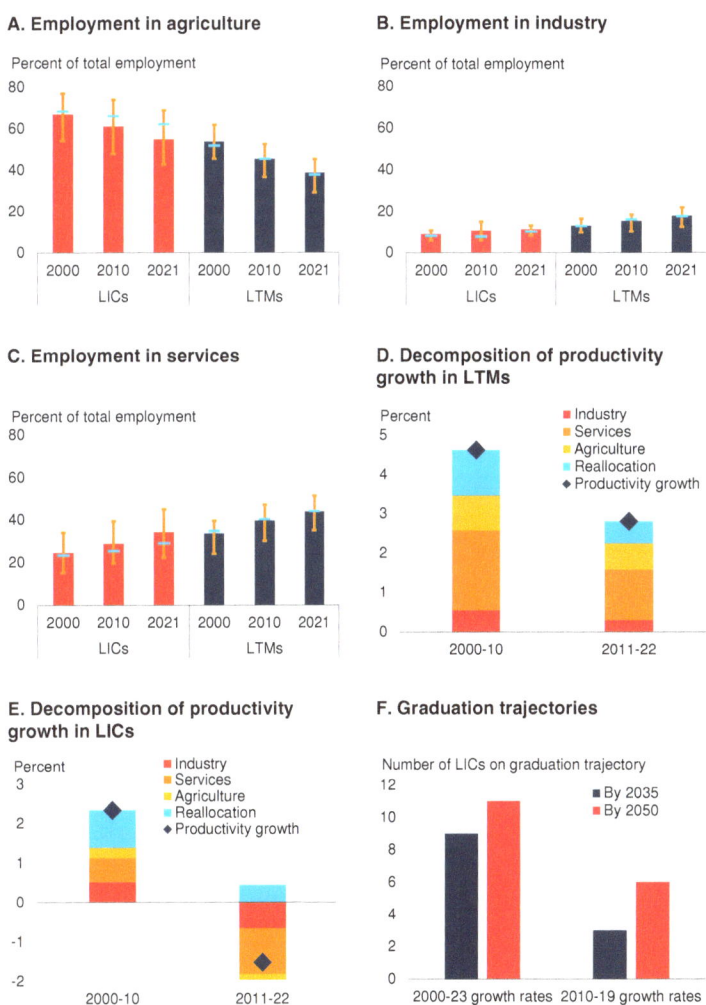

A. Employment in agriculture

B. Employment in industry

C. Employment in services

D. Decomposition of productivity growth in LTMs

E. Decomposition of productivity growth in LICs

F. Graduation trajectories

Sources: International Labor Organization; WDI (database); World Bank.
Note: LICs = low-income countries; LTMs = LICs turned into middle-income countries.
A.-C. The shares of agriculture, industry, and services in total output. Bars show the simple unweighted average. Blue markers show the median. Orange whiskers show the interquartile range.
D.E. Based on ILO estimates. Within-sector contributions to growth are calculated by assuming constant sectoral employment shares across 2000-10 and 2011-22. The reallocation contribution is the residual, due to reallocation of labor across sectors between the first and final year of each period.
F. Graduation trajectories assume that the threshold for middle-income status increases at the same pace as it has on average since 2000.

becoming a large source of employment and output in both country groups—the average services employment share increased by 10 percentage points in both LICs and LTMs in 2000-21. In the same period, the average industrial employment share gained only 2 percentage points in LICs, signifying scant progress on industrialization (figures 4.6.B and 4.6.C). Industrial employment increased more than twice as much in the average LTM, rising 5 percentage points to 18 percent.

Productivity growth. Productivity—measured as output per worker—tends to be highest in the industrial sectors of LICs and LTMs, followed by services, with productivity generally lowest in agriculture.[8] Over the first two decades of this century, the evolution of sectoral employment in LICs and LTMs was accompanied by diverging productivity trends. In the 2000s, mean agricultural productivity growth in LTMs, at 2.8 percent, was about twice the pace in LICs. Thereafter, in the 2010s, agricultural productivity decelerated in LICs while accelerating further in LTMs. Mean industrial productivity growth declined in both country groups across the two decades but was close to a percentage point higher in LTMs throughout. Services sector productivity growth followed a similar pattern in LTMs—declining somewhat after the 2000s but remaining solidly positive. In LICs, however, services productivity declined outright in the 2010s, even as services employment swelled.

Although productivity growth weakened in a large share of LICs in the 2010s, productivity collapsed in some larger LICs amid increased conflict and violence. As such, on a population-weighted basis, LIC productivity declined more than 13 percent between 2010 and 2022. Meanwhile, productivity in LTMs continued to make gains, albeit at a significantly reduced pace compared to the 2000s. Headline labor productivity growth can be disaggregated into growth within sectors, and reallocation between sectors. This decomposition reveals that weakening services productivity trends

accounted for most of the slowdown in LTMs and LICs in the 2010s (figures 4.6.D and 4.6.E). In LTMs, diminishing gains from sectoral reallocation were the second largest contributor, reflecting maturing industrialization. In LICs, sectoral reallocation out of agriculture continued to boost headline productivity in the 2010s, but this effect was outweighed by productivity declines within sectors.

Large gender gaps. LICs have large gender gaps and progress to close them is stalling. Women in LICs are more likely to engage in informal establishments than men (Malta et al. 2019; Ohnsorge and Yu 2022). The pandemic widened gender disparities in LICs: it had a disproportionate economic impact on women, and women led businesses received less government support (ILO 2023; Torres et al. 2021; United Nations 2021). However, gender inequalities in LICs predate the pandemic, and are usually engrained in wider societal and cultural norms. In contexts dominated by patriarchal systems, women are more likely to be less educated, and to engage in low-productivity and uncompensated domestic care activities (World Bank 2012). Female secondary school enrollment rates are lower in LICs than LTMs, on average, and have been declining in recent years. As a percentage of the labor force, female participation is lower in the average LIC than in the average LTM. Discriminatory laws can prevent women from fully and equally contributing to their economies, and the gaps in LICs in this regard are considerable. The average LIC has about two-thirds of the good practice legislation that provides equal status to both men and women (World Bank 2022a). These gender gaps precipitate inequalities in productivity and earnings and put large constraints on overall growth in LICs. On average, in LICs, long-run GDP per capita could potentially be more than 20 percent higher if all gender employment gaps were to be closed (Pennings 2022).

Fading graduation prospects. The recent trend of especially weak growth has seen graduation prospects slip further away in many LICs. However, this pattern is not universal. To advance toward graduation, per capita income only needs

---

[8] Of course, these are inherently broad categories, encompassing subsectors with differing characteristics regarding typical productivity levels and labor intensity.

to grow more quickly than the graduation threshold. Since 2000, the middle-income threshold has increased by 1.8 percent per year, on average. Assuming this trajectory sustains, attaining middle-income status in 2050 will require per capita income of just over $1,800.

Set against this goal, a small number of LICs appear on pace to graduate over the second quarter of this century. Were average growth rates to match those of the 2010s, three LICs (Ethiopia, Rwanda, Uganda) would be expected to graduate by 2035 (figure 4.6.F). By 2050, only another three LICs would be expected to make the transition. In other words, based on 2010-19 average growth rates, the number of LICs would decline by less than one quarter, from 26 this year to 20 in 2050. After graduation became notably rarer in the 2010s than in the 2000s, this would represent a significant further slowdown. Were LICs instead able to lift future growth rates to match their post-2000 average, graduation prospects would be somewhat better. Nine LICs would be expected to graduate over the next decade—roughly in line with the graduation rate since 2010—with a further two becoming middle-income countries by 2050.

Growth accelerations in LICs

For many of today's LICs, graduating in the next 10 or even 25 years would require dramatic improvements in per capita growth rates. This appears a daunting task given the deep challenges the typical LIC has faced over the past 15 years. However, since 1990 there have been many instances in which past and present LICs have achieved growth accelerations—episodes of sizeable and sustained increases in real per capita growth. The following section examines the characteristics of growth accelerations in LICs to illustrate the circumstances under which they have arisen and illuminate the tight link between growth accelerations and broader development successes.

Growth accelerations are defined—following Gootjes et al. (2024)—as spells of eight or more years during which per capita growth rates exceed

a country-specific threshold that incorporates both the long-term average and volatility of per capita growth (see annex 4.1 for methodological details). Identifying growth accelerations in this manner is useful for several reasons. First, growth can be highly volatile in LICs, even over extended periods. Disregarding volatility may generate spurious signals regarding when living standards are durably increasing. Second, growth accelerations provide a simple empirical method to identify periods in which potential growth is likely to have increased. This is beneficial because raising potential growth is a first-order concern for LIC policy makers, but many models of potential growth—often developed for advanced economies—are ill-suited to data-poor environments. Finally, focusing on transformative growth from LIC status avoids equating today's LICs with LTMs that graduated mainly because their income level was already close to the threshold in 2000.

Features of LIC growth accelerations

Small number of growth accelerations in today's LICs. Growth accelerations have been rarer in LICs than in other EMDEs, having taken root in one in four of today's LICs since 1990, compared with one in two LTMs and other EMDEs. Between 1990 and 2023, growth accelerations were recorded in 6 out of 25 LICs for which data are available (Ethiopia, Mali, Mozambique, Rwanda, Chad, and Uganda) while occurring in 22 out of 42 LTMs and 43 out of 87 other EMDEs (figure 4.7.A). In total, 30 growth accelerations have occurred in LTMs and current LICs since 1990, with Indonesia and Mali each experiencing two accelerations over this period. Of these, 26 commenced while countries were classified as LICs, with 19 of those in current LTMs and seven in current LICs.

Accelerations last for many years. Spells of accelerated growth have, on average, tended to last more than 16 years in LTMs and about 14.5 years in current LICs. These spells generally commence and conclude in a distinct manner, with per capita growth rates during spells dramatically exceeding those in other years (figure 4.7.B). Among LTMs, annual per capita growth averaged 6.8 percent during accelerations—sharply higher than the 0.4 percent growth experienced in other years (figure

FIGURE 4.7 Features of growth accelerations

Growth accelerations have been more prevalent among LTMs than LICs. The typical growth acceleration has lasted 16 years in LTMs and 14.5 years in LICs, and accelerations have often exhibited a distinct onset and ending. Average per capita growth exceeds 6 percent per year during these episodes. The COVID-19 pandemic brought all but one ongoing acceleration to an abrupt end. A favorable external environment can help support accelerations, with LIC growth spells in particular occurring in tandem with commodity price pickups.

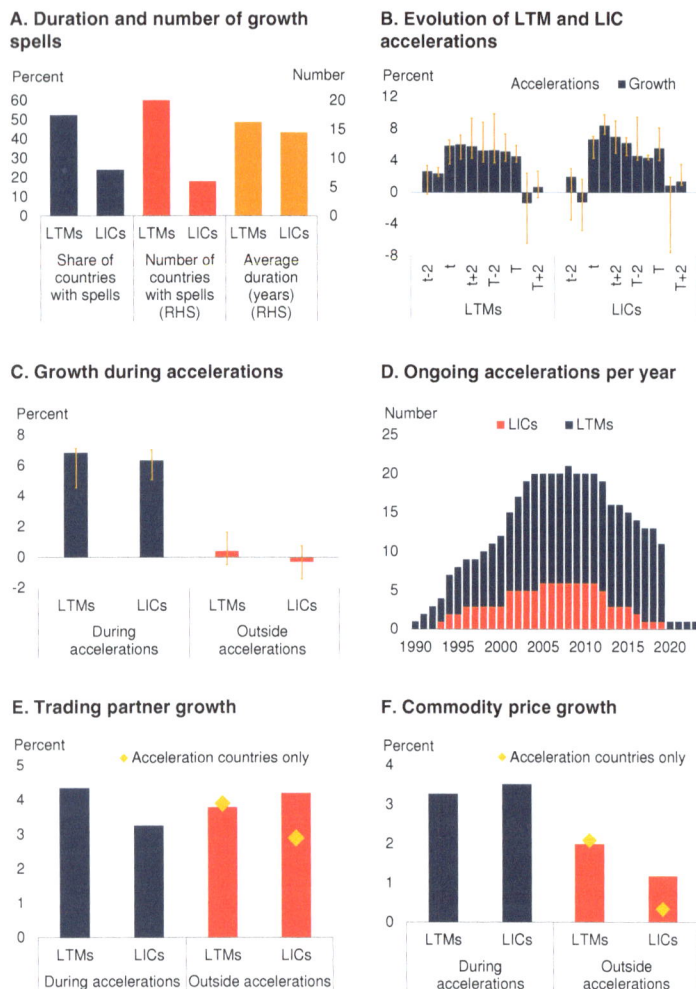

A. Duration and number of growth spells

B. Evolution of LTM and LIC accelerations

C. Growth during accelerations

D. Ongoing accelerations per year

E. Trading partner growth

F. Commodity price growth

Sources: Gootjes et al. (2024); International Monetary Fund; WDI (database); World Bank.

Note: LICs = low-income countries; LTMs = LICs turned into middle-income countries.

A. Based on up to 41 LTMs and 25 LICs.

B. Bars represent average per capita growth; whiskers represent the 20th to 80th percentiles. LTM sample includes 38 countries and 19 accelerations. Indonesia experienced two accelerations. LIC sample includes 21 countries and seven accelerations. Mali experienced two accelerations.

C. Sample includes 19 LTM accelerations and seven LIC accelerations. Whiskers represent the 20th to 80th percentiles. "t" is the first year of an identified growth acceleration, and "T" is the final year.

D. LTMs sample includes 19 growth accelerations; LIC sample includes 7 growth accelerations. The number of accelerations beyond 2016 may be low because as it does not include new accelerations—a minimum of eight years of growth data are required to identify the start of an acceleration.

E. Bars reflect average growth in real GDP of each country's top 10 trading partner economies, weighted by average export shares from 2000-19. Diamonds reflect the average in years outside of growth accelerations for those LTMs and LICs that had experienced accelerations.

F. Bars reflect average real growth in country-specific commodity export price indices. An individual commodity's weight reflects the ratio of that commodity's exports to the country's total commodity exports. Diamonds reflect the average in years outside of growth accelerations for those LTMs and LICs that had experienced accelerations.

4.7.C). Similarly, annual per capita growth in LICs averaged 6.3 percent during growth spells, while incomes contracted by 0.3 percent annually in the years outside of accelerations.[9] Such contrasting growth rates, combined with the length of spells, imply that almost all progress in raising incomes and powering structural transformation occurs during accelerations. In the average growth acceleration, LTM incomes almost tripled—increasing 192 percent—while LIC incomes rose 142 percent.

Many LTM graduations have been aided by accelerations. By the mid-1990s, per capita incomes among the 19 LTMs that were either in a growth acceleration or would enter one in the next 30 years, were on average 29 percent below those of LTMs that would not subsequently experience a growth acceleration. Per capita income in the LTMs that were in, or set to undergo, a growth spell was therefore much further from the graduation threshold, with an average gap of 42 percent compared to 17 percent in the other LTMs. However, by 2010, growth spells had propelled incomes in LTMs with accelerations to 23 percent above those without them.

Accelerations have raised current LICs' prospects of graduation. Per capita incomes have increased to relatively close to the graduation threshold among the six current LICs that have experienced growth accelerations since 1990 (Ethiopia, Chad, Mali, Mozambique, Rwanda, Uganda). On average, per capita incomes in these LICs were 71 percent below the threshold in the year preceding their growth spell's commencement. By the final year of the acceleration, the gap between incomes and the graduation threshold had narrowed by about 48 percentage points to 23 percent. The average gap to graduation in these LICs has since widened slightly, but it remains considerably smaller than the 42 percent average gap for other LICs.

The external environment has played an important role in growth accelerations. The

---

[9] Years outside of accelerations often include periods of sharp contractions. Excluding contractions—to reflect normal times—growth outside of accelerations averaged 3.3 percent and 3.5 percent in LTMs and LICs, respectively.

pattern of low-income accelerations suggests that global growth and commodity prices play important roles seeding accelerations. In the early 1990s, a period of weak global growth, there were no accelerations underway in today's LICs and just a few in LTMs (figure 4.7.D). As global growth picked up in the late 1990s, so did accelerations. During the 2000s—characterized until 2009 by robust global growth and rising commodity prices—saw low-income accelerations proliferate, with 21 ongoing in 2008, albeit disproportionately in LTMs. Compared to LTMs, however, accelerations in today's LICs appear to have aligned more closely with past commodity cycles than with growth cycles in their trading partners (figures 4.7.E and 4.7.F). Of six LICs that experienced growth spells, three (Chad, Mali, Mozambique) are industrial commodity exporters whose accelerations encompassed the commodity price upswing from 2004 to 2011. Accelerations fell away over the 2010s, especially in today's LICs, amid commodity price declines and decelerating global activity. That said, until the extraordinary shock of the COVID-19 pandemic, accelerations were notably persistent, suggesting favorable global developments can be conducive, but should not be seen as determinative relative to domestic factors.

Accelerations have often ended amid crises. Several growth accelerations became casualties of the global financial crisis, partly reflecting slower trading partner growth (Armenia, Azerbaijan), as well as the eventual collapse in oil and other commodity prices in the mid-2010s (Chad, Nigeria). A debt crisis in Mozambique ended its growth spell in 2016. By 2019, there were only 11 ongoing accelerations, of which 10 were in LTMs. All but one of these was cut short in 2020 as the COVID-19 pandemic brought economic activity to a standstill and generated a wave of debt-related stress in vulnerable LTMs and LICs. The growth spell in Bangladesh was not upended by the pandemic and was still ongoing at the last data point in 2023.[10]

---

[10] Although Bangladesh's real GDP growth rate remained positive, it slowed significantly—by 4.5 percentage points to 3.4 percent in FY2020. It gained momentum in the next two years, reaching 7.1 percent in FY2022, but then slowed again in FY2023 and FY2024 (World Bank 2024d).

Macroeconomic and development correlates of growth accelerations

Growth accelerations in LICs have corresponded with rapid improvements in a broad range of macroeconomic and development indicators. In some cases, for example with respect to investment-to-GDP ratios, there are clear theoretical reasons to view these correlates as drivers of accelerations. Other structural correlates—such as trade openness and the sectoral reallocation of labor—are likely to be both outcomes and drivers of accelerations, because while initial improvements in these factors may reflect growth-conducive policy shifts, progress in these regards can also generate a virtuous cycle that helps raise incomes and sustain accelerations. Finally, there are correlates, such as poverty reduction, that are critical for human welfare and economic resilience, but which are likely more properly seen as outcomes of accelerations.

Investment. During growth spells, investment-to-GDP ratios rose at an average of 0.5 percentage point per year in LTMs, compared to an average decline of 0.2 percentage point in other years (figure 4.8.A). Among LICs, the investment ratio increased at a broadly similar pace during accelerations, while barely changing outside of accelerations. The cumulative increase in the investment-to-GDP ratio over an average growth spell was 8.9 percentage points in LTMs, and 6.7 percentage points in LICs—a marked increase in the investment intensity of output. The associated capital deepening in both LTMs and LICs would have lifted potential growth in these economies, likely helping to sustain long accelerations (Kose and Ohnsorge, 2024; World Bank 2024e).

Trade. Historically, increased trade has played a critical role in lifting productivity growth as trade facilitates the transfer of knowledge and other resources across countries. Empirical estimates suggest per capita incomes rise 0.2 percent for every percentage-point rise in the trade-to-GDP ratio (World Bank 2020a). Trade in goods—defined as the ratio of the sum of merchandise exports and imports to GDP—rose 0.6 percentage point per year, on average, during LTM growth spells. In other years, the trade ratio among LTMs

FIGURE 4.8 Correlates of growth accelerations

Growth accelerations are associated with sharp pickups in investment and greater trade openness. During such spells, the pace at which labor reallocates from agriculture to services and industry quickens, with industry gaining a larger share of workers in LTMs than in LICs. Fiscal positions improve, while growth in secondary school enrollment rates triples in LTMs and doubles in LICs. Significant strides in reducing extreme poverty have been made during spells of accelerated growth.

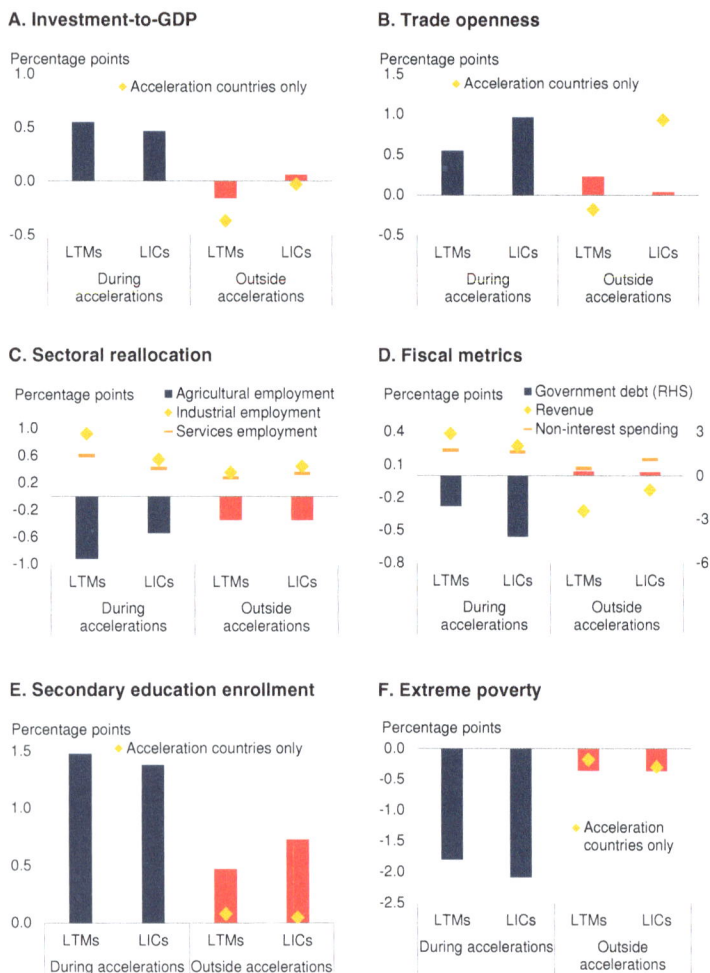

A. Investment-to-GDP

B. Trade openness

C. Sectoral reallocation

D. Fiscal metrics

E. Secondary education enrollment

F. Extreme poverty

Sources: Gootjes et al. (2024); International Monetary Fund; WDI (database); Mahler, Yonzan, and Lakner (2022); WEO (database); World Bank Poverty and Inequality Platform (database); World Bank.

Note: Bars represent averages; diamonds reflect the average in years not outside of growth accelerations for those LTMs and LICs that had experienced accelerations. Sample includes 38 LTMs and 20 LICs. LICs = low-income countries. LTMs = LICs turned into middle income countries.

A. Bars represent the average annual change in the investment-to-GDP ratios.

B. Trade openness is defined as the sum of merchandise exports and imports divided by GDP, all in current U.S. dollars. Bars represent the average annual change in the ratio.

C. Bars and markers represent the average annual change in the ratio of sectoral employment to total employment.

D. Bars represent the average change in the ratio of government debt to GDP. Diamonds represent the average annual change in the revenue-to-GDP ratio. Dashes represent the average annual change in the ratio of government spending (excluding interest payments) to GDP.

E. Annual change in gross secondary enrollment rate. Sample includes 35 LTMs and 20 LICs.

F. Annual change in the ratio of extreme poor to the total population.

rose at less than half this pace (figure 4.8.B). During LIC growth spells, trade growth was substantially faster than outside accelerations, with the goods trade ratio rising 1 percentage point per year compared to stagnant ratios otherwise. While increased dynamism from trade-intensive growth has likely helped sustain accelerations, trade-supporting reforms—including the removal of formal trade barriers and exchange rate reforms—have also often preceded accelerations entered at very low income levels (see box 4.1).

Sectoral reallocation. The reallocation of labor to more productive sectors that occurs during structural transformation provides a boon to economy-wide output per worker and per capita incomes (World Bank 2024e). This process—which can be kick-started by growth-enabling reforms, but also generates a virtuous cycle that sustains rapid growth—has been particularly striking during growth accelerations, especially among LTMs (figure 4.8.C). During the average LTM growth spell, the share of labor devoted to agriculture declined by 0.9 percentage point per year—more than double the pace in other years. Two-thirds of the labor shifting away from agriculture was absorbed by services and the remaining third by industry. In LICs, the agricultural labor share declined by 0.5 percentage point per year, on average, during growth spells, with three-quarters of freed-up labor shifting to services and the remainder to industry. A relatively slower pace of sectoral reallocation in LICs may reflect low starting points for agricultural productivity, with more gains required before surplus labor results.

Fiscal positions. Government debt ratios have declined markedly during growth accelerations, with debt falling 2.1 and 4.2 percentage points per year, on average, in LTMs and LICs respectively (figure 4.8.D). In years outside of accelerations, the debt ratio has increased 0.2 percentage point annually in both groups. While improving debt ratios are a natural consequence of an extended period of above-trend growth, the attendant increase in revenues also allow governments to increase non-interest spending which, when judiciously allocated to areas such as education and infrastructure investment, should help further perpetuate accelerations. In some instances, fiscal reforms efforts may have also generated initial growth impetus preceding the start of an acceleration, including by helping to curtail debt risks and increases the chances of an investment acceleration taking root (World Bank 2024e).

Education. Measures of human capital development correlate strongly with growth accelerations. Outside of growth spells, secondary school enrollment rates have increased by 0.4 and 0.7 percentage point per year in LTMs and current LICs, respectively; however, during growth accelerations, enrollment rates rise by between 1.4 and 1.5 percentage points per year, on average (figure 4.8.E). This implies that over an entire average growth spell, secondary enrollment rates would rise by 24 percentage points in LTMs and 20 percentage points in LICs. Rapid advances in education enrollment during growth spells likely reflect both the greater availability of fiscal resources for education and more families able to support children through school. Among current LICs, where government spending on education has averaged 3.2 percent of GDP since 2000, this ratio has risen by between 0.1 and 0.2 percentage point per year during growth spells and stagnated otherwise. Although improved secondary school enrollment rates are likely to yield economic gains only with a sizeable lag, the average growth spell is long enough that human capital improvements early in an acceleration can yield growth dividends before the acceleration ends. This may help extend accelerations.

Extreme poverty. Rapid declines in poverty rates are a critical development outcome of periods of accelerated growth. During growth spells, extreme poverty rates—the share of the population living on less than $2.15 per day—in LTMs declined by an estimated 1.8 percentage point per year (figure 4.8.F). In LICs, estimated extreme poverty rates fell by 2.1 percentage points per year. In other years, poverty reduction has been slow, with rates falling 0.4 percentage point per year in both LTMs and current LICs. Extreme poverty rates in today's LICs that underwent growth spells average 32 percent—14 percentage points lower than the 46 percent average poverty rate in those LICs that missed out on growth accelerations.

Governance. Indicators of governance quality tend to improve sharply during growth accelerations. In contrast, generally, and in today's LICs especially, institutional quality stagnates or declines outside accelerations (figures 4.9.A-4.9.F). These patterns suggest synergies between stronger growth and better governance. On one hand, peace and a baseline level of political stability is essential for other drivers of growth to operate, and strong institutions are likely to help sustain much needed reform momentum. On the other, large institutional gains do not appear necessary to initially enter an acceleration, with subsequent institutional improvement partly enabled by the social dividends of strong growth.

- *Corruption:* Growth accelerations and improvements in measures of corruption tend to go hand-in-hand. During growth accelerations, control of corruption improves markedly, particularly among LICs. Outside of growth spells, however, it remains stagnant in LTMs and worsens in LICs.

- *Government effectiveness:* Governments tend to become more effective during growth accelerations, likely reflecting greater funding of public services, infrastructure, and administrative capacity afforded by increased fiscal revenues.

- *Political stability:* Improvements in political stability and the absence of violence and terrorism during LTM and LIC growth accelerations underscore that peace and stability enable growth. Deteriorating political stability is strongly associated with periods of low growth.

- *Rule of law:* The rule of law also strengthens during growth spells—particularly in LICs— likely because governments can devote more resources to law enforcement, while improved incomes and opportunities reduce incentives for criminal activities.

- *Regulatory quality:* Regulatory quality improves during LTM and LIC growth spells, with no marked changes in other years. A well calibrated and competently enforced

FIGURE 4.9 Governance and growth accelerations

Improved governance coincides with growth accelerations in both LTMs and LICs. This is reflected in better control of corruption, more effective governments, greater political stability along with reduced incidence of violence or terrorism, enhanced rule of law, and improved quality of regulations. Voice and accountability improves during growth spells in LICs, but not in LTMs—partly as a result of eroding accountability in the later years of some growth spells.

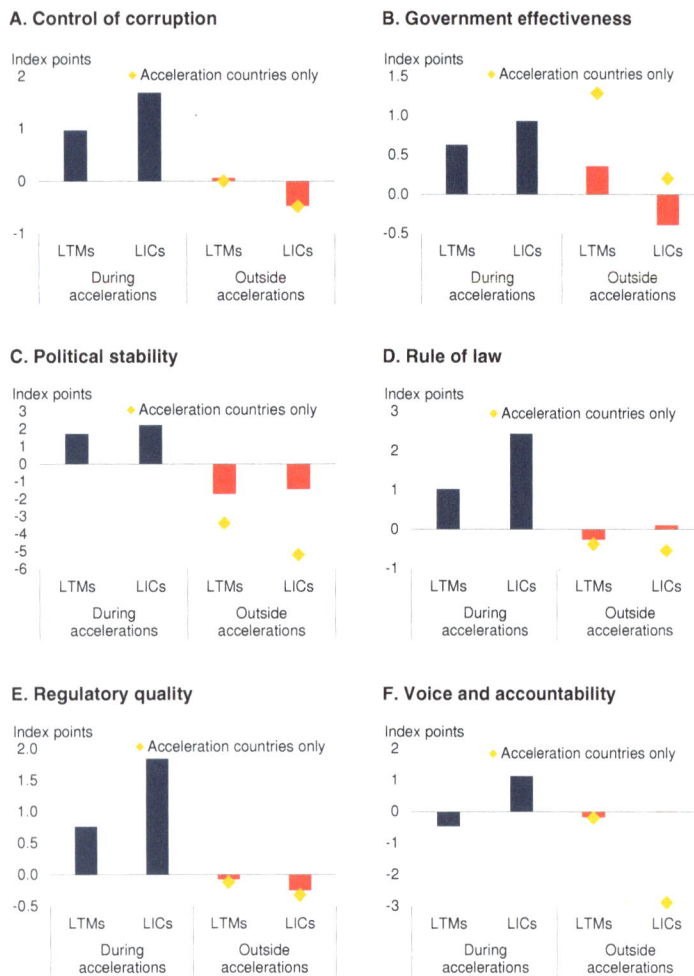

A. Control of corruption

B. Government effectiveness

C. Political stability

D. Rule of law

E. Regulatory quality

F. Voice and accountability

Sources: Gootjes et al. (2024); WGI (database); World Bank.
Note: Bars reflect average annual changes in WGI estimates (z-scores) that have been multiplied by 100 for readability. Diamonds reflect the average in years not outside of growth accelerations for those LTMs and LICs that had experienced accelerations. Sample includes 38 LTMs and 20 LICs. LTMs excludes Indonesia's first acceleration; LICs excludes Mali's second acceleration. LICs = low-income countries; LTMs = LICs-turned-into middle-income countries.
A. Control of corruption reflects perceptions of the extent to which public power is exercised for private gain, including both petty and grand forms of corruption, as well as "capture" of the state by elites and private interests.
B. Government effectiveness reflects perceptions of the quality of public services, the quality of the civil service and the degree of its independence from political pressures, the quality of policy formulation and implementation, and the credibility of the government's commitment to such policies.
C. "Political stability" reflects both political stability and the absence of violence or terrorism. The category measures perceptions of the likelihood of political instability and/or politically motivated violence, including terrorism.
D. Rule of law reflects perceptions of the extent to which agents have confidence in and abide by the rules of society, and in particular the quality of contract enforcement, property rights, the police, and the courts, as well as the likelihood of crime and violence.
E. Regulatory quality captures perceptions of the ability of the government to formulate and implement sound policies and regulations that permit and promote private sector development.
F. Voice and accountability captures perceptions of the extent to which a country's citizens are able to participate in selecting their government, as well as freedom of expression, freedom of association, and a free media.

regulatory framework helps improve the business environment and attract foreign investment.

- *Voice and accountability:* Voice and accountability has improved only during LIC growth spells; it deteriorated somewhat during growth accelerations in LTMs. The worsening among LTMs partly reflects eroding accountability in the latter years of some growth spells.

The accelerations previously discussed all started in countries that were then low-income. However, many were in countries that have long been materially richer than today's LICs—with generally greater levels of human and physical capital and stronger institutions. A fuller understanding of the conditions that could catalyze transformative growth in today's LICs therefore requires delving into a small subset of accelerations—those entered by countries that were, at the time, comfortably within the income distribution of today's LICs.

There are not enough such examples to permit robust statistical analysis, but narrative case studies—as presented in box 4.1—offer important insights. First, sustained strong growth requires peace and a political environment stable enough to foster long-term investment. Encouragingly, in countries with histories of intense conflict, accelerations have sometimes taken root relatively quickly after peace was achieved. Second, rapid investment growth, which can be achieved under a diversity of policy frameworks, tends to yield large dividends in low-income contexts. Third, accelerations were often preceded by reforms that bolstered private sector competitiveness and market incentives. These have included eliminating price controls, curbing the influence of state-owned enterprises, and reforming exchange rate policies. Fourth, continued reform momentum to foster macroeconomic stability and improve conditions for private enterprise helps sustain accelerated growth, especially when backed by a relatively capable public sector.

BOX 4.1 Low-income growth accelerations: Lessons from country case studies

Growth accelerations that started in countries at income levels similar to those prevailing in today's low-income countries (LICs) were often preceded by a mix of country-specific growth-friendly reforms. These reforms usually focused on some combinations of increasing the economy's degree of market orientation, restoring or enhancing macroeconomic stability, channeling greater resources into investment, and upgrading human capital.

The empirical analysis in this chapter documents the features of growth accelerations in low-income countries—spells in which per capita output growth increases at a rapid rate, relative to country-specific growth averages and volatility (see Annex 4.1 for details). However, only a small number of these accelerations occurred in countries that at the time were so poor as to be directly comparable to today's LICs. This box examines several of these spells in detail. It focuses on five growth accelerations in three LICs turned into middle-income countries (LTMs): Nepal (2008-19), Viet Nam (1991-2019), and Kenya (2010-19); and two current LICs: Ethiopia (2004-19), and Rwanda (2001-12). It aims to answer the following questions:

- What types of policy changes helped trigger low-income growth accelerations?

- How did economies structurally evolve during these episodes?

Growth accelerations in LTMs

Nepal (2008-19)

Economic performance. Nepal entered a growth acceleration in 2008, which sustained for 12 years until the COVID-19 pandemic. Relative to many other growth accelerations, the rate of per capita growth during Nepal's acceleration was lower—in part reflecting deep-seated structural challenges such as the country's topography and susceptibility to natural disasters (Cosic, Dahal, and Kitzmuller 2017). However, advancing at more than 4 percent annually—versus 1.6 percent in other years since 1990—real per capita GDP nonetheless increased by about two-thirds between 2007 and 2019. This saw Nepal graduate in 2019, despite starting the century at about the middle of the income distribution of today's LICs. Nepal's recovery from the pandemic has since been weak, however, with real per capita GDP only slightly above its 2019 level in 2023 following commodity import shocks and monetary tightening, and amid a still incomplete recovery in the tourism sector.

Nepal's growth acceleration coincided with strong progress on poverty reduction. Already, by 2010, less than 10 percent of the population lived in extreme poverty (on less than $2.15 per day), but by 2022, three years after the acceleration ended, the proportion had declined to less than 1 percent. Further, the proportion living on less than $3.65 per day was whittled down by more than 30 percentage points between 2010, a couple of years after the acceleration started, and 2022. Income inequality remained on a downward trajectory during the growth acceleration, having decline significantly over the 2000s. The income share of the bottom fifth of the population increased by one-third between 2003 and 2022, reaching 8.7 percent, while the Gini coefficient fell substantially between 2003 and 2010 and continued to more gradually wane thereafter. Wider social indicators also saw a significant improvement during the growth acceleration, as life expectancy increased by more than three years, while infant mortality fell by nearly 40 percent.

While dividends from faster growth contributed to favorable poverty trends, surging remittances also played a key role (Salike, Wang, and Regus 2022). From a structural perspective, the agricultural employment share declined materially, by around 7 percentage points over the acceleration, with about two-thirds of freed up labor absorbed by services and a third by industry. Productivity advanced steadily in all sectors, but traditional industrialization was limited, with upward pressure on the real exchange rate from elevated remittances encumbering export performance. Instead, driven by tourism, transportation, and real estate, the services share of output gradually increased, surpassing 50 percent in the mid-2010s. Key features of Nepal's growth acceleration are illustrated in figure B4.1.

Policy drivers. A substantial degree of growth-enabling reform took place in the late 1980s and early 1990s. Over that period trade and financial sector liberalization started alongside reforms to deregulate access to agricultural inputs (World Bank 2005). Subsequently, in 2004, Nepal joined the WTO as a full member.

BOX 4.1 Low-income growth accelerations: Lessons from country case studies (*continued*)

FIGURE B4.1.1 Nepal's growth acceleration

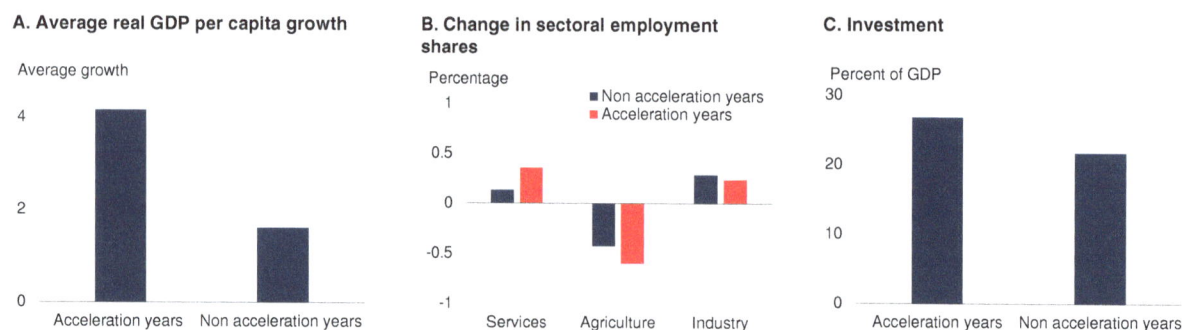

A. Average real GDP per capita growth

B. Change in sectoral employment shares

C. Investment

Source: Gootjes et al. (2024); WDI (database); World Bank.
Note: The sample period is 1990-2023. Acceleration years cover 2008-19. GDP = gross domestic product.
A.C. Bars are simple averages of annual real per capita GDP growth rates, annual changes in sectoral shares of employment, and the share of gross fixed capital formation in GDP during and outside of growth accelerations.

However, the period between 1996 and 2006 was marred by a protracted civil war and extreme political uncertainty, undercutting prospects for significant growth dividends from prior structural reforms. In 2006, a negotiated political settlement gave rise to durable peace. Thereafter, a steady pickup in growth materialized, accompanied by a sizeable increase in the investment to GDP ratio—from about 20 percent to over 30 percent in the late 2010s—concentrated in infrastructure, and particularly in energy, transport, and telecoms (IMF 2020a). Policies supporting trade openness also allowed Nepal to benefit from the economic growth of its neighbors and trading partners. Nepal's economy is deeply intertwined with India's—the countries share a 1750-kilometer border. India accounts for most of Nepal's trade, with the Nepalese rupee pegged to the Indian rupee, and India was also in a growth acceleration for the entirety of Nepal's (Ding and Masaha 2012). Trade between India and Nepal is aided by membership of the South Asian Free Trade Area agreement, signed in 2004, but ratified in India in 2009.

Viet Nam (1991-2019)

Economic performance. Viet Nam started the twenty-first century as one of world's poorest countries, with a per capita GDP in U.S. dollar slightly below the 2000 LIC median. Since then, Viet Nam has achieved rapid economic progress, graduating to lower-middle-income status in 2009, as its real GDP per capita nearly

doubled. Viet Nam's growth acceleration, one of the longest on record, started in 1991 and was upended only by the COVID-19 recession of 2020. Between 1991 and 2019, Viet Nam's real annual GDP growth per capita averaged 5.6 percent, almost twice the rate in non-acceleration years. This sustained period of growth was accompanied by a substantial decline in inflation, low unemployment rates, modest fiscal and current account deficits, and relatively low debt levels. Even during the global recession of 2009, the country maintained positive growth, reflecting the strength of its domestic market and the effectiveness of government policies. Limited exposure to risky financial instruments and Viet Nam's position as a manufacturing hub further insulated the economy, ensuring steady growth acceleration despite global challenges (IMF 2009). During the growth acceleration, the proportion of the population in extreme poverty ($2.15 2017 PPP) fell from 48 percent in 1992 to less than 1 percent in 2020 (World Bank 2022b). Viet Nam's growth spell was both transformative and inclusive. The country ranks in the top quarter of emerging market and developing economies with respect to reaching the Sustainable Development Goals (Baum 2020; World Bank 2024f). Key features of Viet Nam's growth acceleration are illustrated in figure B4.2.

Policy drivers. The 1991 growth spell in Viet Nam was sparked by reforms known as *Doi Moi* or "*renovation*" that started in 1986. These reforms focused on

BOX 4.1 Low-income growth accelerations: Lessons from country case studies (*continued*)

FIGURE B4.1.2 Viet Nam's growth acceleration

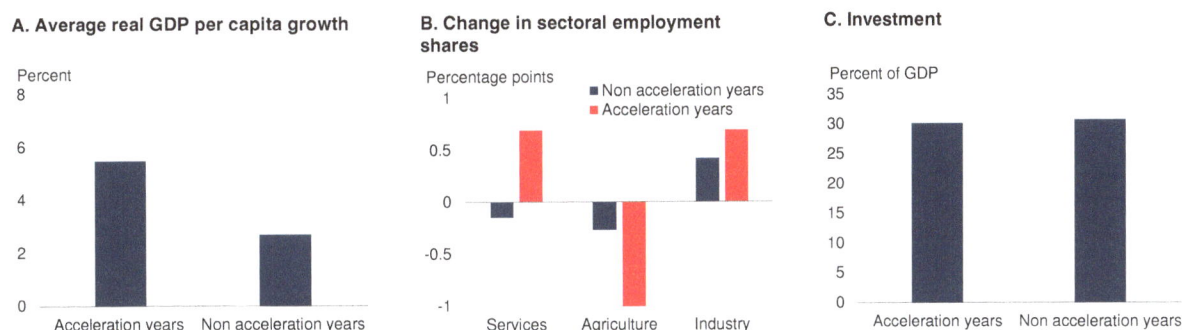

A. Average real GDP per capita growth

B. Change in sectoral employment shares

C. Investment

Source: Gootjes et al. (2024); WDI (database); World Bank.
Note: The sample period is 1990-2023. Acceleration years cover 1991-2019. GDP = gross domestic product.
A.C. Bars are simple averages of annual real per capita GDP growth rates, annual changes in sectoral shares of employment, and the share of gross fixed capital formation in GDP during and outside of growth accelerations.
C. Because of the extended coverage of acceleration years, non-acceleration years coverage is limited. However, when further historical data is considered beyond 1990, the gross fixed capital formation during acceleration years becomes significantly higher than non-acceleration years.

addressing four major economic distortions. First, the reforms sought to facilitate a transition to a market economy, with a focus on trade liberalization and improvements in the business environment (IMF 2019a; Schaumburg-Müller, 2005). Central to this effort were trade reforms that enabled the country's integration into the global economy, with Viet Nam's accession to the WTO in 2007 solidifying its position in global trade (World Bank 2024f). Second, macroeconomic reforms—including the relaxation of price controls, stricter fiscal discipline, and restrictive monetary policy—aimed at achieving price stability, positive real interest rates, and a competitive exchange rate (Bhattacharya 2013; Camen 2006; Irvin 1995). Third, policies were introduced to address key deficits in human capital and public infrastructure, with a focus on the expansion of access to education, health, and electricity (Baum 2020). Fourth, public enterprise reforms, especially the restructuring, liquidation, divestment and equitization of key government-owned enterprises, sought to reduce the role of the government and to encourage private enterprise (Dang et al. 2021; World Bank 2016a). Other reforms were aimed at diversifying the economy to attract foreign direct investment in key sectors, including light manufacturing, energy and extractives, and tourism (Jenkins 2006; World Bank and IFC 2021). Reforms in the agriculture sector sought to increase investment and productivity by removing price controls and strengthening property

rights, while facilitating the adoption of modern technology and access to capital inputs and fertilizer (McCaig and Pavcnik 2013).

Kenya (2010-19)

Economic performance. In 2000, Kenya's GDP per capita in U.S. dollars was close to the median of the LIC income distribution. Kenya's growth acceleration started in 2010 and was ended by the recession caused by the COVID-19 pandemic. Kenya graduated to middle-income status in 2016, halfway into its growth acceleration.[a] During the acceleration, real per capita GDP growth averaged 2.6 percent, compared with 0.3 percent during non-acceleration years. Kenya's real per capita GDP increased by about a third during the acceleration. During this period, Kenya achieved notable macroeconomic stability, with moderate exchange rate volatility and inflation largely within the central bank's target (Alper et al. 2017). Nevertheless, exchange rate appreciation between 2010 and 2019 made exports less competitive and weighed on industrial growth (Owino, Barasa, and Doyle 2024). The services sector was the main driver of growth during the acceleration. The agricultural share of employment declined by 7 percentage points to about 34 percent in

a. Kenya's lower-middle-income status was confirmed after rebasing the country's GDP, which revealed that the size of the economy was 25 percent larger than previously estimated.

BOX 4.1 Low-income growth accelerations: Lessons from country case studies (*continued*)

FIGURE B4.1.3 Kenya's growth acceleration

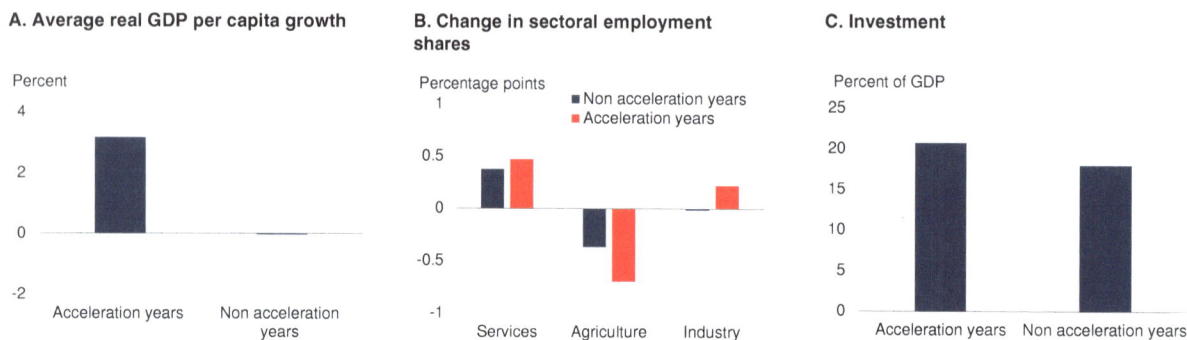

A. Average real GDP per capita growth

B. Change in sectoral employment shares

C. Investment

Source: Gootjes et al. (2024); WDI (database); World Bank.
Note: The sample period is 1990-2023. Acceleration years cover 2010-19.
A.C. Bars are simple averages of annual real per capita GDP growth rates, annual changes in sectoral shares of employment, and the share of gross fixed capital formation in GDP during and outside of growth accelerations.

2019; the employment share in industry increased by 2 percentage points to 15 percent and services grew by 5 percentage points to 51 percent.

Living standards improved somewhat during Kenya's growth acceleration. The share of people living in extreme poverty is estimated to have declined by 2 percentage points to 32 percent in 2019, with marginal reductions in inequality (World Bank 2019, 2023a). Nevertheless, progress on the broader Sustainable Development Goals agenda has stagnated or regressed for 12 of the 17 goals (Sachs, Lafortune, and Fuller 2024). Recent developments—including stalled progress on the broader measures of welfare and sustainable development, as well as high levels of actual and perceived inequality and exclusion—highlight the limitations of public expenditure oversight and the need to improve the quality of growth (IMF 2024b). Key features of Kenya's growth acceleration are illustrated in figure B4.3.

Policy drivers. Kenya's growth acceleration was sparked by a set of policy initiatives, including the implementation of market-oriented reforms, restoration of macroeconomic stability, strengthening of governance institutions, expansion of physical infrastructure, and fostering of financial sector innovations (World Bank 2020b). First, the Economic Recovery Strategy (ERS) of 2003 sought, among other things, to address key macroeconomic vulnerabilities, structural weaknesses, and governance gaps (Sasaoka

2005). The major challenges facing government at the time were how to restore economic growth, reduce poverty, and create jobs. Second, through the 2003-07 Investment Program for Economic Recovery Strategy for Wealth and Employment Creation, Kenya sought to accelerate economic growth and poverty reduction by encouraging private enterprise, improving economic governance, and building human capital by investing in education and health (IMF 2005a).

Kenya made several growth-friendly reforms that encouraged private investment. Price controls were eliminated, interest rates were liberalized, and a competitive exchange rate policy was introduced (Ndungu and Ngugi 1999). The reform of state-owned enterprises reduced the number of parastatals. Further reforms sought to ease the complexity of tax regulations and excessive tax burdens (Karingi and Wanjala 2005). Peace and stability have been key to Kenya's economic performance as the country took advantage of its geographic location to position itself as a regional financial and trade hub (Kimenyi, Mwega, and Ndung'u 2016). Greater structural reform momentum—which was lacking in the 1980s and 1990s—lent impetus to growth in the 2000s. On the supply side, the gains from these reforms were evident in the high growth of the services sector. On the demand side, government expenditure—and particularly greater infrastructure spending—has been a driver of domestic demand (World Bank 2020b).

BOX 4.1 Low-income growth accelerations: Lessons from country case studies (*continued*)

FIGURE B4.1.4 Ethiopia's growth acceleration

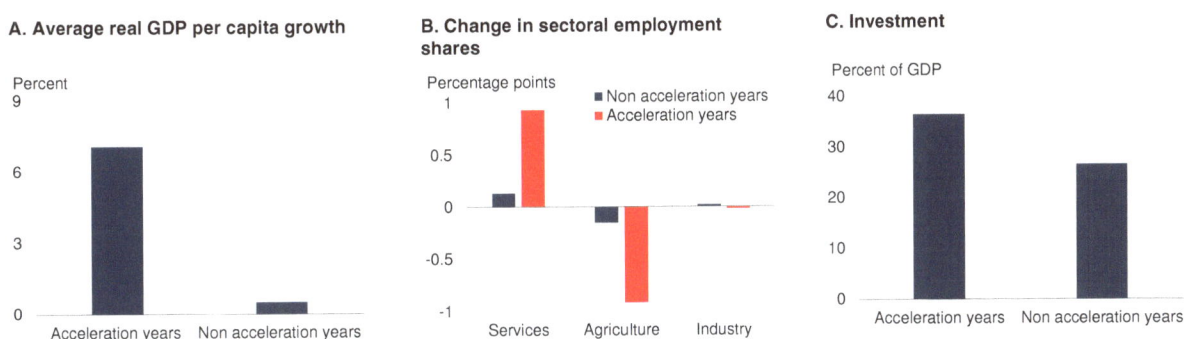

A. Average real GDP per capita growth

B. Change in sectoral employment shares

C. Investment

Source: Gootjes et al. (2024); WDI (database); World Bank.
Note: The sample period is 1990-2023. Acceleration years cover 2004-19.
A.C. Bars are simple averages of annual real per capita GDP growth rates, annual change in sectoral shares of employment, and the share of gross fixed capital formation in GDP during and outside of growth accelerations.

In the 2010s, Kenya's government adopted expansionary fiscal policies to stimulate economic growth and achieve the goals set out in Vision 2030 (IMF 2015).[b] The government prioritized spending on both economic and social infrastructure, aiming to enhance productivity and to reduce poverty (World Bank 2020b). Additionally, investments in education and health have improved labor productivity (World Bank 2014; World Bank 2023b). Kenya's financial sector innovations and the supportive regulatory environment have also significantly advanced financial inclusion, enabled by the rapid expansion of mobile financial services (Gutierrez and Singh 2013; IMF 2018; Jack and Suri 2014). These reforms were supported by a constitutional change in 2010 that decentralized political power and sought to improve governance.

Growth accelerations in LICs

Ethiopia (2004-19)

Economic performance. Ethiopia had a growth acceleration from 2004 to 2019 during which real per capita growth averaged about 7 percent compared to less than 0.5 percent in other years since 1990. Ethiopia started the century as the poorest LIC, but during its

acceleration per capita GDP trebled bringing the country to the brink of middle-income status. During this period extreme poverty also fell notably; about a quarter of the population is estimated to have lived on less than $2.15 a day in 2015, down from more than one-third in 2004. Alongside, life expectancy rose by a decade and infant mortality halved (IMF 2024c). The acceleration was ended by the COVID-19 pandemic although growth had already cooled amid political instability and rising macroeconomic imbalances. Since 2020, Ethiopia's recovery has been severely hampered by civil conflict and unsustainable debt.

The agriculture sector was a key driver of growth during the initial acceleration phase, followed by an increasing contribution from the services sector (Hausmann et al. 2022). In subsequent years, a construction boom, coupled with moderate success in developing textiles and footwear subsectors, saw the industrial share of GDP double. Employment shifted rapidly from agriculture to services during the acceleration. The agricultural share of employment declined by nearly 1 percentage point annually, offset entirely by expanding services employment. This shift was enabled by a doubling of agricultural productivity—facilitated by a combination of improved fertilizer access, extension programs, and an expanding the road network—but services productivity also grew at nearly 4 percent annually (World Bank 2016b). Key features of Ethiopia's growth acceleration are illustrated in figure B4.4.

---

b. While this fiscal expansion contributed to significant improve-ments in infrastructure and spurred economic growth, it also led to rising public debt levels and concerns about fiscal sustainability (Ryan and Maana 2014).

BOX 4.1 Low-income growth accelerations: Lessons from country case studies (*continued*)

Policy drivers. The groundwork for Ethiopia's acceleration was partly laid by reforms in the 1990s that lessened state control of the economy. This included privatizations and a large reduction in average tariff rates (Mengistu 2021). Alongside, the Agriculture Development Led Industrialization strategy of the late 1990s and early 2000s fostered agricultural productivity by improving the availability of agricultural inputs, encouraging crop diversification and investing in supporting infrastructure such as rural transportation and water supply (World Bank 2008a). Ethiopia's land certification program, which aimed to strengthen land tenure security for farming households, also helped to improve investment and productivity in agriculture (Holden, Deininger, and Ghebru 2009). In parallel, an increasing focus on expanding educational access and providing technical and vocational training laid the foundations for a more skilled workforce (Seid, Taffesse, and Ali 2016).

A further critical driver of Ethiopia's acceleration was a sustained public investment drive, encompassing a series of public investment-intensive strategies including the 2005 Plan for Accelerated and Sustained Development to End Poverty, and the first (2010-15) and second (2015-20) Growth and Transformation Plans. The ratio of general government investment to GDP doubled from about 5 percent prior to the acceleration to about 10 percent in the mid-2010s. Moreover, this figure understates total public investment given the prominent role of state-owned enterprises in flagship government strategies.

Extensive investments in communications, energy and transportation infrastructure, as well as education and healthcare, were enabled in part by constrained government consumption. In addition, however, resources were appropriated through a range of heterodox policies, including via financial repression and substantial seigniorage revenues generated by high inflation. As such, private investment was constrained by the implicit rationing of capital, and the real exchange rate appreciated. This reduced the cost of imported capital goods but posed headwinds to export competitiveness and the related accumulation of foreign exchange.

Fiscal space for the public sector-led growth strategy was partly generated by reduced defense spending following the cessation of hostilities with Eritrea in 2000, and by debt relief in the mid-2000s under the Heavily Indebted Poor Countries (HIPC) Initiative and the Multilateral Debt Relief Initiative (MDRI; AfDB 2022; Hausmann et al. 2022). Yet external debt rose rapidly over the 2010s, financing a large current account deficit as the resources required for import- and investment-intensive growth outstripped domestic savings. Even so, from a starting point of extreme capital scarcity, infrastructure investment and associated positive externalities initially outweighed the growth drag from allocative distortions (Moller and Wacker 2017).

That Ethiopia grew so rapidly despite its unusual policy mix exemplifies the large potential benefits of capital accumulation in LICs, especially backed by capable bureaucracy—based on the Worldwide Governance Indicators, since 2010 Ethiopia has consistently been in the top quartile of LICs for government effectiveness. However, the deceleration of growth in the 2020s and an external debt default in 2023 also highlight the limits and risks of a growth model heavily reliant on debt-financed public sector activity. Similarly, tepid export growth and weak private investment underscore the importance of maintaining reform momentum and competitiveness to catalyze new sources of growth, while continued political instability underscores the acute challenge of overcoming conflict.

Rwanda (2001-12)

Economic performance. Rwanda emerged from cycles of conflict and fragility to become one of the fastest growing low-income countries. In 2000, Rwanda's per capita GDP fell to the lowest quartile of LICs. Rwanda's growth spell started in 2001, eight years after the 1994 genocide, and lasted until 2012. Between 2001 and 2012, Rwanda's annual real GDP growth per capita averaged 5.7 percent, 1.5 percentage points higher than in non-acceleration years. Between 2000 and 2013, Rwanda's real GDP per capita doubled. By 2023, real GDP per capita had increased by more than another 50 percent, bringing the country to within 15 percent of the threshold for graduation to middle-income status, on a par with Uganda, and behind only Ethiopia and Togo among LICs with the highest income per capita.

The growth acceleration was associated with broad improvements in living standards, especially in the

BOX 4.1 Low-income growth accelerations: Lessons from country case studies (*continued*)

FIGURE B4.1.5 Rwanda's growth acceleration

A. Average real GDP per capita growth

B. Change in sectoral employment shares

C. Investment

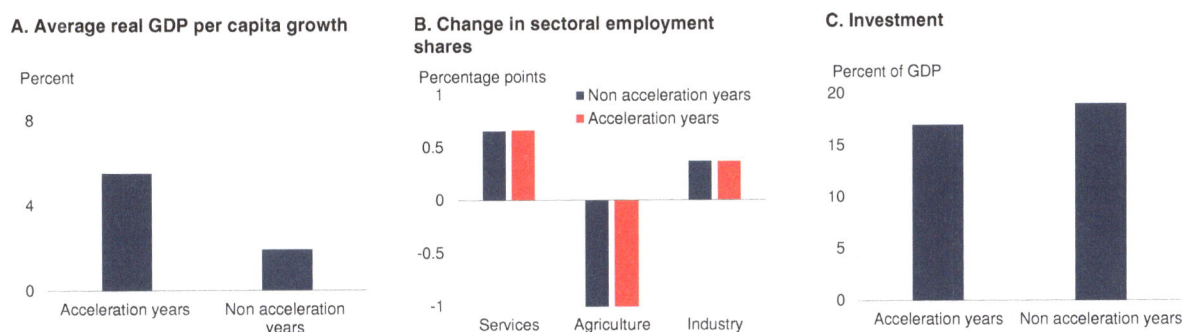

Source: Gootjes et al. (2024); WDI (database); World Bank.
Note: The sample period is 1990-2023. Acceleration years cover 2001-12. GDP = gross domestic product.
A.C. Bars are simple averages of annual real per capita GDP growth rates, annual changes in sectoral shares of employment, and the share of gross fixed capital formation in GDP during and outside of growth accelerations.

earlier years. Between 2000 and 2013, the poverty rate in Rwanda ($2.15 per day) declined by 21 percentage points to less than 55 percent. Accelerated growth also led to significant improvements in non-monetary well-being, particularly in maternal and child health. Since then, however, the relationship between growth and poverty reduction has weakened, resulting in poverty rates that are higher than other African countries with similar income levels. Moreover, inequality remains high, reflecting deeper structural challenges (World Bank 2023c). While structural transformation remained the primary driver of poverty reduction in Rwanda, the labor released from agriculture was mostly absorbed in low-productivity services (World Bank 2020c). Nevertheless, Rwanda has been successful in developing some services-led export sectors, particularly tourism, ICT, and transport (Newfarmer, Page, and Tarp 2018). Key features of Rwanda's growth acceleration are illustrated in figure B1.5.

Policy drivers. Rwanda's growth acceleration was preceded by an ambitious reform effort that sought to stabilize the economy and incentivize private enterprise. Various macroeconomic and structural reforms were implemented to improve efficiency in the banking sector, liberalize the capital account, and reduce trade barriers (Malunda and Musana 2012). These reforms raised productivity by steering the economy from an

administered one to a market-based one (Coulibaly, Ezemenari, and Duffy 2008). Second-generation reforms sought to improve the business environment and sought to eliminate excessive tax, legal, and regulatory burdens on firms. As such, the country emerged as one of the most competitive in the region, ranking above peers on various measures of doing business (Schwab 2019).

Broader institutional reforms strengthened the effectiveness of the public sector. This helped Rwanda develop a bureaucracy capable of maintaining order and efficiently delivering services, with notably little corruption (Chemouni 2017). Among the 50 economies assessed in the 2024 Business Ready report, Rwanda's scores placed the country among the top 10 in the public services and operational efficiency pillars (World Bank 2024g). In addition, the state has been instrumental in driving growth directly, with public investment accounting for approximately 40 percent of the country's GDP growth since 2000 (IMF 2023b).

Debt relief initiatives and development assistance championed by the international community also played a significant role in supporting Rwanda's growth acceleration (IMF 2005b). Rwanda's participation in these initiatives helped create fiscal space that allowed more resources to be channeled into long-term growth enhancing sectors, including education and healthcare.

Challenges to growth and graduation

Following 15 years of intense adversity, many LICs are at risk of further lost decades. The scarring from crises in recent years has compounded pre-existing structural challenges. LICs require substantial investment to accelerate growth and transformation. However, alongside declining growth rates, fiscal positions have deteriorated sharply, limiting available resources (Mawejje 2024a). These challenges are exacerbated by a range of worsening risks that complicate development pathways, including elevated levels of fragility and conflict, advancing climate change, and stalling structural transformation. Moreover, these trends are playing out against a backdrop of a more challenging external environment—one that is characterized by weakening long-term global growth prospects, growing trade restrictions, trade policy fragmentation, and a resurgence of protectionist measures.

Fragility and conflict

Since 2000, years of intense armed conflict—defined as more than 50 battle-related deaths per million people—have been far more common in LICs than elsewhere. Just eight LICs—about one-third—have avoided such conflicts entirely. This compares to more than 90 percent of other EMDEs and more than 80 percent of LTMs. The chance of being in intense conflict in any year during 2000-22, at 16 percent, was 14 times higher in LICs than LTMs (figure 4.10.A). Conflicts have also been more deadly in LICs. Total battle-related deaths in LICs averaged close to 1,400 per million people in 2000-22, more than 20 times the level in other EMDEs. Moreover, civil conflict has increased in LICs since 2010, coinciding with stalling poverty reduction.

Set against a backdrop of heightened geopolitical tensions globally, recent instability and military coups in Burkina Faso, Mali, Niger, and Sudan, and an attempted coup in the Democratic Republic of Congo suggest conflict-related challenges may persist. If they do, graduation prospects will become bleaker. Intense armed conflicts destroy physical and human capital, often generating deep recessions and large persistent output losses (Federle et al. 2024). Conflicts also have severe spillovers, reducing trade flows and weakening private investment in adjacent states (Abdel-Latif et al. 2024; Rauschendorfer and Shepherd 2022). Neighboring countries can be destabilized and become susceptible to conflict themselves (Buhaug and Gleditsch 2008). Higher spending on defense and peace operations often comes at the expense of investment in priority sectors, including education, health, and infrastructure, and heightens fiscal vulnerabilities (Abdel-Latif et al. 2024; Ezeoha et al. 2023).

Economic damages from conflicts in LICs are often enormous. Recent empirical estimates indicate that severe conflicts in LICs are likely to lower GDP per capita by around 15 percent after five years (figure 4.10.B). Some cases can be more extreme. Had there been no conflict, GDP per capita in South Sudan might be as much as three times higher (Mawejje and McSharry 2021). Recent estimates suggest a potentially similar scale of per capita output losses in the Republic of Yemen (World Bank 2024h). Principally, output tends to decline as a result of collapsing private consumption, indicating especially severe welfare effects. Outsized declines in consumption partly reflect that LIC residents have few assets and limited access to credit to smooth these shocks. Conflict also interacts with existing fragility in pernicious ways, such as by undermining already weak institutions and worsening food insecurity—hunger due to conflict is estimated to have nearly doubled between 2018 and 2023 (Chami, Espinoza, and Montiel 2021; FSIN and FNAFC 2024).

Climate change

As climate change has advanced, the frequency and severity of extreme weather events and other natural disasters have intensified in recent decades (Konisky et al. 2016). Natural disasters have become more common in both LICs and LTMs, but the geographical incidence of disasters—especially droughts—is much greater in LICs (figure 4.10.C). The social and economic consequences of disasters are more likely to tip LICs than higher-income economies into economic distress (Mejia et al. 2019). Climate change effects on labor productivity are higher in LICs than in other countries. The median loss of productivity through 2050 could be as high as 6.2 percent in LICs, higher than in lower-middle-income countries (5.7 percent), upper-middle-income countries (1.5 percent), and high-income countries (0.2 percent) World Bank 2024i).[11] LICs with limited financial buffers could experience more adverse effects of climate-change-related disasters on economic stability and growth. With average annual economic losses estimated at 2 percent and adaptation costs estimated at 3.5 percent of GDP, the costs of climate change are higher in LICs than in other EMDEs (Mawejje 2024a).

The effects of drought have been growing in frequency and geographic spread, with large economic losses in low- and middle-income countries. Compared to normal conditions, drought can reduce growth, on average, by as much as 0.85 percentage points in developing countries, compared with 0.3 percentage point in advanced economies (Zaveri, Damania, and Engle 2023). Because agriculture accounts for such a sizeable share of economic activity in LICs, the effects of climate change could be especially severe (Jafino et al., 2020; Adedeji, Gieck-Bricco, and Kehayova 2016). Climate-related destruction of crops and livelihoods could push many LIC populations further into poverty, which would be aggravated by the limited capacity and resources of LICs to counter the adverse effects of climate change (Hallegatte et al. 2016). Recoveries from droughts appear to be taking longer, resulting in less time for livelihoods to be restored between droughts, which renders countries even more vulnerable to shocks of all varieties (Schwalm et al. 2017).

Droughts can have an impact on economies in other ways other than through their effects on agriculture. They can, for example, exacerbate existing vulnerabilities in the business environment, such as by compromising the provision of electricity from hydropower generation. This, in

---

[11] These estimates indicate a pessimistic climate scenario.

FIGURE 4.10 Challenges to growth and graduation to middle-income status in LICs

Intense conflict is far more prevalent in LICs than in LTMs or other EMDEs. In this century, only one-third of LICs have completely avoided intense conflict. The costs of intense conflict are severe, with per capita GDP generally estimated to be about 15 percent lower after five years. LICs are also more likely to experience extreme climate events—especially droughts—than are LTMs. Fiscal space has narrowed significantly in LICs, with more than half in, or at risk of, debt distress.

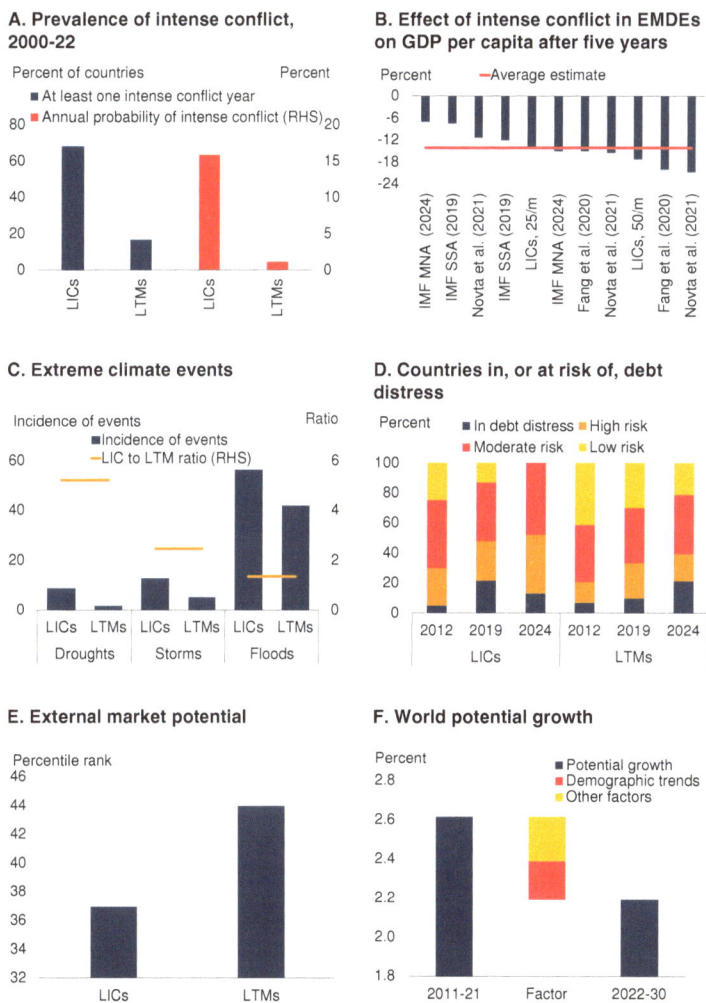

Sources: EM-DAT (database); Fang et al. (2020); IMF (2019b); IMF (2024d); International Monetary Fund; Kose and Ohnsorge (2024); Novta and Pugacheva (2021); Uppsala Conflict Data Program; World Bank.
Note: LICs = low-income countries; LTMs = LICs turned into middle-income countries.
A. Intense conflict years defined as those with more than 50 battle-relate deaths per million people.
B. All estimates are of the decline in GDP per capita in year *t+5*, when year *t* is the onset of intense conflict. Approaches include: local projections; pre-conflict forecast versus outcome; and synthetic control. Where more than one estimate appears from a single publication, this reflects different estimation techniques or country group estimates. All estimates use the "deaths per million" threshold to define intense conflict, ranging from 25/million to 50/million. "LICs 50/m" and "LICs 25/m" are new estimates for current LICs only, based on data from 1990-2022. See Annex 3 for details.
C. Incidence of events is defined as the total number of events per million square kilometers of country area between January 2000 and May 2024.
D. Shares of countries by risk of debt distress, as of Sep 2024. Based on up to 23 LICs and 30 LTMs.
E. External market potential as a measure of trade costs is defined as GDP for all other countries divided by distance between the home country and other countries. The elasticity of the distance effect is assumed at -1.4 (see Carrere et al., 2013). Distances are measured based on capital cities.
F. Based on the production function approach. GDP-weighted averages for a sample of 29 advanced economies and 53 EMDEs. See Kose and Ohnsorge (2024) for details.

turn, can have severely negative implications for output and productivity in services and manufacturing sectors (Falchetta et al. 2019; Mawejje 2024b).

Fiscal vulnerabilities

Fiscal positions are weaker and have deteriorated more rapidly in LICs than in LTMs. LICs entered the 2020 pandemic-caused recession with inadequate fiscal buffers, which, because of their limited market access, made it harder for LICs than LTMs to undertake countercyclical fiscal policy. Since the pandemic, the debt build-up has been faster and more widespread in LICs than in LTMs, so that in 2024, more than half of LICs are either in debt distress or at high risk of it (figure 4.10.D). In addition to increasing their debt ratios, LICs have increased the riskiness of their financing sources. In the decade before the pandemic, non-Paris Club creditors became a more important source of financing, especially in Sub-Saharan Africa (Horn et al. 2023; Mihalyi and Trebesch 2023).

Higher levels of public debt and an increased reliance on riskier sources of financing make many LICs vulnerable to currency, interest rate, and refinancing risks (Essl et al. 2019). Rising debt and interest rates have resulted in a sharp increase in interest payments. In 2023, interest payments in the average LIC exceeded 10 percent of revenue, reaching their highest level in two decades (Mawejje 2024a). In six LICs, government interest payments were higher in 2021 (the latest available data) than spending on health services. Thus, servicing large debt loads is significantly reducing the resources available to invest in growth-enhancing sectors, including in health, education, infrastructure, and climate adaptation.

Geography

Nearly half of LICs today are landlocked, compared to about a quarter of LTMs. Moreover, more than half of today's landlocked LICs are in fragility and conflict-affected situations, and their neighbors are generally other LICs or countries with per capita incomes just above middle-income thresholds. This geographical disadvantage—often

exacerbated by high trade costs and behind-the border non-tariff barriers—limits LICs' ability to catalyze stronger growth by encouraging trade with large trading partner economies (figure 4.10.E; Arvis et al. 2013; Paudel and Cooray 2018). By contrast, among the landlocked LTMs, about half border China, Russia, or both. In many cases, opportunities created via trading relationships with a large and globally connected neighbors—for example through supplying commodities, integrating with regional value chains, or receiving remittances from migrant workers—were integral to attaining middle-income status (Steinbach 2019).

Declining productivity

The broad-based decline in LIC labor productivity since 2010 implies serious obstacles to medium-term growth. In many LICs, productivity across sectors is held back by poor business environments characterized by inadequate provision of public capital, lack of access to finance, political instability, conflict, and policy uncertainty (Bah and Fang 2015; Dabla-Norris, Ho, and Kyobe 2016). In addition, agricultural productivity has been constrained by limited adoption of technology and by climate-related vulnerabilities (World Bank 2008b; Wiggins 2014). High unit labor costs present an obstacle to manufacturing sectors in Sub-Saharan Africa, limiting industrial investment and export growth (Naidoo and Ndikumana 2023; Gelb et al. 2020). Indeed, in Africa, shares of manufacturing in GDP and total employment have declined notably since the 1990s (Balchin et al. 2016). Though workers continue to transition out of agriculture and into services, initial gains in services productivity in the 2000s appear to have lost momentum. This suggests that, because there are few dynamic labor-absorbing industries, the marginal worker is taking up informal low-productivity services work (Fox et al. 2013). As a result, the recent reallocation of resources may have contributed little to aggregate growth in most African economies (Vries, Timmer, and Vries 2013).

The experience of LICs today is consistent with structural change without industrialization, which may have been growth-reducing in some cases (Carmignani and Mandeville 2014; McMillan and

Rodrik 2011). These patterns may reflect broader global forces that are driving trends of premature deindustrialization (Rodrik 2016). With the technological frontier in manufacturing moving ever forward, opportunities to compete in global product markets by substituting comparatively cheap labor and land for technological sophistication may be narrowing (Rodrik and Sandhu 2024). In this context, there could be an emerging trade-off between rapidly increasing manufacturing employment and fostering internationally competitive manufacturing firms, meaning that transitioning workers into manufacturing offers no guarantee of productivity convergence (Diao et al. 2024; Herrendorf, Rogerson, and Valentinyi 2022). That said, there is also some evidence that relatively low-tech manufacturing firms in Sub-Saharan Africa can outperform on productivity metrics when controlling for wider business environment challenges (Harrison, Lin, and Xu 2014).

More challenging external environment

Many LTM graduations, in the 2000s, occurred when there was relatively strong global growth, characterized by a surge in the demand for commodity resources in some large EMDEs. China's unprecedented growth spurt provided demand for commodities, supporting growth in commodity-dependent EMDEs. However, long-term prospects for commodity demand are weakening as growth in China—the largest source of commodity demand—slows and shifts towards less-resource-intensive sectors (World Bank 2018a).

In addition, LTMs benefitted from globalization and greater integration into global value chains by entering into free trade agreements (Steinbach 2019). However, global trade growth has slowed significantly since the global financial crisis and recent overlapping shocks have further disrupted commodity markets and supply chains (Ohnsorge and Quaglietti 2023). A resurgence of trade-restrictive measures, trade policy fragmentation, or moves toward protectionist measures could weaken global trade dynamism further and limit opportunities for LICs to trade more with the rest of the world (World Bank 2024c). Global potential growth is also projected to fall to a three-

decade low of 2.2 percent over the remainder of the 2020s—0.4 percentage point below the average from 2011-21 and continuing a secular deceleration as fundamental drivers are set to weaken further (figure 4.10.F; Kose and Ohnsorge 2024).

Growth opportunities

Enabled by conducive reform efforts, stronger institutions, and greater peace and stability, LICs could take advantage of a range of opportunities linked to their existing characteristics to accelerate growth and development. If effectively harnessed, demographic dividends and natural resource endowments could drive economic growth and transformation, enabling rapid progress. LICs could also accelerate growth by advancing regional trade integration and building up potential export sectors where they have natural advantages, including tourism.

Potential demographic dividends

LICs can reap substantial demographic dividends as the share of their working-age population grows significantly over the next half century (figure 4.11.A). Although steadily declining, fertility rates remain high in LICs, with an annual average of five births per 1,000 people during 2000-21, compared to four births in LTMs, and 3 in other EMDEs. By contrast, the working-age share of the population has been decreasing in advanced economies for more than a decade. The expected growth in LIC working-age populations could have sizable economic impacts (Ahmed and Cruz 2016). As cohorts of children become working age, dependency ratios will decline, and the labor force will swell. By illustration, demographic trends in Sub-Saharan Africa, if combined with effective labor market reforms, could add an estimated 1.2 percentage points a year to potential growth between 2022 and 2030 (Kasyanenko et al. 2023).

Investing in education and skill-training and creating stronger healthcare systems will be critical to ensure greater human capital development capable of driving growth and transformation (World Bank 2018b; World Bank 2021). Beyond the increase in available labor inputs, declining

FIGURE 4.11 Growth opportunities in LICs

To kick-start stronger growth and improve prospects for graduation to middle-income status, today's LICs could find advantage in youthful and growing populations, greater trade integration, tourism potential, and vast natural resource endowments.

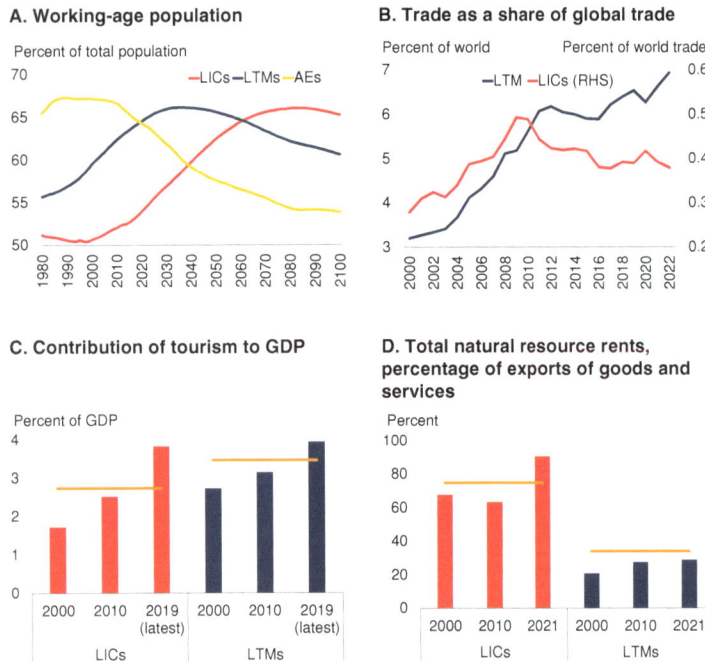

A. Working-age population

B. Trade as a share of global trade

C. Contribution of tourism to GDP

D. Total natural resource rents, percentage of exports of goods and services

Sources: UN World Population Prospects (database); WDI (database); World Bank.
Note: AEs = advanced economies; LICs = low-income countries; LTMs = LICs turned into middle-income countries.
A. Population-weighted averages. Working-age population is defined as people aged 15-64. Based on 25 LICs and 40 LTMs.
B. Solid lines show the share of trade in global trade, by country group. Based on up to 24 LICs and 42 LTMs.
C. International tourism receipts expressed as a percentage of GDP. Solid bars are mean values. Orange bars are the 2010-19 period averages. Sample includes 22 LICs and 41 LTMs.
D. The solid blue bars show simple unweighted year averages. Solid bars are mean values. Orange bars are 2010-19 period averages. Sample includes 25 LICs and 42 LTMs.

dependency ratios can also foster increased domestic savings. Twinned with sufficiently efficient intermediation, higher savings can be channeled into increased investment, supporting rapid capital accumulation. However, the realization of these benefits depends on institutions, labor markets, and financial sectors of sufficient dynamism to generate productive jobs and investment opportunities (Bloom and Canning 2004; Wenjie et al. 2024).

Globalization and trade

The involvement of LICs in global trade has declined since 2010 (figure 4.11.B). As a proportion of world totals, their shares of both

goods and services exports has declined since 2010, while imports flattened out and have been declining since 2015. In part, this reflects low levels of regional trade integration due to the proliferation of non-tariff barriers and weakness in LIC growth prospects—which have softened markedly since 2010. This period has also been associated with wider global trends characterized by weaker global growth, increasing global trade fragmentation, declining foreign direct investment flows, and slowing commodity demand—especially from China. In a context of increasing trade policy uncertainty, these factors have placed large constraints on LIC trade growth and disrupted trade networks (World Bank 2024c). Increasing trade openness and participation in the region could push back against these forces and create opportunities to accelerate growth in LICs. Eliminating barriers to trade can also support wider poverty reduction objectives by lifting demand-side constraints (Goldberg and Reed 2023).

African LICs in particular have a proximate opportunity in the form of the African Continental Free Trade Area (AfCFTA). Created in 2019, the AfCFTA provides a framework for the liberalization of trade in goods and services. The agreement aims to reduce tariffs among member countries and to cover policy areas such as trade facilitation and services, as well as regulatory measures such as sanitary standards and technical barriers to trade. If fully implemented, the free trade area is expected to cover all 55 African countries, including all African LICs. Implementing the AfCFTA could raise income by 7 percent and reduce the number of people living in extreme poverty by 40 million by 2035 (World Bank 2020d).

The creation of a sizeable regional market is a major opportunity for African LICs to take advantage of economies of scale, diversify exports, and attract foreign direct investment (IMF 2020b). The prospects for integration into wider global value chains could also be considerably improved by enhancing the efficiency of intra-African trade. However, implementation of the AfCFTA has been slow, and the focus is currently on merchandise trade only. The Guided Trade

Initiative launched in 2022 aims to test the policy, institutional, legal, and operational environment under the AfCFTA, with a view to facilitating commercially viable trade.[12] Moreover, to realize fully the potential benefits from de jure changes in trade policy, a broader suite of regulatory reforms and infrastructure investments is also necessary.

Natural resource endowments

More than four of five of LICs today are resource dependent—several of them possess plentiful oil and gas resources and mineral deposits, and substantial solar energy and tourism potential. During 2000-21, on average, natural resource-related income accounted for 12 percent of GDP and 76 percent of exports in LICs (figure 4.11.C). Natural resource endowments present both opportunities and risks. Commodity revenues can be transformative if used efficiently for public investment. However, commodity dependence can precipitate macroeconomic management challenges related to so-called Dutch disease, corruption, and fiscal policy volatility, potentially undercutting sustained growth and poverty reduction (Cust, Devarajan, and Mandon 2022; Katoka and Dostal 2022).

Tourism. Many LICs could reap significant benefits by utilizing their natural wealth to foster tourism development. Tourism can be an engine for sustainable economic growth—through job creation, enhanced inclusion, and poverty reduction (Christie et al. 2013). Some African LICs have unique biodiversity and other physical attractions that, under the right conditions, have the potential to develop into premier international destinations (for example, *Democratic Republic of Congo, Rwanda, Uganda*). The contribution of tourism to GDP has increased, on average, by 2 percentage points since 2000 among LICs, compared to just 1 percentage point among LTMs (figure 4.11.D). In a few LICs, the share of tourism receipts in GDP exceeded 5 percent (*Gambia, Madagascar, Rwanda*). In others, such as

those in fragile and conflict-affected situations, it barely reached one-half of a percentage point of GDP (*Burundi, South Sudan, Sudan*), highlighting the drag that conflict can have on sector specific investment and growth.

Because it is a labor-intensive sector, tourism can support jobs and livelihoods. It can also facilitate the development of new infrastructure, helping to boost investment (World Bank 2017). Tourism can be a reliable source of external demand and export growth. Some LTMs have leveraged their tourism potential to generate large economic dividends and growth (Armenia, Cambodia, Comoros, Georgia, Kenya, Kyrgyz Republic, Nepal, Solomon Islands), while Rwanda a fast-growing LIC, has prioritized tourism, among other services exports. The examples of Nepal and Rwanda—both small, landlocked, and post-conflict countries—can serve as encouraging examples of the potential of tourism to drive growth and transformation, even at low levels of development. For both countries, tourism accounted for more than one-quarter of total exports before the pandemic-spawned recession and continues to be a major export sector (World Bank 2022c, 2023d).

Reaching LICs' tourism potential will be contingent on a stable political environment, solid infrastructure, and the provision of reliable ancillary services, which presents considerable challenges. In addition, tourism promotion, if not well calibrated for sustainability, can come with risks related to resource depletion and environmental degradation. Nevertheless, the benefits associated with tourism, such as increased employment, the deepening of local value chains, and enabling infrastructure investment, have the potential to become mutually reinforcing.

Solar energy. Many LICs have substantial potential for the generation of solar power that could provide a sustainable pathway to close the sizeable energy deficits in these countries (ESMAP 2020; Ndubuisi and Avenyo 2024). For example, in almost all LICs, long-term daily photovoltaic power potential averages exceed 4.5 kilowatt hours per installed kilowatt peak (kWh/kWp)—a measure of the average daily energy produced by a solar panel system per unit of peak capacity. By

---

[12] The Guided Trade Initiative is an interim solution to kick-start meaningful trade among interested State Parties that have met the minimum requirements for commencing trade under the Agreement, to test the readiness of the private sector, and to test the operational, institutional, legal and trade policy environment under the AfCFTA.

FIGURE 4.12 The evolution of key macroeconomic variables around commodity discoveries

Oil and gas discoveries are associated with modest increases in primary government spending and real GDP growth among LICs today. Although mineral discoveries have been associated with a modest surge in primary government expenditure, the increase in real GDP growth is insignificant, suggesting an inability to exploit broad economic benefits of these natural resource endowments.

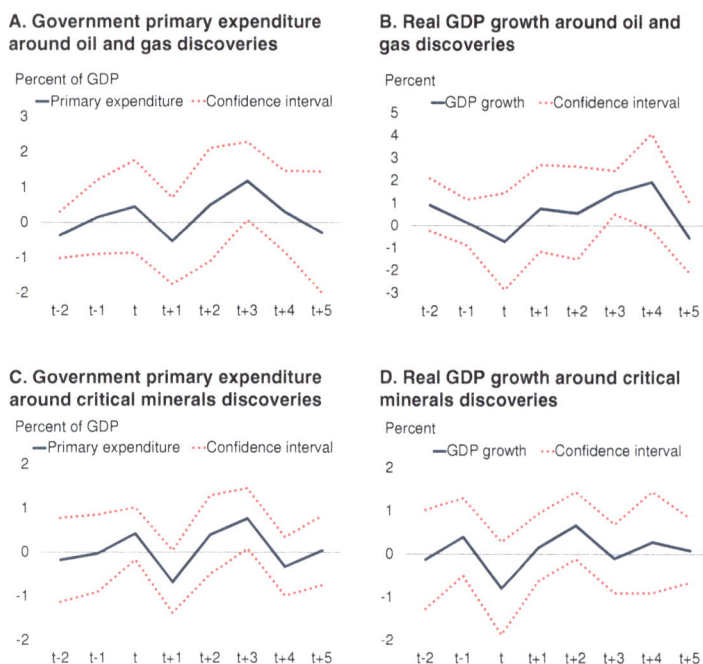

A. Government primary expenditure around oil and gas discoveries

B. Real GDP growth around oil and gas discoveries

C. Government primary expenditure around critical minerals discoveries

D. Real GDP growth around critical minerals discoveries

Sources: Cust, Rivera-Ballesteros, and Mihalyi (2021); International Monetary Fund; Minex Consulting (database); World Bank.

Note: Giant oil and gas field discoveries are defined as those with estimated ultimate recovery (EUR) reserves greater than or equal to 500 million barrels of oil equivalent. Critical minerals are identified as useful in renewable energy technology following World Bank (2020e, 2023e). Four base metals are included in this list: copper, lead, nickel, and zinc. GDP = gross domestic product; LIC = low-income country.

A.-D. The solid blue lines show the point estimates. The dotted red lines show the 90 percent confidence bands. The underlying panel regressions are based on 25 LICs.

and smooth import access to inputs such as solar panels and inverters—could unlock this solar potential and drive down energy costs in LICs. Africa is currently home to only about 1 percent of installed solar PV capacity. By 2030, solar energy is expected to become the dominant source of electricity in Africa, with the potential to contribute 15 to 30 percent of the continent's total electricity generation, primarily because of its abundant solar resources and cost-effectiveness compared to other sources (IEA 2022b). In turn, lower input costs could enhance firm competitiveness and help raise living standards, while susceptibility to international energy price shocks could also be attenuated.

Oil and gas resources. Over the past few years, several low-income countries have discovered sizable oil and gas deposits. Out of 26 LICs, six have had at least one significant oil and /or gas discovery since 1980. The median net present value of the discovery for the period 1980-2020 was 3.9 percent of GDP among today's LICs and 2.8 percent among LTMs. In the past, resource discoveries have supported LIC graduation to middle-income status, with surges of foreign direct investment catalyzing growth in the short run (Toews and Vézina 2017; World Bank 2015). However, countries that used natural resource wealth to achieve higher levels of development over the long term tended to have strong institutional frameworks, with growth disappointments otherwise often following resource discoveries (Cust and Mihalyi 2017). The discovery of natural resources can substantially raise public expectations. In some LICs commodity discoveries have been followed by a deterioration in fiscal positions, with increases in government expenditure, fiscal deficits, and debt (Addison and Roe 2018).

The short-run effects of giant oil and gas discoveries can be investigated by observing how key macroeconomic variables evolved around such events (see annex 4.2 for methodological details). An increase in primary government expenditure follows giant oil and gas discoveries in LICs (figure 4.12.A).[13] Oil and gas discoveries are associated

contrast, some large EMDEs including Brazil, China, and India are assessed as having only mid-range potential (3.4 to 4.5 kWh/kWp). At present, infrastructure shortfalls and low institutional capacity mean comparatively little solar energy is produced in LICs. However, solar-generating capacity can be installed at localized scale in a comparatively decentralized manner, utilizing mature technologies and relatively limited financing. As such, the barriers to broad adoption in LICs may be lower than for many other low-carbon energy technologies.

Appropriate policies—including those that support grid build-out, energy storage solutions

_____

[13] The study investigated impacts on primary government expenditure in a context of low-quality investment data for LICs.

with a modest and short-lived increase in LIC real GDP growth three years after the discovery (figure 4.12.B). Most of the investment in the oil and gas sectors occurs with imported goods and services (Addison and Roe 2018). These results are consistent with the literature that evaluated similar short-run effects in larger samples (Arezki, Ramey, and Sheng 2017). The lead times between discovery and production in LICs can also stretch across many years, in some instances accounting for the weak and delayed growth impacts (Arezki, Ramey, and Sheng 2017; Khan et al. 2016). Harnessing natural resource wealth to drive economic transformation in LIC with persistent effects today will likely require adjustments to structural, fiscal, and monetary policies to foster the transformation of resource rents into wealth-generating assets (Cust and Zeufack 2023).

Base metals and minerals. The energy transition could deliver significant economic dividends for LICs, with increased demand for metals and minerals providing new opportunities for growth and transformation (Andreonia and Avenyo 2023; IEA 2022a). The decarbonization and global energy transition requires substantial amounts of metals and minerals—including cobalt, copper, lithium, and nickel—that are critical to the generation and storage of renewable energy (World Bank 2023e). Some of the largest known deposits of such minerals can be found in LICs. For example, the Democratic Republic of Congo has the largest known reserves of cobalt, accounting for more than 50 percent of the world total, while Guinea boasts 24 percent of global bauxite reserves (Andreoni and Avenyo 2023). Although not currently major lithium producers, the Democratic Republic of Congo and Mali have substantial, yet-to-be-explored lithium deposits (IMF 2024e). Overall, LICs account for more than 60 percent and 50 percent of the known global reserves of cobalt and graphite respectively —two of the minerals that are essential components in many of today's rapidly growing clean energy technologies, but less than 3 percent of current production.

Over recent decades, mineral discoveries have been associated with an increase in primary government expenditure (figure 4.12.C). However, there has not been any systematic relationship between mineral discoveries and real GDP growth (figure 4.12.D). That LICs don't experience growth spurts after giant discoveries of natural resources points to missed opportunities. Current approaches to ownership, governance, transparency, taxation, and investment are likely not configured to provide broad benefits to domestic economies (Ericsson, Löf, and Löf 2020). LICs have the opportunity, however, to better develop metals processing industries, and institute regulatory reforms to maximize the development potential of profitable resource sectors (IMF 2024e). Significant structural changes—such as diversification into downstream and more technologically enabled industries—may be necessary if LICs are to reap sustained benefits from mineral wealth (Andreonia and Avenyob 2023; Karkare and Medinilla 2023).

Policy priorities

There are many challenges that merit urgent policy focus in LICs. However, LIC status is also synonymous with limited resources. As such, prioritization is key, as is recognition of interrelatedness of reforms. If the rate of graduation from LIC to middle-income picks up in coming decades, it will be primarily because national policy makers succeed in creating the conditions for growth. This is likely to require policies focused on catalyzing investment, lifting labor productivity, and improving macroeconomic resilience and governance.

Yet, how these policies are conceived and implemented across countries will depend on widely differing circumstances that mandate tailored solutions. For countries embroiled in conflict, success in reforms will first require attaining at least relative peace and stability. For LICs in debt distress, building fiscal space is paramount. For still other LICs, curbing the volatility that can come with commodity dependence may be key. At the same time, LICs face a range of obstacles to growth the resolution of which will require increased collaboration with, and support from, the international community.

Cross-cutting national policy priorities

Increasing investment. Crafting policies that support a more investment-intensive economy has historically been central to driving growth from low-income levels (World Bank 2024b). Indeed, almost all the drivers of future prosperity in LICs—including human capital development, job creation, infrastructure development, technological advances, and adaptation to climate change — will require much-increased levels of investment. At graduation, the average investment-to-GDP ratio in LTMs was about 5 percentage points higher than recent levels in LICs (figure 4.13.A). While there is no single recipe to deliver rapid investment growth, the conditions that preceded previous EMDE investment accelerations can offer a useful starting point.

In the past, EMDE investment accelerations were more likely to take root when institutional quality is high, and the real exchange rate is competitive (World Bank 2024j). They were often preceded by improvements in fiscal positions and trade liberalization. The adoption or lowering of inflation targets has significantly raised the chances of entering an investment acceleration. These patterns suggest LIC governments should put high priority on bolstering macroeconomic stability, improving institutional quality, and furthering trade integration.

Large increases in private investment often come at the same time that public investment is rising. In part, this reflects that public goods—such as education and healthcare—can raise private investment returns. In LICs, public investment is limited by fiscal constraints, but projects with high potential returns may encourage private investment, suggesting they should be prioritized within sustainable spending envelopes (Eden and Kraay 2014). LICs can also attenuate fiscal constraints that hold back public investment by generating higher revenues through measures to broaden the tax base, increasing the efficiency of spending—including by winding down regressive subsidies—and improving debt management practices (Mawejje 2024a).

LICs could also get more from constrained investment budgets by seeking to improve the quality of investment. The outcomes yielded by public investment can be enhanced by strengthening capacities for project identification, appraisal, preparation, implementation, monitoring, and evaluation. These pillars of public investment management can help to ensure that projects are both financially and economically viable, lowering fiscal risks and increasing the likelihood of securing anticipated economic returns (Adarov, Clements, and Jalles 2024; Adarov and Panizza 2024).

Improving governance and institutions. Enhancing institutions is a multidimensional challenge but is critical to enabling sustained improvements in living standards in LICs. Bearing down on corruption and improving security and the rule of law are necessary to improving the business environment, fostering capital formation and entrepreneurship. At the same time, gradually building public sector capacity—regarding the provision of public services and regulatory oversight, for example—can enhance the state's perceived legitimacy, reduce policy uncertainty, and improve prospects for delivering necessary fiscal reforms. Most LICs will not establish strong institutions by international standards in the near term—and much improvement in institutions tends to occur during growth spurts, underlining the feedback loops between institutional quality and growth. Nevertheless, reversing outright declines in institutional standards is essential if other growth-enhancing reforms, such as greater infrastructure investment, are to succeed (Zergawu, Walle, and Giménez-Gómez 2020).

As to specific policies, digitalizing public sector processes and data could build capacity while also facilitating improved monitoring and transparency—for example, regarding such issues as government procurement (Santiso 2022). Fostering financial inclusion and electronic payments can help improve financial security for businesses and lessen the use of cash for official functions, which may have the benefit of reducing bribery. Increased resources for public sector auditing can disincentivize corruption, but auditors themselves must be sufficiently independent (Olken and Pande 2012). The governance, regulatory oversight, and management incentives of state-owned enterprises merit special attention, given their roles in providing essential services and privileged closeness to governments. Enhanced legal protection for media freedoms can increase political accountability, and thereby representation, buttressing longer-term political stability.

Increasing productivity in agriculture and services. Successful structural transformation in LICs will require much-improved agricultural productivity. In addition, it is nearly certain that the services sector will remain a larger source of employment than the industrial sector for the foreseeable future, even if some LICs overcome concerns regarding premature industrialization. Policies to raise productivity in promising areas of agriculture and services sectors therefore warrant priority. Agricultural productivity-oriented reforms could include improving access to fertilizer and credit, ensuring robust land tenure rights for small farmers, and encouraging crop diversification, including through extension programs.

Fertilizer usage tends to be much lower in LICs than in other EMDEs (figure 4.13.B). Given the evidence of high returns from marginal fertilizer usage in low-income settings, there is a strong case for policy intervention to encourage farmers to adopt fertilizer use (Duflo, Kremer, Robinson 2011). That said, the design of any input subsidy ought to support market development, avoid regressive outcomes, and be calibrated to institutional realities, including risks of illicit diversion. Prioritizing credit access and educational extension programs has been found to bolster the adoption of new crop varieties, which can diversify output, and boost resilience and profits (Ruzzante, Labarta, and Bilton 2021). Where property rights are weak, improving land tenure rights for farmers can incentivize investment, benefitting productivity and incomes (Lawry et al. 2017).

There are several areas of skills and infrastructure development that can help boost productivity in services. Infrastructure to support digitalization—including affordable electricity and remote internet access—can be labor-augmenting with

FIGURE 4.13 National policy priorities

To upgrade growth prospects, LICs will likely need to lift investment-to-GDP ratios closer to levels in LTMs at graduation to middle-income status. Increase used of fertilizer could improve productivity in LIC agriculture, which remains the largest sector by employment. Reduced conflict is essential if development prospects in LICs are to brighten. History shows that LTMs that brought civil conflicts to a durable close experienced sustained higher growth.

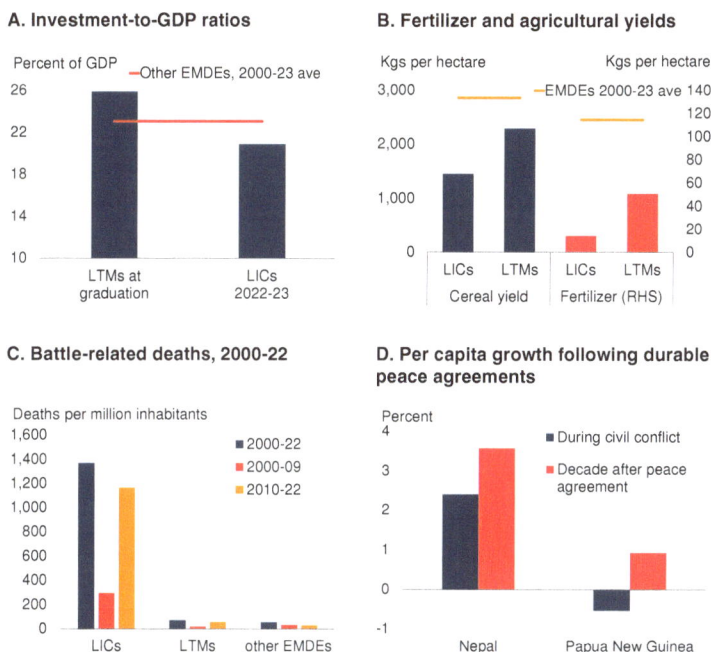

A. Investment-to-GDP ratios

B. Fertilizer and agricultural yields

C. Battle-related deaths, 2000-22

D. Per capita growth following durable peace agreements

Sources: International Monetary Fund; Uppsala Conflict Data Program; WDI (database); World Bank.
Note: EMDEs = emerging market and developing economies; LICs = low-income countries; LTMs = LICs turned into middle-income countries; other EMDEs = emerging market and developing economies excluding LICs.
A. Bar for LTMs indicates the average investment-to-GDP ratio in graduation year. Where countries moved from LIC to middle-income more than once, the final graduation year is used.
B. Bars reflect cereal yields per hectare of harvested land, and fertilizer consumption per hectare of arable land. For LICs, data reflect the sample average in 2022; for LTMs, data reflect the sample average for the respective year of each LTM's graduation.
C. Battle-related deaths per thousand people calculated as the best estimate of battle-related deaths during a time period, divided by the population in the final year of that period.
D. Dates for conflicts are as follows; Nepal, 1996 to 2006; Papua New Guinea, 1987-2001. Dates for the subsequent decade are: Nepal, 2007 to 2016; Papua New Guinea 2002 to 2011.

respect to the productivity and employment of low-skilled workers (Hjort and Tian 2014). Educational quality may be especially critical for services-led growth because employment in higher-value services sectors is likely to be more dependent on the development of transferable skills—such as ICT and linguistic skills—relative to labor-intensive manufacturing. At a broader level, policies supporting sustainable urbanization, such as the development of transportation and sanitation services, can enable urban agglomeration benefits and combat congestion costs

(Grover, Lall, and Timmis 2021). Importantly, while such policies could support productivity growth in services, they can also lay the groundwork for stronger manufacturing sectors.

Unlocking women's economic potential. Economy-wide productivity can also be enhanced by promoting policies that address barriers to female labor force participation and women's labor income. These can include allocating greater resources and higher priority to female education and skills development (Agte et al. 2024). Eliminating gender gaps in the labor market enables broad productivity improvements by facilitating human capital development and a more efficient allocation of talent in the economy (Hsieh et al. 2019). Such policies can support structural transformation, as well as raise total labor supply (Dinkelman and Ngai 2022). Moreover, over the longer term, the lower fertility rates that tend to come with increased female education and labor force involvement can contribute to ushering in a demographic dividend that can help to foster capital accumulation and far-reaching improvements in living standards (Wodon et al. 2020).

Building resilience to macroeconomic shocks. Shocks in LICs are more likely to have long-term adverse consequences reflecting scarring from the knock-on implications of such issues as child malnutrition and sovereign debt distress. The interaction of external shocks with pre-existing fragility also heightens the risk of such extreme outcomes as conflict (Patcharaporn, Castrovillari, and Mineyama 2023). Policies that enhance resilience to economic shocks are therefore key to improving growth and graduation prospects.

Economic diversification can cushion volatility related to global market fluctuations and support resilient, sustainable and inclusive growth (Deléchat et al. 2024). Credible oversight institutions and fiscal frameworks can buttress resilience by helping to build fiscal space and creditor confidence. Robust fiscal and debt management architectures reduce the chances of financial stress and enhance prospects for expeditiously resolving debt-related strains (Rivetti 2021). Fiscal rules can reduce fiscal policy

volatility and the procyclicality of government spending in LICs (Dessus, Diaz-Sanchez, and Varoudakis 2016; Mawejje and Odhiambo 2024). Establishing medium-term budgeting frameworks helps make fiscal rules work and enhances transparency.

To bolster macroeconomic stability, LICs with sufficient institutional capacity can prioritize transitioning to inflation targeting. Currently, very few LIC central banks are full inflation targetters, although several emphasize various inflation measures to guide policy. For other LICs operating with fixed exchange ranges—some within currency unions—it is critical that pegs are commensurate with domestic productivity and backed by prudent fiscal and reserves management policies. By reducing crisis risk and uncertainty, greater macroeconomic stability should serve to attract greater private capital inflows, for example into infrastructure investment, where private participation is low.

Context-specific national policy priorities

Peace and stability. For LICs in fragile and conflict-affected situations, greater peace and stability are necessary conditions for delivering broader reforms. Conflicts can also have significant adverse spillovers to neighboring countries, which compounds aggregate human and economic costs. In LICs, conflicts are widespread—battle-related deaths since 2000 dwarf those recorded in better off countries (figure 4.13.C).

The roots of armed conflict are complex and context-specific but can encompass factors such as a dearth of economic opportunities, inequality, competition over resources—including commodity rents—and economic shocks that threaten livelihoods (Asongu and Nwachukwu 2016; Blattman and Miguel 2010; Vesco et al. 2020). As such, policies promoting inclusive growth in LICs should improve prospects for peace. For example, the benefits of climate adaptation and infrastructure investment may extend to reducing conflict, because climate-related shocks are more likely to tip fragile economies into conflict (Burke et al. 2024). Employment programs targeting ex-combatants may attenuate the risks of resurgent conflict by lessening economic incentives to take up arms (Blattman and Annan 2015). And, in commodity-dependent environments, economic diversification and improved governance over resource extraction may lessen likelihood of fighting for control of resource-rich areas (Berman et al 2017). In addition, social structures characterized by majority-minority ethnic or religious groupings may exacerbate civil conflict risks by entrenching the political dominance of the majority and generating socio-economic exclusion (Collier and Hoeffler 2004; Denny and Walter 2014). Credibly committing to the political representation of minority groups and to safeguards preventing the excessive concentration of political power—for example through constitutional provisions—may diminish such risks.

Resolving long-running conflicts is a daunting challenge for many LICs. All successful efforts at conflict resolution are specific to the situation, but reaching peace has commonly required extensive negotiations, the credibility of which can potentially be bolstered by engagement with neutral facilitators such as international bodies, foreign governments, or non-government organizations. Peace settlements are more likely to endure when they are inclusive, for example by ensuring political representation and the reintegration into society of hostile factions (Call 2012). Case studies of two LTMs that exited civil conflicts without relapsing—Nepal and Papua New Guinea—serve to illustrate these factors:

- *Nepal:* Nepal's civil war ran from 1996-2006, ending with the Comprehensive Peace Accord of November 2006. The agreement established an interim consensus-based government that included former Maoist rebels and other political parties. The interim government gave way to a coalition government following elections 18 months later. The Nepal army, having fought the war, deferred to the political process (Falch and Miklian 2008). Provisions in the accord specified joint responsibility for maintaining peace and prioritized the disarming and rehabilitation of insurgents. International actors such as the

United Nations supported the process. Implementation of the accord has not been without challenges, but Nepal has remained at peace, with regular elections. Nepal's per capita growth rate picked up substantially after 2006, and the country attained middle-income status in 2019 (figure 4.13.D).

- *Papua New Guinea:* The Bougainville Civil War—a secessionist conflict between the government of Papua New Guinea and the Bougainville Revolutionary Army—lasted from 1988 to the late 1990s. The initial cessation of fighting followed peace talks in 1997 that reached a consensus on disarming local forces, withdrawing government forces from the island of Bougainville, and establishing an unarmed monitoring group of neutral observers. The subsequent Bougainville Peace Agreement, signed in 2001, codified regional autonomy and a weapons disposal plan, and laid down parameters for a non-binding independence referendum. With GDP per capita collapsing after 1994, Papua New Guinea became a LIC in 2001. Although the country still faces formidable governance challenges, the end of the conflict proved durable, and growth picked up thereafter. Papua New Guinea regained middle-income status in 2008.

Creating fiscal space. For the roughly half of LICs in or close to debt distress, creating fiscal space is critical to enabling other reforms and crucial for lessening macroeconomic risks. Otherwise, budget constraints and high sovereign risk premiums mean such countries are unlikely to meaningfully raise investment. Similarly, large interest payments and debt redemptions will squeeze out spending on education and healthcare. Moreover, negative shocks could quickly morph into debt crises (Kose et al. 2021; World Bank 2024k). Such circumstances necessitate a multi-pronged approach to generating fiscal space that involves changes in spending and revenue generation. For example, on the spending side, regressive subsidies, including for those for fossil fuels, can be phased out in favor of pro-poor spending. A tight focus on the efficiency of government spending, including bearing down on corruption and curbing sometimes excessive public sector wage bills, can generate stronger economic returns (Mawejje 2024a). On the revenue side, base broadening measures and strategies to promote formalization—such as streamlining cumbersome regulatory hurdles to business expansion—are likely more promising than further taxing small bases of activity. At the same time, investing in improved tax administration can yield large returns (Dom et al. 2022).

Improving natural resources governance. For commodity-exporting LICs, strengthening institutions for natural resource governance is especially important. Resource dependent LICs, and particularly energy exporters, have had disappointing growth outcomes over the past decade. These countries are vulnerable to recurring terms-of-trade shocks, which, because of pre-existing structural vulnerabilities, including weak institutions of governance, poor business environments, and limited human capital, result in persistently low growth outcomes (IMF 2024b).

The prudent management of resource revenues can be enhanced by anchoring fiscal and monetary discipline. Credible and well-designed policy frameworks—including utilization of mechanisms such as fiscal rules, medium-term expenditure frameworks, and stabilization funds—can reduce the procyclicality of fiscal policy, build fiscal space, and strengthen policy outcomes (Arroyo Marioli, Fatas, and Vasishtha 2023; World Bank 2024e). These can also help LICs improve budget management, including management of revenue windfalls. While prudent use of natural resources can drive diversification and transformation in current LICs, the window to take advantage of fossil fuels faces strong headwinds from the climate transition and rapid development of green technologies. Reserves of fossil fuels will soon become stranded assets (Addison and Roe 2018). For countries with rich reserves of green minerals—such as cobalt, lithium and copper—improving current approaches to their extraction and revenue management, including transparency in the allocation of mining rights and enforcement of labor standards, can help drive greater and more inclusive economic benefits.

It is also important that natural resource dependent economies develop robust monetary frameworks able to withstand terms-of-trade volatility. In fixed exchange rate regimes, this necessitates holding substantial foreign exchange reserves to bolster confidence in the system's nominal anchor—which, in turn, requires the institutional capacity to ensure the prudent management of such reserves. Alternatively, where financial markets are sufficiently developed, increased exchange rate flexibility can help buffer economic volatility generated by sudden commodity price movements.

Global policies

The international community can play a proactive role in helping LICs accelerate growth and development. The scale of investment and capacity-building required to meet urgent development challenges is simply too great without increased international support that is well-coordinated and provides tailored financial and technical assistance. Through international efforts LICs can be supported to take advantage of structural growth opportunities, while increasing resilience to a wide range of shocks.

Increasing concessional financing. By some estimates, LICs will require annual investment of 8 percent of GDP through 2030 to meet development objectives, including climate goals (figure 4.14.A). Investment needs are estimated to be particularly high in Sub-Saharan Africa, and those needs likely have grown on account of pandemic-related scarring (Rozenberg and Fay 2019; Benedek et al. 2021). Without greater concessional financing, LICs will lack the resources required to finance such investments at the necessary pace and scale. Some LICs already face liquidity challenges, with interest payments taking a growing share of domestic revenues. More generally, to put in place the scale of programs required to address chronic shortfalls in meeting the sustainable development goals, LICs have a pressing need for steady, predictable, and low-cost financial flows.

The financing challenges in LICs are compounded by declining aid disbursements from the international community. Net official development assistance (ODA), which includes disbursements of loans made on concessional terms, has declined since 2020 by 5 percentage points to 7 percent of GDP in 2022—its lowest level in two decades. Grants from the International Development Association (IDA) have grown significantly over the past decade and have more than doubled since 2015 to 1.2 percent of GDP in 2022 (figure 4.14.B). However, given the large and growing needs, IDA grants will be insufficient even with recent enhancements. Greater global cooperation is essential to help the world's poorest countries restore sustainable fiscal positions that can support their long-term development aspirations. The international community and multilateral development banks should also continue to seek to catalyze financing for LICs, working with the private sector to mobilize additional resources (Chrimes et al. 2024; IEG 2023). This could include mobilizing higher inflows from private creditors, including by providing incentives through credit enhancements, and liability management operations, such as debt-for-development swaps.

Providing debt relief. LIC fiscal positions have weakened significantly over the past decade and many LICs are already in or at high risk of debt distress. A rise in exposure to non-concessional external debt has increased fiscal risks (figure 4.14.C). The increased exposure of LICs to non-Paris Club official creditors and commercial creditors also poses coordination challenges for debt resolutions. For debt that is owed to foreigners, denominated in foreign currency, and adjudicated by foreign courts, default and debt restructuring can become a country's only option—one that usually imposes high long-term costs (Kose et al. 2022). Without quick action, LICs could end up with a situation similar to the 1980s and 1990s when it took decades to solve their debt crisis (Kose et al. 2021). Where debt relief initiatives have been successful, they have sometimes been associated with subsequent investment and growth accelerations in LICs (box 4.1; World Bank 2024e).

For LICs in, or at high risk of, debt distress, providing debt relief should be a high priority.

FIGURE 4.14 Global policy priorities

LICs have large investment needs for resilient and green growth paths and to meet the annual costs of adaptation to climate change. Grants to LICs have recently been falling, with faster declines since 2020, even as International Development Association financing has increased. Because they lack alternative financing means, LICs have taken on much more non-concessional external debt as a share of total external debt since 2000.

A. Investment needs for a resilient and low-carbon growth path

B. Grant financing in LICs

C. Composition of external debt

D. Climate adaptation costs

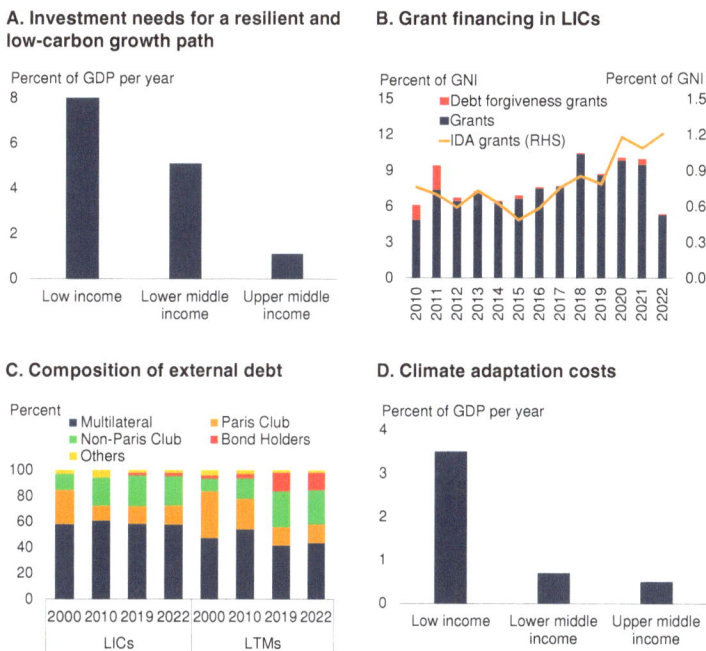

Sources: International Debt Statistics (database); World Bank (2022d); UNEP (2023); WDI (database); World Bank.
Note: GNI = gross national income; LICs = low-income countries; LTMs = LICs turned into middle-income countries. A. Estimates of the annual investment needs to build resilience to climate change and put countries on track to reduce emissions by 70 percent by 2050. Depending on data availability, estimates include investment needs on transport, energy, water, urban adaptations, industry, and landscape.
B. Grants are defined as legally binding commitments allocating funds for disbursement without any requirement for repayment. Data are on a disbursement basis and cover flows from all bilateral and multilateral donors. International Development Association (IDA) grants are net disbursements of grants from IDA.
C. GDP-weighted average of public and publicly guaranteed external debt. "Others" includes multiple lenders. Based on 24 LICs and 41 LTMs.
D. Total undiscounted annual costs of climate change adaptation for the period up to 2030.

There have been several initiatives to do this. In November 2020, following their Debt Service Suspension Initiative (DSSI), the G-20 countries announced the Common Framework to provide debt treatment for DSSI-eligible countries with unsustainable debts (IMF 2021).[14] While the Common Framework initially struggled with creditor coordination and implementation delays, recent developments suggest it is becoming more

---

[14] The Debt Service Suspension Initiative (DSSI) offered the suspension of debt payment obligations on official sector debts for the poorest countries to allow them to create fiscal space to respond to the COVID-19 pandemic.

effective, helped in part by the creation of the Global Sovereign Debt Roundtable (World Bank 2024i).[15] Within the Common Framework, Chad was the first country to conclude an agreement with its official creditors in 2022. In 2023, Zambia became the second country to conclude a debt restructuring agreement, reaching a milestone agreement with bilateral creditors, including China, with a subsequent formal agreement with its sovereign bondholders in March 2024. Ethiopia and Ghana also achieved progress under the Common Framework (World Bank 2024j).

Processes outside the Common Framework are also making progress, as evidenced by agreements on Sri Lanka's debt. Still, timelines remain beyond the typical time frame observed in the past, which hurts both the debtor and its creditors. Where applicable, in particular for Common Framework cases, the timeline to form an official creditor committee could be shortened, to take the best advantage of a format that ensures the efficient sharing of information with all participants. This would also help expedite communication and coordination with private creditors and accelerate their own restructuring processes.

Accelerating climate adaptation. LICs are unusually vulnerable to climate change because of their geographic locations, dependence on agriculture, capacity constraints, and limited macro-financial buffers (IMF 2024a). Without adequate mitigation measures, climate change could precipitate GDP losses of 7 to 12 percentage points by 2050 in some African LICs—higher than other EMDEs (World Bank 2022d). Well-coordinated global efforts are needed to finance the investment required to increase resilience and adaptation capacity. Annual adaptation costs in LICs have been estimated at 3.5 percent of GDP, on average, compared to 0.7 percent in lower-middle-income countries (figure 4.14.D; UNEP 2023). Such needs amount to many times the

United Nations' estimates of current flows of international adaptation finance.

Given the scale of investment required to mitigate climate impacts, LICs will need to mobilize resources at unprecedented scale. However, domestic resources will not be enough and many LICs have weak fiscal positions. It is therefore important that additional climate finance flows take account of any associated fiscal risks. The international community, including multilateral development banks, can work with the private sector to mobilize additional resources at viable costs. Access to a larger pool of concessional financing and grants, including through the IDA, will be vital to supporting climate action in low-income climate vulnerable countries (Bhattacharya et al. 2024).

LICs can also play a crucial role in the global community efforts to achieve broader climate goals by providing metals and minerals critical for the green transition. LICs account for less than 1 percent of global carbon dioxide emissions, but they have significant endowments of such green metals and minerals as lithium and cobalt. Leveraging these resources will require the support of the international community, both to mobilize investment and to develop the institutional architecture that is supportive of long-term growth and helps avoid the so-called resource curse.[16] Ample potential for solar could enable some LICs to model comparatively low-emissions and equitable development pathways without implying any trade-off for the pace of improvements in living standards.

Improving global trade and investment climate. Recent widespread emphasis on industrial policies in advanced economies, a global increase in protectionist measures, and sluggish global trade growth do not portend well for trade-led development (World Bank 2024c). Geopolitical risks have also intensified and threaten more regular disruptions to trade networks and supply chains (World Bank 2024e). To reinvigorate trade

---

[15] Cochaired by the Group of Twenty (G-20), the IMF, and the World Bank, this group includes official creditors, large private creditors, and debtors. It aims to build consensus on debt issues, focusing on such technical matters as restructuring timelines, information sharing, domestic debt treatment (including holdings by nonresidents), assessing comparability of treatment, engaging with credit rating agencies, and suspending debt service (World Bank 2024k; 2024l).

[16] Resource curse refers to the phenomenon of countries with an abundance of natural resources having inferior economic outcomes than resource poor countries (see for example: Sachs and Warner 2001; van der Ploeg 2011).

growth and guard against trade fragmentation, the international community should place greater emphasis on a consistent rules-based multilateral trade system to reduce trade policy uncertainty. At the multilateral level, measures are needed to reinstate and reform the dispute settlement system, and enhance transparency, especially regarding distortions from industrial policies (IMF et al. 2022). Countries could also resume efforts to expand and deepen formal trade agreements.

Landlocked LICs can take advantage of opportunities to deepen regional trade by facilitating regional integration and eliminating trade barriers—as the African Continental Free Trade Area aspires to do (World Bank 2020d). Deepening trade can have additional benefits that include reducing food insecurity, spurring investment, raising productivity, reducing uncertainty, and helping to counteract conflict and violence (IMF 2023a; Martin, Mayer, and Thoenig 2008). The potential benefits from trade in LICs would be enhanced by infrastructure integration and improved domestic business environments, including streamlined customs procedures (Fontagné et al. 2023; Okumu et al. forthcoming). International support in these areas can be enhanced.

Providing technical assistance. How well policy reforms achieve their objectives depends on consistent implementation over years. While some LICs have made progress in many reform areas, including the use of technology in government processes, gains have been uneven. In many cases, implementing the kinds of reforms necessary to improve the policy environment requires substantially increased state capacity. Otherwise, shortcomings in technical and administrative processes may hinder otherwise promising reform agendas. The international community has a critical role to play in supporting LICs through tailored technical assistance and capacity-building interventions. Technical assistance can also support LICs to effectively absorb and utilize additional resources.

Finally, it is important to recognize that today's LICs are data-poor environments in the grip of extremely complex challenges. In that context, judgments over how to best address development gaps—for example, extreme poverty, agricultural productivity, and the scant reach of public services—must be flexible and informed by rigorous on-the-ground empirical assessments. Resourcing such work in today's LICs and similar settings is essential to building a knowledge base that enables the most effective utilization of scarce resources (Banerjee and Duflo 2011; Duflo 2020).

Conclusion

Reducing extreme poverty depends on progress among LICs. Since 2000, substantial strides have been made in raising living standards in EMDEs that are not low-income, including 42 LTMs. Even though growth momentum among middle-income countries has ebbed since the 2010s, most EMDEs are making steady, if unspectacular, gains in per-capita income. In contrast, LICs as a whole have seen feeble growth for 15 years, with structural transformation stalling and institutional quality in decline.

Diagnosing the difficulties facing LICs requires recognizing fundamental differences relative to past cohorts of low-income countries that have graduated to middle-income status. Today's LICs have long been poorer than LTMs. They have less physical and human capital, larger agricultural sectors, and higher poverty levels than LTMs did when they were low-income in 2000. On top of that, they receive less development assistance per person than their LTM peers.

For most LICs, recent trends will not deliver the income gains needed to break out of low-income status any time soon. Less than a quarter of LICs appear on course to graduate by 2050. Improving this outlook will require sustained investment and productivity increases of the type that have only previously occurred in LICs during distinct growth accelerations. Among countries at the lowest income levels, such accelerations occurred following reforms that increased market orientation and channeled resources into capital accumulation, backed by comparatively capable governance.

LICs will need to overcome daunting obstacles, some of which are particular to their generation. Perhaps most important, many LICs need to end recurrent conflicts—a tall order. After the COVID-19 pandemic and subsequent global shocks, LICs' fiscal positions are also precarious. As climate change escalates, LICs face outsized impacts. And, clustered together, they lack the geographical good fortune of wealthy neighbors at a time when global potential growth is declining, and trade fragmentation and geopolitical tensions are escalating.

While the challenges are severe, if they are girded by greater domestic peace and stability, LICs possess endowments that could catalyze growth. Resource rents, properly managed, could be invested in infrastructure, education, and diversification. Ample solar energy could improve competitiveness. Against a backdrop of stronger security, tourism could take off, while low levels of trade openness imply potentially greater gains from trade integration. Such beneficial shifts could be underpinned by a sizeable demographic dividend if education and skills training are improved for swelling LIC labor forces.

If more LICs are to graduate in the coming years, it will principally be because of actions taken in LICs themselves. More LICs will have attained sustained peace. Domestic policy makers will have succeeded in driving up investment growth and delivering institutional reforms, while avoiding economic and governance missteps. However, to help LICs move the needle in several key areas, the international community has a critical role to play. LICs will need the breathing space afforded by increased concessional financing, augmented by technical assistance and, where appropriate, debt relief. In particular, the global community could shoulder more of the burden to prevent climate change from derailing LICs' development. Finally, the global community can re-embrace a fit-for-purpose, rules-based trading system, and not subject LICs to disorderly global fragmentation.

ANNEX 4.1 Identifying growth accelerations

Following Gootjes et al. (2024), growth accelerations are identified as periods in which growth of real GDP per capita in a country exceeds the following country-specific metric for at least eight years:

$$\varphi_i(\mu,\sigma) = \frac{1}{2}(\overline{\mu_{GDPPC_i}} + \overline{\sigma_{GDPPC_i}}) \qquad (4.1.1)$$

where $\overline{\mu_{GDPPC_i}}$ is the historical average real per capita growth rate for country i, and $\overline{\sigma_{GDPPC_i}}$ is the standard deviation of per capita growth over the same period. As such, the metric accounts for long-term trends in growth in real GDP per capita and its volatility. Both the average and the mean exclude the maximum and minimum observations to limit the impact of outliers.[17]

The growth spell's eventual end is identified as the year in which per-capita GDP growth falls below the country-specific metric. However, to avoid a temporary growth dip being identified prematurely as an acceleration's end, a growth episode is considered as ongoing if average growth in the period around—and including—the dip remains above the metric. To prevent cyclical rebounds from being identified growth accelerations, episodes are excluded if the level of real GDP per capita in the final year of the acceleration is lower than in any year prior to the start of the growth spell.

ANNEX 4.2 Resource discovery event studies

The event analyses in this chapter consider the evolution of two key macroeconomic variables: real GDP growth and primary government expenditure (percentage of GDP) around significant resource discoveries. The analysis builds on Kose et al. (2022) who studied the evolution of fiscal space around a set of defined events. The following regression model is estimated:

$$\nu_{i,t} = \alpha_i + \sum_{j=-k}^{p} \beta_j event_{i,t+j} + \gamma_t + \varepsilon_{i,t} \qquad (4.2.1)$$

where $\nu_{i,t}$ is a measure of each of the macroeconomic outcomes in country i and year t, and α_i is the country fixed effect. The variable *event* refers to the occurrence of an event related to the discovery of giant deposits of natural resources and is defined as a dummy taking the value of one if an event occurs in country i and year $t+j$. γ_t are time effects included to control for global factors, and $\varepsilon_{i,t}$ is the error term. Two leads and lags of the dependent variable are included to account for path dependency and control for any anticipation effects. The panel regressions are estimated with Driscol-Kraay standard errors that are robust to autocorrelation and cross-sectional dependence.

A series of coefficients, β, show the effects of adverse events over $(k+p+1)$ years, relative to other non-event years, where p is the number of post-event years included in equation (4.2.1). In this exercise, we use k = 2 and p = 5 to provide a longer horizon. This econometric exercise is not intended to uncover any causal relationships. Instead, the objective is to describe how macroeconomic variables evolve around giant resource discoveries.

Identification of resource discovery events

Oil and gas discoveries. Giant oil discoveries are identified using the data set from Cust, Mihalyi, and Rivera-Ballesteros (2021) and are defined as those with estimated ultimately recoverable reserves of at least 500 million barrels of oil equivalent. In total, 10 giant oil and gas discoveries were identified in five LICs since 1980.

Minerals discoveries. Mineral discoveries are identified using the MinEx Consulting Mineral Deposits Database. The database identifies discoveries classified by size as "Moderate," "Major," "Giant," and "Super Giant." MinEx Consulting maintains a database of more than 62,000 unique mineral deposits worldwide. This

---

[17] Countries with missing GDP data are excluded from the analysis. As a result, there are at most 20 of 26 LICs and 38 of a possible 42 LTMs (see notes to figures 4.7, 4.8, and 4.9).

includes a comprehensive list of 12,837 unique deposits that are "Moderate" in size or bigger. This includes gold, base metals, diamonds, coal, iron ore, bauxite, potash, phosphate and other deposits. In total, 141 giant mineral discoveries have been identified in 21 LICs since 1980. Three LICs (Burkina Faso, Democratic Republic of Congo, Mali) account for more than 40 percent of giant mineral discoveries in LICs since 1980.

ANNEX 4.3 Estimated impact of intense conflict on GDP per capita in LICs

Figure 4.10.B includes a range of estimates of the impact of the onset of intense conflict on GDP per capita in EMDEs after five years (that is, in year t+5, when t is the year when a conflict starts). The figure contains several estimates from past literature for country groups that have material overlap with today's LICs. In addition, the figure contains two new estimates for the effect of intense conflict in today's LICs. In the figure legend, these are labelled "LICs 25/m" and "LICs 50/m," signifying an estimate for intense conflict years—defined as 25 battle-related deaths per

million people, and another with the threshold of 50 deaths per million people.

Data on battle-related deaths are constructed from the best estimates of the Uppsala Conflict Data Program. Intense conflict is defined as starting in the first year with battle-related deaths above the threshold, following at least one year with deaths below the threshold. The following regression model is estimated:

$$
\begin{aligned}
y_{i,t+5} - y_{i,t-1} = {} & \alpha_i + \gamma_t + \Sigma_{j=1}^{3}\theta_j\Delta y_{i,t-j} \\
& + \Sigma_{j=1}^{3}\theta_j C_{i,t-j} + \beta C_{i,t} + \Sigma_{j=1}^{5}\theta_j C_{i,t+j} \\
& + \Sigma_{j=1}^{3}\theta_j D_{i,t-j} + \theta D_{i,t} + \Sigma_{j=1}^{5}\theta_j D_{i,t+j} \\
& + \varepsilon_{i,t+5}
\end{aligned}
\tag{4.3.1}
$$

where $y_{i,t}$ is log GDP per capita and $\alpha_{i,h} + \gamma_{t,h}$ are country and time fixed effects. Three lags of annual GDP growth at t are included as controls. $C_{i,t}$ is a dummy variable for the onset of intense conflict, while $D_{i,t}$ is a dummy variable representing the end of an intense conflict, defined as deaths falling below the conflict threshold for at least five consecutive years. Five leads and three lags are included for both $C_{i,t}$ and $D_{i,t}$. Figure 4.10.B depicts the β estimates, which are statistically significant at the 90 percent level for both thresholds.

TABLE 4.1 List of all LICs

	ISO code	Country Name	GNI per capita in 2000	Latest GNI per capita		ISO code	Country Name	GNI per capita in 2000	Latest GNI per capita
1	AFG	Afghanistan*		360**	14	MWI	Malawi	230	640
2	BDI	Burundi	140	230	15	NER	Niger	220	600
3	BFA	Burkina Faso	260	850	16	PRK	Korea, Dem. People's Rep.*		
4	CAF	Central African Republic	250	470	17	RWA	Rwanda	270	980
5	COD	Congo, Dem. Rep.	130	660	18	SDN	Sudan	350	990
6	ERI	Eritrea*	290		19	SLE	Sierra Leone***	140	560
7	ETH	Ethiopia	130	1,130	20	SOM	Somalia	370	610
8	GMB	Gambia, The	570	830	21	SSD	South Sudan*		
9	GNB	Guinea-Bissau	410	900	22	SYR	Syrian Arab Republic	910	
10	LBR	Liberia	190	730	23	TCD	Chad	180	710
11	MDG	Madagascar	280	530	24	TGO	Togo	430	1,030
12	MLI	Mali	280	860	25	UGA	Uganda	270	980
13	MOZ	Mozambique	330	530	26	YEM	Yemen, Rep.*	400	

Sources: WDI (database); World Bank.
Note: Gross National Income (GNI) per capita, Atlas method (current U.S. dollars). Latest year is 2023 unless stated otherwise.
*Missing data are not publicly available due to insufficient data quality.
**Data are for 2022.
***GDP data for Sierra Leone have recently been re-based and this is expected to lead to a substantial revision of the Atlas GNI series in the near future.

TABLE 4.2 List of LICs that turned into middle-income countries since 2000

	ISO code	Country Name	GNI per capita in 2000	Latest GNI per capita		ISO code	Country Name	GNI per capita in 2000	Latest GNI per capita
1	AGO	Angola	360	2,130	22	LSO	Lesotho	590	1,160
2	ARM	Armenia	640	7,330	23	MDA	Moldova	490	6,110
3	AZE	Azerbaijan	630	6,680	24	MMR	Myanmar	190	1,210
4	BEN	Benin	470	1,440	25	MNG	Mongolia	460	4,950
5	BGD	Bangladesh	430	2,860	26	MRT	Mauritania	710	2,150
6	BTN	Bhutan˙	720	3,740	27	NGA	Nigeria**		1,930
7	CIV	Côte d'Ivoire	640	2,670	28	NIC	Nicaragua	950	2,270
8	CMR	Cameroon	720	1,650	29	NPL	Nepal	220	1,370
9	COG	Congo, Rep.	560	2,470	30	PAK	Pakistan	470	1,500
10	COM	Comoros	730	1,600	31	PNG	Papua New Guinea	600	2,840
11	GEO	Georgia	790	6,680	32	SEN	Senegal	670	1,660
12	GHA	Ghana	330	2,340	33	SLB	Solomon Islands	940	2,270
13	GIN	Guinea	590	1,360	34	STP	São Tomé and Principe	480	2,480
14	GNQ	Equatorial Guinea	680	5,240	35	TJK	Tajikistan	170	1,440
15	HTI	Haiti	550	1,740	36	TLS	Timor-Leste	560	2,140
16	IDN	Indonesia	570	4,870	37	TZA	Tanzania	390	1,210
17	IND	India	440	2,540	38	UKR	Ukraine	680	5,070
18	KEN	Kenya	430	2,110	39	UZB	Uzbekistan	630	2,360
19	KGZ	Kyrgyz Republic	280	1,700	40	VNM	Viet Nam	380	4,180
20	KHM	Cambodia˙	290	2,390	41	ZMB	Zambia	350	1,320
21	LAO	Lao PDR	280	2,120	42	ZWE	Zimbabwe	360	1,740

Sources: WDI (database); World Bank.
Note: GNI per capita, Atlas method (current U.S. dollars). Latest year is 2023 unless stated otherwise.
*Bhutan and Cambodia data were provided by the respective country teams.
**Missing data are not publicly available due to insufficient data quality.

References

Abdel-Latif, H., A. C. David, R. Ouedraogo., and M. Specht. 2024. "Echoes Across Borders: Macroeconomic Spillover Effects of Conflict in Sub-Saharan African Countries." IMF Working Paper 24/100, International Monetary Fund, Washington, DC.

Acemoglu, D., and J. A. Robinson. 2013. *Why Nations Fail: The Origins of Power, Prosperity, and Poverty.* New York: Crown Currency.

Adarov, A., B. Clements, and J. T. Jalles. 2024. "Revisiting Public Investment Multipliers: Nonlinear Effects of the Business Cycle, Fiscal Space, Efficiency, and Capital Stock." Policy Research Working Paper 10954, World Bank, Washington, DC.

Adarov, A., and U. Panizza. 2024. "Public Investment Quality and Its Implications for Sovereign Risk and Debt Sustainability." Policy Research Working Paper 10877, World Bank, Washington, DC.

Addison, T., and A. Roe. eds. 2018. *Extractive Industries: The Management of Resources as a Driver of Sustainable Development.* Oxford: Oxford University Press.

Adedeji, O. S., J. Gieck-Bricco, and V. Kehayova. 2016. "Natural Disasters and Food Crises in Low Income Countries: Macroeconomic Dimensions." IMF Working Paper 16/65, International Monetary Fund, Washington, DC.

AfDB (African Development Bank Group). 2022. "Accelerating Growth in Ethiopia: Key Structural Challenges to Address." Policy Note, African Development Bank Group, Abidjan, Cote d'Ivoire.

Agte, P., O. Attanasio, P. Goldberg, A. Lakshmi Ratan, R. Pande, M. Peters, C. Troyer Moore, and F. Zilibotti. 2024. "Gender Gaps and Economic Growth: Why Haven't Women Won Globally (Yet)?" Discussion Paper 1105, Economic Growth Centre, Yale University, New Haven, CT.

Ahmed, S., and M. Cruz. 2016. "On the Impact of Demographic Change on Growth, Savings, and Poverty." Policy Research Working Paper 7805, World Bank, Washington, DC.

Alper, C. E., R. A. Morales, and F. Yang. 2017. "Monetary Policy Implementation and Volatility Transmission Along the Yield Curve: The Case of Kenya." *South African Journal of Economics* 85 (3): 455-78.

Andreoni, A., and E. Avenyo. 2023. "Critical Minerals and Routes to Diversification in Africa: Linkages,

Pulling Dynamics and Opportunities in Medium-High Tech Supply Chains." Background Paper, Economic Development in Africa Report 2023. United Nations Conference on Trade and Development, Geneva.

Arcand, J.-L., E. Berkes, and U. Panizza. 2012. "Too Much Finance?" IMF Working Paper 12/161, International Monetary Fund, Washington, DC.

Arezki, R., V. A. Ramey, and L. Sheng. 2017. "News Shocks in Open Economies: Evidence From Giant Oil Discoveries." *Quarterly Journal of Economics* 132 (1): 103-55.

Arroyo Marioli, F., A. Fatas, and G. Vasishtha. 2023. "Fiscal Policy Volatility and Growth in Emerging Markets and Developing Economies." Policy Research Working Paper 10409, World Bank, Washington, DC.

Arvis, J. F., Y. Duval, B. Shepherd, and C. Utoktham. 2016. "Trade Costs in the Developing World: 1995-2010." *World Trade Review* 15 (3): 451-74.

Asongu, S. A., and J. C. Nwachukwu. 2016. "Revolution Empirics: Predicting the Arab Spring." *Empirical Economics* 51 (2): 439-82.

Bah, E. H., and L. Fang. 2015. "Impact of The Business Environment on Output and Productivity in Africa." *Journal of Development Economics* 114: 159-71.

Balchin, N., S. Gelb, J. Kennan, H. Martin, D. W. te Velde, and C. Williams. 2016. "Developing Export-Based Manufacturing in Sub-Saharan Africa." Overseas Development Institute, London.

Banerjee, A. V., and E. Duflo. 2011. *Poor Economics: A Radical Rethinking of the Way to Fight Global Poverty.* New York: Public Affairs, Perseus Books.

Barro, R. J. 2012. "Convergence and Modernization Revisited." NBER Working Paper 18295, National Bureau of Economic Research, Cambridge, MA.

Baum, A. 2020. "Vietnam's Development Success Story and the Unfinished SDG Agenda." IMF Working Paper 20/31, International Monetary Fund, Washington, DC.

Benedek, D., E. Gemayel, A. Senhadji, and A. Tieman. 2021. "A Post-pandemic Assessment of the Sustainable Development Goals." IMF Staff Discussion Note 2021/003, International Monetary Fund, Washington, DC.

Berman, N., M. Couttenier, D. Rohner, and M. Thoenig. 2017. "This Mine is Mine! How Minerals Fuel Conflicts in Africa." *American Economic Review* 107 (6): 1564-610.

Bhattacharya, A., V. Songwe, E. Soubeyran, and N. Stern. 2024. "Raising Ambition and Accelerating Delivery of Climate Finance." Grantham Research Institute on Climate Change and the Environment, London School of Economics and Political Science, London.

Bhattacharya, R. 2014. "Inflation Dynamics and Monetary Policy Transmission in Vietnam and Emerging Asia." *Journal of Asian Economics* 34 (October): 16-26.

Blattman, C., and J. Annan. 2015. "Can Employment Reduce Lawlessness and Rebellion? A Field Experiment with High-Risk Men in a Fragile State." NBER Working Paper 21289, National Bureau of Economic Research, Cambridge, MA.

Blattman, C., and E. Miguel. 2010. "Civil War." *Journal of Economic Literature* 48 (1): 3-57.

Bloom, D. E., and D. Canning. 2004. "Global Demographic Change: Dimensions and Economic Significance." NBER Working Paper 10817, National Bureau of Economic Research, Cambridge, MA.

Buhaug, H., and K. S. Gleditsch. 2008. "Contagion or Confusion? Why Conflicts Cluster in Space." *International Studies Quarterly* 52 (2): 215-33.

Burke, M., J. Ferguson, S. Hsiang, and E. Miguel. 2024. "Will Wealth Weaken Weather Wars?" *AEA Papers and Proceedings* 114: 65-69.

Call, C. T. 2012. *Why Peace Fails: The Causes and Prevention of Civil War Recurrence*. Washington, DC: Georgetown University Press.

Camen, U. 2006. "Monetary Policy in Vietnam: The Case of a Transition Country." In *Monetary Policy in Asia: Approaches and Implementation*. BIS Papers, vol. 31, 232-52. Basel, Switzerland: Bank for International Settlements.

Carmignani, F., and T. Mandeville. 2014. "Never Been Industrialized: A Tale of African Structural Change." *Structural Change and Economic Dynamics* 31 (December): 124-37.

Carrere, C., J. De Melo, and J. Wilson., 2013. "The Distance Puzzle and Low-Income Countries: An Update." *Journal of Economic Surveys* 27 (4): 717-42.

Cerdeiro, D. A., and A. Komaromi. 2017. "Trade and Income in the Long Run: Are There Really Gains, and Are They Widely Shared?" IMF Working Paper 2017/231, International Monetary Fund, Washington, DC.

Chami, R., R. Espinoza, and P. J. Montiel. eds. 2021. *Macroeconomic Policy in Fragile States*. Oxford: Oxford University Press.

Chemouni, B. 2017. "The Politics of Core Public Sector Reform in Rwanda." Working Paper 88, Effective States and Inclusive Development Research Centre, University of Manchester, Manchester, England.

Chrimes, T., B. Gootjes, M. A. Kose, and C. Wheeler. 2024. *The Great Reversal: Prospects, Risks, and Policies in International Development Association (IDA) Countries*. Washington, DC: World Bank.

Christie, I., E. Fernandes, H. Messerli, and L. Twining-Ward. 2013. *Tourism in Africa: Harnessing Tourism for Growth and Improved Livelihoods*. Washington, DC: World Bank.

Collier, P., and A. Hoeffler. 2004. "Greed and Grievance in Civil War." *Oxford Economic Papers* 56 (4): 563-95.

Cosic, D., S. Dahal, and M. Kitzmuller. 2017. "Climbing Higher: Toward a Middle-Income Nepal." Country Economic Memorandum, World Bank, Washington, DC.

Coulibaly, K., K. Ezemenari, and N. E. Duffy. 2008. "Productivity Growth and Economic Reform: Evidence from Rwanda." Policy Research Working Paper 4552, World Bank, Washington DC.

Cust, J., S. Devarajan, and P. Mandon. 2022. "Dutch Disease and The Public Sector: How Natural Resources Can Undermine Competitiveness in Africa." *Journal of African Economies* 31 (Supplement 1): i10-i32.

Cust, J., and Mihalyi. D. 2017. "Evidence for a Presource Curse? Oil Discoveries, Elevated Expectations, and Growth Disappointments." Policy Research Working Paper 8140, World Bank, Washington, DC.

Cust, J., A. Rivera-Ballesteros, and D. Mihalyi. 2021. "The Economic Effects of Giant Oil and Gas Discoveries." In *Giant Fields of the Decade: 2010-2020: AAPG Memoir 125*, edited by C. A. Sternbach, R. K. Merrill, and J. C. Dolson, 21-36, Tulsa, OK: American Association of Petroleum Geologists.

Cust, J., and A. Zeufack. eds. 2023. *Africa's Resource Future: Harnessing Natural Resources for Economic Transformation during the Low-Carbon Transition*. Washington, DC: World Bank.

Dabla-Norris, M. E., G. Ho, and M. A. Kyobe. 2016. "Structural Reforms and Productivity Growth in Emerging Market and Developing Economies." IMF

Working Paper 16/15, International Monetary Fund, Washington, DC.

Dang, L. N., D. D. Nguyen, and F. Taghizadeh-Hesary. 2021. "State-Owned Enterprise Reform in Viet Nam: Progress and Challenges." Working Paper 1071, Asian Development Bank Institute, Tokyo.

Davis, S., G. Engstrom, T. Pettersson and M. Oberg. 2024. "Organized Violence 1989-2023, and The Prevalence of Organized Crime Groups." *Journal of Peace Research* 61(4).

Delechat, C., G. Melina, M. Newiak, C. Papageorgiou, and N. Spatafora. 2024. "Economic Diversification in Developing Countries: Lessons from Country Experiences with Broad-Based and Industrial Policies." Departmental Paper 2024/006, International Monetary Fund, Washington, DC.

Denny, E. K., and B. F. Walter. 2014. "Ethnicity and Civil War." *Journal of Peace Research* 51 (2):199-212.

Dessus, S., J. L. Diaz-Sanchez, and A. Varoudakis. 2016. "Fiscal Rules and The Pro-cyclicality of Public Investment in the West African Economic and Monetary Union." *Journal of International Development* 28 (6): 887-901.

Diao, X., M. Ellis, M. McMillan, and D. Rodrik. 2024. "Africa's Manufacturing Puzzle: Evidence from Tanzanian and Ethiopian Firms." *World Bank Economic Review.* https://doi.org/10.1093/wber/lhae029.

Dieppe, A., ed. 2021. *Global Productivity: Trends, Drivers, and Policies.* Washington, DC: World Bank.

Ding, D., and I. Masha. 2012. "India's Growth Spillovers to South Asia." IMF Working Paper 1 2/56, International Monetary Fund, Washington, DC.

Dinkelman, T., and L. R. Ngai. 2022. "Time Use and Gender in Africa in Times of Structural Transformation." *Journal of Economic Perspectives* 36 (1): 57-80.

Dom, R., A. Custers, S. Davenport, and W. Prichard. 2022. *Innovations in Tax Compliance: Building Trust, Navigating Politics, and Tailoring Reform.* Washington, DC: World Bank.

Duflo, E. 2020. "Field Experiments and the Practice of Policy." *American Economic Review* 110 (7): 1952-73.

Duflo, E., M. Kremer, and J. Robinson. 2011. "Nudging Farmers to Use Fertilizer: Theory and Experimental Evidence from Kenya." *American Economic Review* 101 (6): 2350-90.

Eden, M., and A. Kraay. 2014. "Crowding in and the Returns to Government Investment in Low-Income Countries." Policy Research Working Paper 6781, World Bank, Washington, DC.

Ericsson, M., O. Löf, and A. Löf. 2020. "Chinese Control Over African and Global Mining—Past, Present and Future. *Mineral Economics* 33 (1): 153-81.

ESMAP (Energy Sector Management Assistance Program). 2020. *Global Photovoltaic Power Potential by Country.* Washington, DC: World Bank.

Essl, S. M., S. K. Celik, P. Kirby, and A. Proite. 2019. "Debt in Low-Income Countries: Evolution, Implications, and Remedies." Policy Research Working Paper 8794, World Bank, Washington, DC.

Ezeoha, A., A. Igwe, C. Okoyeuzu, and C. Uche. 2023. "The Fiscal Effects of Armed Conflicts in Africa." *African Development Review* 35 (4): 444-56.

Falch, A., and L. Miklian. 2008. "A Transitional Success Story: The Nepali Experience with Powersharing." CSCW Policy Brief 5/2008, Centre for the Study of Civil War, Oslo, Norway.

Falchetta, G., D.E. Gernaat, J. Hunt, and S. Sterl. 2019. "Hydropower Dependency and Climate Change in Sub-Saharan Africa: A Nexus Framework and Evidence-Based Review." *Journal of Cleaner Production* 231 (September): 1399-417.

Fang, X., S. Kothari, C. McLoughlin, and M. Yenice. 2020. "The Economic Consequences of Conflict in Sub-Saharan Africa." IMF Working Paper 20/221, International Monetary Fund, Washington, DC.

Federle, J., A. Meier, G. Muller., W. Mutschler, and M. Schularick. 2024. "The Price of War." Discussion Paper 18834, Centre for Economic Policy Research, London.

Fontagne, L., M. Lebrand, S. Murray, M. Ruta., and G. Santoni. 2023. "Trade and Infrastructure Integration in Africa." Policy Research Working Paper 10609, World Bank, Washington, DC.

Fox, L., C. Haines, J. H. Munoz, and A. Thomas. 2013. "Africa's Got work to Do: Employment Prospects in the New Century." IMF Working Paper 13/201, International Monetary Fund, Washington, DC.

FSIN (Food Security Information Network) and FNAFC (Global Network Against Food Crises). 2024. *Global Report on Food Crises 2024.* Rome: Food Security Information Network and Global Network Against Food Crises.

Gelb, A., V. Ramachandran., C. J. Meyer, D. Wadhwa, and K. Navis. 2020. "Can Sub-Saharan Africa Be a

Manufacturing Destination? Labor Costs, Price Levels, and the Role of Industrial Policy." *Journal of Industry, Competition and Trade* 20 (2): 335-57.

Goldberg, P. K., and T. Reed. 2023. "Presidential Address: Demand-Side Constraints in Development. The Role of Market Size, Trade, and (In) Equality." *Econometrica* 91 (6): 1915-50.

Gootjes, B., J. de Haan, K. Stamm, and S. Yu. 2024. "Identifying Growth Accelerations." Policy Research Working Paper 10945, World Bank, Washington, DC.

Grover, A., S. V. Lall, and J. Timmis. 2021. "Agglomeration Economies in Developing Countries: A Meta-analysis." Policy Research Working Paper 9730, World Bank, Washington, DC.

Gutierrez, E., and S. Singh. 2013. "What Regulatory Frameworks Are More Conducive to Mobile Banking? Empirical Evidence from Findex Data." Policy Research Working Paper 6652, World Bank, Washington, DC.

Hallegatte, S., M. Bangalore, L. Bonzanigo, M. Fay, T. Kane, U. Narloch., J. Rozenberg, D. Treguer, and A. Vogt-Schilb. 2016. "Poverty and Climate Change." In *The Economics of Climate Resilient Development,* edited by S. Fankhauser and T. McDermott. Edward Elgar: Cheltenham, UK.

Hallward-Driemeier, M., and G. Nayyar. 2017. *Trouble in the Making? The Future of Manufacturing-Led Development.* Washington, DC: World Bank.

Harrison, A. E., J. Y. Lin, and L. C. Xu. 2014. "Explaining Africa's (Dis) Advantage." *World Development* 63 (November): 59-77.

Hausmann, R., T. O'Brien, T. Cheston, I. Hassen, C. Soylu, K. Shah, N. Taniparti, P. Prasad, and P. Neumeyer. 2023. "Development in a Complex World: The Case of Ethiopia." CID Faculty Working Paper 423, Harvard University, Cambridge, MA.

Herrendorf, B., R. Rogerson, and A. Valentinyi. 2014. "Growth and Structural Transformation." *Handbook of Economic Growth* 2: 855-941.

Herrendorf, B., R. Rogerson, and A. Valentinyi. 2022. "New Evidence on Sectoral Labor Productivity: Implications for Industrialization and Development." NBER Working Paper 29834, National Bureau of Economic Research, Cambridge, MA.

Hjort, J., and L. Tian. 2014. "The Economic Impact of Internet Connectivity in Developing Countries." Discussion Paper 19371, Centre for Economic Policy Research, London.

Holden, S. T., K. Deininger, and H. Ghebru. 2009. "Impacts of Low^Cost Land Certification on Investment and Productivity." *American Journal of Agricultural Economics* 91 (2): 359-73.

Horn, S., B. C. Parks, C. M. Reinhart, and C. Trebesch. 2023. "China as an International Lender of Last Resort." NBER Working Paper 31105, National Bureau of Economic Research, Cambridge, MA.

Hsieh, C. T., E. Hurst, C. I. Jones, and P. J. Klenow. 2019. "The Allocation of Talent and US Economic Growth." *Econometrica* 87 (5): 1439-74.

IEA (International Energy Agency). 2022a. *The Role of Critical Minerals in Clean Energy Transitions.* World Economic Outlook Special Report. Paris: International Energy Agency.

IEA (International Energy Agency). 2022b. *Africa Energy Outlook 2022.* World Economic Outlook Special Report. Paris: International Energy Agency.

IEG (Independent Expert Group). 2023. *Strengthening Multilateral Development Banks: The Triple Agenda: A Roadmap for Better, Bolder, and Bigger MDBs.* Report of the Independent Expert Group, G20.

ILO (International Labour Organization). "ILO Modelled Estimates (ILOSTAT Database)." Accessed February 07, 2024. ilostat.ilo.org/data.

ILO (International Labour Organization). 2022. *World Employment and Social Outlook: Trends 2022.* Geneva, Switzerland: International Labour Organization.

IMF (International Monetary Fund). 2005a. "Kenya: Poverty Reduction Strategy Paper." IMF Country Report 05/11, International Monetary Fund, Washington, DC.

IMF (International Monetary Fund). 2005b. "Rwanda: Enhanced Initiative for Heavily Indebted Poor Countries—Completion Point Document." IMF Country Report 05/173, International Monetary Fund, Washington, DC.

IMF (International Monetary Fund). 2009. "Vietnam: 2008 Article IV Consultation-Press Release and Staff Report." International Monetary Fund, Washington, DC.

IMF (International Monetary Fund). 2015. "Kenya: Request for Stand-by Arrangement and an Arrangement Under the Standby Credit Facility." IMF Country Report 15/31, International Monetary Fund, Washington, DC.

IMF (International Monetary Fund) 2018. "Kenya: Selected Issues." International Monetary Fund, International Monetary Fund, Washington, DC.

IMF (International Monetary Fund). 2019a. "Vietnam: 2019 Article IV Consultation-Press Release and Staff Report." International Monetary Fund, Washington, DC.

IMF (International Monetary Fund). 2019b. *Regional Economic Outlook: Sub-Saharan Africa—Recovery Amid Elevated Uncertainty.* April. Washington, DC: International Monetary Fund.

IMF (International Monetary Fund). 2020a. "Nepal: Selected Issues." International Monetary Fund, Washington, DC.

IMF (International Monetary Fund). 2020b. "The African Continental Free Trade Area: Potential Economic Impact and Challenges." Staff Discussion Note 20/04, International Monetary Fund, Washington DC.

IMF (International Monetary Fund). 2021. "Questions and Answers on Sovereign Debt Issues." International Monetary Fund, Washington, DC. https://www.imf.org/en/About/FAQ/sovereign-debt.

IMF (International Monetary Fund). 2023a. *World Economic Outlook: Navigating Global Divergences.* October. Washington, DC: International Monetary Fund.

IMF (International Monetary Fund). 2023b. "Rwanda: Technical Assistance Report-Public Investment Management Assessment-PIMA and Climate PIMA." IMF Staff Country 23/300, International Monetary Fund, Washington, DC.

IMF (International Monetary Fund). 2024a. *Macroeconomic Developments and Prospects for Low-Income Countries.* Washington, DC: International Monetary Fund.

IMF (International Monetary Fund). 2024b. *Regional Economic Outlook: Sub-Saharan Africa—Reforms amid Great Expectations.* October. Washington, DC: International Monetary Fund.

IMF (International Monetary Fund). 2024c. "The Federal Democratic Republic of Ethiopia: Request for an Arrangement Under the Extended Credit Facility." IMF Country Report 24/253, International Monetary Fund, Washington, DC.

IMF (International Monetary Fund). 2024d. *Regional Economic Outlook: Middle East and Central Asia—An Uneven Recovery Amid High Uncertainty.* April. Washington, DC: International Monetary Fund.

IMF (International Monetary Fund). 2024e. "Digging for Opportunity: Harnessing Sub-Saharan Africa's Wealth in Critical Minerals." In *Regional Economic Outlook: Sub-Saharan Africa—A Tepid and Pricey Recovery.* April. Washington, DC: International Monetary Fund.

IMF (International Monetary Fund), OECD (Organisation for Economic Co-operation and Development), World Bank, and WTO (World Trade Organization). 2022. *Subsidies, Trade, and International Cooperation.* Washington, DC: IMF, OECD, World Bank, and WTO.

Irvin, G. 1995. "Vietnam: Assessing the Achievements of Doi Moi." *The journal of Development Studies* 31 (5): 725-50.

Jack, W., and Suri, T., 2014. "Risk Sharing and Transactions Costs: Evidence from Kenya's Mobile Money Revolution." *American Economic Review* 104 (1): 183-223.

Jafino, B. A., B. Walsh, J. Rozenberg, and S. Hallegatte. 2020. "Revised Estimates of the Impact of Climate Change on Extreme Poverty by 2030." Policy Research Working Paper 9417, World Bank, Washington, DC.

Jenkins, R. 2006. "Globalization, FDI and Employment in Viet Nam." *Transnational Corporations* 15 (1): 115-42.

Karingi, S. N., and B. Wanjala. 2005. "The Tax Reform Experience of Kenya." WIDER Research Paper 2005/67, The United Nations University World Institute for Development Economics Research (UNU-WIDER), Helsinki.

Karkare, P., and A. Medinilla. 2023. "Green Industrialization: Leveraging Critical Raw Materials for an African Battery Value Chain." Discussion Paper 359, European Centre for Development Policy Management, Maastricht and Brussels.

Kasyanenko, S., P. Kenworthy, S. K. Celik, F. U. Ruch, E. Vashakmadze, and C. Wheeler. 2023. "The Past and Future of Regional Potential Growth: Hopes, Fears, and Realities." Policy Research Working Paper 10368, World Bank, Washington, DC.

Katoka, B., and J. M. Dostal. 2022. "Natural Resources, International Commodity Prices and Economic Performance in Sub-Saharan Africa (1990–2019)." *Journal of African Economies* 31 (1): 53-74.

Khan, T., T. Nguyen, F. Ohnsorge, and R. Schodde. 2016. "From Commodity Discovery to Production."

Policy Research Working Paper 7823, World Bank, Washington, DC.

Kimenyi, M., F. Mwega, and N. Ndung'u. 2016. *The African Lions: Kenya Country Case Study.*

Konisky, D. M., L. Hughes, and C. H. Kaylor. 2016. "Extreme Weather Events and Climate Change Concern." *Climatic Change* 134: 533-47.

Kose, M. A., P. Nagle, F. Ohnsorge, and N. Sugawara. 2021. *Global Waves of Debt: Causes and Consequences.* Washington, DC: World Bank.

Kose, M. A., and F. Ohnsorge, eds. 2020. *A Decade After the Global Recession: Lessons and Challengers for Emerging and Developing Economics.* Washington DC: World Bank.

Kose, M. A., and F. Ohnsorge. eds. 2024. *Falling Long-Term Growth Prospects: Trends, Expectations, and Policies.* Washington, DC: World Bank.

Kose, M. A., F. Ohnsorge, C. M. Reinhart, and K. S. Rogoff. 2022. "The Aftermath of Debt Surges." *Annual Review of Economics* 14 (1): 637-63.

Lawry, S., C. Samii, R. Hall, A. Leopold, D. Hornby, and F. Mtero. 2017. "The Impact of Land Property Rights Interventions on Investment and Agricultural Productivity in Developing Countries: A Systematic Review." *Journal of Development Effectiveness* 9 (1): 61-81.

Mahler, D. G., N. Yonzan, and C. Lakner. 2022. "The Impact of COVID-19 on Global Inequality and Poverty." Policy Research Working Paper 10198, World Bank, Washington, DC.

Malta, V., L. Kolovich, A. Marinez, and M. Tavares. 2019. "Informality and Gender Gaps Going Hand in Hand?" IMF Working Paper 19/112, International Monetary Fund, Washington, DC.

Malunda, D., and S. Musana. 2012. "Rwanda Case Study on Economic Transformation." Report for the African Centre for Economic Transformation (ACET). Institute of Policy Analysis and Research, Kigali, Rwanda.

Martin, P., T. Mayer, and M. Thoenig. 2008. "Make Trade Not War?" *The Review of Economic Studies* 75 (3): 865-900.

Mawejje, J. 2024a. *Fiscal Vulnerabilities in Low-Income Countries: Evolution, Drivers, and Policies.* Washington, DC: World Bank.

Mawejje, J. 2024b. "How Does the Weather and Climate Change Affect Firm Performance in Low-Income Countries? Evidence from Uganda." *Sustainable Futures* 7 (June): 100167.

Mawejje, J., and P. McSharry. 2021. "The Economic Cost of Conflict: Evidence from South Sudan." *Review of Development Economics* 25 (4): 1969-90.

Mawejje, J., and N. M. Odhiambo. 2024. "Fiscal Rules and the Cyclicality of Fiscal Policy in The East African Community." *Applied Economics Letters* 31 (15): 1429-32.

McCaig, B., and N. Pavcnik. 2013. "Moving Out of Agriculture: Structural Change in Vietnam." NBER Working Paper 19616, National Bureau of Economic Research, Cambridge, MA.

McMillan, M., and D. Headey. 2014. "Introduction—Understanding Structural Transformation in Africa." *World Development* 63 (November): 1-10.

McMillan, M., and D. Rodrik. 2011. "Globalization, Structural Change and Productivity Growth." NBER Working Paper 17143, National Bureau of Economic Research, Cambridge, MA.

Mejia, S. A., C. Baccianti, M. Mrkaic, N Novta, E. Pugacheva, and P. Topalova. 2019. "Weather Shocks and Output in Low-Income Countries: Adaptation and the Role of Policies." IMF Working Paper 19/178, International Monetary Fund, Washington, DC.

Mengistu, A. T. 2021. "Ethiopia's Macroeconomic and Finance Policy Framework for Structural Transformation." UNCTAD/BRI PROJECT/RP19, United Nations Conference on Trade and Development, Geneva.

Mihalyi, D., and C. Trebesch. 2023. "Who Lends to Africa and How? Introducing the Africa Debt Database." Kiel Working Paper 2217, Kiel Institute for the World Economy, Kiel, Germany.

Moller, L. C., and K. M. Wacker. 2017. "Explaining Ethiopia's Growth Acceleration—The Role of Infrastructure and Macroeconomic Policy." *World Development* 96: 198-215.

Naidoo, K., and L. Ndikumana. 2023. "The Role of Unit Labor Costs in African Manufacturing Investment and Export Performance." *Review of Development Economics* 27 (3): 1874-909.

Ndubuisi, G., and E. K. Avenyo. 2024. "Solar Photovoltaic Manufacturing in Africa: Opportunity or Mirage?" Policy Paper, Africa Policy Research Institute, Berlin.

Ndung'u, N. S., and R. W. Ngugi. 1999. Adjustment And Liberalization in Kenya: The Financial and Foreign Exchange Markets. *Journal of International Development* 11 (3): 465-91.

Newfarmer, R., J. Page, and F. Tarp, eds. 2018. *Industries without Smokestacks Industrialization in Africa Reconsidered.* Oxford University Press: Oxford.

Novta, N. and E. Pugacheva. 2021. "The Macroeconomic Costs of Conflict." *Journal of Macroeconomics* 68 (June): 103286.

Ohnsorge, F., and L. Quaglietti. 2023. "Trade as an Engine of Growth: Sputtering but Fixable." Policy Research Working Paper 10356, World Bank, Washington, DC.

Ohnsorge, F., and S. Yu, eds. 2022. *The Long Shadow of Informality: Challenges and Policies.* Washington, DC: World Bank.

Okumu, I., J. Mawejje, N. Kilimani, and E. Bbaale. Forthcoming. "Why Do Some African Firms Export? The Role of Regional Economic Communities." *Review of Development Economics.* https:// doi.org/10.1111/ rode.13164.

Olken, B. A., and R. Pande. 2012. "Corruption in Developing Countries." *Annual Review of Economics* 4 (1): 479-509.

Owino, K., M. Barasa, and P. Doyle. 2024. *And Then, Floods: A Critical Macroeconomic Assessment of IMF Conditionality on Kenya, 2021-Present.* Nairobi: Institute of Economic Affairs Kenya.

Patcharaporn, L., C. Castrovillari, and T. Mineyama. 2023. "Macroeconomic Shocks and Conflict." IMF Working Paper 23/68, International Monetary Fund, Washington, DC.

Paudel, R. C., and A. Cooray. 2018. "Export Performance of Developing Countries: Does Landlockedness Matter?" *Review of Development Economics* 22 (3): e36-e62.

Pennings, S. M. 2022. "A Gender Employment Gap Index (GEGI): A Simple Measure of the Economic Gains from Closing Gender Employment Gaps, with an Application to the Pacific Islands." Policy Research Working Paper 9942, World Bank, Washington, DC.

Rauschendorfer, J., and B. Shepherd. 2022. "Trade, Conflict and Informality: Evidence from the South Sudanese Civil War." *The World Economy* 45 (3): 867-94.

Rivetti, D. 2021. *Debt Transparency in Developing Economies.* Washington, DC: World Bank.

Rodrik, D. 2016. "Premature Deindustrialization." *Journal of Economic Growth* 21 (1): 1-33.

Rodrik, D., and R. Sandhu. 2024. "Servicing Development: Productive Upgrading of Labor-Absorbing Services in Developing Economies." Reimagining the Economy Policy Paper. Harvard Kennedy School, Cambridge, MA.

Rozenberg, J., and M. Fay. eds. 2019. *Beyond the Gap: How Countries Can Afford the Infrastructure They Need While Protecting the Planet.* Washington, DC: World Bank.

Ruzzante, S., R. Labarta, and A. Bilton. 2021. "Adoption of Agricultural Technology in the Developing World: A Meta-analysis of the Empirical Literature." *World Development* 146 (1): 105599.

Ryan, T., and I. Maana. 2014. "An Assessment of Kenya's Public Debt Dynamics and Sustainability." Central Bank of Kenya, Nairobi.

Sachs, J. D., G. Lafortune, G. Fuller. 2024. *Sustainable Development Report 2024; The SDGs and the UN Summit of the Future.* Dublin: Dublin University Press.

Sachs, J. D., and A. M. Warner. 2001. "The Curse of Natural Resources." *European Economic Review* 45 (4-6): 827-38.

Sahay, R., M. Čihak, P. N'Diaye, A. Barajas, S. Mitra, A. Kyobe, Y. N. Mooi, and S. R. Yousefi. 2015. "Financial Inclusion: Can It Meet Multiple Macroeconomic Goals?" Staff Discussion Note 15/17, International Monetary Fund, Washington, DC.

Salike, N., J. Wang, and P. Regis. 2022. "Remittance and Its Effect on Poverty and Inequality: A Case of Nepal." *NRB Economic Review* 34 (2): 1-29.

Santiso, C. 2022. "GovTech Against Corruption: What Are The Integrity Dividends of Government Digitalization?" *Data & Policy* 4: e39.

Sasaoka, Y. 2005. "Institution Building for Poverty Reduction and Local Governance: The Cases of Tanzania, Ethiopia and Kenya." GRIPS Development Forum Discussion Paper 13, National Graduate Institute for Policy Studies: Tokyo.

Schaumburg-Muller, H. 2005. "Private Sector Development in a Transition Economy: The Case of Vietnam." *Development in Practice* 15 (3-4): 349-61.

Schwab, K. 2019. *The Global Competitiveness Report.* Geneva: World Economic Forum.

Schwalm, C. R., W. R. L. Anderegg, A. M. Michalak, J. B. Fisher, F. Biondi, G. Koch, and M. Litvak. 2017.

"Global Patterns of Drought Recovery." *Nature* 548: 202-05.

Seid, Y., A. S. Taffesse, and S. N. Ali. 2016. *The African Lions: Ethiopia: An Agrarian Economy in Transition*. Washington, DC: Brookings Institution.

Steinbach, R. 2019. "Growth in Low-Income Countries: Evolution, Prospects, and Policies." Policy Research Working Paper 8949, World Bank, Washington, DC.

Toews, G., and P. L. Vezina. 2017. "Resource Discoveries, FDI Bonanzas, and Local Multipliers: Evidence from Mozambique." *Review of Economics and Statistics* 104 (5): 1046-58.

Torres, J., F. Maduko, I. Gaddis, L. Iacovone, and K. Beegle. 2021. "The Impact of the COVID-19 Pandemic on Women-Led Businesses." Policy Research Working Paper 9817, World Bank, Washington, DC.

UNEP (United Nations Environment Programme). 2023. "Adaptation Gap Report 2023: Underfinanced. Underprepared. Inadequate Investment and Planning on Climate Adaptation Leaves World Exposed." United Nations Environment Programme, Nairobi, Kenya.

United Nations. 2021. *The Sustainable Development Goals Report 2021*. New York: United Nations.

van der Ploeg, F. 2011. "Natural Resources: Curse or Blessing?" *Journal of Economic Literature* 49 (2): 366-420.

Vesco, P., S. Dasgupta, E. De Cian, and C. Carraro. 2020. "Natural Resources and Conflict: A Meta-analysis of The Empirical Literature." *Ecological Economics* 172 (June): 106633.

Vries, G. J. D., M.P. Timmer, and K. D. Vries. 2013. "Structural Transformation in Africa: Static Gains, Dynamic Losses." Working Paper 136, Groningen Growth and Development Centre, Groningen, the Netherlands.

Wenjie, C., K. Khandelwal, A. Laws, F. Saliba, C. Sever, and L. Tucker. 2024. "The Clock is Ticking: Meeting Sub-Saharan Africa's Urgent Job Creation Challenge." In *Regional Economic Outlook: Sub-Saharan Africa—Reforms amid Great Expectations*. October. Washington, DC: International Monetary Fund.

Wiggins, S. 2014. "African Agricultural Development: Lessons and Challenges." *Journal of Agricultural Economics* 65 (3): 529-56.

Wodon, Q., A. Onagoruwa, C. Male, C. Montenegro, H. Nguyen, and B. de la Briere. 2020. "How Large Is the Gender Dividend? Measuring Selected Impacts and Costs of Gender Inequality." The Cost of Gender Inequality Notes Series, World Bank, Washington, DC.

World Bank. 2005. "Nepal Development Policy Review Restarting Growth and Poverty Reduction." Report 29382-NP, World Bank, Washington, DC.

World Bank. 2008a. "Ethiopia—Agriculture and Rural Development Public Expenditure Review 1997/98–2005/06." World Bank, Washington, DC.

World Bank. 2008b. *World Development Report 2008: Agriculture for Development*. Washington, DC: World Bank.

World Bank. 2012. *World Development Report 2012: Gender Equality and Development*. Washington, DC: World Bank.

World Bank. 2014. "Improving Health Outcomes and Services for Kenyans: Sustainable Institutions and Financing for Universal Health Coverage." Final Report on the Proceedings, Kenya Health Policy Forum, Nairobi, March 18-20. World Bank, Washington, DC.

World Bank. 2015. *Global Economic Prospects: Having Fiscal Space and Using It.*" January. Washington, DC: World Bank.

World Bank. 2016a. *Sustaining Success. Priorities for Inclusive and Sustainable Growth*. Vietnam Systematic Country Diagnostic. Washington, DC: World Bank.

World Bank. 2016b. *Ethiopia's Great Run: The Growth Acceleration and How to Pace It*. World Bank, Washington, DC.

World Bank. 2017. "Tourism for Development: 20 Reasons Sustainable Tourism Counts for Development." World Bank, Washington, DC.

World Bank. 2018a. *Global Economic Prospects, The Turning of the Tide*. June. Washington, DC: World Bank.

World Bank. 2018b. *World Development Report 2018: Learning to Realize Education's Promise*. Washington, DC, World Bank.

World Bank. 2019. "Macro Poverty Outlook." World Bank, Washington, DC. https://www.worldbank.org/en/publication/macro-povertyoutlook.

World Bank. 2020a. *World Development Report 2020: Trading for Development in the Age of Global Value Chains.* Washington, DC: World Bank.

World Bank. 2020b. *Systematic Country Diagnostic: Kenya.* World Bank, Washington, DC.

World Bank. 2020c. *Bolstering Poverty Reduction in Rwanda: A Poverty Assessment.* Washington, DC: World Bank.

World Bank. 2020d. *The African Continental Free Trade Area: Economic and Distributional Effects.* Washington, DC: World Bank.

World Bank. 2020e. *Minerals for Climate Action: The Mineral Intensity of the Clean Energy Transition.* Washington, DC: World Bank.

World Bank. 2021. *The Human Capital Index 2020 Update: Human Capital in the Time of COVID-19.* Washington, DC: World Bank.

World Bank. 2022a. *Women, Business and the Law 2022.* Washington, DC: World Bank.

World Bank. 2022b. *From the Last Mile to the Next Mile—2022 Vietnam Poverty & Equity Assessment.* Washington, DC: World Bank.

World Bank. 2022c. *Economic Impacts of Protected Area Tourism on Local Communities in Nepal.* Washington, DC: World Bank.

World Bank. 2022d. "Climate and Development: An Agenda for Action—Emerging Insights from World Bank Group 2021-22 Country Climate and Development Reports." Washington, DC: World Bank

World Bank. 2023a. *Kenya Poverty Assessment 2023—From Poverty to Prosperity: Making Growth More Inclusive.* World Bank: Washington, DC.

World Bank. 2023b. "Digital Skills to Accelerate Human Capital for Youth in Africa." Africa Human Capital Technical Briefs Series. July. Washington, DC: World Bank.

World Bank. 2023c. "Rwanda." Poverty and Equity Brief. World Bank, Washington, DC.

World Bank. 2023d. *Rwanda Economic Update: Making the Most of Nature Based Tourism in Rwanda.* February. Washington, DC: World Bank.

World Bank. 2023e. *Commodity Markets Outlook: Lower Prices, Little Relief.* April. Washington, DC: World Bank.

World Bank. 2024a. *Poverty, Prosperity and Planet Report 2024: Pathways Out of the Polycrisis.* Washington, DC: World Bank.

World Bank. 2024b. *World Development Report 2024: The Middle-Income Trap.* Washington, DC: World Bank.

World Bank. 2024c. *Global Economic Prospects.* June. Washington, DC: World Bank.

World Bank. 2024d. *Bangladesh Development Update: Creating Jobs for a Better Future.* October. Washington, DC: World Bank.

World Bank. 2024e. *Global Economic Prospects.* January. Washington, DC: World Bank.

World Bank. 2024f. *Viet Nam 2045: Trading Up in A Changing World. Pathways to a High-Income Future.* Washington, DC: World Bank.

World Bank. 2024g. *Business Ready 2024.* Washington, DC: World Bank.

World Bank. 2024h. *Growth in the Middle East and North Africa. MENA Economic Update.* October. Washington, DC: World Bank.

World Bank. 2024i. "People in a Changing Climate: From Vulnerability to Action—Insights from World Bank Group Country Climate and Development Reports Covering 72 Economies." World Bank, Washington, DC.

World Bank. 2024j. *South Asia Development Update: Women, Jobs, and Growth.* October. Washington, DC: World Bank.

World Bank. 2024k. "Global Sovereign Debt Roundtable. 3rd Cochairs Progress Report." World Bank, Washington, D.C.

World Bank. 2024l. *International Debt Report 2024.* Washington, DC: World Bank.

World Bank and IFC (International Finance Corporation). 2021. *Creating Markets in Viet Nam.* Country Private Sector Diagnostic. Washington, DC: World Bank and International Finance Corporation.

Zaveri, E., R. Damania, and N. Engle. 2023. *Droughts and Deficits: Summary Evidence of the Global Impact on Economic Growth.* Washington, DC: World Bank.

Zergawu, Y. Z., Y. M. Walle, and J. M. Gimenez-Gomez. 2020. "The Joint Impact of Infrastructure and Institutions on Economic Growth." *Journal of Institutional Economics* 16 (4): 481-502.

STATISTICAL APPENDIX

Real GDP growth

	Annual estimates and forecasts [1] (Percent change)					Quarterly estimates [2] (Percent change, year-on-year)					
	2022	2023	2024e	2025f	2026f	23Q2	23Q3	23Q4	24Q1	24Q2	24Q3e
World	**3.2**	**2.7**	**2.7**	**2.7**	**2.7**	**3.0**	**2.7**	**2.7**	**2.7**	**2.6**	**..**
Advanced economies	**2.8**	**1.7**	**1.7**	**1.7**	**1.8**	**1.7**	**1.6**	**1.6**	**1.5**	**1.6**	**1.7**
United States	2.5	2.9	2.8	2.3	2.0	2.8	3.2	3.2	2.9	3.0	2.7
Euro area	3.5	0.4	0.7	1.0	1.2	0.6	0.0	0.1	0.4	0.5	0.9
Japan	0.9	1.5	0.0	1.2	0.9	1.7	1.1	0.9	-0.9	-0.9	0.5
Emerging market and developing economies	**3.7**	**4.2**	**4.1**	**4.1**	**4.0**	**4.9**	**4.2**	**4.3**	**4.3**	**4.1**	**..**
East Asia and Pacific	**3.4**	**5.1**	**4.9**	**4.6**	**4.1**	**6.0**	**4.8**	**5.1**	**5.2**	**4.7**	**4.7**
Cambodia	5.1	5.0	5.3	5.5	5.5	..	..	..	..	..	..
China	3.0	5.2	4.9	4.5	4.0	6.3	4.9	5.2	5.3	4.7	4.6
Fiji	19.8	7.5	4.0	3.6	3.3	..	..	..	..	..	..
Indonesia	5.3	5.0	5.0	5.1	5.1	5.2	4.9	5.0	5.1	5.0	4.9
Kiribati	3.9	4.2	5.8	4.1	3.3	..	..	..	..	..	..
Lao PDR	2.7	3.7	4.1	3.7	3.7	..	..	..	..	..	..
Malaysia	8.9	3.6	4.9	4.5	4.3	2.8	3.1	2.9	4.2	5.9	5.3
Marshall Islands [3]	-0.6	3.0	3.4	4.0	3.2	..	..	..	..	..	..
Micronesia, Fed. Sts. [3]	-1.4	0.4	1.1	1.7	1.1	..	..	..	..	..	..
Mongolia	5.0	7.2	5.3	6.5	6.1	4.9	8.8	7.2	8.0	3.9	3.5
Myanmar [3][4]	4.0	1.0	-1.0	2.0	..	..	..	..	..	..	..
Nauru [3]	2.8	0.6	1.8	2.0	1.9	..	..	..	..	..	..
Palau [3]	0.0	0.2	12.0	11.0	3.5	..	..	..	..	..	..
Papua New Guinea	5.7	3.0	4.5	4.6	3.5	..	..	..	..	..	..
Philippines	7.6	5.5	5.9	6.1	6.0	4.3	6.0	5.5	5.8	6.4	5.2
Samoa [3]	-5.4	9.2	9.4	5.5	2.8	..	..	..	..	..	..
Solomon Islands	2.3	3.0	2.5	2.9	2.9	..	..	..	..	..	..
Thailand	2.5	1.9	2.6	2.9	2.7	1.8	1.4	1.7	1.6	2.2	3.0
Timor-Leste	4.0	2.3	3.5	3.4	3.6	..	..	..	..	..	..
Tonga [3]	0.1	2.0	1.8	2.4	2.0	..	..	..	..	..	..
Tuvalu	0.4	3.9	3.5	3.0	2.5	..	..	..	..	..	..
Vanuatu	1.9	2.2	0.9	1.5	2.1	..	..	..	..	..	..
Viet Nam	8.1	5.0	6.8	6.6	6.3	4.2	5.5	6.7	5.9	7.1	7.4
Europe and Central Asia	**1.6**	**3.4**	**3.2**	**2.5**	**2.7**	**4.0**	**4.7**	**3.9**	**4.4**	**3.2**	**..**
Albania	4.8	3.9	3.7	3.5	3.3	4.4	4.5	4.2	3.8	4.1	..
Armenia	12.6	8.3	5.5	5.0	4.6	9.3	7.4	6.4	6.6	6.4	5.2
Azerbaijan	4.6	1.1	4.0	2.7	2.4	..	..	..	..	..	..
Belarus	-4.7	3.9	4.0	1.2	0.8	6.1	6.2	4.8	4.3	5.5	..
Bosnia and Herzegovina [5]	4.2	2.1	2.8	3.2	3.9	2.0	2.4	1.7	2.5	2.2	..
Bulgaria	4.0	1.9	2.2	2.8	2.7	2.0	1.6	1.8	1.9	2.3	2.6
Croatia	7.3	3.3	3.5	3.0	2.8	3.9	2.0	5.3	4.0	3.5	3.9
Georgia	11.0	7.5	9.0	6.0	5.0	8.6	6.8	7.3	8.7	9.7	11.0
Kazakhstan	3.2	5.1	4.0	4.7	3.5	5.6	4.1	5.6	3.8	2.6	..
Kosovo	4.3	3.3	3.8	3.9	4.0	..	..	..	..	..	..
Kyrgyz Republic	9.0	6.2	5.8	4.5	4.5	..	..	..	..	..	..
Moldova	-4.6	0.7	2.8	3.9	4.5	-0.3	3.3	-0.2	1.9	2.4	-1.9
Montenegro [2]	6.4	6.3	3.4	3.5	3.2	7.3	7.0	4.7	4.4	2.7	2.6
North Macedonia	2.8	2.1	2.4	3.0	3.2	2.0	2.7	3.1	1.9	2.8	3.0
Poland	5.3	0.1	3.0	3.4	3.2	-0.6	0.5	1.0	2.1	3.2	2.7
Romania	4.0	2.4	1.3	2.1	2.6	3.0	2.9	2.0	2.3	0.9	-0.3
Russian Federation	-1.2	3.6	3.4	1.6	1.1	5.1	5.7	4.9	5.4	4.1	3.1
Serbia	2.6	3.8	3.9	4.2	4.2	3.0	4.8	5.1	4.7	4.2	3.1
Tajikistan	8.0	8.3	8.0	6.0	5.0	..	..	..	..	..	..
Türkiye	5.5	5.1	3.2	2.6	3.8	4.6	6.5	4.6	5.3	2.4	2.1
Ukraine	-28.8	5.3	3.2	2.0	7.0	19.2	9.6	4.7	6.5	3.7	..
Uzbekistan	6.0	6.3	6.0	5.8	5.9	..	..	..	..	..	..

Real GDP growth (*continued*)

	Annual estimates and forecasts [1] (Percent change)					Quarterly estimates [2] (Percent change, year-on-year)					
	2022	2023	2024e	2025f	2026f	23Q2	23Q3	23Q4	24Q1	24Q2	24Q3e
Latin America and the Caribbean	**4.0**	**2.3**	**2.2**	**2.5**	**2.6**	**2.2**	**2.0**	**1.7**	**1.4**	**2.4**	**..**
Argentina	5.3	-1.6	-2.8	5.0	4.7	-5.3	-0.7	-1.2	-5.2	-1.7	-2.1
Bahamas, The	14.4	4.3	2.3	1.8	1.6	..	..	..	..	..	..
Barbados	13.5	4.4	3.9	2.8	2.3	..	..	..	..	..	..
Belize	8.7	4.7	4.3	1.2	0.5	-0.1	-1.5	1.6	8.6	10.5	6.6
Bolivia	3.6	3.1	1.4	1.5	1.5	2.0	2.6	5.1	1.3	3.8	..
Brazil	3.0	2.9	3.2	2.2	2.3	3.9	2.4	2.4	2.6	3.3	4.0
Chile	2.1	0.2	2.4	2.2	2.2	-0.4	0.6	0.4	2.5	1.6	2.3
Colombia	7.3	0.6	1.7	3.0	2.9	0.3	-0.6	0.4	0.7	2.1	2.0
Costa Rica	4.6	5.1	4.0	3.5	3.4	5.9	5.5	4.7	3.6	5.3	3.7
Dominica	5.6	4.7	4.6	4.2	3.2	..	..	..	..	..	..
Dominican Republic	4.9	2.4	5.1	4.7	5.0	1.0	2.6	4.2	4.1	6.0	..
Ecuador	6.2	2.4	-0.7	2.0	2.2	5.0	0.7	-0.7	1.2	-2.2	..
El Salvador	2.8	3.5	2.9	2.7	2.5	4.6	3.3	4.4	3.0	2.3	1.4
Grenada	7.3	4.7	4.2	3.8	3.4	..	..	..	..	..	..
Guatemala	4.2	3.5	3.7	4.0	4.0	4.1	4.0	2.0	3.2	3.7	..
Guyana	63.3	33.8	43.0	12.3	15.7	..	..	..	..	..	..
Haiti [3]	-1.7	-1.9	-4.2	0.5	1.5	..	..	..	..	..	..
Honduras	4.1	3.6	3.7	3.6	3.6	2.8	3.2	5.5	3.3	3.9	..
Jamaica [2]	5.2	2.6	0.8	2.2	1.6	2.3	2.3	1.7	1.2	0.2	..
Mexico	3.7	3.3	1.7	1.5	1.6	3.4	3.5	2.4	1.4	2.2	1.6
Nicaragua	3.8	4.6	3.6	3.5	3.6	3.6	6.0	5.2	4.9	4.4	..
Panama	10.8	7.3	2.6	3.0	3.5	8.2	8.9	3.3	1.8	2.5	2.0
Paraguay	0.2	4.7	4.0	3.6	3.6	5.6	3.7	4.9	4.3	4.8	..
Peru	2.8	-0.4	3.1	2.5	2.5	-0.4	-0.8	-0.2	1.4	3.6	3.8
St. Lucia	20.4	2.2	3.7	2.8	2.3	..	..	..	..	..	..
St. Vincent and the Grenadines	7.2	6.0	5.0	3.5	2.9	..	..	..	..	..	..
Suriname	2.4	2.5	2.9	3.0	3.1	..	..	..	..	..	..
Uruguay	4.7	0.4	3.2	2.6	2.6	-2.1	-0.2	2.0	0.4	4.0	4.1
Middle East and North Africa	**5.4**	**1.7**	**1.8**	**3.4**	**4.1**	**3.4**	**1.0**	**0.3**	**1.4**	**1.8**	**..**
Algeria	3.6	4.1	3.1	3.4	3.3	5.0	6.0	3.0	4.2	3.6	..
Bahrain	6.0	3.0	3.5	3.3	3.3	2.0	3.6	4.3	3.3	1.3	..
Djibouti	3.7	6.7	5.9	5.3	4.9	..	..	..	..	..	..
Egypt, Arab Rep. [3]	6.6	3.8	2.4	3.5	4.2	2.9	2.7	2.3	2.2	2.4	..
Iran, Islamic Rep. [3]	3.8	5.0	3.0	2.7	2.2	6.3	4.1	4.7	5.3	4.2	..
Iraq [5]	7.6	-2.9	-0.8	3.5	3.0	-6.8	-6.4	-0.9	-2.4	..	..
Jordan	2.6	2.7	2.4	2.6	2.6	2.7	2.7	2.3	2.0	2.4	..
Kuwait	6.3	-3.6	-1.0	1.7	2.1	-3.5	-5.8	-4.4	-3.7	-1.5	..
Lebanon [4]	-0.6	-0.8	-5.7	..	..	..	..	..	..	..	..
Libya	-8.3	10.2	-2.7	9.6	8.4	..	..	..	..	..	..
Morocco	1.5	3.4	2.9	3.9	3.4	2.5	3.0	4.2	2.5	2.4	2.8
Oman	9.6	1.3	0.7	2.4	2.8	6.6	4.1	0.3	1.7	2.8	1.1
Qatar	4.2	1.2	2.0	2.7	5.5	4.2	1.5	-3.6	1.5	0.8	..
Saudi Arabia	7.5	-0.8	1.1	3.4	5.4	1.7	-3.2	-4.3	-1.7	-0.3	2.8
Syrian Arab Republic [4]	0.7	-1.2	-1.5	-1.0	..	..	..	..	..	..	..
Tunisia	2.7	0.0	1.2	2.2	2.3	0.3	-0.4	-0.6	0.3	1.0	1.8
United Arab Emirates	7.9	3.2	3.3	4.0	4.1	3.8	2.5	4.3	3.4	3.9	..
West Bank and Gaza	4.1	-5.4	-25.6	4.7	16.5	2.8	2.6	-29.1	-34.9	-32.3	..
Yemen, Rep. [4]	1.5	-2.0	-1.0	1.5	..	..	..	..	..	..	..

Real GDP growth (*continued*)

	Annual estimates and forecasts [1] (Percent change)					Quarterly estimates [2] (Percent change, year-on-year)					
	2022	2023	2024e	2025f	2026f	23Q2	23Q3	23Q4	24Q1	24Q2	24Q3e
South Asia	**5.8**	**6.6**	**6.0**	**6.2**	**6.2**	**6.7**	**7.2**	**7.4**	**6.9**	**6.0**	..
Afghanistan [4]	-6.2	2.7	..	..	..	..	..	..	..	..	..
Bangladesh [3]	7.1	5.8	5.0	4.1	5.4	7.2	6.0	4.8	5.4	3.9	..
Bhutan [3]	4.8	5.0	5.3	7.2	6.6	..	..	..	..	..	..
India [3]	7.0	8.2	6.5	6.7	6.7	8.2	8.1	8.6	7.8	6.7	5.4
Maldives	13.9	4.1	4.7	4.7	4.6	1.3	5.1	6.0	7.7	4.5	..
Nepal [2][3]	5.6	2.0	3.9	5.1	5.5	3.7	4.5	4.6	3.1	2.1	..
Pakistan [2][3][5]	6.2	-0.2	2.5	2.8	3.2	-3.6	2.7	2.0	2.4	3.1	..
Sri Lanka	-7.3	-2.3	4.4	3.5	3.1	-3.0	1.6	4.5	5.3	4.7	5.5
Sub-Saharan Africa	**3.8**	**2.9**	**3.2**	**4.1**	**4.3**	**2.7**	**2.1**	**3.1**	**2.7**	**2.8**	..
Angola	3.0	1.0	3.2	2.9	2.9	0.1	1.8	2.0	4.6	4.1	5.5
Benin	6.3	6.4	6.3	6.4	6.3	..	..	..	..	..	..
Botswana	5.6	2.7	1.0	5.3	4.9	3.3	0.5	1.9	-5.3	-0.4	..
Burkina Faso	1.5	3.0	3.7	3.9	4.1	..	..	..	..	..	..
Burundi	1.8	2.7	2.2	3.5	4.2	..	..	..	..	..	..
Cabo Verde	17.4	5.1	5.2	4.9	4.8	..	..	..	..	..	..
Cameroon	3.6	3.3	3.7	4.0	4.2	..	..	..	..	..	..
Central African Republic	0.5	0.7	0.7	1.1	2.0	..	..	..	..	..	..
Chad	2.8	4.2	3.0	2.1	3.5	..	..	..	..	..	..
Comoros	2.8	3.0	3.5	4.0	4.3	..	..	..	..	..	..
Congo, Dem. Rep.	8.9	8.4	4.9	5.0	4.6	..	..	..	..	..	..
Congo, Rep.	1.5	1.9	2.1	3.5	3.3	..	..	..	..	..	..
Côte d'Ivoire	6.2	6.2	6.5	6.4	6.6	..	..	..	..	..	..
Equatorial Guinea	3.7	-5.7	4.7	-4.4	-0.8	..	..	..	..	..	..
Eritrea	2.5	2.6	2.8	3.0	3.3	..	..	..	..	..	..
Eswatini	0.5	4.8	4.6	3.5	2.9	..	..	..	..	..	..
Ethiopia [3]	6.4	7.2	6.1	6.5	7.1	..	..	..	..	..	..
Gabon	3.1	2.4	3.1	2.4	3.0	..	..	..	..	..	..
Gambia, The	4.9	5.3	5.6	5.8	5.4	..	..	..	..	..	..
Ghana	3.8	2.9	4.0	4.2	4.9	2.5	2.2	3.8	4.7	7.0	7.2
Guinea	4.0	6.7	5.3	6.0	6.4	..	..	..	..	..	..
Guinea-Bissau	4.2	5.2	5.0	5.0	5.0	..	..	..	..	..	..
Kenya	4.9	5.6	4.7	5.0	5.1	5.6	6.0	5.1	5.0	4.6	..
Lesotho	1.3	0.9	2.5	2.3	2.0	4.2	-1.2	3.0	2.0	0.5	..
Liberia	4.8	4.7	5.3	5.7	5.8	..	..	..	..	..	..
Madagascar	4.0	3.8	4.5	4.6	4.7	..	..	..	..	..	..
Malawi	0.9	1.6	1.8	4.2	3.3	..	..	..	..	..	..
Mali	3.5	3.5	3.7	4.0	4.5	..	..	..	..	..	..
Mauritania	6.8	6.5	6.5	7.8	7.5	..	..	..	..	..	..
Mauritius	8.9	7.0	5.6	4.4	3.8	..	..	..	..	..	..
Mozambique	4.4	5.4	4.0	4.0	4.0	5.9	4.4	4.8	3.2	4.5	3.7
Namibia	5.3	4.2	3.1	3.7	3.9	3.4	3.1	5.1	4.4	2.7	2.8
Niger	11.5	2.0	5.7	8.5	4.6	..	..	..	..	..	..
Nigeria	3.3	2.9	3.3	3.5	3.7	2.6	3.1	3.2	2.8	3.0	3.1
Rwanda	8.2	8.2	7.6	7.8	7.5	6.3	7.5	10.0	9.7	9.8	8.1
São Tomé and Príncipe	0.2	0.4	1.1	3.3	3.6	..	..	..	..	..	..
Senegal	3.8	4.6	6.1	9.7	6.0	..	..	..	..	..	..
Seychelles	14.9	3.2	3.7	4.1	3.5	0.5	-8.5	-6.6	-7.4	1.5	..
Sierra Leone	5.3	5.7	4.3	4.7	4.7	..	..	..	..	..	..

Real GDP growth (*continued*)

	Annual estimates and forecasts[1] (Percent change)					Quarterly estimates[2] (Percent change, year-on-year)					
	2022	2023	2024e	2025f	2026f	23Q2	23Q3	23Q4	24Q1	24Q2	24Q3e
Sub-Saharan Africa (*continued*)											
Somalia	2.7	4.2	4.4	4.5	4.5	..	..	..	..	..	..
South Africa	1.9	0.7	0.8	1.8	1.9	1.8	-0.9	1.4	0.5	0.3	0.3
South Sudan [3]	-2.3	-1.3	-7.8	-11.4	6.1	..	..	..	..	..	..
Sudan	-1.0	-20.1	-15.1	1.3	2.9	..	..	..	..	..	..
Tanzania	4.6	5.1	5.4	5.8	6.2	..	..	..	..	..	..
Togo	5.8	6.4	5.3	5.4	5.8	..	..	..	..	..	..
Uganda [3]	4.7	5.3	6.0	6.2	10.8	5.7	5.6	5.8	7.1	6.2	6.7
Zambia	5.2	5.4	1.2	6.2	6.6	5.1	5.0	7.5	2.2	1.7	..
Zimbabwe	6.1	5.3	2.0	6.2	4.8	..	..	..	..	..	..

Sources: Haver Analytics; World Bank.

Note: e = estimate; f = forecast. Since Croatia became a member of the euro area on January 1, 2023, it has been added to the euro area aggregate and removed from the EMDE and ECA aggregate in all tables to avoid double counting.

1. Aggregate growth rates calculated using GDP weights at average 2010-19 prices and market exchange rates.

2. Quarterly estimates are on a calendar year basis and based on non-seasonally-adjusted real GDP, except for advanced economies, as well as Algeria, Ecuador, Morocco, and Tunisia. In some instances, quarterly growth paths may not align to annual growth estimates, owing to the timing of GDP releases. Quarterly data for Jamaica, Nepal, and Pakistan are gross value added. Data for Timor-Leste represent non-oil GDP.

Regional averages are calculated based on data from the following economies.

East Asia and Pacific: China, Indonesia, Malaysia, Mongolia, the Philippines, Thailand, and Viet Nam.

Europe and Central Asia: Albania, Armenia, Belarus, Bosnia and Herzegovina, Bulgaria, Georgia, Hungary, Kazakhstan, Moldova, Montenegro, North Macedonia, Poland, Romania, the Russian Federation, Serbia, Türkiye, and Ukraine.

Latin America and the Caribbean: Argentina, Belize, Bolivia, Brazil, Chile, Colombia, Costa Rica, the Dominican Republic, Ecuador, El Salvador, Guatemala, Honduras, Jamaica, Mexico, Nicaragua, Panama, Paraguay, Peru, and Uruguay.

Middle East and North Africa: Bahrain, the Arab Republic of Egypt, the Islamic Republic of Iran, Jordan, Morocco, Oman, Qatar, Saudi Arabia, Tunisia, the United Arab Emirates, and West Bank and Gaza.

South Asia: Bangladesh, India, Maldives, Nepal, Pakistan, and Sri Lanka.

Sub-Saharan Africa: Angola, Botswana, Ghana, Kenya, Lesotho, Mozambique, Namibia, Nigeria, Rwanda, the Seychelles, South Africa, Uganda, and Zambia.

3. Annual GDP is on fiscal year basis, as per reporting practice in the country. For Bangladesh, Bhutan, Egypt, Nepal, and Pakistan, the column for 2023 refers to FY2022/23—covering 2022Q3 to 2023Q2. For India and the Islamic Republic of Iran, the column for 2023 refers to FY2023/24—covering 2023Q2 to 2024Q1.

4. Data for Afghanistan (beyond 2023), Lebanon (beyond 2024), Myanmar (beyond 2025), the Syrian Arab Republic (beyond 2025), and the Republic of Yemen (beyond 2025) are excluded because of a high degree of uncertainty.

5. Data for Bosnia and Herzegovina are from the production approach. Annual GDP for Pakistan is based on factor cost, and both annual and quarterly GDP for Iraq is also reported on a factor cost basis.

Data and Forecast Conventions

The macroeconomic forecasts presented in this report are prepared by staff of the Prospects Group of the Development Economics Vice Presidency, in coordination with staff from the Macroeconomics, Trade, and Investment Global Practice of the Equitable Growth, Finance and Institutions Vice Presidency and from regional and country offices, and with input from regional Chief Economist offices. They are the result of an iterative process that incorporates data, macroeconometric models, and judgment.

Data. Data used to prepare country forecasts come from a variety of sources. National Income Accounts (NIA), Balance of Payments (BOP), and fiscal data are from Haver Analytics; the World Development Indicators by the World Bank; the *World Economic Outlook*, *Balance of Payments Statistics*, and *International Financial Statistics* by the International Monetary Fund. Population data and forecasts are from the United Nations World Population Prospects. Country- and lending-group classifications are from the World Bank. The Prospects Group's internal databases include high-frequency indicators such as industrial production, consumer price indexes, emerging markets bond index (EMBI), exchange rates, exports, imports, policy rates, and stock market indexes, based on data from Bloomberg, Haver Analytics, IMF *Balance of Payments Statistics*, IMF *International Financial Statistics*, and J.P. Morgan.

Aggregations. Aggregate growth rates for the world and all subgroups of countries (such as regions and income groups) are weighted averages of country-specific growth rates, calculated using GDP weights at average 2010-19 prices and market exchange rates. Income groups are defined as in the World Bank's classification of country groups.

Output growth forecast process. The process starts with initial assumptions about advanced-economy growth and commodity price forecasts. These are used as conditioning assumptions for the first set of growth forecasts for EMDEs, which are produced using macroeconometric models, accounting frameworks to ensure national account identities and global consistency, estimates of spillovers from major economies, and high-frequency indicators. These forecasts are then evaluated to ensure consistency of treatment across similar EMDEs. This is followed by extensive discussions with World Bank country teams, who conduct continuous macroeconomic monitoring and dialogue with country authorities and finalize growth forecasts for EMDEs. The Prospects Group prepares advanced-economy and commodity price forecasts. Throughout the forecasting process, staff use macroeconometric models that allow the combination of judgment and consistency with model-based insights.

Global trade growth forecast process. Global trade growth is calculated as the percentage change in the average of global exports and imports of goods and nonfactor services, both measured in real U.S. dollars. Forecasts for global exports and imports are derived from a bottom-up approach, using country-level forecasts for real exports and imports produced during the forecasting process as described above.

Global Economic Prospects: Selected Topics, 2015-25

Global Economic Prospects: Selected Topics, 2015-25

Global Economic Prospects: Selected Topics, 2015-25

Fiscal policies

Fiscal policy in commodity exporters: An enduring challenge	January 2024, chapter 4
How does procyclical fiscal policy affect output growth?	January 2024, box 4.1
Do fiscal rules and sovereign wealth funds make a difference? Lessons from country case studies	January 2024, box 4.2
Fiscal policy challenges in low-income countries	June 2023, chapter 4
Resolving high debt after the pandemic: lessons from past episodes of debt relief	January 2022, special focus
How has the pandemic made the fourth wave of debt more dangerous?	January 2021, box 1.1
The fourth wave: Rapid debt buildup	January 2020, chapter 4
Debt: No free lunch	June 2019, box 1.1
Debt in low-income countries: Evolution, implications, and remedies	January 2019, chapter 4
Debt dynamics in emerging market and developing economies: Time to act?	June 2017, special focus 1
Having fiscal space and using it: FiscFal challenges in developing economies	January 2015, chapter 3
Revenue mobilization in South Asia: Policy challenges and recommendations	January 2015, box 2.3
Fiscal policy in low-income countries	January 2015, box 3.1
What affects the size of fiscal multipliers?	January 2015, box 3.2
Chile's fiscal rule—an example of success	January 2015, box 3.3
Narrow fiscal space and the risk of a debt crisis	January 2015, box 3.4

Commodity markets

Russia's invasion of Ukraine: Implications for energy markets and activity	June 2022, special focus 2
Commodity price cycles: Underlying drivers and policy options	January 2022, chapter 3
Reforms after the 2014-16 oil price plunge	June 2020, box 4.1
Adding fuel to the fire: Cheap oil in the pandemic	June 2020, chapter 4
The role of major emerging markets in global commodity demand	June 2018, special focus 1
The role of the EM7 in commodity production	June 2018, SF1, box SF1.1
Commodity consumption: Implications of government policies	June 2018, SF1, box SF1.2
With the benefit of hindsight: The impact of the 2014–16 oil price collapse	January 2018, special focus 1
From commodity discovery to production: Vulnerabilities and policies in LICs	January 2016, special focus
After the commodities boom: What next for low-income countries?	June 2015, special focus 2
Low oil prices in perspective	June 2015, box 1.2
Understanding the plunge in oil prices: Sources and implications	January 2015, chapter 4
What do we know about the impact of oil prices on output and inflation? A brief survey	January 2015, box 4.1

Globalization of trade and financial flows

High trade costs: causes and remedies	June 2021, chapter 3
The impact of COVID-19 on global value chains	June 2020, box SF1
Poverty impact of food price shocks and policies	January 2019, chapter 4
Arm's-length trade: A source of post-crisis trade weakness	June 2017, Special Focus 2
The U.S. economy and the world	January 2017, Special Focus
Potential macroeconomic implications of the Trans-Pacific Partnership Agreement	January 2016, chapter 4
Regulatory convergence in mega-regional trade agreements	January 2016, box 4.1.1
China's integration in global supply chains: Review and implications	January 2015, box 2.1
Can remittances help promote consumption stability?	January 2015, chapter 4
What lies behind the global trade slowdown?	January 2015, chapter 4

Prospects Group:
Selected Other Publications on the Global Economy, 2015-25

Commodity Markets Outlook	
Potential near-term implications of the conflict in the Middle East for commodity markets: A preliminary assessment	October 2023
Forecasting industrial commodity prices	April 2023
Pandemic, war, recession: Drivers of aluminum and copper prices	October 2022
The impact of the war in Ukraine on commodity markets	April 2022
Urbanization and commodity demand	October 2021
Causes and consequences of metal price shocks	April 2021
Persistence of commodity shocks	October 2020
Food price shocks: Channels and implications	April 2019
The implications of tariffs for commodity markets	October 2018, box
The changing of the guard: Shifts in industrial commodity demand	October 2018
Oil exporters: Policies and challenges	April 2018
Investment weakness in commodity exporters	January 2017
OPEC in historical context: Commodity agreements and market fundamentals	October 2016
From energy prices to food prices: Moving in tandem?	July 2016
Resource development in an era of cheap commodities	April 2016
Weak growth in emerging market economies: What does it imply for commodity markets?	January 2016
Understanding El Niño: What does it mean for commodity markets?	October 2015
How important are China and India in global commodity consumption?	July 2015
Anatomy of the last four oil price crashes	April 2015
Putting the recent plunge in oil prices in perspective	January 2015

Inflation in Emerging and Developing Economies: Evolution, Drivers, and Policies	
Inflation: Concepts, evolution, and correlates	Chapter 1
Understanding global inflation synchronization	Chapter 2
Sources of inflation: Global and domestic drivers	Chapter 3
Inflation expectations: Review and evidence	Chapter 4
Inflation and exchange rate pass-through	Chapter 5
Inflation in low-income countries	Chapter 6
Poverty impact of food price shocks and policies	Chapter 7

A Decade After the Global Recession: Lessons and Challenges for Emerging and Developing Economies	
A decade after the global recession: Lessons and challenges	Chapter 1
What happens during global recessions?	Chapter 2
Macroeconomic developments	Chapter 3
Financial market developments	Chapter 4
Macroeconomic and financial sector policies	Chapter 5
Prospects, risks, and vulnerabilities	Chapter 6
Policy challenges	Chapter 7
The role of the World Bank Group	Chapter 8

Global Waves of Debt: Causes and Consequences	
Debt: Evolution, causes, and consequences	Chapter 1
Benefits and costs of debt: The dose makes the poison	Chapter 2
Global waves of debt: What goes up must come down?	Chapter 3
The fourth wave: Ripple or tsunami?	Chapter 4
Debt and financial crises: From euphoria to distress	Chapter 5
Policies: Turning mistakes into experience	Chapter 6

Prospects Group:
Selected Other Publications on the Global Economy, 2015-25

www.ingramcontent.com/pod-product-compliance
Lightning Source LLC
Chambersburg PA
CBHW050906210326
41597CB00002B/42